FOUNDATIONS OF SOCIAL WORK PRACTICE IN THE FIELD OF AGING

A Competency-Based Approach

FOUNDATIONS OF SOCIAL WORK PRACTICE IN THE FIELD OF AGING

A Competency-Based Approach

ROBERTA R. GREENE, HARRIET L. COHEN,
COLLEEN M. GALAMBOS & NANCY P. KROPF

NASW PRESS

NATIONAL ASSOCIATION OF SOCIAL WORKERS
WASHINGTON, DC

ELVIRA CRAIG DE SILVA, DSW, ACSW, PRESIDENT
ELIZABETH J. CLARK, PHD, ACSW, MPH, EXECUTIVE DIRECTOR

Cheryl Y. Bradley, Publisher
Marcia D. Roman, Managing Editor, Journals and Books
Sarah Lowman, Editor
Louise Rosenblatt Goines, Copy Editor
Cara Schumacher, Proofreader
Bernice Eisen, Indexer

Cover design by Eye to Eye Design, Bristow, VA
Interior design by Circle Graphics, Columbia, MD
Printed and bound by Port City Press, Baltimore, MD

First Impression, October 2007
Second Impression, February 2013

Library of Congress Cataloging-in-Publication Data

Foundations of social work practice in the field of aging : a
competency-based approach / Roberta R. Greene ... [et al.].
     p. cm.
  Includes bibliographical references and index.
  ISBN 978-0-87101-378-1
  1. Social work with older people—United States. 2.
Gerontology. 3. Older people. I. Greene, Roberta R. (Roberta
Rubin), 1940-
  HV1451.F68 2007
  362.6—dc22
                                                    2007020730

Contents

Acknowledgments

This book did not begin when we started writing it more than a year ago. It was made possible because we, who have known each other for many years, have been dedicated to enhancing geriatric social work practice and increasing the number of practitioners in the field. Our particular thanks to Dr. JoAnn Damron-Rodriquez who wrote the introduction and has always rolled up her sleeves and worked in the trenches.

I (Roberta R. Greene) would like to thank Dr. Olivia Lopez and Youjung Lee, contributors to chapter 3, with whom I have had the delight to know as doctoral students and new professionals joining the ranks. I would also like to thank my family and friends, especially my spouse, David, and gerontologist Dr. Sandra Graham, who kept the sometimes frustrating book details to a minimum.

I (Colleen C. Galambos) would like to thank Mark Miller for his research assistance and for his work on designing the policy analysis tables and Stephanie Sinn and Fresa Jacobs for their administrative support. I would also like to thank Doug and Kevin Grove for helping fix computer glitches and for supporting my involvement in this project.

Introduction

Social Work Practice in Aging

A Competency-Based Approach for the 21st Century

JOANN DAMRON-RODRIGUEZ

A competency-based approach to social work practice in the field of aging requires practitioners, educators, and students to be grounded in the requisite knowledge and offer evidence of the effectiveness of their work. The Geriatric Social Work Competencies, developed through the collaboration of the John A. Hartford Foundation Geriatric Social Work Initiative programs—the Council on Social Work Education (CSWE) first Strengthening Aging and Gerontological Education in Social Work (SAGE–SW), then Gero-Rich and now the National GeroEd Center and the Social Work Leadership Institute (SWLI) of the New York Academy of Medicine (NYAM) Practicum Partnership Program (PPP), are now nationally adopted and have been incorporated in this text (see Appendix). This introduction familiarizes the reader with these competencies and addresses the need for social workers to

- prepare for practice in a 21st-century aging society
- access knowledge for contemporary practice
- define social work practice in aging
- identify evidence of the effectiveness of social work in the field of aging
- develop a competency-based approach to learning
- recognize core geriatric social work competencies
- self-assess individual growth in social work competence in aging.

The rationale for competency-based education and the need for students and practitioners to evaluate the effectiveness of their interventions are also discussed. This introduction advocates the use of the most current knowledge and best practices in the field of aging.

The book provides a strengths-based multisystemic orientation to foundation social work content for all social workers, as well as those concentrating on the field of aging. Each chapter opens with the geriatric social work competencies thought necessary to carry out effective practice and issued by the CSWE Gero-Ed Center (www.Gero-EdCenter.org).

Chapter 1 discusses the present context of social work practice in the field of gerontology. Chapter 2 provides theoretical constructs to guide geriatric practice, and chapter 3 describes the heterogeneity of the aging population; chapters 4, 5, and 6 focus on the individual, families, and informal support systems. The orientation in chapter 7 is on group work. Chapter 8 on case management discusses both direct individual and family practice skills as well as the need to be able to navigate the services system at the organizational level. Chapters 9 and 10 relate to macro practice within organizations and the community. Finally, chapter 11 addresses policy practice at the state and national levels. These chapters further describe the impact of an aging society on its institutions and culture, including family structure, intergenerational and gender roles, work and retirement, dependency ratios, community engagement, and health and social services.

Factors Effecting Geriatric Social Work Practice in the 21st Century

Increased Life Expectancy

Educators have developed geriatric social work competencies in large measure as a response to the changing context of social work practice. Social work practice in the 21st century takes place in the midst of two major societal changes. First is the dramatic increase in life expectancy and the aging of society. Increased human longevity, a hallmark achievement of the 20th century, will have worldwide impact in the 21st century. The 28-year gain in average life expectancy since 1900 is unprecedented over the preceding 5,000 years of human history (see chapter 1). It is not only the dramatic increase in the number of older people that presents an imperative for social work practice in aging, but also the increased diversity of the older population in chronological age (65 to 120 years), birth cohort, race and ethnicity, socioeconomic status, immigration status, functional level, and cognitive capacity that require psychosocial assessment, intervention planning, program development, and policy advocacy (Torres-Gil & Moga, 2001; see chapter 2).

The aging of societies is a global phenomenon. The United Nations International Year of Older Persons in 1999 proclaimed that with thoughtful planning an aging society could become a "society for all ages" that would embrace multigenerational equity and meaningful involvement at all life stages. A society for all ages would acknowledge the interdependence of the individual and society (Lubben & Damron-Rodriguez, 2006). Scharlach and colleagues (2000) stated: "Overarching social work goals in an aging society include preservation of maximum independence, optimal functioning, dignity, and quality of life, through personal empowerment and effective and efficient service utilization" (p. 525).

Increase in Knowledge

The second societal change affecting contemporary social work practice is the exponential increase in knowledge. The explosion of knowledge about the human condition, particularly the aging process, forms the context for the competency-based approach for contemporary practice.

The Knowledge Age

The 21st century following the Industrial Revolution and the brief transitional period of the "information age" of the late 20th century have been conceptualized as the "knowledge age" (Haag, Cummings, McCubbrey, Pinsonneault, & Donovan, 2006). Social work practitioners entering the workforce or continuing to work in the knowledge age must be equipped with distinct professional knowledge and the skills and the ability to acquire more knowledge continuously to serve their clients and society best.

In the knowledge age, information is often disseminated by technology. Computer technology and the Internet make the acquisition of information or the "use of science" more available for practitioners. Thus, social work education must prepare practitioners to be intelligent consumers of research. Using science also requires that the nuance and contextual application of findings be put into practice (Webb, 2001).

Individuals are living longer and healthier lives in part because of the extraordinary growth of biomedical knowledge and public health initiatives. The confluence of the rapid and large increase of the older population and the exponential increase in the dissemination of knowledge create an imperative for social workers to employ the most recent advances in knowledge in their practice with people living increasingly longer lives.

Developing countries cannot age successfully without the use of public health initiatives and population-based interventions such as improved sanitation methods and immunizations. It is these fundamental public health interventions that lead to the increased well-being of the populations of less-developed countries. Their demographic transition involves a shift from high fertility and mortality rates to those of more developed societies with lower fertility and mortality rates (Lubben & Damron-Rodriguez, 2006). This developmental transition takes place in two major stages (Rowe & Kahn, 1999). The first is a marked reduction in infant mortality and early childhood death rates; the second is a significant decrease in death rates among middle-aged and older adults. This reduction of mortality is attributable to an expansion of public health, nutrition, and health care. In an aging society, therefore, individuals have the potential to live longer and healthier lives (see chapter 1 for the use of knowledge and scientific thinking).

Social Workers as Knowledge Workers

Social workers are specialized knowledge workers. Over 30 years ago, Drucker (1998) defined *knowledge workers* as those who develop and use knowledge to accomplish their work. Social work can be defined by its specialized knowledge, values, and competencies, and social workers can be recognized as a special subset of knowledge workers with the requisite professional knowledge to create and improve policies, programs, and services for communities and individuals.

Drucker (1998) further stated that knowledge workers add value by processing existing information to create new information that can be used to define and solve problems better. Reflective practice, program evaluation, and social work research are good examples of this. Social work may be considered a problem-solving profession with practitioners using applied knowledge. The practitioner may be thought of as

- a problem solver rather than a production worker or functionary
- a person who uses intellectual rather than manual skills to earn a living
- an individual who requires a high level of autonomy
- a manipulator of symbols; someone paid for quality of judgment
- someone who possess un-codified knowledge that is difficult to duplicate
- someone who uses knowledge and information to add to deeper knowledge and information. (Western Management Consultants, 2002)

Definition of Social Work in Aging

The development of geriatric social work competencies coincides with the profession's interest in defining our practice domain. The bureau of health professions white paper definition of social work in aging is based on the generic description of the profession as described in the *Standards for the Classification of Social Work Practice* (NASW, 1981) (see Berkman, Dobrof, Damron-Rodriguez, & Harry, 1997). This definition of social work in aging relates essential social work roles to the needs of older people and their families as is described in the purposes of geriatric social work practice section. Terms for professional practice with older adults used throughout this book are "gerontological" (founded in knowledge of the aging process) and "geriatric" (based in interventions with older people with health-related issues), sometimes used interchangeably.

Geriatric practice is consumer directed, with the client given the choice in type of service, provider, and timing of care provision (Benjamin, 2001). It focuses on family caregiving. Although 80 percent of the care of older adults is provided by their informal support systems, social workers play a key role in assisting families in their caregiving role (Rizzo & Rowe, 2005; Stone, Reinhard, Achemer, & Rudin, 2002). Another major emphasis is on community care by hospitals or institutions or homes and communities.

Purposes of Geriatric Social Work Practice

Gerontological social workers should have the professional competence to

- enhance developmental, problem solving, and coping capacities of older adults and their families
- promote effective and humane operation of delivery systems that provide resources and services to older people and their families

- link older clients with systems that provide them with resources, services, and opportunities
- contribute to the development and improvement of social policies that enhance individual functioning throughout the life span. (Berkman et al., 1997)

Values of Geriatric Practice

In addition to having specialized professional knowledge, social work practice in the field of aging embodies values unique to the profession, adding a dimension that is a signature element of the profession as described in this book. These professional ethics and values are delineated in the NASW *Code of Ethics* (NASW, 2000) and are used along with knowledge and skills to accomplish the mission of the profession—"to enhance human well-being and help meet the basic human needs of all people, with particular attention to the needs and empowerment of people who are vulnerable, oppressed, and living in poverty" (p. 1).

The resilience-enhancing model (REM) (Greene, 2002) that forms the conceptual foundation for this text develops the new tenets of practice in aging for the present era and a philosophy for a new gerontology. Rather than an "aging as a problem" perspective of earlier gerontology and geriatric practice, resilience interventions are based on the self-direction and self-advocacy of older adults.

Evidence of Effectiveness

Social work decisions should be based on the best available evidence. The development of geriatric social work competencies is congruent with the profession's interest in providing consumers with evidence of effectiveness (www.socialworkleadership.org). Social work is garnering evidence of the value added by the profession's interventions to older adults' quality of life (Duke, 2005; Grimier & Gorey, 1998; Morrow-Howell & Burnette, 2001). Rizzo and Rowe (2005), in a comprehensive review of research on social work intervention with older people, reported the following intervention outcomes: shorter lengths of hospital stays; decrease in inappropriate use of emergency rooms; overall better coordination of health care; and greater ability of caregivers to cope. Several terms are used to describe the optimal use of outcomes research in practice. Evidence-based practice, practice guidelines, and best practices are types of knowledge (research) that can be applied to interventions.

Evidence-Based Practice

Evidence-based practice is

- practice supported by research findings and demonstrated as being effective through a critical examination of current and past practices (www.cona-nurse.org/standards/glossary.htm)

- clinical decision making based on a systematic review of the scientific evidence of the risks, benefits, and costs of alternative forms of diagnosis or treatment (www.moh.govt.nz/moh.nsf/0/15f5c5045e7a1dd4cc256b6b0002b038)
- an approach to decision making in which the clinician uses the best evidence available, in consultation with the patient, to decide on which course of action suits the patient best (www.nhstayside.scot.nhs.uk/FoISA/Glossary.htm).

For example, the evidence of the effectiveness of community-based case management is based on its relatively low cost and the improved quality of life it provides for the frail elderly population (Duke, 2005).

Practice Guidelines

Practice guidelines are systematically developed statements to assist practitioners and patients in making decisions about appropriate health care for specific clinical circumstances (Institute of Medicine, Committee to Advise the Public Health Service on Clinical Practice Guidelines, 1990). Sets of practice techniques that have been evaluated and proved efficacious are practice guidelines.

Best Practices

Best practices are those that have been systematically identified, described, combined, and disseminated as effective and efficient clinical or management strategies for practicing clinicians (Mold & Gregory, 2003).

Competency-Based Approach

A competency-based approach requires the demonstration of core knowledge, values, and skills in social work practice (Vass, 1996). Competency is measured along a continuum or a range of skill levels. The competence level can be adequate or highly qualified in a skill domain. Competency-based education and evaluation (CBE) as defined by Bogo and colleagues (2002) first requires an adoption of a set of defined skills as described in the Development of Geriatric Social Work Competencies section. A CBE approach also leads to the establishment of learning goals and the measurement of their achievement in classroom and field education (Bogo et al., 2002).

Geriatric Social Work Competencies

The social work profession did not recognize the need for specific gerontological or geriatric knowledge until the mid-20th century. Lowy (1979) acknowledged that "prior to 1945, not much had been happening in social work with the aging" (p. 9). Social welfare was initially founded to carry out child welfare functions. It was not until the late 1960s and early 1970s that older people were considered a target population. This was a time when many professions began to recognize that specialized knowledge and training were required to serve older people (Damron-Rodriguez, 2006).

In 1995 the Bureau of Health Professions held a National Forum for Geriatric Education in which social work was one of the key professions. Each profession produced a white paper outlining a strategy for education and training (Berkman et al., 1997). In the late 1990s, the John A. Hartford Foundation, whose goal is to improve the care of older people by strengthening geriatrics in the health professions, turned its attention to social work continuing to fund projects in medicine and nursing geriatric education. Through forums with social work leaders and production of white papers (Scharlach et al., 2000), the Hartford Geriatric Social Work Initiative was crafted. This initiative has had a major impact on the field of geriatric social work (Robbins & Rieder, 2002).

The Council on Higher Education Accreditation (CHEA), which oversees standards for 76 different specializations and professions including nursing, public health, pharmacy, medicine, counseling, education, pastoral care, and social work, reported that nationally 46 percent of these schools are competency based. The CHEA has now adopted a competency-driven model for accreditation of all professional schools (National Center for Higher Education Management Systems, 2000). Competence is used not only as a measure of education and training, but also as a measure for accreditation. The Joint Commission on Accreditation of Healthcare Organizations (2001), for example, stressed the value of competency-based geriatric education in preparing professionals for practice in health care. By establishing geriatric competencies, the field could shape curriculum, field training, and continuing education to prepare practitioners effectively to address the needs of older adults and their families.

Development of Geriatric Social Work Competencies

Research Development

Gerontological social work competencies have been developed over a multiyear period through several of the John A. Hartford social work initiatives. In 1999, CSWE received a grant, SAGE-SW. The project delineated 65 competencies based on a literature review, expert opinion, and a comprehensive survey of the field (Rosen, Zlotnik, & Singer, 2002). These competencies have been applied to aging curriculum development (Greene & Galambos, 2002). In 2000 competencies were being developed for the measurement of geriatric social work enhanced field education (Fortune & Damron-Rodriguez, 2002) by the NYAM PPP and resulted in the PPP Geriatric Social Work Competency Scale I. Scale I incorporated and condensed SAGE-SW competencies and focus group feedback from providers (Naito-Chan, Damron-Rodriguez. & Simmons, 2004). The Geriatric Social Work Competency Scale II is the most recent shorter measurement tool and is presented at the end of this chapter for use in the measurement of student's assessment of skill level (see chapter appendix for Scale II). The Gero-Rich program and now the National GeroEd Center has brought the competencies to curriculum infusion for generalist practice (Hooyman, 2006).

The Hartford Geriatric Social Work Initiative has adopted a common list of geriatric competencies composed of knowledge, skills, and values in four domains. These competencies, whether stated as learning objectives (GeroEd) or measurable skills (PPP), are the adopted skills set now available to guide curriculum development at schools and departments of social work (www.Gero-EdCenter.org and www.socialworkleadership.org). The four domains of competencies are (1) values, ethics, and theoretical perspectives; (2) assessment; (3) intervention; and (4) aging services, programs, and policies. The competencies are presented in their totality in chapter 1 and the appropriate competencies are listed at the beginning of each chapter of the book to guide course development and discussion.

Classroom Infusion and Integration

Competencies have been related to curricula in the following ways:

- Basic course descriptions are stated in competency-based terms.
- Course objectives now specify competencies are targeted for aging infusion.
- Aging content in courses supports geriatric competencies.
- Teaching resources are used for educational supports and activities.
- Assessments of skill development are identified and a part of each course.

Student Assessment: Geriatric Social Work Competency Scale II

To assess student competency, instructors must distinguish the level of student performance. Students may also assess their own progress by using the PPP Geriatric Social Work Competency Scale II provided in the Appendix (Chung, Damron-Rodriguez, Lawrance, & Volland, 2007; Damron-Rodriguez, 2006). The PPP Geriatric Social Work Competency Scale II is a self assessment of skill that is currently used in more than 35 schools of social work for measurement of competence. These evaluations at the various PPP sites have consistently demonstrated student increase in geriatric competence over the training period (Damron-Rodriguez, Lawrance, Barnett, & Simmons, 2007). The five levels of social work competence are categorized as

1. not skilled at all (I have no experience with this skill)
2. beginning skill (I have to consciously work at this skill)
3. moderate skill (This skill is becoming more integrated in my practice)
4. advanced skill (This skill is done with confidence and is an integral part of my practice)
5. expert skill (I complete this skill with sufficient mastery to teach others).

Thus, evaluation and measurement are central dimensions of competency development. The PPP Geriatric Social Work Competency Scale II can also be used to enrich field experience to

- define learning objectives based on outcomes
- structure student contracts identifying competencies
- design field rotations to enhance experiences for competency development
- develop or use modules and teaching resources to link field and classroom
- provide integrative seminars
- train field instructors to use competencies in structuring field experience.

Further Measurement

The validity of assessment of competency through self-efficacy measures has been substantiated through research (Holden, Meenaghan, Anastas, & Metry, 2002). Bandura (1997) defined *self-efficacy* as belief in one's capability to perform actions required to produce certain results or outcomes. Self-efficacy has been established as a reliable and valid construct for predicting performance in a variety of health disciplines. Self-efficacy is conceived to be task or domain specific. It is not measured by the number of skills acquired, but by the level of confidence felt necessary to accomplish specific outcomes. It requires organizing many subskills, including ones that are cognitive, social, emotional, and behavioral, into the competence to meet goal-directed outcomes (Bandura). Self-efficacy has a positive and significant relationship to academic performance and consistent goal accomplishment across multiple research studies (Multon, Brown, & Lent, 1991). The further development of this and other constructs to measure educational outcomes is imperative (Holden et al.; McKinley, Fraser, & Baker, 2000).

Other more objective measures are needed as the profession continues on the path of competency-based education (Bogo et al., 2002). Practice for the 21st century will require knowledge utilization at an unprecedented level. Competency-based evaluation of educational outcomes is therefore an important aspect of the movement toward best practices in aging. It can be used in educational planning for setting educational goals. Collaboration with and learning from other professions as they move toward geriatric competency measurement will be beneficial as well as provide additional benefits for social work education (American Geriatrics Society, 2000). As CSWE continues its revision of the Educational Policy Statement and Accreditation Standards, it is anticipated that social work educators will join the ranks of those using a competency-based approach. This book is intended to contribute to that endeavor.

Suggested Web Sites

- Projects funded by the Hartford Geriatric Social Work Initiative may be accessed at http://www.jhartfound.org.

- The CSWE Gero-Ed Center funded by the John A. Hartford Foundation provides extensive resources for infusing content on gerontology in the social work curriculum and can be accessed at www.Gero-EdCenter.org.
- The Social Work Leadership Institute of the New York Academy of Medicine provides access to PPP resources, evidence-based practice for geriatric social work through the Center for Aging Policy Evidence Database and Public Policy Clearing House at www.socialworkleadership.org.
- The California Social Work Education Center Aging Initiative, a consortium of all California schools that have developed an aging competency-based curriculum for the state. Their work is described at http://calswec.berkley.edu/aging_post04summit_execsummary.pdf.

The author wishes to acknowledge the contributions to the competency model of Patricia J. Volland, MSW, MBA, principle investigator of the Social Work Leadership Institute PPP and vice president, New York Academy of Medicine, and Frances P. Lawrance, consultant on the evaluation of PPP.

References

American Geriatrics Society. (2000). Core competencies for the care of older patients: Recommendations of the American Geriatrics Society. *Academic Medicine, 75,* 252–255.

Bandura, A. (1997). *Self-efficacy: The exercise of control.* New York: Freeman Press.

Benjamin, A. E. (2001). Consumer-directed services at home: A new model for persons with disabilities. *Health Affairs, 20*(6), 80–95.

Berkman, B., Dobrof, R., Damron-Rodriguez, J. A., & Harry, L. (1997). Social work. In S. M. Klein (Ed.), *A national agenda for geriatric education: White papers* (pp. 53–85). New York: Springer.

Bogo, M., Regehr, C., Hughes, J., Power, R., & Globerman, J. (2002). Evaluating a measure of student field performance in direct service: Testing reliability and validity of explicit criteria. *Journal of Social Work Education, 38,* 385–401.

Chung, G., Damron-Rodriguez, J., Lawrance, F. P., & Volland, P. (2007, February 2–4). *Geriatric social work competence: Learning partnership involving student self-assessment and field instructor evaluation.* Paper presented at CSWE Gero-Ed Forum, Charleston, SC.

Damron-Rodriguez, J. A. (2006). Moving ahead: Developing geriatric social work competencies. In B. Berkman (Ed.), *Handbook of social work in health and aging* (pp. 1051–1068). New York: Oxford University Press.

Damron-Rodriguez, J. A., Lawrance, F. P., Barnett, D., & Simmons, J. (2007). Developing geriatric social work competencies for field education. *Journal of Gerontological Social Work, 48*(1/2), 139–169.

Drucker, P. (1998, October 5). Management new paradigms. *Forbes, 162*(7), 152–177.

Duke, C. (2005). The frail elderly community-based case management project. *Geriatric Nursing, 26*(2), 122–127.

Fortune, A. E., & Damron-Rodriguez, J. A. (2002). *Model for geriatric social work practicum partnership program.* New York: New York Academy of Medicine.

Greene, R. R. (2002). Resiliency: An integrated approach to practice, policy, and research. Washington, DC: NASW Press.

Greene, R., & Galambos, C. (2002). *Social work's pursuit of a common professional framework: Have we reached a milestone? Advancing gerontological social work education.* New York: Haworth Press.

Grimier, A., & Gorey, K. (1998). The effectiveness of social work with older people: A meta-analysis of conference proceedings. *Social Work Research, 22,* 60–64.

Haag, S., Cummings, M., McCubbrey, D., Pinsonneault, A., & Donavan, R. (2006). *Management information systems for the information age* (3rd Canadian ed.). Whitby, Ontario, Canada: McGraw Hill Ryerson.

Holden, G., Meenaghan, T., Anastas, J., & Metry, G. (2002). Outcomes of social work education: The case for social work self-efficacy. *Journal of Social Work Education, 38,* 115.

Hooyman, N. R. (2006). *Achieving curricular and organizational change: Impact of the CSWE geriatric enrichment in social work education project.* Alexandria, VA: Council on Social Work Education.

Institute of Medicine, Committee to Advise the Public Health Service on Clinical Practice Guidelines. (1990). *Clinical practice guidelines: Directions for a new program.* Washington, DC: Author.

Joint Commission on Accreditation in Healthcare Organizations. (2001). *Comprehensive JCAHO accreditation manual for hospitals: The official handbook.* Oakbrook Terrace, IL: Author.

Lowy, L. (1979). *Social work with the aging: The challenge and promise of the later years.* New York: Harper & Row.

Lubben, J. E., & Damron-Rodriguez, J. A. (2006). World population aging. In B. Berkman (Ed.), *Handbook of social work in health and aging* (pp. 939–946). New York: Oxford University Press.

McKinley, R. K., Fraser, R. C., & Baker, R. (2000). Model for directly assessing and improving clinical competence and performance in revalidation of clinicians. *British Medical Journal, 32,* 712–715.

Mold, J. W., & Gregory, M. E. (2003). Best practices research. *Family Medicine, 35*(2), 131–134.

Morrow-Howell, N., & Burnette, D. (2001). Gerontological social work research: Current status and future directions. *Journal of Gerontological Social Work, 36,* 63–81.

Multon, K. D., Brown, S. D., & Lent, R. W. (1991). Relation of self-efficacy beliefs to academic outcomes: A meta-analytic investigation. *Journal of Counseling Psychology, 38,* 53–63.

Naito-Chan, E., Damron-Rodriguez, J. A., & Simmons, W. J. (2004). Identifying competencies for geriatric social work practice. *Journal of Gerontological Social Work, 43*(4), 59–78.

National Association of Social Workers. (1981). *NASW standards for the classification of social work practice* (Policy Statement 4). Silver Spring, MD: Author.

National Association of Social Workers. (2000). *Code of ethics of the National Association of Social Workers.* Washington, DC: Author.

National Center for Higher Education Management Systems. (2000). *Competency standards model: Another approach to accreditation review.* Washington, DC: Council on Higher Education Accreditation.

Rizzo, V. M., & Rowe, J. (2005). *Studies of the efficacy and cost-effectiveness of social work services in aging: A report commissioned by the National Leadership Council.* Retrieved September 1, 2005, from http://socialwork.nyam.org/pdf/Efficacy Final_Report.pdf

Robbins, L. A., & Rieder, C. H. (2002). The John A. Harford Foundation geriatric social work initiative. *Journal of Gerontological Social Work, 39*(3), 71–90.

Rosen, A. L., Zlotnik, J. L., & Singer, T. (2002). Basic gerontological competence for all social workers: The need to "gerontologize" social work education. *Journal of Gerontological Social Work, 39*, 25–36.

Rowe, J. W., & Kahn, R. L. (1999). *Successful aging.* New York: Pantheon.

Scharlach, A., Damron-Rodriguez, J., Robinson, B., & Feldman, R. (2000). Educating social workers for an aging society: A vision for the 21st century. *Journal of Social Work Education, 36*, 521–538.

Stone, R., Reinhard, S. C., Achemer, J., & Rudin, D. (2002). *Geriatric care managers: A profile of an emerging profession* [Research Report]. Washington, DC: American Association of Retired Persons.

Torres-Gil, F., & Moga, K. B. (2001). Multiculturalism, social policy and the new aging. *Journal of Gerontological Social Work, 36*(3/4), 13–31.

Vass, A. A. (Ed.). (1996). *Social work competencies: Core knowledge, values, and skills.* London: Sage Publications.

Webb, S. A. (2001). Some considerations on the validity of evidence-based practice in social work. *British Journal of Social Work, 31*, 57–79.

Western Management Consultants. (2002). *Herding knowledge workers.* Retrieved May 15, 2007, from http://www.wmc.on.ca/articles/article06.htm

HARTFORD PRACTICUM PARTNERSHIP PROGRAM
GERIATRIC SOCIAL WORK COMPETENCY SCALE II

Developed by the Hartford Practicum Partnership Program and revised/adopted
by the CSWE Gero-Ed Center

To Be Used For Rating Student Competency Attainment

The following is a listing of *skills* recognized by gerontological social workers as important to social workers effectively working with and on behalf of older adults and their families. Completion of this scale requires careful self-assessment and recognition that few practitioners would receive the rating of 4 for all skills. This scale can capture self-assessment of scale development across the learning continuum, from BSW, to MSW and post-MSW.

Please use the scale below to thoughtfully rate your current skill:

0 = Not skilled at all (I have no experience with this skill)
1 = Beginning skill (I have to consciously work at this skill)
2 = Moderate skill (This skill is becoming more integrated in my practice)
3 = Advanced skill (This skill is done with confidence and is an integral part of my practice)
4 = Expert skill (I complete this skill with sufficient mastery to teach others)

Please note that field supervisors could also use this scale to assess students' competencies.

0	1	2	3	4
Not skilled at all	Beginning skill	Moderate skill	Advanced skill	Expert skill

Please add any comments and/ or suggestions regarding the skills in each section.

I. VALUES, ETHICS AND THEORETICAL PERSPECTIVES   Skill Level
(Knowledge and value base, which is applied through skills/competencies)   (0–4)

1. Assess and address values and biases regarding aging.   _____

2. Respect and promote older adult clients' right to dignity and self-determination.   _____

3. Apply ethical principles to *decisions* on behalf of all older clients with special attention to those who have limited decisional capacity.   _____

4. Respect diversity among older adult clients, families, and professionals (e.g., class, race, ethnicity, gender, and sexual orientation).   _____

5. Address the cultural, spiritual, and ethnic values and beliefs of older adults and families.   _____

6. Relate concepts and theories of aging to social work practice (e.g., cohorts, normal aging, life course perspective).   _____

**Skill Level
(0–4)**

7. Relate social work perspectives and related theories to practice with older adults (e.g., person-in environment, social justice). _____

8. Identify issues related to losses, changes and transitions over their life cycle in designing interventions. _____

9. Support persons and families dealing with end-of-life issues related to dying, death, and bereavement. _____

10. Understand the perspective and values of social work in relation to working effectively with other disciplines in geriatric interdisciplinary practice. _____

Comments _____

_____

_____

_____

II. ASSESSMENT

1. Use empathy and sensitive interviewing skills to engage older clients in identifying their strengths and problems. _____

2. Adapt interviewing methods to potential sensory, language, and cognitive limitations of the older adult. _____

3. Conduct a comprehensive geriatric assessment (bio-psychosocial evaluation). _____

4. Ascertain health status and assess physical functioning (e.g., ADLs and IADLs) of older clients. _____

5. Assess cognitive functioning and mental health status of older clients (e.g., depression, dementia). _____

6. Assess social functioning (e.g., social skills, social activity level) and social support of older clients. _____

7. Assess caregivers needs and level of stress. _____

8. Administer and interpret standardized assessment and diagnostic tools that are appropriate for use with older adults (e.g., depression scale, Mini-Mental Status Exam). _____

9. Develop clear, timely, and appropriate service plans with measurable objectives for older adults. _____

10. Reevaluate and adjust service plans for older adults on a continuing basis. _____

Comments _____

_____

_____

_____

	Skill Level (0–4)

III. INTERVENTION

1. Establish rapport and maintain an effective working relationship with older adults and family members. _____

2. Enhance the coping capacities and mental health of older persons through a variety of therapy modalities (e.g., supportive, psychodynamic). _____

3. Utilize group interventions with older adults and their families (e.g., bereavement groups, reminiscence groups). _____

4. Mediate situations with angry or hostile older adults and/or family members. _____

5. Assist caregivers to reduce their stress levels and maintain their own mental and physical health. _____

6. Provide social work case management to link elders and their families to resources and services. _____

7. Use educational strategies to provide older persons and their families with information related to wellness and disease management (e.g. Alzheimers disease, end of life care). _____

8. Apply skills in termination in work with older adults and their families. _____

9. Advocate on behalf of clients with agencies and other professionals to help elders obtain quality services. _____

10. Adhere to laws and public policies related to older adults (e.g., elder abuse reporting, legal guardianship, advance directives). _____

Comments _____

_____

_____

_____

IV. AGING SERVICES, PROGRAMS AND POLICIES

1. Provide outreach to older adults and their families to ensure appropriate use of the service continuum. _____

2. Adapt organizational policies, procedures, and resources to facilitate the provision of services to diverse older adults and their family caregivers. _____

3. Identify and develop strategies to address service gaps, fragmentation, discrimination, and barriers that impact older persons. _____

4. Include older adults in planning and designing programs. _____

5. Develop program budgets that take into account diverse sources of financial support for the older population. _____

Skill Level
(0–4)

6. Evaluate the effectiveness of practice and programs in achieving intended outcomes for older adults. _____

7. Apply evaluation and research findings to improve practice and program outcomes. _____

8. Advocate and organize with the service providers, community organizations, policy makers, and the public to meet the needs and issues of a growing aging population. _____

9. Identify the availability of resources and resource systems for older adults and their families. _____

10. Assess and address any negative impacts of social and health care policies on practice with historically disadvantaged populations. _____

Comments _____

_____

_____

_____

_____

_____

Source: Retrieved August 17, 2007, from http://www.socialworkleadership.org/nsw/resources/products/ gsw_competencies_scale_ii.pdf

Context and Philosophy of Practice | 1

RATIONALE: Social work practice is guided by an ever-evolving person-in-environment perspective. Practice is carried out within multiple contexts—social, cultural, political, and historical—that affect the lives of client (systems) and the design of social services delivery systems. The demographic imperative—a rapidly expanding aging population—suggests all social workers need to be prepared to serve older adults and their families.

COMPETENCY: Students will describe and attend to practice contexts and the environments in which clients live.

Gerontology, the multidisciplinary study of aging, encompasses biology, sociology, and psychology. Gerontologists study the physical, mental, and social changes associated with the aging process and provide an understanding of the life course, that is, how a client has functioned over time, the timing of family life events, and the historical and cultural changes associated with those events (Greene, 2000; Hareven, 1996). Geriatric social workers combine this body of knowledge with social work content to practice with and deliver services to their clients.

To appreciate the context of geriatric social work practice in the 21st century, it is important to consider the factors shaping the society in which we age and to recognize movements within the behavioral health and social sciences that emphasize effective functioning in old age. Societal changes in the past quarter century have brought about a significant shift in the challenges confronting social workers and other practitioners serving the older population (Hudson, 2005). "Not since more than half a century ago have the political, economic, cultural, and ideological views of the time so dramatically affected how social work practice is defined" (Greene, 2005b, p. 37).

Sociocultural changes have been accompanied by an interest in strengths-based human behavior theory and positive psychological frameworks (see chapter 2 for further discussion of theoretical concepts). As the result of societal influences and decades of research, a "new gerontology" has emerged: Instead of viewing old age as solely a time of deterioration and decline, it examines how people can and do experience a healthy and engaged old age (Holstein & Minkler, 2003; Kiyak & Hooyman, 1999; Rowe & Kahn, 1998; Scharlach & Kaye, 1997).

The new gerontology provides an exciting view of older adults in expanded roles and increased opportunities (see chapters 9 and 10). It is only as effective as a practitioner's commitment to a strengths-based orientation: It is all too easy for a social worker interviewing a frail older adult to ignore that client's abilities. But as Kivnick and Murray (2001) have pointed out, social workers who wish to keep elderly people as "independent" or "in the community" as long as possible must learn about each client's personal values, lifelong commitments, and how the client wants to live out his or her life. They must focus on a client's life strengths that allow the client to remain engaged in the world. Social work students should evaluate their own commitment to strengths-based assessment (see how you approach practice by using the questionnaire in Appendix 1-A; see also chapter 5 for assessment information).

Demographic Imperative

The need for social workers who are prepared to serve older adults is escalating. Why this rise in career opportunities in geriatric social work? A "longevity revolution" is under way (Figure 1-1). In the United States, life expectancy at birth is now 72.5 years for men and 79.3 years for women, and it is anticipated that life expectancy for both genders will continue to increase. By 2030 the population over 65 years of age is projected to be twice as large as in 2000—growing from 35 million to 71.5 million—and will represent nearly 20 percent of the total U.S. population (Gonyea, Hudson, & Curley, 2004).

With the swelling numbers will come an increasingly ethnically diverse elderly population, adding to the complexity of services needs (Takamura, 2001; Torres-Gil & Moga, 2001). The most dramatic changes will be the rise in the proportion of black and Hispanic older adults and the decline of the non-Hispanic white population. According to the U.S. surgeon general's report on mental health (U.S. Department of Health and Human Services, 1999), by 2030 the population of older adults will be the most heterogeneous generational cohort in history in terms of ethnic mix, gender balance, living arrangements, and general quality of life health. These older adults will have differing social, cultural, and political experiences as well as general worldviews. Clearly, social workers have a demographic imperative to attend to the old and very old (85 years and older), some of whom may be frail or may suffer from chronic health and cognitive impairments. A practitioner's ability to understand—and respect—the differences in a client's meaning and perception of old age will be paramount (see chapter 3 for a discussion of culture).

FIGURE 1-1 Longevity Projections

Numbers of Persons 65+, 1900–2030 (numbers in millions)

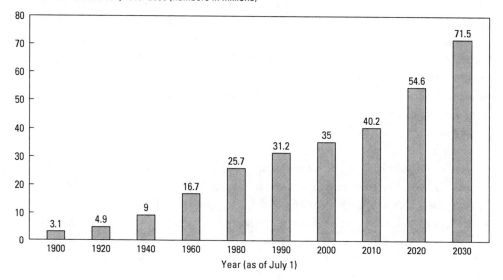

Year (as of July 1)

Note: Increments in years are uneven.
Sources: Projections of the population by Age are taken from the January 2004 Census Internet Release. Historical data are taken from "65+ in the United States,"Current Population Reports, Special Studies, P23-190 data for 2000 are from the 2000 Census and 2003 data are taken from the Census estimates for 2003. U.S. Department of Health and Human Services, Administration on Aging. (2004). *A profile of older Americans: 2004* (p. 3). Retrieved January 16, 2006, from http://www.amsa.org/ger/facts.cfm.

Ageism

To successfully work in the field of aging, practitioners must first explore, identify, and resolve their own biases, myths, and stereotypes about older adults and the aging process. Thinking in negative ways about older adults and considering them poor candidates for various forms of psychosocial treatments are biases that have long permeated the helping professions. Freud's belief that older adults were poor candidates for psychotherapy was adopted by most mental health professionals and continued well into the 1980s. In addition, human behavior theories (such as Piaget's) only addressed childhood learning. Moreover, some physicians still attribute forgetfulness to natural processes of old age without critically exploring possible causative factors (Greene, 1986/2000).

Robert Butler, the first director of the National Institute on Aging, coined the term *ageism* to refer to blatant prejudice of stereotyping older adults as helpless and nonproductive. Ageism, he said, is a process of systematic stereotyping of and discrimination against people because they are old, just as racism and sexism have this effect with skin color and gender. Ageism allows the younger generations to see older people as different from themselves. Thus, they subtly cease to identify with their elders as human beings (Butler, 1975).

Try filling out the checklist of common old-age stereotypes in Appendix 1-B to see what myths you may believe. You may also want to take the Palmore Facts on Aging Quiz in Appendix 1-C to evaluate your beliefs about the aging process (Palmore, 1998).

Ageism, like other forms of prejudice, carries with it the risk of spreading and becoming institutionalized. When this form of discrimination becomes widespread, it can influence practitioners' attitudes about the employment of older adults and their rights to health care. Indeed, some social workers may internalize societal misconceptions and hence view older adults negatively (Greene, 1986/2000). Their self-views and ageist attitudes may interfere with the range and types of choices they present to their older adult clients.

To avoid falling into the ageism trap, social workers should analyze their older client's views of their own aging process (see chapter 5 for a discussion of self-awareness). In addition, older adults' perceptions of the aging process influence expectations about future health (Sarkisian, Steers, Hays, & Mangione, 2005). One tool to assist practitioners in this regard is developed from the Sarkisian et al. 12-Item Expectations Regarding Aging Survey (ERA-12; see Appendix 1-D). Through client self-reports, the ERA-12 measures client expectations about their physical and mental health and cognitive functioning, as well as their global expectations for old age. You may take questions from the ERA-12 to learn more about your clients' perceptions of their health.

Ethics and the Aging Population

Historical Overview

Ethical dilemmas permeate our society. They may occur at multiple systems levels in the social work or biomedical communities, legal system, social policy arena, or broader societal contexts (Greene, 1988; Figure 1-2). At the broadest societal level, tensions between the powers of the state and an individual's rights contribute to public policy debates about ethical issues, such as the right to die or decision to forgo life-sustaining treatment.

In the 1970s and 1980s, two federal groups, the National Commission for the Protection of Human Subjects of Biomedical and Behavioral Research (National Commission) and the President's Commission for the Study of Ethical Problems in Medicine and Biomedical and Behavioral Research (President's Commission), considered many issues that social workers still encounter today. Those commissions issued a series of reports and proposed state statutes to guide professionals' ethical decision making.

Especially important to geriatrics was the first issue examined by the President's Commission: whether the law ought to recognize a new means for officially establishing that death has occurred. In studying the definition of death, the commission was struck by the "depth of public concern about life-sustaining treatment of patients who are dying or permanently unconscious" (President's Commission, 1983b, p. 31). As

FIGURE 1-2 Multiple Layers of Influences on Ethical Decision Making

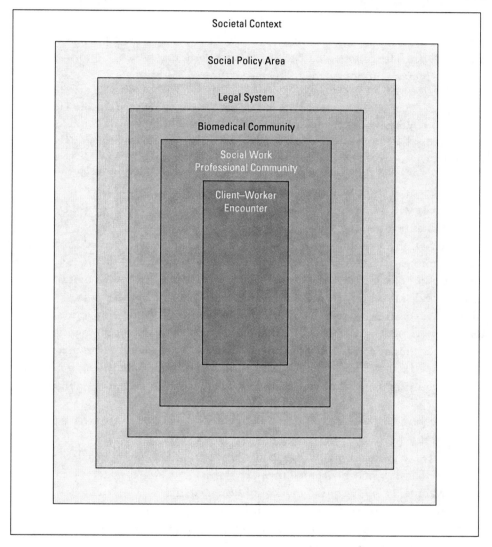

Source: Adapted with permission from Greene, R. R. (1988). *Continuing education for gerontological careers* (p. 92). Alexandria, VA: Council on Social Work Education.

the President's Commission became aware that "conflicting values between physicians and patients, between patients and their families, or among family members are not uncommon" (p. 32), it decided it was necessary to "clarify the rights, duties, and liabilities of all concerned" (p. 32). Furthermore, it decided to clarify the nature of death because medical technology enables an individual's heart and lungs to function when the patient's brain may not. Such technology poses a dilemma in that sometimes it is difficult to distinguish between patients who are clinically dead and those who are dying or severely injured.

The President's Commission (1983b) concluded that developments in medical treatment necessitated a restatement of traditionally recognized standards for determining death. The commission decided the standards ought to be uniform across all 50 states, thereby proposing the following statute:

> An individual who has sustained either (1) irreversible cessation of circulatory and respiratory function, or (2) irreversible cessation of all functions of the entire brain, including the brain stem, is dead. A determination of death must be made in accordance with accepted medical standards. (p. 16)

The commission also concluded that defining death should be a matter for each state legislature; a state's health and judiciary subcommittees would be responsible for coordinating that task.

The National Commission and the President's Commission studied another issue important to geriatric social workers: when and how patients and their families might forgo life-sustaining treatment. Of the people who die in the United States, the vast majority will have been treated by health care professionals who possess, through advanced medical technology, a powerful means to forestall death. Sometimes, though, that objective may so dominate care that the therapy or treatment those professionals provide may not be consistent with patients' own goals and values. Therefore, attempts to postpone death should, at times, yield to other, more important patient goals. Overall, the following themes flowed through the final reports of the two commissions:

- Respect the choice of competent individuals who decide to forgo life-sustaining treatment.
- Provide mechanisms and guidelines for decision making on behalf of patients so that they may make their own decisions.
- Maintain a presumption in favor of sustained life.
- Improve the medical options available to dying patients.
- Provide respectful, responsive, and supportive care to patients for whom no further medical therapies are available or elected.
- Encourage health care institutions to take responsibility for ensuring that adequate procedures for decision making are available for all patients. (President's Commission, 1983a)

Although professionals debate ethical issues at the societal and biomedical community levels, ethical topics are the focus of debate among members of the social work community who may hold differing values about client care. Ethical dilemmas typically surface during the client–social worker encounter, when issues such as autonomy and how to treat client self-determination may arise. For example, should a client who appears to be unsafe be allowed to continue to live alone, or should the social worker attempt to have the client protected? Or, when a social worker and the client's family differ in their views about the right to reject heroic life-saving interventions, how shall the parties involved resolve this matter? The frameworks presented in chapter 4 are intended to facilitate the deliberation of such ethical dilemmas and their possible resolution.

Ethics and Values

According to the NASW *Code of Ethics* (2000), ethics and professional values guide professional conduct; that is, social worker integrity and self-understanding are essential for practitioners to act in the best interest of their clients or client system. An ethical social worker tolerates ambiguity, respects divergent opinions, and recognizes a client's right to self-determination.

Skills, the behaviors that bring knowledge and values together and put them into action, may also be thought of as knowledge in action (Schon, 1983). Within the larger sociopolitical context, professional social work practitioners use the skills of interpreting complex situations and reflecting on how to conduct their practice (Laird, 1993). To enhance their skills, practitioners have traditionally imparted client-centered, relationship-building qualities, including empathy, the ability to deal sensitively and accurately with client feelings; nonpossessive warmth, acceptance of the client as an individual; and genuineness, or authenticity (Rogers & Dymond, 1957). These process-oriented skills are necessary for client—or system—engagement, assessment, intervention, and evaluation (see chapter 6).

Embracing Diversity

Competencies are not just knowledge and skills for student practitioners to master. Rather, the work of applying content in our chosen field of practice begins before the social worker ever sees the client. That is, the intake interview begins before the participants ever meet (Greene, 1986/2000).

Variations in Help-Seeking Behaviors

Clients bring to the social worker–client relationship expectations about the helping process that are based on their own and their family's beliefs and norms (Greene, 1986/2000). Moreover, they frequently will describe their requests and needs in terms used within their own cultural milieu. The events these clients have experienced throughout their lifetimes will have shaped their thoughts about specific services and acceptable solutions. They also will express their own unique views about the world at large (see chapter 3).

For the social worker to "begin where the client is," the practitioner must use critical and reflective thinking to gain an awareness of his or her own personal biases before being able to act on a client's concerns (see chapter 5 for further details on assessing practitioner self-awareness). Furthermore, the practitioner must have knowledge of the client's aging process within his or her particular historical and sociocultural contexts.

Having an awareness of clients' help-seeking behaviors—one way of embracing their diversity—helps to remove barriers to a client-centered relationship. Practitioners might also use the following strategies to ensure that services are client centered:

- Maintain a positive and affirmative attitude toward the client.
- Engage in active listening—listen to discern client concerns and realize client possibilities for a positive future.
- Conduct client meetings in environments familiar to them.
- Talk candidly about behavior and activities.
- Remain nonjudgmental.
- Express a willingness to assist.
- Initiate the helping process according to client directions. (Tice & Perkins, 1996).

When the social worker asks about the client's conception of a better tomorrow, the client is motivated to think about his or her future and the helping relationship is on its way.

Changes in Family Structure

Among the early decisions the social worker makes in working with an older client is deciding who the client is. Although the social worker may address an older adult's particular concern, family members may be relevant to the problem and its solution. An important part of this assessment is determining who in the client's family or social support system is the most active and available to the client (chapter 5 further describes the tools used in making an assessment). The practitioner, though, needs to be aware that family structures have taken on different shapes owing to the longevity of the population, decreased fertility rates, and higher divorce rates (Bengtson, Giarrusso, Silverstein, & Wang, 2000). At the beginning of the 20th century, the structure of most families was akin to a pyramid, with usually one elderly grandparent at the top. The 21st-century family, in contrast, is shaped more like a beanpole, with great-grandparents who are still living at the top, but with fewer branches, that is, members of their children's, grandchildren's, and great-grandchildren's generations (Kiyak & Hooyman, 1999). The narrowing of the family means there is less potential for intrafamily support and caregiving.

Because of cultural and socioeconomic differences, the extent to which families and friends provide help to older adults varies across racial and ethnic groups. The social worker may observe cultural differences between clients' household and living arrangements. An American Association of Retired Persons (2001) survey, for example, found that Asian, black, and Hispanic people are more likely than white people to have three generations under one roof or an extended family living in one home. Because the effects a family's structure has on family members' ability to care for their older adults remains unclear (Greene, 2005a), social workers, during their assessment of the client and family system, must determine how families carry out various role demands (Tennstedt, 1999; see also chapter 6 for a discussion of interventions).

Essential Elements of Practice

Informed and effective action with individuals, families, groups, organizations, and communities is required for competent social work practice (Council on Social Work Education [CSWE], 1992). The following essential elements of curriculum proposed for the new CSWE Educational Policy and Accreditation Standards should inform practice. Students should be able to

- identify practice contexts—The social worker appraises and addresses current and future risks, assets, and solutions in an environment of ongoing local, national, and global change.
- apply ethics and professional values—The social worker is able to tolerate ambiguity and resolve ethical dilemmas.
- embrace diversity—The practitioner appreciates and delivers services to clients whose worldviews are different from his or her own.
- promote social and economic justice.
- incorporate theories and knowledge about the human condition.
- analyze and advocate for policies that redress inequitable conditions.
- use conceptual thinking and analytical reasoning—The social worker has the capacity to identify personal biases and myths, think critically, and formulate professional judgments.
- use science—The practitioner develops practice strategies that incorporate new knowledge and technological advances.
- establish a professional identity—The social worker demonstrates an ability to grow and carry out responsibilities professionally. (Black, 2007)

Practice Contexts

To prepare themselves to serve older adults effectively, students must learn about the changing nature of the aging population. For example, many of the baby-boomer population, those born in the post-World War II years between 1946 and 1964, will be well educated and have the financial means to take more control over their own care (Silverstone, 1996, 2000). Others, however, will not have that choice because of a lifetime of economic hardships and discrimination. As social workers contemplate new designs for social services and health care systems, we must address this two-tiered nature of opportunity (Greene, 2005a; see also chapter 11 for a discussion of policy practice).

Shifting Health and Human Services Delivery Systems

The demographic shifts in the aging population combined with dramatic changes in the shape, delivery, and financing of health and human services are influencing both the skills that social workers must bring to practice and their ability to provide quality care to older adults (Berkman & Harootyan, 2003). For example, privatization; the use of technology, especially in health care delivery; and a greater focus on quality, cost-effectiveness, and outcome measures are significant factors affecting health and human services delivery systems.

Although some of these factors may have resulted in improved care, practitioners must be aware that particular changes, such as cost containment, have led to skewed access to and distribution of health care and other services (Gardner & Zodikoff, 2003). Because clients may have had a difficult time accessing and receiving help from various services systems, social workers may want to ask clients what other agencies they have used. Frequently the practitioner acts as case manager—advocating for and coordinating the delivery of services (for more on competencies for case management practice, see chapter 8). However, a key intervention for the practitioner is to empower clients to traverse delivery systems on their own.

Using Conceptual Thinking and Analytical Reasoning

An essential element of the social work curriculum that informs practice is the use of conceptual thinking—the practitioner identifies underlying issues in a complex problem—and analytical reasoning—the social worker systematically and logically examines the problem to determine its implications and identifies strategies for resolving the problem. These skills enable social workers to carry out an open-minded assessment of a client's situation.

Using Science

In addition to learning about a client's views on aging, practitioners must acquire knowledge of current social concerns. For example, recent scientific research provides findings about diseases and treatments that involve older clients. Technological advances have revolutionized home health care with families assuming more medical follow-up at home after hospitalization. The ability to integrate and apply science, technology, and empirically based innovations into practice is a characteristic of contemporary social work.

Social workers use critical thinking to synthesize research findings and to develop a deeper understanding of social issues. In assessing a client's situation and to gain a deeper understanding of how recent scientific information may affect the client, practitioners may ask several questions (Gibbs & Gambrill, 1996):

- How do I know a claim is true?
- Who said the claim was accurate? What could their motivation be? How reliable are these sources?

- Are the presented facts correct?
- Have any facts been omitted?
- Have there been any critical tests of this claim? Have any experimental results been replicated? Were these studies relatively free of bias? What samples were used? How representative were they? Was random assignment used?
- Are there other plausible explanations?
- If correlations are presented, how strong are they?
- What weak appeals are used (for example, to emotion or special interest)?

Competency-Based Education

An array of issues and practice areas needed for competent practice with older adults and their families and support systems are presented. They are based on CSWE Foundation competencies and those developed by the CSWE Gero-Ed Center. They are rooted in resilience theory and the strengths-based perspective as described in the Resilience-Enhancing Model (REM) (Greene, 2007).

Foundation Competencies

To meet the demand for social services in contemporary society, students must acquire the knowledge, values, and skills embedded in foundation content. This content allows students to return to the historical mission of social work, which is composed of two complementary ideals—to enhance individual well-being and to improve or change social conditions (CSWE, 2001). The attention to both person and environment has been a continuing and unifying theme in the historical development of social work and is fundamental to geriatric practice. This multisystemic approach, also known as the ecological perspective, focuses on enhancing social functioning and creating the strongest mutually beneficial interaction between people and their environments (Bronfenbrenner, 1989; Cournoyer, 2000; Greene & Barnes, 1998; see chapter 2). The ecological perspective also acts as a guide for social workers in the helping process, suggesting practitioners address issues involving individuals, families, groups, organizations, communities, and society. Moreover, the person-in-environment perspective examines how the person fits into his or her environment to understand how environments can be supportive or hostile. When environments are not supportive, an important social work role is to advocate for social justice and for better access to services for marginalized groups, including older adults (U.S. Department of Health and Human Services, 1999).

Aging-Related Competencies

CSWE Foundation competencies provide the initial framework for the social work curriculum. However, within that framework are specific competencies that social workers in a particular field must acquire and demonstrate for informed and effective practice. In the field of aging, there has been a long-standing problem of an inadequate number of well-educated social work professionals to serve older adults and their families (Gonyea et al., 2004; Greene, 1989; Hudson, Gonyea, & Curley, 2003). Gerontological social workers have long struggled to ensure that competencies for geriatric practice would find a place in the social work curriculum, and their efforts seem to have paid off. The recent integration of aging competencies into foundation content has notably influenced social work education (Greene & Galambos, 2002; Rosen, Zlotnik, & Singer, 2002). Faced with an aging baby-boomer generation and the growing need for geriatric social workers, the John A. Hartford Foundation has committed to a number of projects to sustain, focus, and centralize efforts to strengthen the social work profession's response to this need (CSWE, 2001). In 1999, the Hartford Foundation established the Hartford Geriatric Social Work Initiative culminating in the competencies provided in this book (see the introduction to this book for the CSWE Gero-Ed Center Geriatric Social Work Competencies used as a scale in student self-assessment). Competencies in the field of aging presented at the beginning of each chapter are designed to prepare practitioners to carry out skills specific to geriatric practice. They include values, ethics, and theoretical perspectives; assessment of older adults, families, and support systems; intervention with older adults and their families; and aging services, programs, and policies (see Appendix 1-E for the CSWE Gero-Ed Center Geriatric Social Work Competencies stated in the form of curriculum outcomes).

Strengths-Based Competencies

The strengths-based social work movement emphasizes client assets and capabilities (Saleebey, 1997, 2005). The philosophy of the movement draws a practitioner's attention to positive aspects of aging well. *Aging well* means staying healthy and productive, living independently, and engaging in enjoyable activities. A person who ages well maintains ties with family, friends, and a circle of social supports (Antonucci & Akiyama, 1991). To help in this application, several strengths-based models are presented with an emphasis on the practice model—the Resilience-Enhancing Model (Greene, 2002, 2007).

In the strengths-based, positive approach, organizing constructs center around a philosophy that emphasizes resilience and how the social worker can help older clients to negotiate life transitions competently (Cohen & Greene, 2005; Diehl, 1998; Fraser, Richman, & Galinsky, 1999; Saul, 2003; Willis, 1991). This philosophy builds on the body of literature that underscores that a successful treatment outcome is the product of a client's own strengths and resources (Duncan & Miller, 2000; Miller, Duncan, & Hubble, 1997) and his or her worldview, culture, and life experiences (Ronch & Goldfield, 2003).

Of the numerous other concepts promoting everyday competence among older adults is Antonovsky's (1998) "salutogenesis" orientation, a paradigm focusing on how people naturally use available resources—within themselves or their environment—to foster mental and physical well-being. Similarly, the gerontologist Atchley's (1999) continuity theory contends that no matter how strong the societal forces are, an adult's thought and behavioral patterns over time are central to his or her ability to adapt. That is, the person's adaptive or continuity strategies help him or her maintain life satisfaction across the spectrum of life experiences from wellness to disability.

Productive aging is a theoretical construct looking at a person's capacity to remain in paid employment (Kaye, 2005). From a broader person-in-environment perspective, this concept refers to any activity "that produces goods and services such as housework, child care, volunteer work, help to family and friends, along with training and skills to enhance the capacity to perform such tasks" (Hooyman, 2005, p. 39). Another useful construct centering on a resilience philosophy that goes hand in hand with productive aging is successful aging. According to Rowe and Kahn (1998), successful aging is characterized by older adults adopting a disease prevention orientation, engaging in life by continuing social involvement, and maintaining high cognitive and physical functioning through ongoing activities (Figures 1-3 and 1-4). Crowther and colleagues (2002) have expanded the conceptualization of successful aging to include positive spirituality.

Conclusion

Finally, whatever the term—positive aging, wellness in aging, or successful aging—a movement is afoot to approach older clients in a positive, hopeful, and strengths-based fashion. This shift in focus from viewing aging as a time of decline to having a more

FIGURE 1-3 Components of Successful Aging

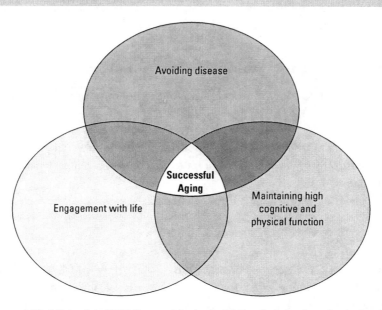

Sources: Rowe, J. W., & Kahn, R. L. (1998). Successful aging (p. 39).New York: Pantheon Books. Reprinted by permission of International Creative Management, Inc. Copyright © 1998 by J. W. Rowe and R. L. Kahn.

FIGURE 1-4 Revised Rowe and Kahn Model of Successful Aging

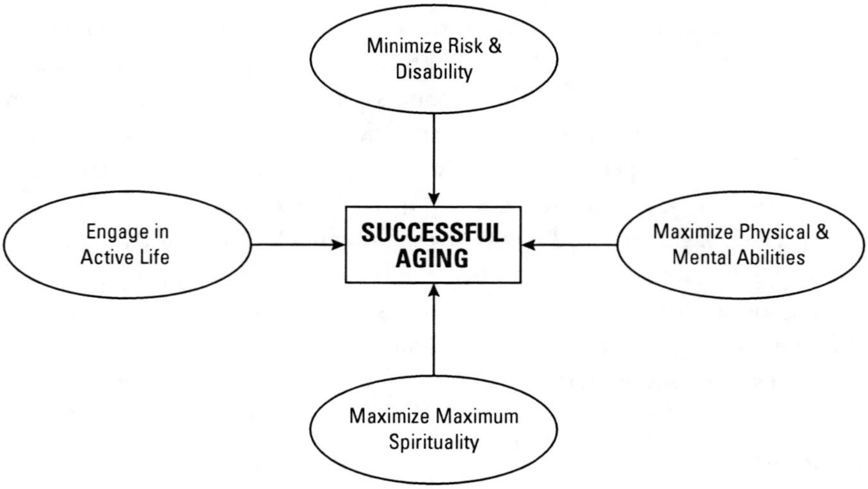

Source: Reprinted with permission from Crowther, M. R., Parker, M, W., Achenbaum, W. A., Larimore, W. L., & Koenig, H. G. (2002). Rowe and Kahn's model of successful aging revisited: Positive spirituality—The forgotten factor. *Gerontologist*, 42, 613–620.

positive view is a signal to the social work profession to develop programs that specifically promote health and psychosocial well-being among older adults and their families and use assertive rehabilitation strategies (Lewis & Harrell, 2002).

Suggested Exercise to Evaluate Student Competency

Students will conduct an environmental scan of their community demonstrating their ability to

- collect data on the economic and political trends in their geographic locale
- use census information and social indicators to describe local social, economic, and demographic trends
- describe their local client base in asset terms.

References

American Association of Retired Persons. (2001, July). *In the middle: A report on multicultural boomers coping with family and aging issues.* Washington, DC: Author.

Antonovsky, A. (1998). The sense of coherence: An historical and future perspective. In H. I. McCubbin, E. A. Thompson, A. I. Thompson, & J. E. Fromer (Eds.), *Stress, coping, and health in families* (pp. 3–20). Boston: Allyn & Bacon.

Antonucci, T., & Akiyama, H. (1991, Winter). Social relationships and aging well. *Generations,* pp. 39–44.

Atchley, R. C. (1999). *Continuity and adaptation in aging.* Baltimore: Johns Hopkins University Press.

Bengtson, V. L., Giarrusso, R., Silverstein, M., & Wang, H. (2000). Families and intergenerational relationships in aging societies. *Hallym International Journal of Aging, 2,* 3–10.

Berkman, B., & Harootyan, L. (2003). *Social work and health care in an aging society.* New York: Springer.

Black, P. (2007, February 2). *Evolution or revolution.* Paper presented at the CSWE Leadership Meeting, Charleston, South Carolina.

Bronfenbrenner, U. (1989). Ecological systems theory. *Annals of Child Development, 6,* 187–249.

Butler, R. N. (1975). *Why survive? Being old in America.* New York: Harper & Row.

Cohen, H. L., & Greene, R. R. (2005). Older adults who overcame oppression. *Families in Society, 87,* 1–8.

Council on Social Work Education. (1992). *Handbook of accreditation standards and procedures* (rev. ed.). Alexandria, VA: Author.

Council on Social Work Education. (2001). *A blueprint for the new millennium.* Alexandria, VA: Author.

Council on Social Work Education, National Center for Gerontological Social Work Education. (n.d.). *Foundation gerontological social work competencies.* Retrieved November 16, 2006, from http://depts.washington.edu/geroctr/Curriculum3/ Competencies/FdnComp.doc

Cournoyer, B. (2000). *The social work skills workbook.* Belmont, CA: Wadsworth.

Cowger, C. D. (1994). Assessing client strengths: Clinical assessment for client empowerment. *Social Work, 39,* 262–268.

Crowther, M. R., Parker, M, W., Achenbaum, W. A., Larimore, W. L., & Koenig, H. G. (2002). Rowe and Kahn's model of successful aging revisited: Positive spirituality—The forgotten factor. *Gerontologist, 42,* 613–620.

Diehl, M. (1998). Everyday competence in later life: Current status and future directions. *Gerontologist, 38,* 422–433.

Duncan, B. L., & Miller, S. D. (2000). *The heroic client.* San Francisco: Jossey-Bass.

Fraser, M. W., Richman, J. M., & Galinsky, M. J. (1999). Risk, protection, and resilience: Toward a conceptual framework for social work practice. *Social Work Research, 23,* 129–208.

Gardner, D., & Zodikoff, B. (2003). Meeting the challenges of social work practice in health care and aging in the 21st century. In B. Berkman & L. Harootyan (Eds.), *Social work and health care in an aging society* (pp. 377–392). New York: Springer.

Gibbs, L., & Gambrill, E. (1996). *Critical thinking for social workers: A workbook.* Thousand Oaks, CA: Pine Forge Press.

Gonyea, J. G., Hudson, R. B., & Curley, A. (2004, Spring). The geriatric social work labor force: Challenges and opportunities in responding to an aging society. In *Institute for geriatric social work issue brief* (pp. 1–7). Boston: Boston University School of Social Work.

Greene, R. (1988). *Continuing education for gerontological careers.* Alexandria, VA: Council on Social Work Education.

Greene, R. R. (1989). The growing need for social work services for the aged in 2020. In B. S. Vourlekis & C. G. Leukefeld (Eds.), *Making our case* (pp. 11–20). Silver Spring, MD: NASW Press.

Greene, R. R. (2000). *Social work with the aged and their families* (2nd ed.). New York: Aldine de Gruyter. (Original work published 1986)

Greene, R. R. (2002). *Resiliency: An integrated approach to practice, policy, and research.* Washington: DC: NASW Press.

Greene, R. R. (2005a). Family life. In L. W. Kaye (Ed.), *Perspectives on productive aging: Social work with the new aged* (pp. 107–122). Washington, DC: NASW Press.

Greene, R. R. (2005b). Redefining social work for the new millennium: Setting a context. *Journal of Human Behavior and the Social Environment, 10,* 37–54.

Greene, R. R. (2007). *Social work practice: A risk and resilience perspective.* Monterey, CA: Brooks/Cole.

Greene, R. R., & Barnes, G. (1998). The ecological perspective and social work practice: Applying the ecological perspective. In R. R. Greene & M. Watkins (Eds.), *Serving diverse constituencies* (pp. 63–96). New York: Aldine de Gruyter.

Greene, R. R., & Galambos, C. (2002). Social work's pursuit of a common professional framework: Have we reached a milestone? *Journal of Gerontological Social Work, 39,* 7–23.

Hareven, T. K. (1996). *Aging and generational relations over the life course: A historical and cross-cultural perspective.* Hawthorne, NY: Aldine de Gruyter.

Holstein, M. B., & Minkler, M. (2003). Self, society, and the "new" gerontology. *Gerontologist, 43,* 787–796.

Hooyman, N. (2005). Conceptualizing productive aging. In L. W. Kaye (Ed.), *Perspectives on productive aging: Social work with the new aged* (pp. 37–57). Washington, DC: NASW Press.

Hudson, R. B. (2005). The new political environment in aging: Challenges to policy and practice. *Families in Society, 86,* 321–327.

Hudson, R. B., Gonyea, J. G., & Curley, A. (2003, Spring). The geriatric social work labor force: Challenges and opportunities. *Public Policy 7 Aging Report, 13*(2), 12–16.

Kaye, L. W. (2005). *Perspectives on productive aging: Social work with the new aged.* Washington, DC: NASW Press.

Kivnick, H., & Murray, S. (2001). Life strengths interview guide: Assessing elder client's strengths. *Journal of Gerontological Social Work, 34*(4), 7–32.

Kiyak, H., & Hooyman, N. (1999). Aging in the twenty-first century. *Hallym International Journal of Aging, 1,* 56–66.

Laird, J. (1993). *Revisioning social work education: A social constructionist approach.* New York: Haworth Press.

Lewis, J. S., & Harrell, E. B. (2002). Resilience and the older adult. In R. R. Greene (Ed.), *Resilience theory and research for social work practice* (pp. 277–292). Washington, DC: NASW Press.

Miller, S. D., Duncan, B. L., & Hubble, M. A. (1997). *Escape from Babel: Toward a unifying language for psychotherapy practice.* New York: W. W. Norton.

National Association of Social Workers. (2000). *Code of ethics of the National Association of Social Workers.* Washington, DC: Author.

Palmore, E. B. (1998). *The facts on aging quiz* (2nd ed.). *The facts on aging quiz: Part 1* (pp. 3–4). New York: Springer.

President's Commission for the Study of Ethical Problems in Medicine and Biomedical and Behavioral Research. (1983a). *Deciding to forego life-sustaining treatment: A report on the ethical, medical, and legal issues in treatment decisions.* Washington, DC: Author.

President's Commission for the Study of Ethical Problems in Medicine and Biomedical and Behavioral Research. (1983b). *Summing up: Final report on studies of the ethical and legal problems in medicine and biomedical and behavioral research.* Washington, DC: Author.

Rogers, C. R., & Dymond, R. F. (1957). *Psychotherapy and personality change.* Chicago: University of Chicago Press.

Ronch, J., & Goldfield, J. A. (Eds.). (2003). *Mental wellness in aging: Strengths-based approaches.* Baltimore: Health Professions Press.

Rosen, A. L., Zlotnik, J. L., & Singer, T. (2002). Basic gerontological competence for all social workers: The need to "gerontologize" social work education. *Journal of Gerontological Social Work, 39*(1/2), 25–36.

Rowe, J. W., & Kahn, R. L. (1998). *Successful aging.* New York: Pantheon Books.

Saleebey, D. (1997). *The strengths perspective in social work practice* (2nd ed.). New York: Longman.

Saleebey, D. (2005). *The strengths perspective in social work practice* (4th ed.). Boston: Allyn & Bacon.

Sarkisian, C., Steers, W. N., Hays, R. D., & Mangione, C. M. (2005). Development of the 12-item expectations regarding aging survey. *Gerontologist, 45,* 240–248.

Saul, J. (2003). Strengths-based approaches to trauma in the aging. In J. Ronch & J. A. Goldfield (Eds.), *Mental wellness in aging: Strengths-based approaches* (pp. 299–314). Baltimore: Health Professions Press.

Scharlach, A. E., & Kaye, L. W. (Eds.). (1997). *Controversial issues in aging.* Boston: Allyn & Bacon.

Schneider, E. L., & Kropf, N. P. (1992). *Gerontological social work: Knowledge, service settings, and special populations.* Chicago: Nelson-Hall.

Schon, D. A. (1983). *The reflective practitioner: How professionals think in action.* New York: Basic Books.

Silverstone, B. (1996). Older people of tomorrow: A psychosocial profile. *Gerontologist, 36*, 27–32.

Silverstone, B. (2000). The old and the new in aging: Implications for social work practice. *Journal of Gerontological Social Work, 33*(4), 35–50.

Takamura, J. C. (2001). Towards a new era in aging and social work. *Journal of Gerontological Social Work, 36*(3/4), 1–11.

Tennstedt, S. (1999, March). *Family caregiving in an aging society.* Paper presented at the U.S. Administration on Aging Symposium: Longevity in the New American Century, Baltimore.

Tice, C. J., & Perkins, K. (1996). *Mental health issues and aging: Building on the strengths of older persons.* Pacific Grove, CA: Brooks/Cole.

Torres-Gil, F., & Moga, K. B. (2001). Multiculturalism, social policy, and the new aging. *Journal of Gerontological Social Work, 36*(3/4), 13–31.

U.S. Department of Health and Human Services. (1999). *Mental health: A report of the surgeon general.* Rockville, MD: U.S. Department of Health and Human Services.

Willis, S. L. (1991). Cognition and everyday competence. In K. W. Schaie (Ed.), *Annual review of gerontology and geriatrics* (Vol. 11, pp. 80–109). New York: Springer.

APPENDIX 1-A To What Extent Do I Assess Client Strengths?

Using a Likert-type scale, answer the following questions about your approach to social work practice:

	Low				High
When I meet with a client, I will					
give preeminence to client's understanding of the facts.	□ 1	□ 2	□ 3	□ 4	□ 5
believe the client.	□ 1	□ 2	□ 3	□ 4	□ 5
discover what the client wants.	□ 1	□ 2	□ 3	□ 4	□ 5
move the assessment toward personal and environmental strengths.	□ 1	□ 2	□ 3	□ 4	□ 5
make the assessment of strengths multidimensional.	□ 1	□ 2	□ 3	□ 4	□ 5
use the assessment to discover uniqueness.	□ 1	□ 2	□ 3	□ 4	□ 5
use language the client can understand.	□ 1	□ 2	□ 3	□ 4	□ 5
make assessment a joint activity between social worker and client.	□ 1	□ 2	□ 3	□ 4	□ 5
reach a mutual agreement on the assessment.	□ 1	□ 2	□ 3	□ 4	□ 5
avoid blame and blaming.	□ 1	□ 2	□ 3	□ 4	□ 5
avoid cause-and-effect thinking.	□ 1	□ 2	□ 3	□ 4	□ 5
assess and not diagnose.	□ 1	□ 2	□ 3	□ 4	□ 5

Source: Adapted with permission from Cowger, C. D. (1994). Assessing client strengths: Clinical assessment for client empowerment. *Social Work, 39,* 262–268.

APPENDIX 1-B Myths of Aging Checklist

To which of these myths do you subscribe? Use this checklist to find out!

Biological myths

☐ Getting to be old means a life fraught with physical complaints and illness.

☐ Older people are not attractive. They smell, have no teeth, can hardly see or hear, and are underweight.

☐ Older people should not exert themselves; they may have a heart attack or fall and break a bone.

☐ Older people sleep all the time.

☐ Sex ends at age 60. Older adults are asexual, have no interest in sex, and are unable to function as sexual beings.

Psychological myths

☐ Most older adults are set in their ways and unable to change.

☐ Old age is a time of relative peace and tranquility when people can relax and enjoy the fruits of their labor after the stressors of life have passed.

☐ Older adults are not responsive to counseling.

☐ Dementia is inevitable in old age. Older people cannot learn anything new. Intelligence declines with advancing age.

☐ Older people cannot solve day-to-day problems.

Social myths

☐ Older people are very dependent and need someone to take care of them. Older adults are socially isolated and neglected by their families.

☐ Older people inevitably withdraw from the mainstream of society as they grow older.

☐ Older adults do not want to work. Older people are poor.

☐ Older adults want to be left alone and spend most of their time watching television.

☐ The generation gap between young and old leads to alienation.

Source: Adapted from Schneider, E. L., & Kropf, N. P. (1992). *Gerontological social work: Knowledge, service settings, and special populations.* Chicago: Nelson-Hall.

APPENDIX 1-C The Palmore Facts on Aging Quiz

Answer true or false (check one box) for each statement:

	True	False
1. The majority of old people—65 years and over—are senile.	☐	☐
2. The five senses (sight, hearing, taste, touch, smell) all tend to weaken in old age.	☐	☐
3. The majority of old people have no interest in, or capacity for, sexual relations.	☐	☐
4. Lung vital capacity tends to decline with old age.	☐	☐
5. The majority of old people feel miserable most of the time.	☐	☐
6. Physical strength tends to decline with age.	☐	☐
7. At least one-tenth of the aged are living in long-stay institutions, such as nursing homes, mental hospitals, and homes for the aged.	☐	☐
8. Older drivers have fewer accidents per driver than those under age 65.	☐	☐
9. Older workers usually cannot work as effectively as younger workers.	☐	☐
10. Over three-fourths of the aged are healthy enough to do their normal activities without help.	☐	☐
11. The majority of old people are unable to adapt to change.	☐	☐
12. Older people usually take longer to learn something new.	☐	☐
13. Depression is more frequent among the elderly than among younger people.	☐	☐
14. Older people tend to react slower than younger people.	☐	☐
15. In general, old people tend to be pretty much alike.	☐	☐
16. The majority of old people say they are seldom bored.	☐	☐
17. The majority of older people are socially isolated.	☐	☐
18. Older workers have fewer accidents than younger workers.	☐	☐
19. More than 20 percent of the population is now 65 and older.	☐	☐
20. The majority of medical practitioners tend to give low priority to the aged.	☐	☐
21. The majority of old people have incomes below the poverty line, as defined by the U.S. federal government.	☐	☐
22. The majority of old people are working or would like to have some kind of work to do, including housework and volunteer work.	☐	☐
23. Old people tend to become more religious as they age.	☐	☐
24. The majority of old people say they are seldom irritated or angry.	☐	☐
25. The health and economic status of old people will be about the same or worse in the year 2010 compared with younger people.	☐	☐

Note: All odd-numbered statements are false; all even-numbered statements are true.

Source: Palmore, E. B. (1998). *The facts on aging quiz* (2nd ed.). *The facts on aging quiz: Part 1,* pp 3–4. New York: Springer. Reproduced with the permission of Springer Publishing Company, LLC, New York, NY 10036.

APPENDIX 1-D Expectations Regarding Aging Survey (12 items)

This survey measures what you expect will happen as people age. Please check the one box to the right of the statement that best corresponds with how you feel about the statement. If you are not sure, check the box that you think best corresponds with your feelings.

	Definitely True 1	Somewhat True 2	Somewhat False 3	Definitely False 4
1. When people get older, they need to lower their expectations of how healthy they can be.	☐	☐	☐	☐
2. The human body is like a car: When it gets old, it gets worn out.	☐	☐	☐	☐
3. Having more aches and pains is an accepted part of aging.	☐	☐	☐	☐
4. Every year that people age, their energy levels go down a little more.	☐	☐	☐	☐
5. I expect that as I get older I will spend less time with family and friends.	☐	☐	☐	☐
6. Being lonely is just something that happens when people get old.	☐	☐	☐	☐
7. As people get older they worry more.	☐	☐	☐	☐
8. It is normal to be depressed when you are old.	☐	☐	☐	☐
9. I expect that as I get older I will become more forgetful.	☐	☐	☐	☐
10. It is an accepted part of aging to have trouble remembering names.	☐	☐	☐	☐
11. Forgetfulness is a natural occurrence just from growing old.	☐	☐	☐	☐
12. It is impossible to escape the mental slowness that happens with aging.	☐	☐	☐	☐

Source: Adapted with permission from Sarkisian, C., Steers, W. N., Hays, R. D., & Mangione, C. M. (2005). Development of the 12-item expectations regarding aging survey. *Gerontologist, 45,* 240–248.

 COUNCIL ON SOCIAL WORK EDUCATION

GERO-ED CENTER NATIONAL CENTER FOR GERONTOLOGICAL SOCIAL WORK EDUCATION
GERIATRIC SOCIAL WORK INITIATIVE • *Funded by The John A. Hartford Foundation*

APPENDIX 1-E CSWE Gero-Ed Center Foundation Gerontological Social Work Competencies

The following is a list of foundation knowledge, values, and competencies (e.g., skills) to help form classroom learning objectives for BSW and 1st year MSW students. This represents a synthesis of the SAGE-SW competencies and the Practicum Partnership Program (PPP) Scale. It is not a scale, but rather a list of competencies to guide curriculum development in the BSW and MSW foundation years.

I. Values, Ethics, and Theoretical Perspectives (knowledge and value base, which is applied through skills/competencies)

1. Identify and assess one's own values and biases regarding aging and, as necessary, take steps to dispel myths about aging.
2. Respect and promote older adult clients' right to dignity and self-determination within the context of the law and safety concerns.
3. Apply ethical principles to decisions on behalf of all older clients with special attention to those who have limited decisional capacity.
   This competency includes professional boundary issues in work with older adults, client self-determination, end-of-life decisions, family conflicts, and guardianship.
4. Respect diversity among older adult clients, families, and professionals (e.g., class, race, ethnicity, gender, and sexual orientation).
   This competency encompasses understanding how diversity relates to variations in the aging process.
5. Address respectfully the cultural, spiritual, and ethnic values and beliefs of older adults and their families.
6. Relate concepts and theories of biological and social aging to social work practice.
   This competency includes understanding the effects of cohort and generational experiences on older adults, the normal aging process, and the life course perspective.
7. Relate social work perspectives and related theories to practice with older adults (e.g., person-in-environment, social justice).
8. Identify issues related to grief and loss, transitions, and adaptations to change over the life cycle.
9. Support individuals and families dealing with end-of-life issues related to dying, death, other losses, and grief.
10. Understand the perspectives and values of social work in relation to working effectively with other disciplines in geriatric interdisciplinary practice with older adults, their caregivers, and the community.

II. Assessment

1. Use empathy and sensitive interviewing skills (e.g., reminiscence or life review, support groups, counseling) to assess social functioning (e.g., social skills, social activity level) and social support of older adults.

(Continued)

APPENDIX 1-E CSWE Gero-Ed Center Foundation Gerontological Social Work Competencies (*Continued*)

II. Assessment (*Continued*)

This competency includes being able to conduct a social history that identifies family, agency, community, and societal factors that contribute to and support the older adult's independence and develop a service plan that builds on strengths and meets the needs of older persons, their families, or significant others.

2. Adapt interviewing methods to potential sensory, language, and cognitive limitations of the older adult.
3. Conduct a comprehensive evaluation of psychosocial factors that affect older people's physical and mental well-being.
   This competency includes evaluating safety issues and degree of risk for older clients.
4. Identify ways to ascertain the health status and physical functioning (e.g., ADLs and IADLS) of older adults.
5. Assess cognitive functioning and mental health status of older adults (e.g., depression, dementia).
   This competency includes knowing how to gather information regarding mental status (particularly memory), history of any past or current mental health problems, life satisfaction, coping abilities, mood or affect, and spirituality of older adults.
6. Assess caregivers' needs and stress levels.
7. Be aware of standardized assessment and diagnostic tools that are appropriate for use with older adults (e.g., depression scale, Mini-Mental Status Exam).
8. Develop clear, timely, and appropriate service or care plans with measurable objectives for older adults.
   Such plans are to be based on functional status, life goals, symptoms management, and financial and social supports of older people and their families and are to address financial, legal, housing, medical, and social needs.
9. Reevaluate and adjust services or care plans for older adults on a continuing basis.

III. Intervention

1. Establish rapport and maintain an effective working relationship with older adults and family members.
   This competency encompasses engaging and working with older adults and their families within the home, community-based settings, and institutions.
2. Adapt psycho-educational approaches to enhance older people's coping capacities and mental health.
3. Utilize group interventions with older adults and their families (e.g., bereavement groups, reminiscence groups).
4. Mediate situations with angry or hostile older adults and family members.
5. Assist caregivers to reduce their stress levels and maintain their own mental and physical health.

(*Continued*)

APPENDIX 1-E CSWE Gero-Ed Center Foundation Gerontological Social Work Competencies (*Continued*)

III. Intervention (*Continued*)

This competency encompasses assisting families that are in crisis situations regarding their older family members, providing information to support family caregivers, and engaging family caregivers in maintaining their own mental and physical health.

6. Provide social work case management to link elders and their families to resources and services and to conduct long-term planning.
7. Use educational strategies to provide older persons and their families with information related to wellness and disease management (e.g., Alzheimer's disease, end of life care).
8. Understand how to terminate work with older clients and their families.
9. Advocate on behalf of older adults with agencies and other professionals to help them obtain quality services.
10. Adhere to laws and public policies related to older adults (e.g., elder-abuse reporting, legal guardianship, powers of attorney, wills, advance directives, and do-not-resuscitate orders).

IV. Aging Services, Programs, and Policies

1. Identify how policies, regulations, and programs impact older adults and their caregivers, particularly among historically disadvantaged populations (e.g., women and elders of color).
2. Identify ways to reach out to older adults and their families to ensure appropriate use of the service continuum (e.g., health promotion, long-term care, mental health).
3. Adapt organizational policies, procedures, and resources to facilitate the provision of services to diverse older adults and their family caregivers.
   This competency can encompass health, mental health, and long-term care policies.
4. Identify and develop strategies, including intergenerational approaches, to address services gaps, fragmentation, discrimination, and barriers that impact older persons.
5. Include older adults in planning and designing programs.
6. Evaluate the effectiveness of practice and programs in achieving intended outcomes for older adults.
7. Apply evaluation and research findings to improve practice and program outcomes.
8. Advocate and organize with services providers, community organizations, policymakers, and the public to meet the needs and issues of a growing aging population.
   This competency encompasses strategies to address age discrimination in relation to health, housing, employment, and transportation.

(*Continued*)

APPENDIX 1-E CSWE Gero-Ed Center Foundation Gerontological Social Work Competencies (*Continued*)

IV. Aging Services, Programs, and Policies (*Continued*)

    9. Identify the availability of resources and resource systems for older adults and their families.

   10. Identify the major sources of funding for meeting the needs of older adults.

Note: This list of competencies reflects a blending of the Council on Social Work Education's Strengthening Aging and Gerontology Education in Social Work (SAGE-SW competencies and the Practicum Partnership Program Scale (PPP) (a project funded by the John A. Hartford Foundation). It is not a scale, but rather a list of competencies to guide curriculum development in the BSW and MSW foundation years. (The PPP Geriatric Social Work Competency Scale II used in field education can be found in the Introduction to the text).

Source: From Council on Social Work Education, Gero-Ed Center. (2004). *Foundation gerontological social work competencies.* Retrieved November 16, 2006, from http://depts.washington.edu/geroctr/Curriculum3/Competencies/FdnComp.doc

Theory and Concepts Underpinning Assessment in Practice

2

RATIONALE: Social workers must stay on the forefront of an expanding knowledge base and take advantage of scientific advances. Perspectives from the humanities and social and life sciences should be applied critically to understand complex human and social concerns. Whenever possible, social workers should use empirical content on the reciprocal relationships between human behavior and social environments to assess biological, psychological, sociological, and spiritual development across the life span. They should be able to use a life course perspective to inform practice with diverse clients within a sociocultural and historical context.

COMPETENCY: Students will critique and use conceptual frameworks to guide the process of assessment. They will demonstrate that they can

- relate social work perspectives and related theories to practice with older adults (e.g., person in environment, social justice).
- relate concepts and theories of biological and social aging to social work practice.
  This competency includes understanding the effects of cohort and generational experiences on older adults, the normal aging process, and the life course perspective.
- identify issues related to losses, changes, and transitions over the life cycle in designing interventions. (Council on Social Work Education, Gero-Ed Center, 2004)

Social work educators have debated how to use theories in social work practice. Some have contended (Laird, 1993; Saleebey, 2004) that theories offer social workers perspectives—not truth—and hence contribute narratives and interpretive devices. For example, Dennis Saleebey (2005), a pioneer in the strengths-based approach to social work practice, has characterized theories as follows:

- Theories are associated with power and the dominant culture. The origins of theories of human behavior are sociocultural, political, and relational.
- Theories offer multiple, not singular, views. Practitioners must consider theories in light of the uniqueness of individuals and cultures.
- Theories best address individuals as social phenomena. Theories need to address people as interdependent beings or as persons-in-environments.
- Theories reflect language and intersubjectivity. Language is the basis for the exchange and creation of meanings. Theories imply or reflect values.

On the other hand, educators have argued that theories ought to organize practitioners' observations logically and bind facts and data together to provide explanatory power (Newman & Newman, 2005). That is, there should be empirical support for their major assumptions. Throughout this book, we have suggested a working knowledge of theory, following the definition that a theory is a "framework to structure professional activities, to guide the practitioner through the social work processes of conducting assessments and selecting interventive strategies, and creating new meanings through discourse" (Greene, 1999, p. 2).

As you understand and adopt conceptual frameworks from various theories, you will develop the competencies that comprise the building blocks of your resilience-enhancing practice. You will first want to consider whether the concept you have adopted will be effective with older adults. For example, you may come to realize that the life course perspective suggests that your clients have faced and overcome many life challenges before entering their later years. This positive perspective may lead you to adopt resilience-enhancing interventions that help you tap your clients' current strengths (see chapter 6).

Foundation Knowledge

Ecological Perspective

Ecological theory views human behavior in a person-in-environment context; that is, the mutual accommodation of an active, growing human (in this specific situation the older adult) to his or her environment (Bronfenbrenner, 1979). The person-in-environment orientation that guides foundation practice is compatible with social work's long-standing concern for individual well-being and improved societal or environmental conditions. An ecological viewpoint expands social workers' worldview so that they may better understand their clients' psychological concerns, material needs, and economic and social conditions (Greene & Watkins, 1998). Approaching assessment of client systems from an ecological standpoint is congruent with resilience-enhancing social work practice and advantageous to practitioners in the field of aging for a number of reasons discussed below. The principles of an ecological assessment, as adapted from Greene and Barnes (1998), are

- Assessment requires identification of a focal system to receive primary attention—the person, housing complex, or neighborhood.
- Practitioners need to comprehend clients' stress levels and ability to cope with stress and the imbalance between demands and the use of resources.
- Social workers need to assess client efficacy or confidence to act on the environment.
- Assessment encompasses how clients engage with people and their natural environment, that is, the extent and quality of their relationships, and social and emotional ties.
- Key to the assessment process is determining the goodness of fit between the older adult and the older adult's family and their environment and whether the client family is in a position to exercise their self-determination or choices.
- Agency assessment should address the climate for services for diverse client populations and whether agency services are culturally sensitive.
- Assessment at the macro level should explore the large-scale societal context and how the client's family is affected by legal regulations or policies.

Multisystemic View

One important advantage of the ecological perspective is that it enables practitioners to delineate clearly not only who the case or the client is, but also what the systemic boundaries are:

> The case may be defined as a person, a family, a hospital ward, a housing complex, a particular neighborhood, a school population, a group with particular problems and needs, or a community with common concerns. . . . The drawing of a systemic boundary rather than a linear one provides for the true psychosocial perception of a case, because it includes the significant inputs into the lives of the individuals involved. (Meyer, 1973, p. 50)

The ecological perspective emphasizes the connections between the older adult and the various systems levels with which he or she interacts (Bronfenbrenner, 1979; see Figure 2-1). From this perspective, multilevel client assessments allow geriatric social workers to gain an understanding of how older clients function within their total environment and to plan a range of helpful interventions that promote continued competence (see chapter 5).

When deciding on which system to focus, practitioners may ask: What are the older adult's risks? Where do his or her solutions lie? Because the ecological perspective is a multisystemic approach, social workers may apply it to their work with small-scale

FIGURE 2-1 Bronfenbrenner's Model of the Ecology of Human Development

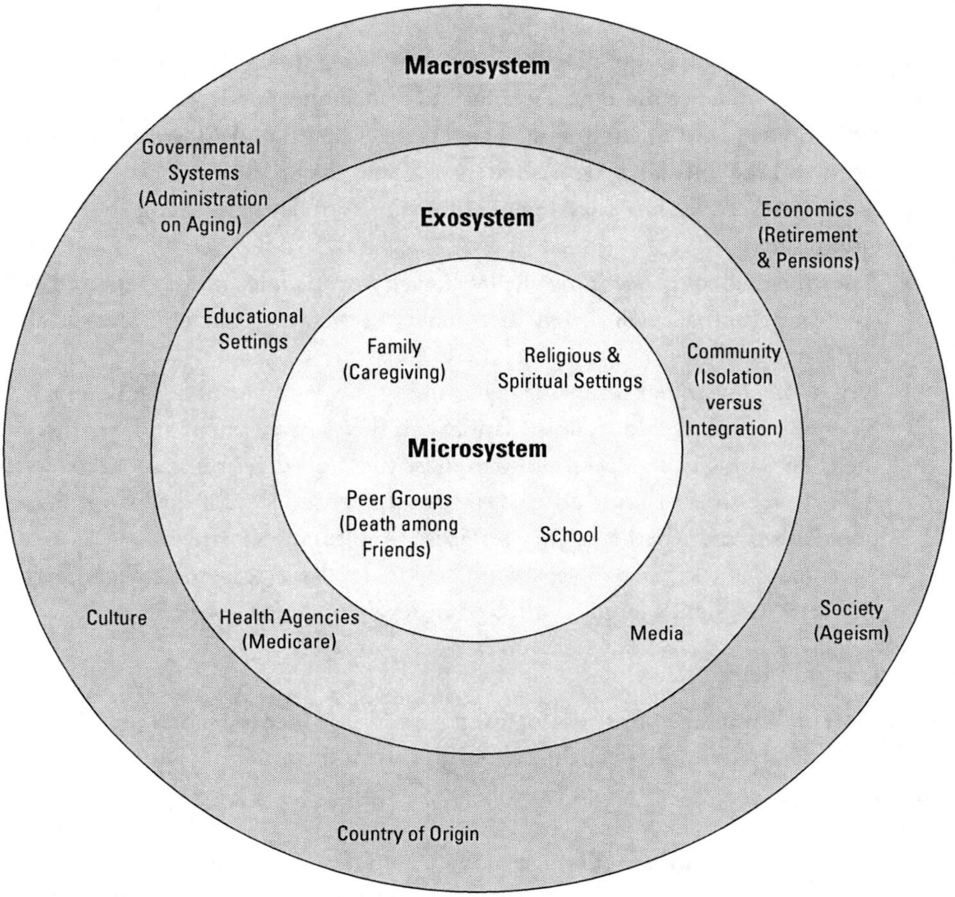

Source: Adapted from Bronfenbrenner, U. (1979). The ecology of human development. Cambridge, MA: Harvard University Press.

microsystems, which involve face-to-face relationships (for example, in families and peer groups); *mesosystems,* which are the connections between systems (for example, the linkages between the family and senior centers); *exosystems,* which encompass the connections between systems—at least one of which does not directly involve the developing person (for example, the area agency on aging or the adult child's workplace); and *macrosystems,* which are overarching large-scale systems (for example, the legal and political systems that enact and administer policies affecting client systems).

From this perspective, practitioners are able to better understand the multiple forces affecting an older adult's concerns and opportunities. For example, an older adult may have interpersonal issues that are exacerbated by the political environment;

or the political environment may contribute to a lack of social support. You may also learn how older adults can work to improve their environments.

What are the relative risks and protective factors? Using an ecological approach as reflected in resilience-enhancing practice, practitioners learn how each system functions so that they may target a particular system or systems for intervention. They may need to engage in "boundary-spanning practice," in which they secure resources for an older client from several different systems to maintain his or her well-being (for more on this process, see chapters 6 and 8).

In addition to deciding on which system or systems to devote their primary attention, practitioners must settle on how to best use their skills. Will they engage in face-to-face dialogue with their older clients? Will they engage with and attempt to change other client systems? Will they plan programs on their clients' behalf or advocate for policy changes that might improve access to services? On the other hand, social workers may carry out any or all of these roles and functions.

During the assessment and intervention process with older adults, their families, and support systems, then, social workers would typically follow six steps (Longres, 1990) by identifying the

1. client system to be assessed
2. condition in the client system that the practitioner needs to understand
3. factors about the client system itself that contribute to the condition
4. factors in the social context of the client system that contribute to, or assist with, the condition
5. resources available to the client system that exist within the system itself
6. resources that exist within the environment of the particular system. (pp. 47–48)

Life Course Perspective

Another useful feature of ecological theory is that it assumes people will experience growth throughout the *life course*. The life course concept provides a way for social workers to view and appreciate a client's key life events. This approach reveals the experiences that the client has shared with his or her *cohort*, or group of people born in the same era. Was he or she shaped by the Great Depression, wars, or the civil rights movement? The life course concept is a useful approach for working with older adults and their families because it considers individual life transitions within family and social contexts (Hareven, 1982). It also helps to explain the critical events people faced during their lifetime (Figure 2-2). This information about coping can enlighten the practitioner as he or she plans present interventions (chapter 6 will discuss this idea further).

The life course concept does not just look at events chronologically. Rather it considers a person's life within multiple contexts including gender, race, ethnicity, sexual orientation and so forth. The life course contrasts with the *life stage approach* in which social workers gather a detailed social history to determine if a person has successfully negotiated the developmental tasks or milestones associated with life transitions (Masten,

FIGURE 2-2 Example of a Timeline

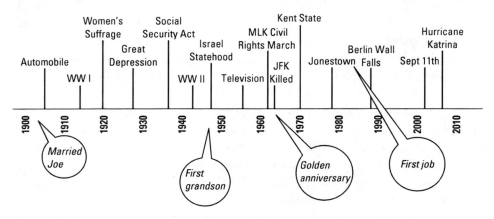

Source: Adapted from Frank, C., Kurland, J., and Goldman, B. (1978). Tips for getting the best from the rest (p. 13). Baltimore: Jewish Family & Children's Service.

1994). Some theorists (Germain, 1991; Greene, 1999; Hareven, 1982) adopt a more universal approach in which the practitioner explores a client's life story to discover the timing of personal and family life events, and the historical and cultural changes associated with them. You may want to adapt the time line provided in Figure 2-2 to examine critical events in your client's life history.

Stress and Adaptation to Problems in Living

The ecological perspective calls our attention to how older adults, their families, and their communities deal with the stressful events of life. Carter and McGoldrick (1999) have provided a schema, or a pictorial representation, allowing us to visualize two dimensions of stress including the developmental path of the individual, family, and society, and the multiple systems levels along which development takes place (Figure 2-3). As you examine the figure, think about the many obstacles in life resilient that older adults and their social support systems have had to overcome.

The vertical axis of systems levels in Figure 2-3 reflects the individual's biological and genetic makeup. The horizontal axis defines the individual's emotional, cognitive, interpersonal, and physical development over the life course, taking into account the person's sociohistorical context. At the family level, the vertical axis depicts the family history and intergenerational patterns of relating. The horizontal axis or time line refers to family changes over time, as members move through family life transitions. At the sociocultural level, the vertical axis relates cultural and societal history, stereotypes, power, privileges, and oppression (chapter 3 will further discuss diversity issues). The horizontal axis encompasses community connections, current events, and social policy (chapters 10 and 11 will discuss community and policy issues in depth).

FIGURE 2-3 Flow of Stress Through the Family

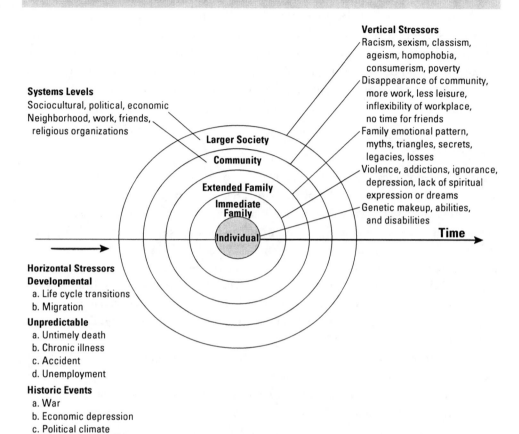

Sources: From Carter, Betty & Monica McGoldrick (Eds.). *The expanded family life cycle: Individual, family, and social perspective, 3/e*. Published by Allyn and Bacon, Boston, MA. Copyright © 1998 by Pearson Education. Reprinted by permission of the publisher.

A resilience-enhancing model can be used to explain the sources of an older client's stress and how to alleviate them (Greene, 2007). When does stress occur? What precipitates it? According to Germain and Gitterman (1995), people will meet natural stressors at any time over the life course. These include:

- difficult life transitions, developmental or social changes such as retirement or widowhood
- traumatic life events, including grave losses—such as those experienced by survivors of Hurricane Katrina—or illness—for example, people who live with cancer or human immunodeficiency virus
- environmental pressures, such as poverty and violence.

As ecological approaches emerged in the 1970s and 1980s, social workers began to emphasize healthy, realistic adaptation to problems in living (Kirschner, 1986). A clear benefit of the ecological perspective as a building block in a resilience-enhancing approach is that it directs the social worker's attention to the way in which older adults meet everyday life tasks, and the support they receive and provide to their social support systems (Germain & Gitterman, 1995). A successful contemporary practitioner is one who understands how older clients handle the stresses imposed daily by their environment and the steps they take to remain competent.

Relatedness

A successful ecological assessment involves not only examining how the older adult adapts to stress, but also how he or she forms relationships and continues to connect with others. Social workers who practice with intergenerational families need to learn about how issues, such as loyalty obligations and indebtedness to family members, influence or affect family dynamics (Boszormenyi-Nagy & Spark, 1973). The perspective is helpful to social workers in the field of aging because it recognizes that relationships can positively influence the development of resilience. Clearly, the bonding of infants and children with their parents is an important developmental task. However, bonding continues to be important as the family develops, and as the individual ages and participates in social networks (Brody, 1985).

Practitioners will also want to learn more about the older client's (and family's) connection to other social systems. By using the ecomap shown in chapter 5, you can facilitate this. As people age and their contemporaries die, support networks often diminish. These losses can precipitate difficulties, particularly depression. Therefore, knowledge about the people available to the client (family) is important to the assessment process.

General Systems Theory

Practitioners often use general systems theory, a set of abstract assumptions—adopted from biology—about how systems work, to understand and assess older adults within family systems. The word "families" is understood to encompass multiple forms, including blended families, single-parent families, and partners (Greene, 1999). From the systemic point of view, the social worker sees that the whole is more than the sum of its parts. According to Buckley (1967), a pioneer in the development of systems thinking, the "more than" points to family organization that is different from looking at each member alone. General systems theory suggests, then, that to understand a family, it is necessary to examine the relationships among family members, and any one individual's behavior should be considered to be a consequence of the total social situation. This can clearly be seen in caregiving families and whether they work together effectively.

Other systems theory theoretical assumptions include:

- Each family (of later years) has a unique, discernible "structure," or a pattern of stable relationships, among family members based on the functions that each person carries out.
- The nature of family relationships is reflected in its "organization," or the groupings or working arrangements of the system members.
- All social systems have two interrelated systems of roles: the "instrumental," dealing with socioeconomic tasks, and the "expressive," dealing with emotions. Family members may play different roles at different times in the life of the family. The caretaking role, for example, may be fulfilled by the parent for a child or by an adult child for a parent.
- "Complementarity" of family roles, which refers to the fit of role relationships and the growth and creative adaptability of the family group, is of major importance to family functioning. To achieve complementarity of roles, one member of the family system acts to provide something that is needed by another. When there is failure in role complementarity, stress is placed on the family system.
- Throughout the life cycle, family members must be able to negotiate the required changes, shifting and altering their relationships to meet the needs of all. This movement through the life cycle is called "family development".
- As family systems develop, they can be resilient in their own right. Their resilience is dependent on the meaning that the collective attributes to life events.

Such abstract assumptions can enable practitioners to better understand how the family group behaves as an organized social system and whether the group is meeting the needs of family members (Greene, 1999).

Collective Identity

A social system is an organization of people united in some form of regular interaction and interdependence. As practitioners conduct a family assessment, it is important that they remain mindful of the collective identity of individuals who are members of the social system. According to the systems model, to comprehend collective behavior, social workers must examine the relationship between members and focus on the social system's properties in its own right (Greene, 1999). How does the adult child perceive his or her aging parent? How does the aging parent perceive his or her child? Are they able to communicate effectively?

In many instances, particularly when communication is less than effective, the practitioner might decide that the family system itself is the client. The practitioner will understand the family as a social system consisting of individuals that influence one another. Thus, individuals and their roles are interdependent. Family rules develop over time, such as who is in charge of certain functions. To fully understand the caregiving provided within a family, the social worker must appreciate the development of the family as a group of interacting, interdependent individuals (Klein & White, 1996).

Functional-Age Model of Intergenerational Family Treatment

The functional-age model of intergenerational family treatment developed by Greene (1986/2000) allows social workers to assess and intervene with older adults and their families in caregiving situations. In this model, the social worker views the family as a mutually dependent unit with a shared past and future. During assessment, the social worker explores the functional capacity of the person needing care. The family is assessed as a social system with an emphasis on how members carry out their roles and deal with life transitions. When these general systems theory assumptions are joined with resilience-enhancing principles, they direct the practitioners' attention to "the adaptive qualities of families as they encounter stress" (Hawley & DeHaan, 1996, p. 284; see chapter 5 for more details on how the assessment is carried out.).

Theorists interested in family resilience will also focus on the family's natural resources, patterns of functioning, and capabilities that enable the family to meet and even thrive in the face of crisis. A family is not only a social system, but also a boundary-maintaining system, that is, it is open to societal or environmental resources and demands. Can a family link with other social systems and adapt to changing situations? What external forces has a family faced over time? Has it obtained needed resources?

Using family systems theory, as outlined above, practitioners may begin to observe and understand how family structure may be changed through planned interventions. Systems theory guides social workers in their assessment of a family by

- working with the family to define its membership
- learning about the family's culture
- assuming each family is a unique structure with its own communication patterns
- observing how the family is organized and what roles each family member fulfills
- assessing how the family deals with stress
- determining how the family uses its internal resources and what resources it needs to acquire from other social systems
- ascertaining what are mutually acceptable interventions.

Family Meanings and Stress

Families can be understood by exploring family meanings that have developed over time. Families share collective meanings that are distinct from individual meanings.

Family meanings are collective constructs created through the life experiences of family members as they interact over time. Patterson and Garwick (1998) have suggested that there are two levels of meaning: (1) situational meaning, involving the individual's and family's perceptions of their daily demands and capabilities; and (2) global meaning, encompassing a transcendent set of beliefs about the relationships of family members and the family to the community. The social worker can learn about a family's global beliefs as it explores the family's sense of common purpose. Do members accept that they are part of a collective? Are they able to view their situation optimistically? How do they perceive demands? Do they share control and trust?

Family Transitions

An important aspect of a family assessment is learning how members have functioned as a group over time. Families may go through normative (usual and expected) transitions, such as births, marriages, and deaths, or they may have to handle unexpected events, such as the death of a child. The more difficult transitions families in Western culture face are dying, death, and bereavement. Social workers must have the appropriate preparation and skills to work with families in such difficult times.

Caregiving

The family continues to be the primary caregiver to disabled and frail older adults (Riley, 2007). This is a normative task that represents a major family transition, is one that is expected of all families, and can be difficult and time consuming, particularly when an older relative has advance-stage dementia or is incontinent. Family members who care for an impaired relative may develop physical or psychological difficulties of their own. For example, they may become depressed or experience deterioration in their own health. This is referred to as *caregiver burden*. Therefore, assessing family stress and exploring how to lessen caregiver burden are central social work functions in dealing with the family of later years.

One means of helping caregivers reduce their burden is to explore the possible rewards of caregiving. Recent research has shed light on the fact that caregiving can increase psychological well-being and resiliency (Riley, 2007). The literature (Hunt, 2003) indicates that caregiving has five positive aspects:

1. caregiver satisfaction—caregiving experiences that provide a positive feeling about life
2. uplift of caregiving—daily events that can make the caregiver feel good
3. caregiver esteem—the confidence caregivers can gain as a direct result of their caregiving
4. any positive return—any return caregivers receive because of the experience
5. ability to find or make a positive appraisal of caregiving—transforms the meaning of the caregiving experience.

Although each of these benefits offers the social worker a slightly different view of the personal rewards of caregiving, they provide an avenue to pursue during assessment interviews (Gaugler, Kane, & Newcomer, 2007) (see chapter 5 for discussion of assessment strategies).

End-of-Life Issues

One of the most difficult challenges geriatric social workers face is helping a family make end-of-life decisions, face the death of a loved one, or go through the bereavement process. They will often help families make ethical decisions involving advanced directives—documents signed by a competent person giving direction to health care providers about treatment choices in certain circumstances (see chapter 4 for a discussion of ethical issues).

Practitioners must recognize that end-of-life decision making—another major family transition—may vary given a client family's culture (see chapter 4 for how cultural differences influence end-of-life decisions). For example, how an older adult and his or her family perceive the meaning of dying may differ depending on how members have been socialized to think about death. Are they fearful, or do they consider death to be a natural part of life? Furthermore, family members may have varying reactions to the loss of a loved one who has died after a prolonged illness or peacefully during sleep.

Bereavement

A universal response to the loss of a loved one, bereavement is the ability to sustain, integrate, and recover from loss. Although bereavement is a natural part of growth and development throughout life, affective or emotional reactions may range from sadness, restraint, to even anger. The acceptance of various expressions of grief requires social workers to view mourning responses as resilient acts of healing (Greene, 2002).

Social Support Networks

In assessment, geriatric practitioners will want to include information about the structure and content of their clients' social support networks or potential "helpers"—that is, biological and extended family members, friends, partners, and others who have established relationships with the individual or family. This information may indicate how people's attachments and support systems contribute to resilience. The structure of support systems refers to the number of ties, types of ties, and the interconnectedness of ties, and content includes information about the type of assistance a person has received. When people need help, they may turn to neighbors and friends to provide counseling or emotional support (Farris, 2007). Such social support has been found to be related to well-being. For example, social integration may positively affect physical or mental health; furthermore, it provides a buffer against damages a person may suffer because of a major life crisis (Thoits, 1995).

In the future, older clients' social support networks will include fewer adult children who are available to care for them. In fact, today an estimated one-fifth of Americans 65 years of age and older have no children and one-third of the baby boomer generation will have no children. We are increasingly living in a "small-family society." Consequently, this "thinning of the caregiving cohort" places a greater reliance on other members of one's social support networks for the well-being and care of older adults (Gironda, Lubben, & Atchison, 1999). How do these data affect our client family?

Gerontological Knowledge

Most older adults prefer to age in place—that is, in their own homes. They desire to grow old in a familiar environment, a place they have established over time and to which they have developed a psychological and physical attachment. Such familiarity may assist an older adult in overcoming the limitations posed by his or her physiological and sensory conditions. Our homes are often an expression of who we are: Home, for example, may be in a neighborhood that is linked to one's personal history and life events. This may explain why some older adults are reluctant to relocate (Rowles, 1993). To help geriatric social workers better assess the feasibility of an older adult's desire to age in place and that adult's readiness to remain competent in his or her home environment, we must first understand the concept of *environmental press,* how the environmental context places demands on the older adult.

Environmental Press–Competence Model

Like other social work theoretical approaches, an ecological model of aging examines behavior as the function of a person and the environment. The person is viewed in terms of a set of competencies, and the environment is defined in terms of demands. Thus, the fit between the two involves the interaction between the older individual and the environment.

Environment

Just as Bronfenbrenner (1979) classified environmental systems by their size and linkages to the individual, environments may be characterized by their influences on behavior. Will the risks in an older adult's environment be *proximal,* those closer to the individual, or *distal,* those situated further away, such as the political climate of the day (Kirby & Fraser, 1997)? "Personal environments" consist of significant others, such as family or friends, who engage in a one-to-one personal relationship with the older adult. Does the older adult maintain friendships? "Suprapersonal environments" are the modal characteristics of all the people in physical proximity to an older person, including his or her neighbors or ethnic group (Lawton, 1982). Is the older adult living close to his or her cultural group? "Social environments" comprise the norms or values (such as the wish to live independently) and institutions operating in the individual's subgroup, society, or culture. Do the norms of the social environment promote independence or interdependence? "Physical environments" refer to the nonpersonal, nonsocial aspects of the environment, such as space, noise, and pollution. Does the older adult, for example, live in a neglected neighborhood? When using this model, the social worker's assessment is based on the client's positive behavioral outcome, exploring whether the older adult is able to balance capabilities with the demands—or press—of his or her environment (Lawton & Nahemow, 1973; see Figure 2-4).

Competence

How does the social worker decide that a client appears competent in his or her environment? Historically, competence has been defined by an individual's "attributes associated with a white middle-class type of success in school or society . . . commonly involving the performance of a culturally specified task" (Ogbu, 1981, p. 414). From the perspective of environmental press, competence is defined "as the theoretical upper limit of capacity of the individual to function in the areas of biological health, sensation–perception, motoric behavior, and cognition" (Lawton, 1982, p. 38). When social workers examine the upper limit of an individual's capacity to function in the environment, they are exploring the least restrictive environment in which the person is able to function. If a client prefers to stay in his or her home, can he or she remain there? Does the client need or want additional help?

FIGURE 2-4 Environmental Press–Competence Model

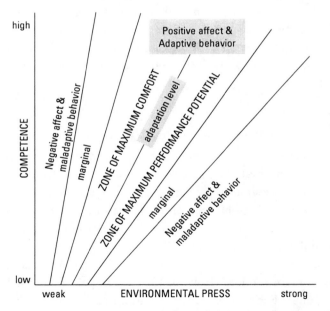

Source: Reprinted with permission from Lawton, M. P., & Nahemow, L. (1973). Ecology and the aging process. In C. Eisdorfer & M. P. Lawton (Eds.), *The psychology of adult development and aging* (p. 661). Washington, DC: American Psychological Association.

Factors that the geriatric social worker will examine to assess client competence (Lawton, 1982) are

- biological health—absence of disease states that prohibit functioning in the home
- sensory–perceptual capacity—processes of vision, audition, olfaction, gestation, somesthesis (bodily perception), and kinesthesis (the ability to sense the position, orientation, and movement of one's body parts) that make movement in the home extremely difficult
- motor skills—muscular strength and complex coordination that are necessary to perform on one's own
- cognitive capacity—ability to comprehend, process, and cope with the external world required to live alone
- ego strength—internal psychological strength that enhances independence.

In "relativistic models," competencies are carried out within the context of a particular culture. Social workers are concerned with the person-in-environment fit, that is, how well a client is able to function within his or her home environment. Goodness of fit refers to an appropriately supportive environment (see chapter 3 on how discrimination and oppression affect goodness of fit). From this viewpoint, geriatric social workers recognize that competence is not static, but is subject to interventions that improve functional capacity. In an assessment of the person-in-environment fit, the practitioner examines the older adult's functional limitations, such as severe loss of sight, or loss of upper extremity skills, and environmental barriers, such as inaccessible bathrooms or bedrooms or unsafe stairways (see chapter 5 for a home safety survey). The practitioner and client then develop a plan of care that includes what interventions will be taken (see chapter 6).

Biopsychosocial and Spiritual Function

Another way of assessing the person-in-environment fit is to explore an older client's biopsychosocial and spiritual functioning. "Functional-age assessment," which provides indications of a person's competence, resilience, or both, involves understanding the biopsychosocial and spiritual behaviors that affect a person's ability to perform behaviors central to everyday life. The geriatric social worker must examine the client's biological factors, or functional capacity, including health, physical capacity, or vital life-limiting organ systems. Psychological factors also come into play during assessment; they encompass an older adult's affective state or mood, cognitive or mental status, and the person's behavioral dimensions. Sociocultural aspects to consider are the cultural, political, and economic aspects of life events (Birren, 1959; Greene, 2000; McInnis-Dittrich, 2002). Spiritual factors may include a person's relationship with his or her faith or religious community or an inner system of beliefs. The importance of spiritual functioning is that it contributes to a person's ability to transcend the immediate situation and to discover life's meaning.

From a systems standpoint, social workers will consider an older adult's biopsychosocial and spiritual functioning as intertwined (Berger & Federico, 1982). The outcome of the holistic assessment when viewed from the vantage point of ecological press will allow the practitioner to help the older adult (and his or her family) to come to a decision about resources and services that may be required for an older adult to remain living in his or her home. They will also indicate how well a client system has overcome difficulties in past and current functioning that may positively affect resilience.

Knowledge: The Resilience Perspective

Resilience as Competence

Risk and resilience theory explains why some people better withstand adversity or high levels of stress than others. Risk and resilience theory has its roots in a public health model that explored risk factors for heart and lung disease. For example, in the Framingham Heart Study that started in the 1950s (http://www.nhlbi.nih.gov/index.htm), risk was defined as the statistical probability that smoking behavior would likely increase the development of a problem condition, namely, heart disease. Researchers informed participants in the study of the risks resulting from inactivity, smoking, and a high-fat diet. The study outcome—many but not all smokers would develop heart disease. The question was why.

Investigations of how people have overcome adversity have influenced theories of human development (Fraser, Richman, & Galinsky, 1999; Greene, 2002, 2007). What protective factors provided a defense against the risks or reduced them altogether? What allowed a person to successfully negotiate these risks? The research suggested that people who are able to overcome adverse or stressful events have protective factors that defend them, such as a supportive family member (Garmezy, 1991; Masten, 1994). People who readily overcome adversity are called resilient.

The most important aspect of resilience-based practice models is that they view older adults as advocating for themselves, directing their own care, and working hand in hand with the social worker to explore the options available in their environment or community. Consumer-directed care allows older adults to exercise their choices and preferences in the services they have requested and received. Practitioners who are considering using this care approach, though, must be mindful that some family cultures may prefer more family-centered decision-making processes rather than individual decision making. For example, the head of the family may be the designated person to contact the physician. Knowing what to expect in caregiving situations will better prepare the practitioner in assisting caregivers as consumers.

In addition, resiliency is often attributed to family and other support systems in which cultural groups experience strong communal and spiritual ties (Cross, 1998; see chapter 3 for a further discussion). Knowledge of how people successfully adapt despite stressful experiences can help practitioners better work with older adults. Such asset-focused research has led social workers in the field of aging to understand how an increase in the number or quality of resources may improve an older adult's quality of life. Resilience-enhancing strategies that have emerged from this theory base have provided practitioners with a set of practice skills that address how they can better maintain and enhance client competence within the client's environment (Cohen & Greene, 2005).

Risk and resilience theory represents a shift in thinking about human behavior in the social environment to positive aspects of human development across the life course. This book incorporates this emerging theory as a wellness approach to highlight the older adult's adaptability and capacity to meet life challenges, giving attention to culturally specific personal stories. The risk and resilience perspective adds to the gerontological stock of knowledge because it is based on an ecological metaphor, helping geriatric practitioners understand the network of influences—family, peer group, school, neighborhood, and society—on an older adult's sources of strength (Brooks, Nomura, & Cohen, 1989). By comprehending these influences, practitioners may recognize the social context in which individual resilience is embedded, that is, the larger social systems that act "as nested contexts for social competence" (Walsh, 1998, p. 12).

Defining Risk and Resilience

Fraser and colleagues (1999) have argued that the social work profession should reserve the term resilience for "unpredicted or markedly successful adaptations to negative life events, trauma, stress, and other forms of risk" (p. 136). They contend that if "we can understand what helps some people to function well in the context of high adversity, we may be able to incorporate this knowledge into new practice strategies" (p. 136). Definitions of resilience vary, as can be seen from the following:

- Resilience is concerned with individual variations in response to risk. Resilience refers to the positive pole of individual differences in people's response to stress and adversity, as well as hope and optimism in the face of adversity. (Rutter, 1987, pp. 316–317)
- Resilience is not defined in terms of the absence of pathology or heroics. Rather, it is an ability to cope with adversity, stress, and deprivation. (Begun, 1993, pp. 28–29)
- Resilience is the ability to maintain continuity of one's personal narrative and a coherent sense of self following traumatic events. (Borden, 1992, p. 125)
- Resilience is normal development under difficult conditions. (Fonagy, Steele, Steele, Higgitt, & Target, 1994, p. 233)

Although definitions differ, associating resilience with risk—the probability that a problem may emerge—can be useful in the assessment of older adults when safety issues are of concern.

In her research, Masten (1994) has focused on the protective factors or circumstances that moderate the effects of risks and enhance adaptation. This approach, originally used with children and youths, is also useful to geriatric social workers because it gives us a way to think about what critical events or traumas an older adult may have overcome over his or her life course. For example, a client who has lived through the Great Depression or World War II may have developed various coping strategies that he or she can tap in old age. Furthermore, life review and other storytelling techniques, such as narrative therapy, are particularly applicable in working with an older adult because they reveal their resilience—the client's ability to maintain the continuity of his or her personal story (Borden, 1992; see chapter 6 for more information on interventions).

Philosophy

An interest in risk and resilience theory can be traced to several social science movements, including the positive psychology movement (based on positive emotions of hope, humor, and joy) and the demand for evidence-based practice (based on research findings and protocols) and prevention (based on interventions that attempt to avert a problem) (Greene & Cohen, 2005). The positive psychology movement is "a science based on the idea that if . . . people are taught resilience, hope, and optimism, they will be less susceptible to depression and will lead happier, more productive lives" (Seligman, 2002, p. 3). Positive psychology refocuses practitioners' attention to assess clients' adaptive functioning—how people maintain well-being despite stumbling blocks or trauma.

The health and wellness movement invites social workers to promote health and well-being among their clients. This may be accomplished by using positive thinking techniques (Ryff & Singer, 2002). Combining this philosophy with other theoretical information about normal functioning of older adults may enable the social worker to be more likely to see the client from a strengths-based perspective (see chapter 6 for interventions that follow a resilience-enhancing philosophy).

Resilience-Enhancing Model of Social Work Practice

These shifts in beliefs and scientific understanding about human development contribute to a different kind of understanding of clients and to a changed view of social work practice. This alternative type of practice is proposed by the resilience-enhancing model (REM), which centers on promoting and maintaining client competence or self-efficacy. According to Greene (2007), REM

> embodies a philosophy of hope, instilling positive expectations for the future. It is based on the belief that people have an innate capacity to lead productive lives, and offers practitioners the means of fostering health-promoting behaviors across the life course. As a model that centers on a client's assets and propensity to grow and heal, it generally avoids problem-saturated client descriptions. (p. 70)

Although the model suggests that practitioners pay attention to client loss, vulnerability, and stress, it also emphasizes that they help clients take as much control over their life decisions as possible. In addition to ensuring that older clients have basic life necessities, the social worker uses various techniques—for instance, listening for the signs of positive emotions such as humor and hope—to mobilize clients. In some cases, practitioners using REM enable their clients to make meaning of negative events so they are better able to transcend the difficulties of the immediate situation.

Many of the intervention strategies in REM are derived from social construction theory, which suggests that one's views of social reality grow out of his or her interaction and discourse in daily life experiences (Gergen, 1985). Accordingly, REM focuses on how people retain a sense of competence as they age. In large measure, this ability is attributed to a client's facility at making meaning of critical life events, that is, the older adult has "a sense of direction, a sense of order, and a reason for existence, a clear sense of personal identity, a greater sense of social conscious" (Reker, 1997, p. 710).

When an adverse event first occurs, a client may feel the world is meaningless. However, as time passes, an older adult may begin to understand the meaning and significance of the event, depending on his or her appraisal of it (Janoff-Bulman & Berger, 2000). Thus, an important social work role is to interview the client to help that individual appraise his or her life story to determine whether it is a loss or a challenge (Lazarus & Folkman, 1984). This interviewing process is described further in chapter 5.

Theory Critiquing

The preceding key theoretical concepts delineate the knowledge a successful social worker will need to conduct assessments of older adults, their families, and their social support networks effectively. However, when using these theories, one should assume a critical stance (Laird, 1993). During assessment, it is important to evaluate theories to determine how well they apply to a particular client situation. Theory critiquing will help the practitioner gain confidence in his or her knowledge about a theory and the interweaving of its components.

To evaluate a model or theory fully, the practitioner needs to examine first the model or theory author's background, credentials, and demographic characteristics. The social worker must then ask the following questions about the model or theory:

■ When was it developed? What prompted the author to develop it? What important social, cultural, or historical events surrounded the development?
■ Are the ideological biases articulated? If so, what are they (for example, a differential emphasis on person and the environment or use of a particular knowledge base)? On what psychological or social sciences theory or theories does it draw?
■ What is its purpose or direction?

- What is its value system? What consideration does it give to the role of race or ethnicity, gender, sexual orientation, age, physical or mental challenge, or socioeconomic class?
- What are the client characteristics (for example, demographics, skills, knowledge, or personality type) thought to be necessary for appropriate use?
- What unit or units of attention are addressed?
- How does it define problems?
- What causes psychological or interpersonal problems?
- How is assessment defined and conducted?
- What interventions are described? What skills are required by the practitioner?
- What is the role of the practitioner and that of the client? How is the professional relationship defined and described?
- What are the desirable outcomes or goals?
- How is time structured?
- Are there any personnel exclusions stated or implied by it?
- Is it consistent with collaboration and referral to other agencies or practitioners?
- To what extent can it be evaluated for effectiveness? What research has been done to evaluate it?
- How is it similar to or different from social work's person-in-situation paradigm?
- How is it consistent or inconsistent with the NASW *Code of Ethics* (NASW, 2000)? (Meyer, 1983)

Conclusion

Finally, a theory should help you configure or put together the various factors involved in a client's situation. What are the challenges? What are the opportunities? Has the theoretical information used in assessment helped you and your client make meaning of the situation? Do you understand your client's situation and mutually agree on a future direction? (See chapter 5 for more assessment information.) Have you embarked on a path that uses theory in the strengths tradition of social work practice?

Suggested Exercise to Evaluate Student Competency

Students will critique a theory by using the following conceptual framework, considering whether a theory has a balance between

- pathology–health (Do concepts focus on deficits or on well-being?)
- practitioner–client control (Does the theory allow for mutual or shared control?)
- personal–societal impact (Does the theory see the client difficulty as client based or societal?)
- internal–external change (Does the theory emphasize personal or societal change?)

▪ rigidity–flexibility (Does the theory allow for adjustments for diverse clients?) (Trader, 1977)

References

Begun, A. (1993). Human behavior and the social environment: The vulnerability, risk, and resilience model. *Journal of Social Work Education, 29,* 26–35.

Berger, R., & Federico, R. (1982). *Human behavior: A social work perspective.* New York: Longman.

Birren, J. E. (1959). Principles of research on aging. In J. E. Birren (Ed.), *The handbook of aging and the individual* (pp. 3–42). Chicago: University of Chicago Press.

Borden, W. (1992). Narrative perspectives in psychosocial intervention following adverse life events. *Social Work, 37,* 125–141.

Boszormenyi-Nagy, I., & Spark, G. (1973). *Invisible loyalties.* New York: Harper & Row.

Brody, E. (1985). Parent care as normative family stress. *Gerontologist, 25,* 19–29.

Bronfenbrenner, U. (1979). *The ecology of human development.* Cambridge, MA: Harvard University Press.

Brooks, J. S., Nomura, C., & Cohen, P. (1989). A network of influences on adolescent drug involvement: Neighborhood, school, peer, and family. *Genetic, Social, and General Psychology Monographs, 115,* 125–145.

Buckley, W. (1967). Systems and entities. In W. Buckley (Ed.), *Sociology and modern systems theory* (pp. 42–66). Englewood Cliffs, NJ: Prentice Hall.

Carter, E. A., & McGoldrick, M. (1999). *The expanded family life cycle: Individual, family, and social perspectives* (3rd ed.). Boston: Allyn & Bacon.

Cohen, H., & Greene, R. R. (2005). Older adults who overcame oppression. *Families in Society, 87,* 1–8.

Council on Social Work Education, Gero-Ed Center. (2004). *Foundation gerontological social work competencies.* Retrieved November 16, 2006, from http://depts. washington.edu/geroctr/Curriculum3/ Competencies/FdnComp.doc

Cross, T. (1998). Understanding family resiliency from a relational worldview. In H. I. McCubbin, E. A. Thompson, A. I. Thompson, & J. E. Fromer (Eds.), *Resiliency in Native American and immigrant families* (pp. 143–158). Thousand Oaks, CA: Sage Publications.

Farris, K. (2006). The role of African-American pastors in mental health care. In R. R. Greene (Ed.), *Contemporary issues of care.* New York: Haworth Press.

Fonagy, P., Steele, M., Steele, H., Higgitt, A., & Target, M. (1994). The Emanuel Miller memorial lecture 1992: The theory and practice of resilience. *Journal of Child Psychology and Psychiatry and Allied Disciplines, 35,* 231–257.

Frank, C., Kurland, J., & Goldman, B. (1978). Tips for getting the best from the rest (p.13). Baltimore: Jewish Family & Children's Service.

Fraser, M. W., Richman, J. M., & Galinsky, M. J. (1999). Risk, protection, and resilience: Toward a conceptual framework for social work practice. *Social Work Research, 23,* 129–208.

Garmezy, N. (1991). Resiliency and vulnerability to adverse developmental outcomes associated with poverty. *American Behavioral Scientist, 34,* 416–430.

Gaugler, J. E., Kane, R. J., & Newcomer, R. (2007). Resilience and transitions from dementia caregiving. *Journal of Gerontology: Psychological Sciences, 62B*(1), 38–44.

Gergen, K. J. (1985). The social construction movement in modern psychology. *American Psychologist, 40,* 266–275.

Germain, C. B. (1991). *Human behavior in the social environment.* New York: Columbia University Press.

Germain, C. B., & Gitterman, A. (1995). *The life model of social work practice* (2nd ed.). New York: Columbia University Press.

Gironda, M., Lubben, J., & Atchison, K. (1999). Social networks of elders without children. *Journal of Gerontological Social Work, 31*(1/2), 63–83.

Greene, R. R. (1999). *Human behavior theory and social work practice* (2nd ed.). Hawthorne, NY: Aldine Transaction.

Greene, R. R. (2000). *Social work with the aged and their families.* New York: Aldine de Gruyter.

Greene, R. R. (2002). *Resiliency theory: An integrated framework for practice, research, and policy.* Washington, DC: NASW Press.

Greene, R. R. (2007). *Social work practice: A risk and resilience perspective.* Monterey, CA: Brooks/Cole.

Greene, R. R., & Barnes, G. (1998). The ecological perspective and social work practice. In R. R. Greene & M. Watkins (Eds.), *Serving diverse constituencies: Applying the ecological perspective* (pp. 63–96). New York: Aldine de Gruyter.

Greene, R. R., & Cohen, H. L. (2005). Social work with older adults and their families: Changing practice paradigms. *Families in Society, 86,* 367–373.

Greene, R. R., & Watkins, M. (1998). *Serving diverse constituencies: Applying the ecological perspective.* New York: Aldine de Gruyter.

Hareven, T. L. (1982). The life course and aging in historical perspective. In T. K. Hareven & K. J. Adams (Eds.), *Aging and life course transitions: An interdisciplinary perspective* (pp. 1–26). New York: Guilford Press.

Hawley, D. R., & DeHaan, L. (1996). Towards a definition of family resilience: Integrating the life span. *Family Process, 35,* 283–298.

Hunt, C. K. (2003). Concepts in caregiver research. *Journal of Nursing Scholarship, 35,* 27–32.

Janoff-Bulman, R., & Berger, A. R. (2000). The other side of trauma: Towards a psychology of appreciation. In J. H. Harvey & E. D. Miller (Eds.), *Loss and trauma: General and close relationship perspectives* (pp. 29–44). Philadelphia: Brunner-Routledge.

Kirschner, J. D. (1986). Context and process: An ecological view of the interdependence of practice and research. *American Journal of Community Psychology, 14,* 581–589.

Klein, D. M., & White, J. M. (1996). *Family theories: An introduction.* Thousand Oaks, CA: Sage Publications.

Laird, J. (1993). *Revisioning social work education: A social constructionist approach.* New York: Haworth Press.

Lawton, M. P. (1982). Competence, environmental press, and the adaptation of older people. In M. P. Lawton, P. G. Windley, & T. O. Byerts (Eds.), *Aging and the environment: Theoretical approaches* (pp. 33–59). New York: Springer.

Lawton, M. P., & Nahemow, L. (1973). Ecology and the aging process. In C. Eisdorfer & M. P. Lawton (Eds.), *The psychology of adult development and aging* (pp. 619–674). Washington, DC: American Psychological Association.

Lazarus, R. S., & Folkman, S. (1984). *Stress, appraisal, and coping.* New York: Springer.

Longres, J. F. (1990). *Human behavior in the social environment.* Itasca, IL: F. E. Peacock.

Masten, A. (1994). Resilience in individual development: Successful adaptation despite risk and adversity. In M. C. Wang & E. W. Gordon (Eds.), *Educational resilience in inner-city America: Challenges and prospects* (pp. 3–25). Hillsdale, NJ: Lawrence Erlbaum.

McInnis–Dittrich, K. (2002). *Social work with elders: A biopsychosocial approach to assessment and intervention.* Boston: Allyn & Bacon.

Meyer, C. (1973). Direct services in new and old contexts. In A. J. Kahn (Ed.), *Shaping the new social work* (pp. 26–54). New York: Columbia University Press.

Meyer, C. (1983). Selecting appropriate practice models. In A. Rosenblatt & D. Waldfogel (Eds.), *Handbook of clinical social work* (pp. 731–749). San Francisco: Jossey-Bass.

National Association of Social Workers. (2000). *Code of ethics of the National Association of Social Workers.* Washington, DC: Author.

Newman, B. M., & Newman, P. R. (2005). *Development through life: A psychosocial approach* (8th ed.). Pacific Grove, CA: Brooks/Cole.

Ogbu, J. U. (1981). Origins of human competence: A cultural–ecological perspective. *Child Development, 52,* 413–429.

Patterson, J. M., & Garwick, A. W. (1998). Theoretical linkages: Family meanings and sense of coherence. In H. I. McCubbin, E. A. Thompson, A. I. Thompson, & J. E. Fromer (Eds.), *Stress, coping and health in families: Sense of coherence and resiliency* (pp. 71–90). Thousand Oaks, CA: Sage Publications.

Reker, G. T. (1997). Personal meaning, optimism, and choice: Existential predictors of depression in community and institutional elderly. *Gerontologist, 37,* 709–716.

Riley, J. (2007). Caregiving: A risk and resilience perspective. In R. R. Greene (Ed.), *Social work practice: A risk and resilience perspective* (pp. 239–262). Monterey, CA: Brooks/Cole.

Rowles, G. (1993). Evolving images of place in aging and "aging in place." *Generations, 17,* 65–71.

Rutter, M. (1987). Psychosocial resilience and protective mechanisms. *American Journal of Orthopsychiatry, 57,* 316–330.

Ryff, C. D., & Singer, B. (2002). From social structure to biology: Integrative science in pursuit of human health and well-being. In C. R. Snyder & S. J. Lopez (Eds.), *Handbook of positive psychology* (pp. 541–555). New York: Oxford University Press.

Saleebey, D. (2004). "The power of place": Another look at the environment. *Families in Society, 85,* 7–16.

Saleebey, D. (2005). *The strengths perspective in social work practice* (4th ed.). Boston: Allyn & Bacon.

Seligman, M. E. P. (2002). Positive psychology, positive prevention, and positive therapy. In C. R. Snyder & S. J. Lopez (Eds.), *Handbook of positive psychology* (pp. 3–7). New York: Oxford University Press.

Thoits, P. (1995). Stress, coping, and social support processes: Where are we? What next? *Journal of Health and Social Behavior, 36*(Suppl.), 53–79.

Trader, H. P. (1977). Survival strategies for oppressed minorities. *Social Work, 22,* 10–13.

Walsh, F. (1998). *Strengthening family resilience.* New York: Guilford Press.

Diversity, Difference, and Redress

3

RATIONALE: Social workers should be prepared to practice without discrimination, respecting people from diverse backgrounds. They should appreciate, celebrate, and skillfully engage people who are different from them, recognizing the complex nature of culture and personal identity. There are multiple dimensions to difference that must be learned by the social worker to ensure practice effectiveness and the applicability of the design and implementation of social services programs. Social workers must also be prepared to promote nondiscriminatory social and economic systems.

COMPETENCY: Students should be able to engage, learn from, and incorporate new knowledge gained from their client informants. They will

- respect diversity among older adult clients, families, and professionals (e.g., class, race, ethnicity, gender, and sexual orientation).
  This competency encompases understanding how diversity relates to variations in the aging process.
- address respectfully the cultural, spiritual, and ethnic values and beliefs of older adults and families. (Council on Social Work Education, Gero-Ed Center, 2004)

Practice with Diverse Older Adults: An Overview

You are beginning your social work career at a time when the United States is becoming increasingly multicultural. Immigrants and people of color continue to make up an increasingly greater percentage of the population in this country (Grantmakers in Aging,

---

Note: Youjung Lee and Olivia Lopez contributed to this chapter.

2002; U.S. Census Bureau, 2000). Furthermore, older adults are becoming more ethnically diverse (Takamura, 2001; Torres-Gil & Moga, 2001). By 2050, the population of Asians 65 years of age and older will have grown by approximately 720 percent; Hispanic elders by 553 percent; black elders by 262 percent; and white elders by 116.7 percent (Min, 2005; U.S. Department of Health and Human Services, Substance Abuse and Mental Health Services Administration [HHS, SAMHSA], 1999). Today's geriatric social workers will also need to address how clients' lives are influenced by gender, religion, sexual orientation, socioeconomic status, geographic location, immigration status, and physical and mental ability. As Hooyman (1996) so aptly put it, a social worker's mandate is "to promote the full humanity of all voices which have been marginalized in our society" (p. 20).

Older adults of racial and ethnic groups encounter more barriers to health and human services than their mainstream counterparts (Institute of Medicine, 1994, 2003; Min, 2005; see Appendix 3-A). Cultural barriers and differences in attitude about accessing health and mental health services include older adults' feelings of shame and stigma, their fear and mistrust of the treatment system, and their limited financial and transportation resources (Choi & Gonzalez, 2005). Moreover, models of community health based on a person-in-environment perspective continue to document that health outcomes are disproportionately unfavorable among older adults in minority groups, frequently bringing about a more rapid decline in their functional status compared with white older adults (Institute of Medicine, 2003; Johnson & Smith, 2002; HHS, SAMHSA, 1999). High blood pressure, for example, affects a disproportionate number of black American older adults relative to their white counterparts, putting them at greater risk of other health complications (Ford & Hatchett, 2001).

Yet, an ethnic family's resilience may be enhanced by cultural values and the provision of mutual psychological support (Genero, 1998; McCubbin, Thompson, Thompson, & Futrell, 1998). Evidence increasingly suggests that the capacity to transcend the risks of oppressive environments can be enhanced by strengthening a family's unique cultural protective factors (Greene, 2002). For example, religiosity, particularly among elders of racial and ethnic groups, can be a mediating factor in reducing caregiver stress (Chadiha & Fisher, 2002; Morano & King, 2005).

The new multicultural aging population requires that social workers rethink the complex nature of diversity (Torres-Gil & Moga, 2001). Cultural competence is a major challenge that each new social worker will face in his or her career (de Anda, 1997; Greene & Watkins, 1998). This chapter outlines a culturally sensitive approach to social work practice that can help the new practitioner begin that process.

On the Road to Cultural Competence

Cultural diversity, according to Fong (2001), "embraces the multiple dimensions of human identity, biculturalism, and culturally defined social behaviors. In the broadest sense, it encompasses people of color, women, the aged, gays and lesbians, physically and emotionally challenged, the poor and homeless, and a host of other disenfranchised groups" (p. 1). Cultural competence, on the other hand, is the ability to "provide services, conduct assessments, and implement interventions that are reflective of the clients' cultural values and norms, congruent with their natural help-seeking behaviors, and inclusive of existing indigenous solutions" (Fong, p. 1). In effective cross-cultural practice, then, social workers recognize that they and their clients are from different cultures, and therefore culturally specific information must be infused into the helping process (Greene, 1994).

What these definitions mean for geriatric social workers is that they will need to craft their assessments to gain a better understanding of an older client's worldview and work together with the client to select culturally appropriate interventions. "Social services can and should be provided to people in ways that are culturally acceptable to them and that enhance their sense of [ethnic] group participation and power" (Green, 1999, p. 5).

Preparation for Competent Practice

Social workers who strive to be culturally competent have to undergo a lifelong process of acquiring the requisite knowledge, attitudes, and skills. Even before seeing their first client, practitioners can begin to gain knowledge associated with culturally competent practice—that is, information they will need to develop an informed understanding of the client's life experiences. Social workers should ask themselves: What do I already know about my client's culture? What more can I learn more about my client's community? What symbols and rituals must I know?

As the practitioner listens to clients' life stories, he or she begins to learn how clients' personal, political, and economic factors influence their lives. Other knowledge gained may include an understanding of clients' cultural norms, religion and spirituality, place in the life cycle, finances, and medical needs. Because such knowledge is individualized, it is used differentially with each client. This knowledge-seeking process will stretch the practitioner's ability to be more inclusive of the different people who will enter his or her practice.

The attitude dimension of culturally competent practice requires that practitioners be open minded and learn to appreciate other cultures (Okayama, Furuto, & Edmondson, 2001). A social worker who is proficient in diversity practice recognizes that older clients and social workers may have different attitudes about autonomy, self-determination, and choice. Furthermore, each client has a different comfort level when it comes to disclosing personal information. Moreover, the broader societal attitudes that clients have encountered will influence their developmental path to resilience in later years; practitioners must consider, for instance, whether an older client has faced discrimination and oppression. Because U.S. mainstream values or beliefs may clash with those of other cultures—for example, how clients approach death and dying—the geriatric social worker must create an atmosphere of acceptance and learn about the client's worldview on such matters (Ramirez, 1999; Rothman, 1999). Most theorists agree that knowledge of a repertoire of skills is essential to reinforce cultural values and support appropriate interventions (Fong, 2001), as practitioners use culturally competent skills along each step of the social services delivery process (Okayama et al., 2001).

Exploration of Cultural Influences on Self and Client

NASW (2001) has mandated that all social workers strive to be culturally competent (see Appendix 3-B). Cultural competence requires self-awareness and an acknowledgment of how culture shapes a client's life experiences.

Self-Awareness

Most professionals today, including social workers, are white, English-speaking, middle-class people (Green, 1999). (Eighty-six percent of licensed social workers are non-Hispanic white, compared with 68 percent of the U.S. population.) Yet, they increasingly serve diverse constituencies. To work effectively across cultures, social workers must possess a heightened sense of self-awareness, the ability to reflect on one's own thoughts and actions. This process involves taking stock of "white privilege," a term sometimes used to describe the advantages granted to the white, middle-class population, including freedom of movement in housing, jobs, and recreation, and access to resources such as education and health care (see Appendix 3-C). Furthermore, self-awareness entails conducting a self-inventory to determine how we as practitioners perceive other cultures and self-examination to see whether we believe in the power of family and culture as protective factors that can buffer people from adverse events and thus heighten resilience (see Appendix 3-D for an ethnic-sensitive inventory).

Acknowledgment of Cultural Influences

Culture is "a way of life of a society and comprises institutions, language, artistic expression, and patterns of social and interpersonal relationships" (Greene, 1994, p. 28). It encompasses the values and beliefs that people learn are valuable, appropriate, and desirable. Because of the important role culture plays in affecting people's life experiences, social work educators have advocated for "ever-expanding parameters related to cultural diversity" (Tully, 1994, p. 235). For example, Green (1999) recommended that social workers take a broad view and consider culture as a community of interest that includes communities not explicitly racial or ethnic, such as a school for deaf people, a drug house, or street people. Culture, he added, is not a specific value, physical appearance, or something that people have; rather, it is people's shared cognitive map, their discourse, and how they go about their lives—their life perspective.

As people grow up in families, they become socialized into cultural norms and behavioral expectations. Such teachings will have also influenced older clients. Culture, for example, may affect caregiving of family members with dementia. It may shape how a family designates a primary caregiver, uses outside help, makes decisions about placement in a nursing home, and heals through the bereavement process.

Meaning Making

An important aspect of culture is that it sets the general parameters of how group members structure behavior and guides the meaning they ascribe to life events. Cultures differ in their worldview and in their "concept of the essential nature of the human condition" (Devore & Schlesinger, 1996, p. 9). For example, a Western (mainstream) orientation to the view of the self is that people should aspire to be autonomous or independent. However, some black American, Indian, and Asian older adults may be more comfortable with a relational worldview model—a world in which people strive for a unified community and collective responsibility such as those expressed in the symbolism of Kwanza (Daly, Jennings, Beckett, & Leashore, 1995; see http://officialkwanzaawebsite.org). Discerning how a client thinks about his or her independence is a key feature in geriatric assessment. Does he or she expect to live independently or with extended family?

Help-Seeking Models

Help-seeking models are used to understand how an older adult's culture has influenced his or her patterns of asking for help. These models also shed light on the meaning attributed to using social work services. Meaning making takes a personal and communal course. As individuals process life events, they develop a sense of direction and purpose (Krause, 2004). They also create a life story that embodies a larger cultural and historical context, and they bring their stories with them when seeking help.

Help-seeking models were originally designed to account for cultural differences in describing and understanding illness. How do differing cultural views of sickness and treatment affect communication among an older client, family, and practitioner? Are there culturally specific and universal characteristics of the healing process? These models suggest that various cultures have their own ideas about the nature of illnesses, treatments, and types of healers. Such models also portray health care systems as culturally based systems with their own symbolic meanings, particular patterns of social interactions, and institutional arrangements. Because helping systems are an outgrowth of culture, they are governed by cultural rules that shape beliefs and behaviors. People's awareness of their cultural life becomes more relevant or heightened when they contrast their culture with another by crossing a social boundary, such as class, education, religious affiliation, ethnicity, occupation, or social network (Kleinman, 1978, 1992; see Appendix 3-E for a list of the principles of diversity). This contrast in culture can present conflicts for older adults and their families as they work their way through bureaucratic requirements in health care settings. It is often the social worker who can help negotiate these transactions.

Kleinman's Help-Seeking Model

Kleinman's (1980) work on the meaning of illness focuses on the cognitive and belief systems of different cultures. This model has been defined by various social sciences, such as anthropology, and used in various helping professions. The primary characteristic of this model is that it stresses understanding the experience of illness from the subjective culturally based view of the client (McSweeney, 1990). This approach to understanding the meaning of illness is holistic, focusing on cultural belief systems.

Help-seeking models suggest that episodes of sickness and their treatment are tied to systems of knowledge and values. Such models are, however, characterized by vagueness, multiple meanings, frequent changes, and lack of sharp boundaries. They are unconsciously formed; tend to change over time; and are influenced by environment, ethnicity, individual interpretation, familial illness experience, exposure to Western medical practices, and tacit knowledge (Luyas, 1990; McSweeney, 1990).

Because such models incorporate the personal beliefs people use to recognize, interpret, and respond to a particular illness, social workers will have to learn how older adults perceive their medical diagnosis. People construct these models through interaction with the sociocultural environment, creating a common sense understanding of body function (McSweeney, Alan, & Mayo, 1997; Schoenberg, Amey, & Coward, 1998). This accounts for why the meaning of an illness among patients and health practitioners may often differ or conflict.

As a particular instance, when farm-working women interact with a social work professional, they bring with them medical "philosophies" related to cultural beliefs and practices based on long-standing traditions and notions about sickness and treatment (Lopez, 2006; Thompson & Wiggins, 2002). This cultural system of health and healing often differs from the more accepted and recognized Western medical model (Kleinman, 1980). For these women, the meaning of illness rests on the interpretation of symptoms, and an understanding of diagnosis based on a cultural understanding of illness, experiences of family members, and social networks.

It is important for social workers to explore clients' cultural interpretations of illness and treatment in a respectful manner to gain an understanding of their orientation toward and acceptance of Western medical practices. For example, Holland and Courtney (1998) reported that many Mexican Americans do not think of their cultural health beliefs and practices as "folk" medicine. For example, rather than asking patients if they use folk medicine, social workers can ask how a particular illness is treated in their home community. This may demonstrate cultural sensitivity and help create a positive partnership between patients and practitioners. Social workers must also explore how Western health systems relate to local folk meanings. It will be at these intersections that patients and Western medical practitioners can help move toward a more unified health care plan.

Multigenerational legacies and stories often shape a family's beliefs and responses to illness and treatment. Furthermore, they convey beliefs about illness and treatment patterns across generations (Scollan-Koliopoulos, O'Connell, & Walker, 2005). Thus, family expectations become another very important component of health-seeking models and cultural health systems. It is likely that a patient has expectations about illness, treatment, and caregiving linked to familial history. It is also likely that a patient has provided care to a parent or grandparent and has clear ideas about caregiving. As a result, this patient may have expectations about who should provide care for him or her as well. Therefore, social workers will need to address this area during the preliminary evaluation of care and pay careful attention to the client's familial experience of illness, treatment, and the suitability of any care plan.

Green's Model

The notion that the helping process is imbued with cultural elements of both clients and professionals has been applied to the social services (Green, 1999). The schema in Figure 3-1 depicts how a client's culture contrasts with that of the professional subculture. When an older adult of a racial or ethnic group meets with a social work professional, both parties are communicating across cultural boundaries. The client brings a distinct set of assumptions about his or her own difficulties, such as beliefs about the cause of a problem. The professional has his or her own perceptions and interpretations. The greater the cultural distance between social worker and client, the greater the discrepancies in meaning and more important the need to build a relationship based on good communication and trust.

FIGURE 3-1 A Help-Seeking Behavior Model

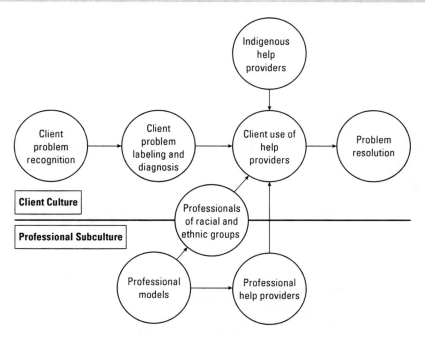

Sources: Green, J. W. (1999). *Cultural awareness in the human services: A multi-ethnic approach* (3rd ed.) p. 55. Boston: Allyn & Bacon. Reprinted with permission from Pearson Education.

Relational Worldview

The relational worldview model offers another aspect of health found among indigenous peoples—that is, the model illustrates how Indian clients may view "dis-ease" and health (Cross, 1998; Figure 3-2). The model depicts culture as a circle resembling a medicine wheel consisting of four factors: (1) context, including family, culture, and history; (2) mind, embodying intellect, emotion, and memory; (3) spirit, encompassing dreams, symbols, and stories; and (4) body, involving genetics, condition, and age. Indians believe that when a person keeps all four parts in balance, he or she experiences harmony or health. But a person has a sense of imbalance when he or she feels disharmony or dis-ease. Learning about such cultural meanings related to well-being is central to the helping process with older adults and their families.

FIGURE 3-2 A Relational Worldview Model

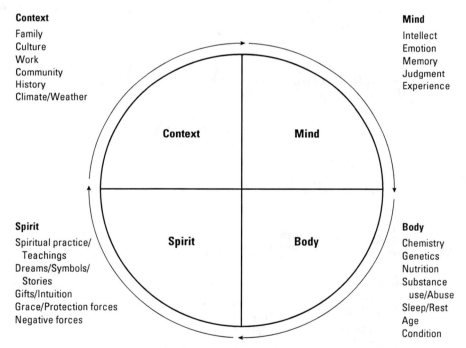

Context
Family
Culture
Work
Community
History
Climate/Weather

Mind
Intellect
Emotion
Memory
Judgment
Experience

Spirit
Spiritual practice/
  Teachings
Dreams/Symbols/
  Stories
Gifts/Intuition
Grace/Protection forces
Negative forces

Body
Chemistry
Genetics
Nutrition
Substance
  use/Abuse
Sleep/Rest
Age
Condition

Note: The items listed are examples only. All of life and existence is included in the circle. Balance among all four parts brings harmony, and harmony equals health. Nothing in the circle can change without every other thing in the circle changing as well. The circle is constantly changing because of the cycles of the days, weeks, and seasons and because of development and different experiences. Individuals are considered ill if the circle becomes out of balance. Lack of balance causes "dis-ease." In this view of health and mental health, healing may come from any or all of the four parts of the circle.
Source: Cross, T. (1998). Understanding family resiliency from a relational world view. In H. I. McCubbin, E. A. Thompson, A. I. Thompson, & J. E. Fromer (Eds.), *Resiliency in Native American and immigrant families* (p. 148). Thousand Oaks, CA: Sage Publications. Reprinted with permission of Sage Publications, Inc.

Practice Within a Cultural Context

The Relationship

One of the most challenging aspects of forming a helping relationship with clients from cultures other than one's own is the perceived power differential (Pinderhughes, 1983; 1989). Pinderhughes has suggested that both clients and practitioners bring feelings and behaviors to the helping encounter that are related to social markers of power, including social class, age, race, and ethnicity. Empathy, she argues, is the key ingredient to neutralizing the client's feelings of powerlessness.

Kadushin (1992) advised that practitioners working across cultures be ready to listen and be open to correction. Social workers should be prepared to accept that they will be "sized up" by clients of racial and ethnic groups. They might ask themselves: Am I being perceived as genuine? Will I demonstrate a nonjudgmental attitude?

Interview

The social work interview is a vehicle for learning about cultural differences. A successful interview involves suspending habitual judgments and engaging in dialogue that explores differences. For most practitioners, this process involves taking risks during the interaction, especially when asking for clarification or when admitting ignorance (Okayama et al., 2001). Conducting a skillful interview with diverse populations requires the selective and differential use of human behavior theory and practice methods (Greene, 1994). For example, can practitioners be empathetic if we share few of the client's life experiences (Kadushin, 1992)? Can social workers protect a client's right to self-determination and informed consent in situations such as working with Korean American families who believe they must shield their elderly parents from difficult events and "unseemly" information (Fong, 2001)?

Narrative

An increasingly popular way of obtaining client information, particularly people's recollection of memories, is through the narrative. In *narrative gerontology*, the focus is on eliciting a story or an account of critical life events as told by an older adult in his or her specific sociocultural context (Diehl, 1999; Kenyon & Randall, 2001). This approach offers several benefits: An individual's story, told in his or her own words, can "uncover how life reflects cultural themes of the society, personal themes, institutional themes, and social histories" (Creswell, 1998, p. 49). Personal stories are a link to one's personal past and to collective historical events (Andersen, Reznik, & Chen, 1997). Moreover, a narrative provides a means of understanding an individual's life course through the unfolding of critical life events, such as unemployment, an accident, or experiences with discrimination and its associated risks (Cohen, Greene, Lee, Gonzalez, & Evans, 2006). Critical life events—changes in a person's health, for instance—may also affect their sense of control and self-efficacy (see chapter 6 for a discussion of a client's feelings following a heart attack).

Cross-Cultural Models and Concepts

An assumption common among cross-cultural models of social work practice is that social workers cannot possibly have detailed and comprehensive knowledge about every diverse group or client. Rather, these models offer an overarching framework for learning about a specific client's concerns. Models do not put clients into categories or describe a list of traits that characterize people of a certain culture, but they do provide methods that enable practitioners to clarify the client's help-seeking behaviors.

When learning about unfamiliar people and places, every social worker should take the following steps in cross-cultural learning (Green, 1999):

- read ethnographic descriptions
- prepare a social map
- act as a participant and observer
- plan community contacts
- meet key respondents
- conduct formal interviews
- identify specific culturally competent skills for the particular community. (p. 94)

In the social services, according to Green (1999), "we do not want or need to know everything about the cultural background of every client. What is needed is cultural data bearing on the presenting issue" (p. 133). When working with a family of later years, determine the family's expectations for care. For example, the practitioner may learn that for Asian or Latino families *familism*—"the perceived strength of family bonds and sense of loyalty to family" (Luna et al., 1996, p. 267; for more on familism, see the section "Work with Families" later in this chapter)—brings with it the expectation that the extended family will care for an older relative or that the family will consult specially trained folk healers for advice. As described by Green, to successfully engage in cross-cultural social work, practitioners must have the following five competencies:

1. ethnic competence as awareness of one's own cultural limitations
2. ethnic competence as openness to cultural differences
3. ethnic competence as a client-oriented, systematic learning style
4. ethnic competence as using cultural resources
5. ethnic competence as acknowledging cultural integrity.

Dual Perspective

As practitioners cross social boundaries, cultural differences become more apparent. Norton (1976) has provided a tool to help practitioners learn about these differences: This is the dual perspective, a "conscious and systematic process of perceiving, understanding, and comparing simultaneously the larger societal system with those of the client's immediate family and community system" (p. 3; see Figure 3-3). According to

FIGURE 3-3 Dual System of All Individuals

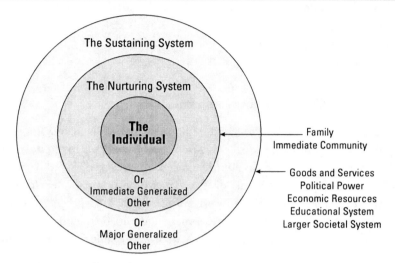

Source: Adapted with permission from Norton, D. (1976). *The dual perspective of ethnic minority content in the social work curriculum* (p. 5). New York: Council on Social Work Education.

Norton's model, all people are a part of two systems: (1) the dominant or sustaining (mainstream) system, which is the source of power and economic resources; and (2) the nurturing (racial and ethnic group) system, which is the immediate social environment of the family and community. Individuals first learn about their immediate culture in the nurturing family system. They later encounter the mainstream, sustaining cultural system as they interact with the institutions, such as schools and health and human services agencies that control the provision of goods and services.

From the dual perspective, evaluation involves assessing two disparate systems to determine the source of the client's major stressors (Norton, 1976). Social work practice often focuses on the risks—that is, the tensions and conflicts—that a client experiences because of the dissonance between the client's sustaining and nurturing systems. That focus, however, must factor in culture. Culture can serve as an insulator, offering comfort and affirmation. For example, elderly Latino clients often feel a sense of belonging, purpose, and pride in their *comunidad* (community). They develop a "blueprint for their behavior" within this immediate environment (Applewhite, 1998, p. 11). Because a client may describe his or her difficulties in terms familiar in that person's nurturing culture, the practitioner will want to learn more about the client's meanings, symbols, and rituals.

The dual perspective is particularly important when working with new Americans. A culturally competent social worker will more effectively engage a family by using a *culturagram,* an instrument that allows the practitioner to examine a family's culture in a nonjudgmental manner (see Figure 3-4). This tool enables practitioners to better understand culturally diverse families by gathering information from them on such factors as reasons for immigration, contact with cultural institutions, and language spoken at home and in the community. Social workers usually discover that there are intergenerational differences in families that sometimes can cause conflict when grandparents are far less acculturated than their grandchildren.

Competence in an Oppressive Environment

Competence is the ability to remain effective in one's environment over the life course. A critical issue in examining personal competence is how people living in hostile environments—characterized by "social injustice, societal inconsistency, and personal impotence" (Chestang, 1972, p.105)—are able to cope. Environments that limit personal opportunity—that may be directed toward minority groups or people who are gay or lesbian—have the potential to inhibit development and impede the fulfillment of human potential. At the same time, minority cultures can promote adaptive strategies and foster

FIGURE 3-4 A Culturagram

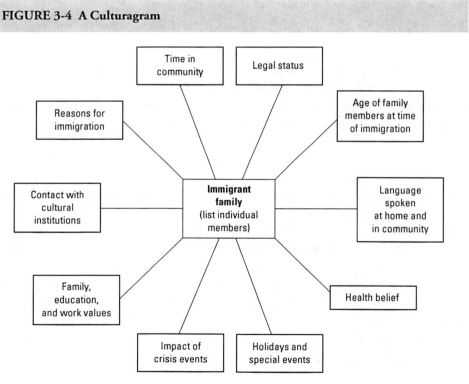

Source: Congress, E. P. (1994). The use of culturagrams to assess and empower culturally diverse families. *Families in Society, 75,* 532. Reprinted with permission from *Families in Society* (www.familiesinsociety.org), published by the Alliance for Children and Families.

resilience. Therefore, practitioners must consider what resources and coping strategies clients have developed for surviving hostile environments (Greene, 1999, 2002).

Some research suggests that institutional *homophobia,* the irrational fear and hatred of those who love and sexually desire someone of the same sex, may not necessarily lead to negative coping. Researchers have found that older lesbians and gay men have developed affirming and positive images of themselves as they have deconstructed negative stereotypes from the past. The term *crisis competence* is used to describe how older lesbians and gay men restructured homosexuality from societal negativity to something positive in their lives (Kimmel, 1978). In fact, they may be better prepared to handle a crisis and become more resilient—or more able to deal with losses associated with the aging process (Barranti, C., & Cohen, H. 2000; Cohen & Greene, 2005).

Acculturation

Acculturation is the process of acquiring the language, customs, and values of a dominant or alternative culture (Skinner, 2002). It is a "phenomena which results when groups of individuals having different cultures come into continuous first-hand contact, with subsequent changes in the original cultural patterns of either or both groups" (Redfield, Linton, & Herskovits, 1936, p. 149).

To assess the extent to which an older client is acculturated, the practitioner must find answers to several questions: Does the client have a degree of acceptance of mainstream culture? Does that person feel loss for certain aspects of his or her original cultural heritage? Has the client adapted, thus combining mainstream and ethnic cultures? Has he or she had a negative reaction to mainstream culture? There often is a generational effect when considering the degree to which an older client is acculturated, with some older clients preferring to keep traditional cultural patterns that are more easily given up by their grandchildren.

Biculturalism

Biculturalism is the ability to conduct oneself in two different cultures. The ability to move between two different cultures differs from person to person (Greene, 1999). Some may feel a high sense of success entering the mainstream culture, whereas others might experience discomfort. Usually, members of the younger generation are more bicultural and able to reach out and participate in mainstream culture.

Work with Families

Contemporary social workers will find themselves practicing with a family unit that no longer is the "traditional" nuclear unit comprising blood relatives. Today's families may differ in structure, form, and culture (Greene, 1994). Racial and ethnic group households may consist of multiple generations. Or a practitioner might work with a "blended family," in which a woman with children marries a man with children (resulting in two sets of grandparents). Social workers might also serve aging gay men and lesbian couples.

These self-defined families are bound together by the same emotional relationships, interdependence, and loyalty that characterize traditional families.

Interdependence

Family-focused social work is based on the premise that over time each family develops a network of relationships with discernible structural and communication patterns (Greene, 1994). How members interact and relate is reflected in observable structures and is influenced by the standards of what is considered acceptable in that family's culture. How interdependent is the family? When difficulties arise, how does the family expect to come up with solutions? What conflicts persist?

Familism

Familism is a protective factor that buffers the effects of risk and enhances adaptation commonly experienced by racial and ethnic groups in the United States (Bullock, Crawford, & Tennstedt, 2003; Hinton, Guo, & Hillygus, 2000). As an abstract term, it incorporates several cultural aspects of family dynamics. In a review of familism among Latino family caregivers, Magana (2006) identified three such dynamics: (1) support from family members, (2) obligations to family, and (3) family members as referents. She found that the informal support network of Latino family caregivers consisted primarily of family members. Those informal caregivers made an exceptional commitment to their ill family members—besides the principal caregiver, the rest of the family was obliged to care for ill relatives. Furthermore, Latino family members tended to seek advice from other family members rather than outside sources. Magana argued, although more similarities than differences exist across Latino family cultures, diversity within this ethnic group was apparent because families have varying countries of origin, primary language, and religion.

Familism guides families in racial and ethnic cultures in their decision making about whether to seek assistance from social workers. Frequently, families decide to reject outside help because they do not wish to disclose sensitive issues. Such decisions are influenced by a widely held cultural value that families are the first, and possibly the only, source of help (Hicks & Lam, 1999). For example, some Asian American families may choose to keep an ill parent or spouse home despite burdensome caregiving tasks because of the strength of their philosophy. Researchers have found that, in the caregiving process, caregivers from racial and ethnic groups prefer to rely on extended family networks rather than formal services (Bullock et al., 2003; Dilworth-Anderson, Williams, & Gibson, 2002). Thus, many Asian American family caregivers limit the handling of issues to within the family network until the need for professional assistance is inescapable (Moon, Lubben, & Villa, 1998; Watari & Gatz, 2004).

The family unit has protected many immigrant families from racial discrimination in mainstream U.S. culture and has provided families with the strength to survive. Familism has allowed those families to celebrate their lives and to think positively about themselves in a foreign country. They may perceive that discussions about a family member's health problems with outsiders would tarnish the family's image in the community. That perception and cultural barriers to the use of health care systems influence many families of racial and ethnic groups to decide not to replace informal care with outside services (Bullock et al., 2003).

Filial Piety

Filial piety is a social value that deeply affects the parent–child relationship of much of the East Asian population (Sung, 1997). Like familism, this cultural factor now shapes the dynamics of Asian American families. It is a core idea in Confucian ethics (Hwang, 1999; Yeh & Bedford, 2003). *Confucianism* is "the tradition and doctrine of *literati/* scholars. In fact, [Confucianism] is more than the values of a group of people. It contains a socio-political programme, an ethical system, and a religious tradition" (Yao, 2000, p. 31). From a Confucianistic perspective, humans are "part of the natural order and the natural state . . . one of harmony, not discord" (Ihara, 2004, p. 23). This tradition, in which family cohesion and continuity are the most important components for sustaining the community and the state, has strongly influenced China and other Asian countries (Park & Cho, 1995).

Originally, the philosophy of filial piety was that children have responsibilities to their parents; that is, offspring will respect and care for their aging parents (Yeh & Bedford, 2003). Modern filial piety continues this tradition, although in a modified form because of the cultural exchange with the West. In a study of 1,227 Korean adults and preadults, Sung (1997) identified two dimensions of modern filial piety: (1) *behaviorally oriented filial piety,* which involves sacrifice, responsibility, and repayment; and (2) *emotionally oriented filial piety,* which is characterized by family harmony, love or affection, and respect. Yeh and Bedford (2003) have proposed a dual model that distinguishes *reciprocal filial piety,* when a child emotionally and spiritually attends to a parent, from *authoritarian filial piety,* when a child suppresses his or her own wishes and follows the parents' requests.

Knowledge about familism and filial piety will assist those social workers who are members of mainstream culture to be aware of how these philosophies may influence family dynamics, such as the emergence of a proxy decision maker or the selection of primary caregivers. For example, in mainstream culture, a spouse is more likely to be the primary caregiver of aging parents (Janevic & Connell, 2001), but in Asian culture, in observance of Confucian values, the eldest son and his wife typically provide care to parents (Brown & Browne, 1998), a practice that is common in Korean culture. Even when the first son and his wife do not reside with the older adult client, they are assumed to be the main caregivers (Youn, Knight, Jeong, & Benton, 1999). In contrast, daughters in Latino and African American cultures play a larger role as alternative decision makers (Hornung et al., 1998) and main caregivers. Research has suggested that those caregiving patterns may account for lower caregiving burden because family roles are clear (Lee & Sung, 1998).

When the family and social worker mutually decide to arrange for outside services, the practitioner should attempt to complement the informal family assistance. The social worker should begin the assessment of client families by asking about their perceptions and expectations of familism and filial piety in their culture. For example, the family might report they expect their Asian American oldest child or daughters-in-law to be major care providers for their parent with dementia. Even though such expectations may be modified in today's society, some caregivers may still hold to more traditional beliefs.

During assessment, the practitioner must respect heterogeneity within a racial or ethnic group by attending to factors such as a caregiver's country of origin, reason for immigration to the United States, socioeconomic status, and educational attainment. An immigrant family's level of acculturation is a significant factor contributing to that family's adjusted norm and lifestyle in a foreign country. Because acculturation is a process rather than a product (Berry, 1997; Skinner, 2002), the practitioner must conduct a multidimensional assessment for the acculturation level of families of racial and ethnic groups. That assessment needs to include socioeconomic factors, education in the United States, income, and other factors that may strongly influence the family's level of acculturation.

End-of-Life Decisions

Asian culture usually considers death to be a part of life and a time of family decision making. Therefore, Asian families might feel uncomfortable in planning procedures related to death. Research has suggested that familism and filial piety are particularly powerful influences on end-of-life decision making, such as the knowledge and use of advance directives (Kwak & Haley, 2005). When a family in a racial and ethnic group faces end-of-life decisions, then the social work staff must be sensitive to the family's cultural and linguistic concerns. For example, in some cultures, an adult child translating a parent's concern to an English-speaking social worker may be perceived by the parent as a form of disrespect. Thus, the social worker must pay special attention to building trust and establishing a connection with families of racial and ethnic groups to overcome language and cultural barriers.

Personal and Institutional Oppression

Power differentials continue to exist between the mainstream population and members of racial and ethnic groups. On a personal level, power is related to the goodness of fit between person and environment. Thus, a social worker should assess an older adult's environment to determine if it is sufficiently nutritive, providing the necessary resources, security, and support to enhance the client's well-being (Greene, 1994; Solomon, 1976). Unfortunately, many older clients of racial and ethnic groups, with limited political power, may have experienced a lifetime of discrimination and have lived in marginalized neighborhoods (Lum, 1999).

On entering a field placement or new place of employment, it is advisable for the social worker to strive for an understanding of the ecological context in which he or she will practice. The practitioner may want to complete a mental ecomap (see chapter 5) for, or needs assessment of, the community (see chapter 10), and ask himself or herself: Can I imagine my older client's environment? What ethnic and cultural groups exist in my service community? What social classes? What family types? The practitioner will need to seek information to determine whether a client is experiencing

- inequality in social resources, social position, or political and cultural influences
- inequality in opportunities to make use of existing resources
- inequality in the division of rights and duties
- inequality in implicit or explicit standards of judgment that often lead to differential treatment in law, the labor market, educational practices, and so forth
- inequality in cultural representations, that is, devaluation of the powerless group, stereotyping, references to the nature (or biological) essence of the less powerful
- inequality in psychological consequences, that is, a "psychology of inferiority" (such as insecurity, "double-bind" experiences, and sometimes identification with the dominant group) versus a "psychology of superiority" (such as arrogance or an inability to abandon the dominant perspective)
- social and cultural tendency to minimize or deny power inequality such that potential conflict is represented as consensus and one views power inequality as "normal." (Davis, Leijenaar, & Oldersma, 1991, p. 52)

Conclusion

A critical task when examining personal competence is to discover how people who live in hostile environments—those characterized by "social injustice, societal inconsistency, and personal impotence" (Chestang, 1972, p. 105)—are able to cope. Environments limiting personal opportunity may potentially inhibit development and impede the fulfillment of human potential. Therefore, practitioners must consider what resources and coping strategies clients have developed for surviving under such hostile conditions (Greene, 2002).

Suggested Exercise to Evaluate Student Competency

Students will conduct research to increase their knowledge of a culture other than their own. They will

- use empirical research to understand and give a presentation on disparities in health care, relying on the following sources: Institute of Medicine (1994, 2003); HHS, SAMHSA (1999)

- research the cultural end-of-life beliefs among an ethnic minority population and write a paper reflecting on how these beliefs may differ from their own
- write an agency plan on adapting organizational policies, procedures, and resources to facilitate the provision of services to diverse older adults and their family caregivers.

References

Andersen, S. M., Reznik, I., & Chen, S. (1997). The self in relation to others: Cognitive and motivational underpinnings. In J. G. Snodgrass & R. L. Thompson (Eds.), *The self across psychology: Self-recognition, self-awareness, and the self-concept* (pp. 233–275). New York: New York Academy of Sciences.

Applewhite, S. L. (1998). Culturally competent practice with elderly Latinos. *Journal of Gerontological Social Work, 30*(1/2), 1–15.

Barranti, C., & Cohen, H. (2000). Lesbian and gay elders: An invisible minority. In R. Schneider, N. Kropf, & A. Kisor (Eds.), *Gerontological social work* (pp. 343–368). Belmont, CA: Wadsworth.

Berry, J. (1997). Immigration, acculturation, and adaptation. *Applied Psychology: An International Review, 46*, 5–33.

Brown, K., & Browne, C. (1998). Perceptions of dementia, caregiving, and help seeking among Asian and Pacific Islander Americans. *Health & Social Work, 23*, 262–275.

Bullock, K., Crawford, S., & Tennstedt, S. (2003). Employment and caregiving: Exploration of African American caregivers. *Social Work, 48*, 150–162.

Chadiha, L. A., & Fisher, R. H. (2002). Contributing factors to African American women caregivers' mental well-being. *African American Research Perspectives, 8*(1), 72–84.

Chestang, L. W. (1972). *Character development in a hostile society* (Occasional Paper No. 3). Chicago: School of Social Services Administration, University of Chicago.

Choi, N., & Gonzalez, J. (2005). Barriers and contributors to minority older adult's access to mental health treatment: Perceptions of geriatric mental health clinicians. *Journal of Gerontological Social Work, 44*, 115–135.

Cohen, H. L., Greene, R. R., Lee, Y., Gonzalez, J., & Evans, M. (2006). Older adults who overcame oppression. *Families in Society, 87*, 1–8.

Congress, E. P. (1994). The use of culturagrams to assess and empower culturally diverse families. *Families in Society, 75*, 531–540.

Council on Social Work Education, Gero-Ed Center. (2004). *Foundation gerontological social work competencies.* Retrieved November 16, 2006, from http://depts. washington.edu/geroctr/Curriculum3/ Competencies/FdnComp.doc

Creswell, J. W. (1998). Qualitative inquiry and research design: Choosing among five traditions. Thousand Oaks, CA: Sage Publications.

Cross, T. (1998). Understanding family resiliency from a relational world view. In H. I. McCubbin, E. A. Thompson, A. I. Thompson, & J. E. Fromer (Eds.),

Resiliency in Native American and immigrant families (pp. 143–158). Thousand Oaks, CA: Sage Publications.

Daly, A., Jennings, J., Beckett, J., & Leashore, B. R. (1995). Effective coping strategies of African Americans. *Social Work, 40,* 240–248.

Davis, K., Leijenaar, M., & Oldersma, J. (Eds.). (1991). *The gender of power.* Newbury Park, CA: Sage Publications.

de Anda, D. (Ed.). (1997). *Controversial issues in multiculturalism.* Needham Heights, MA: Allyn & Bacon.

Devore, W., & Schlesinger, E. G. (1996). *Ethnic-sensitive social work practice.* Boston: Allyn & Bacon.

Diehl, M. (1999). Self-development in adulthood and aging: The role of critical life events. In C. D. Ryff & V. W. Marshall (Eds.), *The self and society in aging processes* (pp. 150–183). New York: Springer.

Dilworth-Anderson, P., Williams, I., & Gibson, B. (2002). Issues of race, ethnicity, and culture in caregiving research: A 20-year review (1980–2000). *Gerontologist, 42,* 237–272.

Fong, R. (2001). Culturally competent social work practice: Past and present. In R. F. Fong & S. Furuto (Eds.), *Culturally competent practice: Skills, interventions, and evaluations* (pp. 1–9). Needham Heights, MA: Allyn & Bacon.

Ford, M. E., & Hatchett, B. (2001). Gerontological social work with older African American adults. *Journal of Gerontological Social Work, 36,* 141–155.

Genero, N. P. (1998). Culture, resiliency, and mutual psychological development. In H. I. McCubbin, E. A. Thompson, A. I. Thompson, & J. A. Futrell (Eds.), *Resiliency in African-American families* (pp. 31–48). Thousand Oaks, CA: Sage Publications.

Grantmakers in Aging. (2002, October). *Exploring diversity from multiple perspectives. The changing face of America: Aging realities in the 21st century.* Paper presented at the Grantmakers in Aging annual conference, Long Beach, CA.

Green, J. (1999). *Cultural awareness in the human services: A multi-ethnic approach* (3rd ed.). Needham Heights, MA: Allyn & Bacon.

Greene, R. R. (1994). *Human behavior theory: A diversity framework.* Hawthorne, NY: Aldine de Gruyter.

Greene, R. R. (1999). *Human behavior theory and social work practice.* New Brunswick, NJ: Aldine Transaction Press.

Greene, R. R. (Ed.). (2002). *Resiliency: An integrated approach to practice, policy, and research.* Washington, DC: NASW Press.

Greene, R. R., & Watkins, M. (1998). *Serving diverse constituencies: Applying the ecological perspective.* New York: Aldine de Gruyter.

Greene, R. R., Watkins, M., Evans, M., David, V., & Clark, E. J. (2003). Defining diversity: A practitioner survey. *Arête, 27,* 51–71.

Hicks, M., & Lam, M. (1999). Decision-making within the social course of dementia: Accounts by Chinese-American caregivers. *Culture, Medicine & Psychiatry, 23,* 415–452.

Hinton, L., Guo, Z., & Hillygus, J. (2000). Working with culture: A qualitative analysis of barriers to the recruitment of Chinese-American family caregivers for dementia research. *Journal of Cross-Cultural Gerontology, 15,* 119–137.

Ho, M. K. (1991). Use of ethnic-sensitive inventory to enhance practitioner skills with minority clients. *Journal of Multicultural Social Work, 1,* 60–61.

Holland, L., & Courtney, R. (1998). Increasing cultural competence with the Latino community. *Journal of Community Health Nursing, 23,* 49–64.

Hooyman, N. R. (1996). Curriculum and teaching: Today and tomorrow. In Mandel School of Applied Social Sciences (Ed.), *White paper on social work education— Today and tomorrow* (pp. 11–24). Cleveland: Case Western Reserve University Press.

Hornung, C., Eleazer, G., Strongers, H., Wieland, G., Eng, C., McCann, R., & Sapir, M. (1998). Ethnicity and decision-makers in a group of frail older people. *Journal of the American Geriatrics Society, 46,* 280–286.

Hwang, K. (1999). Filial piety and loyalty: Two types of social identification in Confucianism. *Asian Journal of Social Psychology, 2,* 163–183.

Ihara, C. (2004). Are individual rights necessary? A Confucian perspective. In K. Shun & D. B. Wong (Eds.), *Confucian ethics: A comparative study of self, autonomy, and community* (pp. 11–30). New York: Cambridge University Press.

Institute of Medicine. (1994). *Balancing the scales of opportunity: Ensuring racial and ethnic diversity in the health professions.* Washington, DC: National Academies Press.

Institute of Medicine. (2003). *Unequal treatment: Confronting racial and ethnic disparities in health care.* Washington, DC: National Academies Press.

Janevic, M., & Connell, C. (2001). Racial, ethnic, and culture differences in the dementia caregiving experience: Recent findings. *Gerontologist, 41,* 334–347.

Johnson, J. C., & Smith, N. H. (2002, Fall). Health and social issues associated with racial, ethnic, and cultural disparities. *Generations,* pp. 25–32.

Kadushin, A. (1992). *Supervision in social work* (3rd ed.). New York: Columbia University Press.

Kenyon, G. M., & Randall, W. (2001). Narrative gerontology: An overview. In G. Kenyon, P. Clark, & B. de Vries (Eds.), *Narrative gerontology* (pp. 3–18). New York: Springer.

Kimmel, D. C. (1978). Adult development and aging: A gay perspective. *Journal of Social Issues, 34,* 113–130.

Kleinman, A. M. (1978). Rethinking the social and cultural context of psychopathology and psychiatric care. In T. C. Manschreck & A. M. Klunman (Eds.), *Renewal in psychiatry: A critical rationale perspective* (pp. 97–138). New York: John Wiley & Sons.

Kleinman, A. M. (1980). *Patients and healers in the context of culture.* Berkley, CA: University of California Press.

Kleinman, A. M. (1992). Pain as a human experience: An introduction. In M. DelVecchio, P. E., Brodwin, B. Good, & A. Kleinman (Eds.), *Pain as a human experience: An anthropological perspective* (pp. 169–197). Berkeley: University of California Press.

Krause, N. (2004). Stressors arising in highly valued roles, meaning in life, and the physical health status of older adults. *Journals of Gerontology; Series B: Psychological Sciences & Social Sciences, 59B*(5), S287–S297.

Kwak, J., & Haley, W. (2005). Current research findings on end-of-life decision making among racially or ethnically diverse groups. *Gerontologist, 45,* 634–641.

Lee, Y., & Sung, K. (1998). Cultural influences on caregiving burden: Cases of Koreans and Americans. *International Journal of Aging & Human Development, 46,* 125–141.

Lopez, O. (2006). Self-care practices and Hispanic women with diabetes. In R. R. Greene (Ed.), *Contemporary issues of care* (183–200). New York: Haworth Press.

Lum, D. (1999). *Culturally competent practice.* Pacific Grove, CA: Brooks/Cole.

Luna, I., Ardon, E., Lim, Y., Cromwell, S., Phillips, L., & Russell, C. (1996). The relevance of familism in cross-cultural studies of family caregiving. *Western Journal of Nursing Research, 18,* 267–274.

Luyas, G. T. (1990). *An explanatory model of diabetes.* New York: Sage Publications.

Magana, S. (2006). Older Latino family caregivers. In B. Burkman (Ed.), *Handbook of social work in health and aging* (pp. 327–380). New York: Oxford University Press.

McCubbin, H. I., Thompson, E. A., Thompson, A. I., & Futrell, J. A. (1998). *Resiliency in African American families.* Thousand Oaks, CA: Sage Publications.

McIntosh, P. (1988). *White privilege and male privilege: A personal account of coming to see correspondences through work in women's studies* (Working Paper No. 189, pp. 5–8). Wellesley, MA: Center for Research on Women, Wellesley College.

McSweeney, J. C. (1990). *Making behavior changes after myocardial infarction: A naturalistic study.* Published doctoral dissertation, University of Texas at Austin.

McSweeney, J. C., Alan, J. D., & Mayo, K. (1997). Exploring the use of explanatory models in nursing and research practice. *Image Journal of Nursing Scholarship, 29,* 243–248.

Min, J. W. (2005). Cultural competency: A key to effective future social work with racially and ethnically diverse elders. *Families in Society, 86,* 347–357.

Moon, A., Lubben, J., & Villa, V. (1998). Awareness and utilization of community long-term care services by elderly Korean and non-Hispanic white Americans. *Gerontologist, 38,* 309–316.

Morano, C L., & King, D. (2005). Religiosity as a mediator of caregiver well-being: Does ethnicity make a difference? *Journal of Gerontological Social Work, 45*(1/2), 69–84.

National Association of Social Workers. (2001). *NASW standards for cultural competence in social work practice.* Washington, DC: Author.

Norton, D. (1976). *Dual perspectives: The inclusion of ethnic minority content in social work curriculum.* New York: Council on Social Work Education.

Okayama, C. M., Furuto, S. B. C. L., & Edmondson, J. (2001). Components of cultural competence: Attitudes, knowledge, and skills. In R. Fong & S. Furuto (Eds.),

Culturally competent practice: Skills, interventions, and evaluations (pp. 89–131). Boston: Allyn & Bacon.

Park, I., & Cho, L-J. (1995). Confucianism and the Korean family. *Journal of Comparative Family Studies, 26,* 117–134.

Pinderhughes, E. (1983). Empowerment for our clients and for ourselves. *Social Casework, 64,* 331–338.

Pinderhughes, E. (1989). *Understanding race, ethnicity, and power: The key to efficacy in clinical practice.* New York: Free Press.

Ramirez, M. (1999). *Multicultural psychotherapy: An approach to individual and cultural differences.* Needham Heights, MA: Allyn & Bacon.

Redfield, R., Linton, R., & Herskovits, M. J. (1936). Memorandum of the study of acculturation. *American Anthropologist, 3,* 149–152.

Rothman, J. C. (1999). *The self-awareness workbook for social workers.* Boston: Allyn & Bacon.

Schoenberg, N. E., Amey, C. H., & Coward, R. T. (1998). Stories of meaning: Lay perspectives on the origin and management of noninsulin dependent diabetes mellitus among older women in the United States. *Social Science and Medicine, 47,* 2113–2125.

Scollan-Koliopoulos, M., O'Connell, K. A, & Walker, E. A. (2005). The first diabetes educator is the family: Using illness representation to recognize a multigenerational legacy of diabetes. *Clinical Nurse Specialist, 19,* 302–307.

Skinner, J. (2002). Acculturation: Measures of ethnic accommodation to the dominant American culture. In J. H. Skinner, H. John, J. A. Teresi, D. Holmes, S. M. Stahl, & A. L. Stewart (Eds.), *Multicultural measurement in older populations* (pp. 37–51). New York: Springer.

Solomon, B. B. (1976). *Black empowerment: Social work in oppressed communities.* New York: Columbia University Press.

Sung, K. (1997). Filial piety in modern times: Timely adaptation and practice patterns. *Australasian Journal on Ageing, 17*(1, Suppl.), 88–92.

Takamura, J. C. (2001). Towards a new era in aging and social work. *Journal of Gerontological Social Work, 36*(3/4), 1–11.

Thompson, C. D., & Wiggins, M. F. (2002). *The human cost of food: Farm workers' lives, labor and advocacy.* Austin: University of Texas Press.

Torres-Gil, F., & Moga, K. B. (2001). Multiculturalism, social policy, and the new aging. *Journal of Gerontological Social Work, 36*(3/4), 13–31.

Tully, C. T. (1994). Epilogue: Power and the social work profession. In R. R. Greene (Ed.), *Human behavior a diversity framework* (pp. 235–244). New York: Aldine de Gruyter.

U.S. Census Bureau. (2000). 65+ in the United States. *Current population reports* (Special Studies, pp. 23–190). Washington, DC: Author.

U.S. Census Bureau. (2003). *Current population reports.* Washington, DC: Author.

U.S. Department of Health and Human Services, Substance Abuse and Mental Health Services Administration. (1999). *Mental health: A report of the surgeon general.* Rockville, MD: Center for Mental Health Services, National Institute of Mental Health, National Institutes of Health.

Watari, K., & Gatz, M. (2004). Pathways to care for Alzheimer's disease among Korean Americans. *Cultural Diversity and Ethnic Minority Psychology, 10,* 23–38.

Yao, X. (2000). *An introduction to Confucianism.* Cambridge, England: Cambridge University Press.

Yeh, K., & Bedford, O. (2003). A test of the dual filial piety model. *Asian Journal of Social Psychology, 6,* 215–228.

Youn, G., Knight, B., Jeong, H., & Benton, D. (1999). Differences in familism values and caregiving outcomes among Korean, Korean American, and white American dementia caregivers. *Psychology & Aging, 14,* 355–364.

APPENDIX 3-A Changing Demographics in the 21st Century

The first half of the 21st century will witness a dramatic increase in the size and racial and ethnic composition of the 65 years of age and older population of the United States. These changes will have profound implications for the scale and delivery of social services to the elderly population and for the education of geriatric social workers.

As the baby-boom generation—those born between 1946 and 1964—begins to celebrate their 65th birthdays in 2011, the **over-65 population will surge**. By 2030, an estimated 71.5 million people aged 65 years and older, almost twice the number in 2004, will live in the United States. That is 20 percent of the total population. Moreover, the 85 years and over population is projected to increase from 4.6 million in 2002 to 9.6 million in 2030. In 2004, the latest year for which data were available, 36.3 million people aged 65 years and older represented 12.4 percent of the U.S. population, or about one in every eight Americans.

Racial and ethnic groups, that is, all people other than the non-Hispanic white population, will account for nearly 90 percent of the total growth in the U.S. population in the first half of the 21st century. Currently, elders of racial and ethnic groups compose more than 16.1 percent of all older Americans (those aged 65 years and older). In the future, their numbers will increase dramatically. By 2030, members of racial and ethnic groups are projected to represent 26.4 percent of the older population.

Between 1999 and 2030, the total population of adults 65 years of age and older in racial and ethnic groups is projected to increase by 217 percent, compared with 81 percent for the older white population. Reflecting continued immigration and larger family sizes, the Hispanic population will be the most rapidly increasing racial and ethnic group, growing by 322 percent, compared with 128 percent for black American elders, 301 percent for Asian American elders, and roughly 193 percent for American Indian and Alaska Natives.

In 2003, **older men** were much more likely to be **married** than older women—71 percent of men compared with 41 percent of women. Almost half (43 percent) of all older women in 2003 were widows. More than four times as many widows (8.2 million) compared with widowers (2.0 million) resided in the United States in 2003. Divorced and separated (including married, but spouse absent) older people represented only 10.7 percent of all older people in 2003, but that percentage has increased from 1980, when approximately 5.3 percent of the older population was divorced or separated, or married with a spouse absent.

The **proportion of individuals living alone** increases with advanced age. In 2003, among women aged 75 years and older, about half (49.8 percent) lived alone and about 30.8 percent (10.5 million) of all noninstitutionalized older people lived alone (7.8 million women and 2.7 million men). The proportion of adults living with their spouse decreases with age, especially for women. Only 28.7 percent of women at least 75 years old lived with a spouse.

Although a relatively small number (1.56 million) and percentage (4.5 percent) of the population that was at least 65 years old lived in nursing homes in 2000, the percentage

(Continued)

APPENDIX 3-A Changing Demographics in the 21st Century (*Continued*)

increases dramatically with age, ranging from 1.1 percent for people aged 65 years to 74 years to 4.7 percent for people aged 75 years to 84 years and 18.2 percent for people aged 85 or more years. In addition, approximately 5 percent of elderly people lived in self-described senior housing of various types, many of which have supportive services available to their residents.

About 3.6 million (10.2 percent) elderly people in 2003 were living **below the poverty level**. Another 2.3 million (6.7 percent) elderly people were classified as "near poor" (income between the poverty level and 125 percent of that level). One of every 12 (8.8 percent) elderly white Americans was poor in 2003 compared with 23.7 percent of elderly black Americans, 14.3 percent of Asian Americans, and 19.5 percent of the elderly Hispanic population. Higher-than-average poverty rates for older people were found among those who lived in central cities (13.1 percent), outside metropolitan areas (that is, rural areas—11.0 percent), and in the South (11.9 percent).

Older women had a higher poverty rate (12.5 percent) than older men (7.3 percent) in 2003. Older people living alone were much more likely to be poor (18.6 percent) than were older people living with families (5.8 percent). The highest poverty rates (40.8 percent) were experienced by older Hispanic women who lived alone.

For one-third of Americans older than 65 years of age in 2002, **social security benefits** constituted 90 percent of their income. Other major sources of income as reported by the Social Security Administration for older people in that year were from assets (reported by 55 percent), private pensions (reported by 29 percent), government employee pensions (reported by 14 percent), and earnings (reported by 22 percent).

Despite the overall increase in **educational attainment** among older Americans, substantial educational differences still exist among racial and ethnic groups. In 1998, about 72 percent of the non-Hispanic white population aged 65 years and older had finished high school compared with 65 percent of the non-Hispanic Asian and Pacific Islander population, 44 percent of the non-Hispanic black older population, and 29 percent of the Hispanic older population. The educational level of the older population is increasing, however. Between 1970 and 2003, the percentage of older Americans who had completed high school rose from 28 percent to 71 percent. But the percentage who had completed high school varied considerably by race and ethnic origin in 2003: 76 percent of white Americans, 70 percent of Asians and Pacific Islanders, 52 percent of black Americans, and 36 percent of the Hispanic population.

In 2004, 37.4 percent of noninstitutionalized older people assessed their **health** as excellent or very good (compared with 65.8 percent for people from 18 years to 64 years of age). Little difference existed between the genders on this measure, but older black people (57.7 percent) and older Hispanic adults (60.1 percent) were less likely to rate their health as excellent or good than were older white people (76.9 percent).

In 1997, more than half (54.5 percent) of the older population reported having at least one **disability** (physical or nonphysical). More than one-third (37.7 percent)

(Continued)

APPENDIX 3-A Changing Demographics in the 21st Century (*Continued*)

reported at least one severe disability. Disability takes a much heavier toll on the very old. Almost three-fourths of those aged 80 years and older reported at least one disability. More than half of people aged 80 years and older had one or more severe disabilities, and more than a third of the population aged at least 80 years of age reported needing assistance as a result of disability.

In 1999, more than 27.3 percent of community-resident Medicare beneficiaries older than 65 years of age had difficulty performing one or more **activities of daily living** (ADLs). An additional 13.0 percent reported difficulties with instrumental activities of daily living (IADLs). (ADLs include bathing, dressing, eating, and getting around the house. IADLs include preparing meals, shopping, managing money, using the telephone, doing housework, and taking medication.) By contrast, 93.3 percent of institutionalized Medicare beneficiaries had difficulties with one or more ADLs and 76.3 percent of them had difficulty with three or more ADLs. Limitations on activities because of chronic conditions apparently increase with age: Among those aged 65 years to 74 years, 19.9 percent had difficulties with ADLs. In contrast, more than half (52.5 percent) of people 85 years and older had difficulties with ADLs.

About 11 percent (3.7 million) of older Medicare enrollees received **personal care** from a paid or unpaid source in 1999. Almost all community-resident older people with chronic disabilities received either informal care (from family or friends) or formal care (from services provider agencies). More than 90 percent of all those older people with chronic disabilities received informal or formal care, and about two-thirds received only informal care. About 9 percent of that chronically disabled group received only formal services.

Sources: All statistics, data, and projections are compiled from U.S. Bureau of the Census, U.S. Bureau of Labor Statistics, National Center for Health Statistics, and Social Security Administration publications and related Web sites.

APPENDIX 3-B NASW Standards for Cultural Competence in Practice

Standard 1. Ethics and Values
Social workers shall function in accordance with the values, ethics, and standards of the profession, recognizing how personal and professional values may conflict with or accommodate the needs of diverse clients.

Standard 2. Self-Awareness
Social workers shall seek to develop an understanding of their own personal and cultural values and beliefs as one way of appreciating the importance of multicultural identities in the lives of people.

Standard 3. Cross-Cultural Knowledge
Social workers shall have and continue to develop specialized knowledge and understanding about the history, traditions, values, family systems, and artistic expressions of major client groups that they serve.

Standard 4. Cross-Cultural Skills
Social workers shall use appropriate methodological approaches, skills, and techniques that reflect the workers' understanding of the role of culture in the helping process.

Standard 5. Services Delivery
Social workers shall be knowledgeable about and skillful in the use of services available in the community and broader society and be able to make appropriate referrals for their diverse clients.

Standard 6. Empowerment and Advocacy
Social workers shall be aware of the effect of social policies and programs on diverse client populations, advocating for and with clients whenever appropriate.

Standard 7. Diverse Workforce
Social workers shall support and advocate for recruitment, admissions and hiring, and retention efforts in social work programs and agencies that ensure diversity within the profession.

Standard 8. Professional Education
Social workers shall advocate for and participate in educational and training programs that help advance cultural competence within the profession.

Standard 9. Language Diversity
Social workers shall seek to provide or advocate for the provision of information, referrals, and services in the language appropriate to the client, which may include use of interpreters.

Standard 10. Cross-Cultural Leadership
Social workers shall be able to communicate information about diverse client groups to other professionals.

Note: The NASW National Committee on Racial and Ethnic Diversity proposed standards were approved by the NASW Board of Directors on June 23, 2001.
Source: National Association of Social Workers. (2001). *NASW standards for cultural competence in social work practice.* Washington, DC: Author.

APPENDIX 3-C Types of Privilege Reflected in Statements

Type of Privilege	Sample Statement
The freedom to associate exclusively or primarily with members of your own group.	I can, if I wish, arrange to be in the company of people of my race most of the of the time. (p. 5)
The level of social acceptance one can presume across varying contexts.	If I should need to move, I can be pretty sure of renting or purchasing housing in an area where I want to live. (p. 5)
	Whether I use checks, credit cards, or cash, I can count on my skin color not to work against the appearance of financial reliability. (p. 6)
	I do not have to educate my children to be aware of systemic racism for their own daily protection. (p. 6)
The ability to see members of your group in a positive light in history records, in texts, in media, and as role models.	When I am told about our national heritage or about civilization, I am shown that people of my color made it what it is. (p. 6)
	I can be pretty sure that if I ask to speak to the person in charge, I will be facing a person of my own race. (p. 7)
Freedom from stereotyping.	I can swear, or dress in second-hand clothes or not answer letters, without having people attribute these choices to the bad morale, poverty, or illiteracy of my race. (p. 7)
	I can do well in a challenging situation without being called a credit to my race. (p. 7)
	I can be late to a meeting without having the lateness reflect on my race. (p. 8)
The ability to be oblivious of other groups in a culture.	I can remain oblivious of the language and customs of people of color who constitute the world's majority without feeling any penalty for such oblivion. (p. 7)

Source: Adapted from McIntosh, P. (1988). *White privilege and male privilege: A personal account of coming to see correspondences through work in women's studies* (Working Paper No. 189, pp. 5–8). Wellesley, MA: Center for Research on Women, Wellesley College.

APPENDIX 3-D Ethnic-Sensitive Inventory

In working with (older adult) clients of racial and ethnic groups, I

- realize that my own ethnic and class background may influence my effectiveness

- am aware of the systemic sources (racism, poverty, and prejudice) of their problems

- can identify the links between systemic problems and individual concerns

- assist them to understand whether the problem is of an individual or a collective nature

- am able to engage them in identifying major progress that has taken place

- consider it an obligation to familiarize myself with their culture, history, and other ethnically related responses to the problems

- am able to understand and "tune in" to the meaning of their ethnic dispositions, behaviors, and experiences

- am able, at the termination phase, to help them consider alternative sources of support

- am sensitive to their fears of racism or prejudiced orientations

- am able to move more slowly in the effort to actively "reach for feelings"

- consider the implications of what is being suggested in relation to each client's ethnic reality (unique dispositions, behaviors, and experiences)

- clearly delineate agency functions and respectfully inform clients of my professional expectations of them

- am able to understand that the worker–client relationship may last a long time

- am able to explain clearly the nature of the interview

- am respectful of their definition of the problem to be solved

- am able to specify the problem in practical, concrete terms

- am sensitive to treatment goals consonant with their cultures

- am able to mobilize social and extended family networks

- am sensitive to the client's premature termination of service.

Source: Adapted from Ho, M. K. (1991). Use of ethnic-sensitive inventory (ESI) to enhance practitioner skills with minority clients. *Journal of Multicultural Social Work, 1*(1), 60–61.

APPENDIX 3-E Diversity Principles

- Sound diversity practice requires a model.

- Diversity practice requires the ability to think critically.

- Diversity practice requires that social workers be learners.

- Diversity content encompasses practice methods, social policy, ethics, social justice, human behavior in the social environment, research, and field education.

- Diversity content encompasses the selective and differential use of knowledge, skills, and attitudes pertaining to all areas of social work practice.

- Theory building for social work practice with diverse constituencies should reevaluate concepts such as normalcy and deviance.

- Diversity practice involves the use of knowledge or research conducted in a culturally congruent manner to people involved in the study.

- Diversity practice requires an understanding of multiple theories, such as systems theory and the ecological perspective.

- Diversity practice requires an understanding of concepts such as privacy and space.

- Using a diversity framework, one views culture as a source of cohesion, identity, and strength as well as strain and discordance.

- A diversity framework needs to provide an understanding of a culture's adaptive strategies.

- Diversity practice requires an understanding of bicultural status.

- The scope of diversity practice encompasses all populations at risk affected by social, economic, and legal biases, distribution of rights and resources, and oppression.

- Diversity practice requires an understanding of a person's behavior as a member of his or her family, various groups and organizations, and his or her community.

- Diversity practice requires that social workers understand the process of inclusion and exclusion.

- Diversity practice requires that social workers understand that individuals and groups may have limited access to resources, live in unsafe environments damaging to self-esteem, and experience their environments as hostile.

(Continued)

APPENDIX 3-E Diversity Principles (*Continued*)

- Diversity practice requires an understanding of the effects of institutional racism, ageism, homophobia, and sexism.

- Diversity practice recognizes that social work practice cannot be neutral, value free, or objective.

- Diversity practice requires an appreciation for attitudinal differences between clients and social workers regarding autonomy or self-determination.

- Social workers who are culturally sensitive appreciate differences.

- Diversity practice requires that social workers understand that their decisions may be culture bound or ethnocentric.

- Diversity practice requires that social workers be self-aware, open to cultural differences, and aware of their own preconceived assumptions of diverse groups' values and biases.

- Diversity practice requires that social workers understand their own and the client's belief systems, customs, norms, ideologies, rituals, traditions, and so forth.

- Diversity practice requires social workers to uphold the profession's commitment to social justice.

- Diversity practice involves the integration of skills and theory grounded in the client's reality.

- Diversity practice recognizes differences in help-seeking patterns, definition of the problem, selection of solutions, and interventions.

- Diversity practice promotes a client's sense of self-efficacy and mastery of his or her environment.

- The most effective social workers in diversity practice differentially use assessment and intervention strategies.

- The most effective workers in diversity practice use a blend of formal and informal resources.

Source: Adapted from Greene, R. R., Watkins, M., Evans, M., David, V., & Clark, E. J. (2003). Defining diversity: A practitioner survey. *Arête*, 27(1), 70–71.

Incorporation of Values and Ethics in Practice with Older Adults

4

RATIONALE: Social work is grounded in the NASW *Code of Ethics* and a set of core values—service, social and economic justice, dignity, and the worth of the person—that define the profession's commitment to ethical standards. When ethical dilemmas occur, practitioners attempt to resolve their ambiguity, using professional tools and guidelines. These values are congruent with fostering the optimal development of human capacity and supporting the mission to promote societal well-being. To be competent practitioners, social workers must be aware of personal values, be self-critical, uphold professional responsibilities, deal with ethical dilemmas, and advocate for a just society.

COMPETENCY: Students must be able to apply ethical reasoning models and resolution strategies. They will

- respect and promote older clients' right to dignity and self-determination within the context of the law and safety concerns
- apply ethical principles to decisions on behalf of all older clients, with special attention to those with limited decisional capacity.
  This competency includes professional boundary issues in work with older adults, client self-determination, end-of-life decisions, family conflicts, and guardianship.
- adhere to laws and public policies related to older adults (e.g., elder abuse reporting, legal guardianship, powers of attorney, wills, advance directives, and Do-Not-Resuscitate orders). (Council on Social Work Education, Gero-Ed Center, 2004)

What Are the Core Values and Ethical Standards and Principles?

The social work profession is built on a set of values that influence and direct practice. As professionals, social workers are responsible for working within the parameters of ethics set forth by their profession. This chapter describes the specific values, knowledge, and skills—or competencies—required of practitioners to effectively apply ethical standards and principles in their work with older adults. Their practice must be built on the profession's core values that guide and underpin interventions with the client population. Pincus and Minahan (1973) have defined values as

> beliefs, preferences, or assumptions about what is desirable or good. An example is the belief that society has an obligation to help each individual realize his fullest potential. They are not assertions about how the world is and what we know about it, but how the world should be. As such, value statements cannot be subjected to scientific investigation; they must be accepted on faith. Thus, we can speak of a value as being right or wrong, only in relation to the particular belief system or ethical code being used as a standard. (p. 38)

Values guide and shape social workers' responses to, and interventions with, older adults.

According to Levy (1973), social workers, agencies, and professional associations must have a set of values on which to base their choices and decisions related to client interventions or their deliberations with regard to institutions and society. Levy (1984) developed a framework with four core values—societal, organizational and institutional, professional, and human services practice—and pointed out the importance of the profession's adopting a set of outcomes with the goal of achieving standards for practice. Levy's values framework may be applied to any of the practice levels—micro, meso, or macro.

The NASW *Code of Ethics* identifies the following key values of the profession:

- service—service to others takes precedence over self-interest
- social justice—advocate for the rights of clients, particularly the most vulnerable in society, and pursue social change when indicated
- dignity and worth of the person—treat people courteously and in a caring manner and respect individual differences, as well as cultural and ethnic diversity
- importance of human relationships—hold relationships among people in the highest regard and recognize that those relationships may be catalysts for change
- integrity—be mindful of the profession's mission, values, ethical principles, and standards, and apply them in practice
- competence—obligation to increase professional knowledge and skills and use them in practice. (NASW, 2000)

Although values play a central role in social work practice, professional ethics, according to Dolgoff, Loewenberg, and Harrington (2005), guide social workers to transform professional values into practice activities. The distinction between ethics and values is that values relate to what is good and desirable, whereas ethics pertain to what is right and correct.

Social workers must be mindful of professional values and ethics when working with older adults. For example, when facing circumstances in which it appears clients may be a danger to themselves, practitioners may find it challenging to remain objective. Their objectivity may be further tested if they perceive clients are not making the best decisions that further their own well-being or are being exploited by family members or neighbors. To remain objective, it is essential that practitioners use tools such as those presented in this chapter to help them in clarifying the dynamics and factors involved in each client's particular situation.

Aids for Ethical Practice

Assessment Tools

A number of tools are available to practitioners working with older adults. Dolgoff and colleagues (2005) designed an assessment screen to help social workers engage in a rational planning process that emphasizes ethics (Figure 4-1). This tool is designed to assist gerontological social workers in the intervention phase. Consider, for example, the case of an 80-year-old woman who lives alone in an apartment building for older adults. It is her choice to live independently; however, her cognitive functioning has declined over the years. One day, unaware that she has not turned off the stove, she places a tea towel on the stove top, resulting in a kitchen fire. The assessment screen allows the practitioner to weigh the importance of honoring the client's independence and autonomy against the need to protect the safety and well-being of the client and other residents.

Another aid for ethical decision making is Kitchener's (1984) critical evaluation model. Four ethical principles form the basis of this model: (1) *autonomy*—the promotion of self-determination or the freedom to make choices for oneself; (2) *beneficence*—the promotion of goodness, kindness, or charity, and the prevention or removal of harm; (3) *nonmaleficence*—the act of doing no harm; and (4) *justice*—the provision of equal treatment to all. When applying this model to practice, the social worker factors into the assessment personal and environmental influences affecting the client's situation. For instance, certain cultures may emphasize family decision making over individual decision making. With such a cultural dynamic, autonomy is less important for the older adult than the other three principles.

The model designed by Corey, Corey, and Callanan (1993) allows practitioners to assess those factors that may affect the older adult's situation thoroughly and systematically. Using their model, practitioners would follow these seven steps:

1. Identify the problem or dilemma. The practitioner gathers information about the older adult's situation. Is the conflict an ethical, legal, or moral one?

FIGURE 4-1 Ethical Assessment Screen

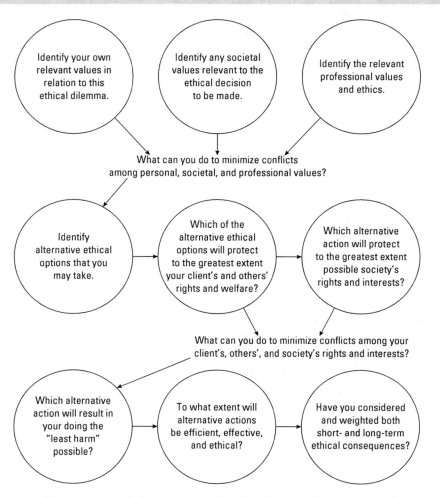

Source: From *Ethical decisions for social work practice* (7th ed.) by Dolgoff, R., Loewenberg, F. M., Harrington, D. (2005). Reprinted with permission of Wadsworth, a division of Thomson Learning: www.thomsonrights.com. Fax 800-730-2215.

2. Identify the issues. What are the critical issues that pertain to the situation? What are the rights, responsibilities, and welfare of all concerned? Are there competing factors that embody the moral principles of autonomy, beneficence, nonmalfeasance, and justice?

3. Review relevant ethical guidelines. What are the relevant aspects of professional codes of ethics that would apply in the particular situation?

4. Obtain consultation. Acquire a different perspective on the situation by conferring with colleagues.

5. Consider possible or probable courses of action. List them.
6. Enumerate the consequences of various decisions. Ask, What are the implications of each course of action for the older adult? For the family? For the community? For the social worker? Use the principles of autonomy, beneficence, nonmalfeasance, and justice as a framework for evaluation.
7. Decide on the best course of action. Assess the information obtained in steps 1–6 and come to a decision.

Corey et al.'s model encourages practitioners to include existing codes of ethics and colleagues' opinions in the assessment process. The use of codes of ethics provides clear guidelines and outlines considerations to be made in the decision-making process with older adults and their families.

The model developed by Congress (1999) specifically helps social workers to resolve ethical dilemmas. This five-step model that can be used with older adults is called ETHIC:

Examine relevant personal, societal, agency, client, and professional values.
Think about what ethical standard of the NASW *Code of Ethics* (2000) applies to the situation, and consider relevant laws and case decisions.
Hypothesize about possible consequences of different decisions.
Identify who will benefit and who will be harmed in view of social work's commitment to the most vulnerable people.
Consult with one's supervisor and colleagues about the most ethical choice. (pp. 31–33)

The model encourages social workers to examine all values that may influence their decision making methodically and to review the available options systematically. The advantage in using ETHIC is that it includes input from the NASW *Code of Ethics* and colleagues before the practitioner reaches a decision to bring to the older adult.

As society copes with a growing aging population, gerontological social workers will need to balance the rights of older adults against those of others. Issues requiring attention include how to allow clients as much autonomy as possible and also protect them and others from harm. As older adults lose physical and cognitive capacity, such ethical decision making becomes more complicated.

Codes of Ethics

Many professional organizations have established codes of ethics, which usually include standards and principles to guide practice. For example, the NASW *Code of Ethics* (2000) serves six purposes. It

1. identifies core values on which social work's mission is based
2. summarizes broad ethical principles that reflect the profession's core values and establishes a set of specific ethical standards that should be used to guide social work practice

3. is designed to help social workers identify relevant considerations when professional obligations conflict or ethical uncertainties arise
4. provides ethical standards to which the general public can hold the social work profession accountable
5. socializes practitioners new to the field to social work's mission, values, ethical principles, and ethical standards
6. articulates standards that the social work profession itself can use to assess whether social workers have engaged in unethical conduct. NASW has formal procedures to adjudicate ethics complaints filed against its members. In subscribing to this *Code,* social workers are required to cooperate in its implementation, participate in NASW adjudication proceedings, and abide by any NASW disciplinary rulings or sanctions. (Dogoff et al., p. 257)

The values, principles, and standards in the NASW *Code of Ethics* guide practitioners' decision making and conduct. When social workers apply the code to practice, however, they must consider the context of a situation and any conflicts between the code and the practice situation. For example, the *Code of Ethics* cannot resolve all ethical issues. An important component of the ethical decision-making process is the social worker's informed judgment. In addition, social workers may avail themselves of various tools to help them with their ethical decision making. Such tools include ethical theory or state regulations, laws, and other professional codes that might provide additional guidance on working through a dilemma.

Dolgoff and colleagues (2005) have developed two tools that help practitioners presented with an ethical dilemma prioritize the elements of that conflict. The first tool is an ethical rules screen (Figure 4-2). This screen helps social workers determine if the NASW *Code of Ethics* applies to a situation and if it provides sufficient guidance to resolve the dilemma.

If a social worker is unsuccessful in applying the NASW *Code of Ethics* to a practice situation, he or she may use the ethical principles screen (Dolgoff et al., 2005) to rank order principles (Figure 4-3). Using this tool, the social worker decides which principle applies to the case and the location of that principle on the screen. Fulfilling a higher order principle takes precedence over fulfilling a lower order one.

Because the NASW *Code of Ethics* is not a blueprint for professional conduct, practitioners must be prepared to engage actively in ethical decision making when working with older adults. Particular challenges gerontological social workers may face include allowing older adults as much autonomy in the decision-making process as possible while promoting the best approach that avoids harm, advocating for fair and equitable treatment of older adults, and encouraging interventions that promote the most good. To respect a person's autonomy is to recognize that person as a self-determining agent who is entitled to decide his or her own destiny. It is to recognize that the individual has the right to his or her own opinions and to act on them. It is to acknowledge that the person has the right to his or her own judgments. An autonomous person

FIGURE 4-2 Ethical Rules Screen

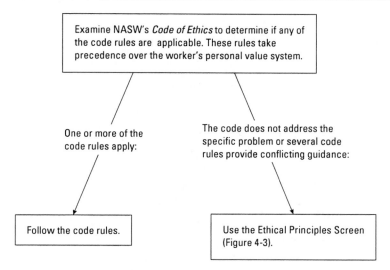

Source: From *Ethical decisions for social work practice* (7th ed.) by Dolgoff, R., Loewenberg, F. M., Harrington, D. (2005).Reprinted with permission of Wadsworth, a division of Thomson Learning: www.thomsonrights.com. Fax 800-730-2215.

is free from external constraints and can handle his or her own affairs (Beauchamp & Walters, 1989).

Liberty-Limiting Principles

Although practitioners ought to respect autonomous decision making whenever possible, sometimes it is necessary to restrict an individual's freedoms to protect the older person and others affected by the individual's behavior. Four liberty-limiting principles identified by Beauchamp and Walters (1989) justifying such action are

1. The principle of paternalism: A person's liberty is justifiably restricted to prevent the individual from harming self.
2. The harm principle: A person's liberty is justifiably restricted to prevent harm to others caused by that person.
3. The principle of legal moralism: A person's liberty is justifiably restricted to prevent that person's immoral behavior.
4. The offense principle: A person's liberty is justifiably restricted to prevent offense caused by that person to others. (p. 39)

The first two liberty-limiting principles are the two principles that most often are applied to practice with older adults. Ethical conflicts occur when an older adult has

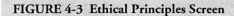

FIGURE 4-3 Ethical Principles Screen

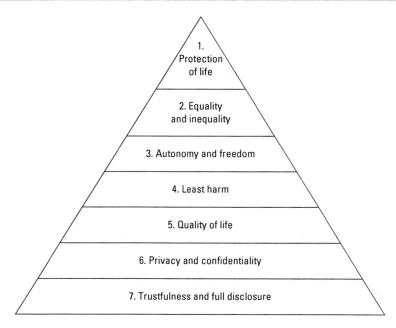

1. Protection of life

2. Equality and inequality

3. Autonomy and freedom

4. Least harm

5. Quality of life

6. Privacy and confidentiality

7. Trustfulness and full disclosure

Source: From *Ethical Decisions for Social Work Practice* (7th ed.) by Dolgoff, F., Loewenberg, F. M., Harrington, D. (2005). Reprinted with permission of Wadsworth, a division of Thomson Learning: www.thomsonrights.com. Fax 800-730-2215.

compromised internal capacities for self-governance, for instance, when the individual has dementia, temporary memory loss, or a developmental disability. In such situations, the principle of beneficence applies, directing social workers to prevent or remove possible harm to the individual. This may lead to application of the liberty-limiting principle paternalism, one form of beneficence. According to Beauchamp and Walters (1989), "the person who limits autonomy appeals exclusively to grounds of beneficence for the person whose autonomy is limited" (p. 39).

Another liberty-limiting principle social workers may encounter in their work with older adults is the harm principle, which addresses life-safety issues. A practitioner might apply this principle, for example, in the case of an older adult male who has a diagnosis of schizophrenia and has threatened the safety of another person because the voices in his head have directed him to harm that person. Using the ethical principles screen outlined in Figure 4-3, the social worker could examine whether the protection of life is a more compelling principle than autonomy and freedom. Therefore, both that tool and the liberty-limiting principle might direct the practitioner to intervene in the older adult's autonomous decision making because another person's life might be at stake.

Sometimes the issue of whether an older adult is capable of self-governance arises, thus leading to a question of legal competence. A person who is legally incompetent performs below a minimum level of cognitive ability. To make an initial evaluation of the cognitive functional capacity of an older adult, the social worker might ask several assessment questions, adapted from Herr and Weber (1999), Kapp (1998), and Linzer (2002):

- Can the older adult make and communicate by spoken words (or by other means) his or her decisions or choices?
- Can he or she provide reasons why these choices were made?
- Are the reasons underlying the choices rational?
- Is the individual able to understand the implications or the risks and benefits of the choices he or she has made?
- Are the choices consistent with the older adult's values and preferences?

The answers will reveal a sense of the client's legal competence. If the older adult appears able to articulate and understand the reasons for selecting a course of action and no obvious harm or safety issues are present, then the social worker ought to respect the individual's autonomy even if the choices conflict with the practitioner's own or society's expectations.

To further protect an older person's right to autonomous decision making, social workers and other practitioners should apply informed consent procedures to every intervention or treatment decision. Informed consent enables the older adult to accept or refuse treatment; however, informed consent involves three elements (Herr & Weber, 1999):

1. Competency—The individual or surrogate decision maker must be legally capable of giving consent.
2. Knowledge—The social worker needs to furnish adequate information so that the individual can evaluate and understand the benefits and risks of an intervention. The social worker also needs to provide an opportunity for the client to ask questions and receive understandable answers.
3. Voluntariness—The individual should not be coerced to make a decision one way or another. He or she ought to have the option to abstain from the intervention.

Informed consent must occur before the intervention. Informed consent requires practitioners to explain each intervention and procedure thoroughly so that clients will understand the risks and benefits, and will be in a position to make informed decisions. Health care or social work practitioners may convey the following information to older adults (Herr & Weber, 1999):

- diagnosis
- nature and purpose of the intervention

- risks or consequences of the intervention
- prognosis or probability of success
- alternatives to the intervention
- possible outcomes if procedure is not done
- provider limitations, if any
- professional advice or recommendations. (p. 48)

If the three elements—competency, knowledge, and voluntariness—are present and the social worker or health care practitioner has provided a reasonable amount of information to the older adult, then informed consent has been achieved.

Obtaining informed consent from an older adult whose cognitive functioning fluctuates may be difficult. In such cases, the practitioner should wait for a good day—when cognitive functioning is optimal—to provide that client with information. It is recommended that a trusted family member or friend observe the informed consent session and lend support to the older adult.

As Congress (1999) has pointed out, "ethical social work with older persons begins with the client" (p. 97). Thus, in all situations, social workers need to maximize older adults' participation in decision making to the fullest extent possible.

Thorough Decision Making

It is important for professional social workers to gather as much information as possible about a client's situation, using that information to conduct a thorough assessment. In cases involving ethical conflicts or dilemmas with older adults, this step in the assessment process is a key to the deliberations that must occur before deciding on the right course of action. It is essential that social workers facilitate the decision-making process in a thoughtful and inclusive manner, especially when older adults and their families are considering whether to pursue life-sustaining treatment or to relinquish decision-making responsibilities.

A Decision-Making Model

Loewenberg and colleagues (2000) proposed the general decision-making model shown in Appendix 4-A to serve as a practice guide. One intent of their model is to keep social workers mindful that the input of several people, including family members, neighbors, and health care workers, can be useful before rendering a decision. Practitioners may apply Loewenberg et al.'s model to any practice situation, even one that does not involve an ethical problem.

Each person in the decision-making process has the potential to present new information, suggest options, and provide or withdraw support, all of which can alter or refine decision making. Because ethical decision making is a complex process, practitioners must remain flexible and thoughtful, often using more than one problem-solving approach.

Consultation with Committees and Teams

The most prominent use of ethics committees is within hospital settings, although such committees are now appearing in long-term care facilities (Agich, 1993; Beauchamp & Walters, 1989). When medical and treatment decisions are at hand, social workers may seek opinions from an ethics committee or ethics consultation group to ensure the thoroughness of the decision-making process. Ethics committees serve a number of purposes. They can provide education, develop institutional policies and guidelines, or are available for consultation, often with cases involving the withholding, withdrawing, or continuation of life-sustaining medical care. A typical ethics committee comprises a physician, nurse, social worker, attorney, hospital administrators, clergy, a community member, an advocate for the aged population, and a medical ethicist. Some committees include the client and family in their membership (Beauchamp & Walters).

In the social services agency setting, practitioners may use peer review and services plan committees to oversee delivery of services (Galambos, 1999). Such committees monitor client services and handle ethical conflicts as they emerge within an agency. They determine whether the services provided are reasonable, too few, or too costly, or whether the social worker's use of services is reasonable to meet a client's needs. In essence this process is a form of ethical consideration in the delivery of services (Galambos, 1997). Research has shown that peer review and interdisciplinary collaboration have positive effects on services delivery (Netting & Williams, 1995).

Administrative teams composed of administrators and services providers also may assist with ethical deliberations. These teams meet periodically to discuss issues and practices related to quality of care, consumer choice, and service delivery. This type of interdisciplinary dialogue raises awareness about the constraints, problems, and successes of client services provided within an agency (Galambos, 1999).

Principles of Autonomy and Paternalism

Trying to balance an older adult's right to autonomy and the professional's responsibility to intervene in situations potentially harmful to the older adult and others—and responding effectively to everyone's needs—may lead to an ethical conflict, that is, a clash between opposing obligations (Galambos, 1997) or an ethical dilemma. Ethical dilemmas typically occur when the social worker chooses between two or more relevant, but contradictory, ethical directives, or when every alternative results in an undesirable outcome for one or more people. Each party to an ethical disagreement may put forth moral principles to support his or her competing conclusions.

In matters of client self-determination, guardianship, and end-of-life decision making, the ethical conflict is that of autonomy versus paternalism. Autonomy supports an older adult's independence in terms of decision making and living arrangements, and it encourages respect of an older adult's preferences. Paternalism obligates the practitioner to help others and to prevent harm or ameliorate harmful situations. A paternalistic approach deprives an older person of his or her own free choice; rather, others make decisions out of concern for the elder's own good. Following the principle of paternalism, the social worker's concept of what constitutes benefits and harm prevails over the client's view, which may differ. For example, on learning that an elderly client with a history of chronic depression has admitted to having a concrete suicide plan, the social worker would arrange for the client's psychiatric hospitalization.

Autonomy–paternalism conflicts occur when practitioners must judge whether an elder is competent to make independent decisions about, for instance, living in a community with limited resources or in an unsafe or unhealthy environment, or whether or not to comply with medical treatment. One risk in making such a judgment is that the social worker may discount an elder's competency as a decision maker if his or her viewpoint differs from his or her own (Kane, 1992).

Furthermore, autonomy–paternalism conflicts may be exacerbated by boundary issues, that is, when "human service professionals encounter actual or potential conflicts between their professional duties and their social, sexual, religious, or business relationships" (Reamer, 2001, p.1). A particular challenge in maintaining boundaries is protecting the client's right to confidentiality and privacy. A social worker has an ethical obligation to maintain confidences; therefore, sharing information with anyone without the client's consent is a boundary violation (Galambos, Watt, Anderson, & Danis, 2005). In their guidelines for protecting client confidentiality, Galambos and colleagues have recommended that practitioners use informed consent procedures, discuss potential boundary issues during the assessment process, and explain how they will handle confidentiality. They should periodically assess if they are treating confidentiality in a manner that is acceptable to their clients.

Sometimes a care provider's and an elderly client's autonomies compete (Kane, 1992). For example, a frail, older adult may choose to return home after a hospitalization, yet that community placement may create hardships—increased care and support, and increased financial responsibilities—for the care provider. In such circumstances, the social worker must delicately balance the needs of the care provider with those of the elderly client. In considering the family unit as a whole, while being mindful of any boundary issues, the social worker might decide that prompt paternalism should take precedence over the client's autonomy. It is essential, though, that the parties involved clearly communicate with each other about the issues and options available to the older adult and that they ensure the older adult has an equal voice in the decision making.

Involving Clients in the Care Plan

Practitioners may use several techniques to increase an elderly client's autonomy. One is to encourage the client's active participation in the development of the care plan and to ensure that participation continues throughout the goal planning, implementation, and monitoring processes (Galambos, 1997). Practitioners are encouraging independent decision making by soliciting client input.

Atchley and Barusch's (2004) concept of negotiated risk is gaining popularity within assisted living facilities and home care programs as a means of preserving client autonomy. In this model, the social worker gives the older adult an opportunity to state what risks he or she is willing to assume as a condition of providing less strict procedures and close monitoring of the client's situation.

Following Informed Consent Procedures

Another technique for encouraging client autonomy is to use informed consent procedures, discussed earlier. Informed consent assists clients in understanding available options, thereby enabling them to weigh the pros and cons of a decision. It also provides social workers with a structured form for dissemination of information.

The informed consent process is ongoing and "includes the systematic disclosure of information to a client over time, along with an opportunity to engage in dialogue with the client about forthcoming treatment and service" (Reamer, 1987, p. 428). Informed consent allows social workers to offer ongoing information about the type of services recommended to functionally and legally competent clients, and provides an opportunity for clients to refuse services (Reamer, 1987, 1990). In cases in which an elder has been legally declared incompetent, informed consent procedures may be extended to legal guardians or surrogates (Reamer, 1990).

Including Clients and Others in Care-Planning Process

Another approach to protecting the rights of all people involved in a case is to include the relevant parties in deliberations. Whenever possible, the social worker should involve family members and care providers in the assessment process and in the development of treatment or care plans. When an elderly client's care needs have increased or in cases in which the elder's functional and cognitive functioning has decreased, it is particularly important to include care providers in the planning process.

Considering Guardianship

Practitioners who have determined through mental status exams and medical testing that an older adult is marginally competent may pursue "guardianship," a legal mechanism by which a person is invested with the power and responsibility to assume control and decision-making responsibility over another person adjudicated to be unable or incompetent to manage his or her own affairs (Bell, Schmidt, & Miller, 1981). There are two types of guardianship: (1) property, in which the guardian controls financial and property affairs; and (2) person, in which the guardian makes personal decisions for the client about, for example, medical care, social services, and the like. Guardianship often is beneficial in situations in which a frail elder requires protection and is unable to manage his or her own affairs.

Some forms of personal guardianship protect the older adult's rights more than others. A "limited" guardianship allows for increased autonomy; it supports independence and self-control; and it provides the elder an opportunity to participate in the decision-making process. A "full" guardianship, on the other hand, severely limits a person's autonomy, and social workers should pursue this legal status judiciously. Because full guardianship reduces the legal status of the elder to that of a minor, social workers ought to pursue this legal status only as a last resort. Under full guardianship status, older adults may lose control over their property and are unable to act independently. Furthermore, guardianship removes an older adult's right to vote or to refuse medical treatment, manage their finances, drive a car, or make other independent decisions, including treatment decisions (Bell et al., 1981).

Discussing Advance Directives

An inclusive alternative to decision making about medical care is an approach that supports client autonomy—the enactment of *advance directives,* or written instructions, "such as a living will or durable power of attorney for health care recognized under State law and relating to the provision of such care when the individual is incapacitated" (Osman & Perlin, 1994, p. 246). When appropriate, social workers can encourage elderly clients to discuss, and assist in executing, advance directives. These documents will aid in the decision making on medical issues should the client have a terminal illness or is in a persistent and vegetative state and is consequently unable to communicate his or her wishes (Galambos, 1998; Kapp, 1998).

Advance directives fall into two categories: (1) an instruction directive, written by the principal, that details the life-sustaining treatments the person desires under certain types of clinical situations; and (2) a proxy directive, by which the principal appoints an individual to make health care decisions for him or her in the event of incapacitation. The proxy decision maker is obligated to make the same decision that the incapacitated elder would make, thus preserving some autonomy. The proxy approach works well in situations in which an older adult's wishes are known.

Because older adults sometimes defer end-of-life decision making to family members, social workers can support their clients' autonomy by offering information on end-of-life options. In addition, research has indicated that the provision of educational programs on advance directives to older adults and their family members increases the frequency and intensity of discussions about end-of-life decision making (Bailey & DePoy, 1995). Social workers are in an excellent position to coordinate such programs.

Conclusion

In today's practice world, ethical challenges are becoming more prevalent as people live longer and medical advances create new and different treatment approaches. As society faces declining resources and simultaneously confronts an increasing demand for services, social workers will find themselves involved in ethical dilemmas requiring their thoughtful responses, so that they may resolve conflicts in practice situations.

When applied consistently, the models and tools presented in this chapter can assist practitioners in working through competing ethical principles, at the same time ensuring a fair process for their older adult clients. Mastery of the ethics competencies highlighted in this book will help social workers develop the skills necessary to work effectively with an aging population.

Suggested Exercise to Evaluate Student Competency

Students will use Dolgoff et al.'s (2005) ethical assessment tool to evaluate a case involving ethical practice issues. Referring to Figure 4-1, answer the following questions:

1. What can you do to minimize conflicts among your personal, societal, and professional values?
2. What can you do to minimize conflicts among your client's, other's, and society's rights and interests?

References

Agich, G. J. (1993). *Autonomy and long-term care.* New York: Oxford University Press.

Atchley, R. C., & Barusch, A. S. (2004). *Social forces and aging.* Belmont, CA: Wadsworth.

Bailey, D. J., & DePoy, E. (1995). Older people's responses to education about advance directives. *Health & Social Work, 20,* 223–228.

Beauchamp, T. L., & Walters, L. (1989). *Contemporary issues in bioethics.* Belmont, CA: Wadsworth.

Bell, W. G., Schmidt, W., & Miller, K. (1981). Public guardianship and the elderly: Findings from a national study. *Gerontologist, 2,* 194–202.

Congress, E. P. (1999). *Social work values and ethics.* Belmont, CA: Wadsworth.

Corey, G., Corey, M., & Callanan, P. (1993). *Issues and ethics in the helping professions* (4th ed.). Pacific Grove, CA: Brooks/Cole.

Council on Social Work Education, Gero-Ed Center. (2004). *Foundation gerontological social work competencies.* Retrieved November 16, 2006, from http://depts.washington.edu/geroctr/Curriculum3/ Competencies/FdnComp.doc

Dolgoff, R., Loewenberg, F. M., & Harrington, D. (2005). *Ethical decisions for social work practice* (7th ed.). Belmont, CA: Brooks/Cole–Thomson Learning.

Galambos, C. M. (1997). Resolving ethical conflicts in providing case management services to the elderly. *Journal of Gerontological Social Work, 27*(4), 57–67.

Galambos, C. (1998). Preserving end-of-life autonomy: The Patient Self-Determination Act and the Uniform Health Care Decisions Act. *Health & Social Work, 2,* 275–281.

Galambos, C. (1999). Resolving ethical conflicts in a managed health care environment. *Health & Social Work, 24,* 191–197.

Galambos, C., Watt, J. W., Anderson, K., & Danis, F. (2005). Rural social work practice: Maintaining confidentiality in the face of dual relationships. *Journal of Social Work Values and Ethics, 2*(2), 1–5.

Herr, S. S., & Weber, G. (1999). *Aging, rights, and quality of life.* Baltimore: Paul H. Brookes.

Kane, R. (1992). Case management: Ethical pitfalls on the road to high-quality managed care. In S. Rose (Ed.), *Case management and social work practice* (pp. 219–228). White Plains, NY: Longman.

Kapp, M. B. (1998). Forcing services on at-risk older adults: When doing good is not so good. *Social Work in Health Care, 13,* 1–13.

Kitchener, K. S. (1984). Intuition, critical evaluation, and ethical principles: The foundation for ethical decisions in counseling psychology. *Counseling Psychologist, 12,* 43–55.

Levy, C. S. (1973). The value base of social work. *Journal of Education for Social Work, 9,* 34–42.

Levy, C. S. (1984). Values and ethics. In S. Dillick (Ed.), *Value foundations of social work* (pp. 17–29). Detroit: Wayne State University, School of Social Work.

Linzer, N. (2002). An ethical dilemma in home care. *Journal of Gerontological Social Work, 37*(2), 23–34.

Loewenberg, F. M., Dolgoff, R., & Harrington, D. (2000). *Ethical decisions for social work practice* (6th ed.). Itasca, IL: F. E. Peacock.

National Association of Social Workers. (2000). *Code of ethics of the National Association of Social Workers.* Washington, DC: Author.

Netting, E., & Williams, F. G. (1995). Integrating geriatric case management into primary care physician practices. *Health & Social Work, 20,* 152–155.

Osman, H., & Perlin, T. M. (1994). Patient self-determination and the artificial prolongation of life. *Health & Social Work, 19,* 245–252.

Pincus, A., & Minahan, A. (1973). *Social work practice: Model and method.* Itasca, IL: F. E. Peacock.

Reamer, F. E. (1987). Informed consent in social work. *Social Work, 32,* 425–429.

Reamer, F. E. (1990). *Ethical dilemmas in social service.* New York: Columbia University Press.

Reamer, F. E. (2001). *Tangled relationships: Managing boundary issues in the human services.* New York: Columbia University Press.

APPENDIX 4-A General Decision-Making Model

Step 1.   Identify the problem and the factors that contribute to its maintenance.

Step 2.   Identify all of the people and institutions involved in this problem, such as clients, victims, support systems, other professionals, and others.

Step 3.   Determine who should be involved in decision making.

Step 4.   Identify the values relevant to this problem that are held by the several participants identified in Step 2, including the client's and worker's personal values, as well as relevant professional, group, and societal values.

Step 5.   Identify the goals and objectives whose attainment you believe may resolve (or at least reduce) the problem.

Step 6.   Identify alternate intervention strategies and targets.

Step 7.   Assess the effectiveness and efficiency of each alternative in terms of the identified goals.

Step 8.   Select the most appropriate strategy.

Step 9.   Implement the strategy selected.

Step 10.   Monitor the implementation, paying particular attention to unanticipated consequences.

Step 11.   Evaluate the results and identify additional problems.

Source: Ethical decisions for social work practice (6th ed.) by Loewenberg, F. M., Dolgoff, R., & Harrington, D. (2000). Reprinted with permission of Wadsworth, a division of Thomson Learning: www.thomsonrights.com. Fax 800-730-2215

Assessment of Older Adults, Their Families, and Their Social Supports

5

RATIONALE: Social work foundation practice focuses on client strengths and resources relative to the broader environment. Practitioners work with systems of all sizes (individuals, families, groups, communities, and societies) to bring about planned change and general well-being. Professional practice encompasses ample preparation, engagement, and assessment as well as intervention strategies and evaluation of practice. Practitioners should use effective communication skills, collaboration, and supervision to achieve their goals.

COMPETENCY: Students are able to conduct multidimensional assessments. They

- assess and address values and biases regarding aging.
- use empathy and sensitive interviewing skills (e.g., reminiscence or life review, support groups, counseling) to assess social functioning (e.g., social skills, social activity level) and social support of older adults.
- adapt interviewing methods to potential sensory, language, and cognitive limitations of the older adult.
- conduct a comprehensive evaluation of psychosocial factors that affect older persons' physical and mental well being.
  This competency includes evaluating safety issues and degree of risk for older clients.
- identify ways to ascertain health status and assess physical functioning (e.g., ADLs and IADLS) of older adults.
- assess cognitive functioning and mental health needs of older adults (e.g., depression, dementia).
  This competency includes knowing how to gather information regarding mental status (particularly memory), history of any past or current mental health problems, life satisfaction, coping abilities, mood or affect, and spirituality f older adults.

- understand the perspective and values of social work in relation to working effectively with other disciplines in geriatric interdisciplinary practice.
- assess caregivers' needs and level of stress.
- be aware of standardized assessment and diagnostic tools that are appropriate for use with older adults (e.g., depression scale, Mini-Mental Status Exam). (Council on Social Work Education, Gero-Ed Center, 2004)

This chapter focuses on the initial assessment interviews for working with older adults. Special techniques and adjustments are described that can make interviews more comfortable for older clients. The chapter also presents tools and instruments commonly used in geriatric assessment. These tools can be used selectively to ascertain a client's functional capacity. The use of the interview as shaped by various schools of intervention is discussed in depth in chapter 6, as are accompanying intervention strategies. Evaluation methods are explored in chapters 7 through 11.

The Helping Process

The helping process starts with a preparatory process in which the practitioner becomes well grounded in the theory necessary for geriatric social work practice (see chapter 2). Practitioners may also become more aware of the client context in which they will work (see chapter 1). After gathering potential information and knowledge about the client situation, social work practice generally goes through four stages: (1) engaging the older client; (2) assessing the older client; (3) intervening with the older client; and (4) evaluating client outcomes or goals. These stages often overlap. For example, a client's request for help may be characterized as a form of self-change or intervention.

Engaging Client and Client System

Practitioner–Client Relationship

The practitioner–client relationship is the key to effective social work assessment and intervention (Kirst-Ashman & Hull, 1999). The client-centered social work tradition suggests that practitioners can develop relationships and foster an older client's constructive personal growth by imparting *empathy:* the ability to deal sensitively and accurately with client feelings; *nonpossessive warmth:* acceptance of the older client as an individual; and *genuineness:* authenticity (Rogers & Dymond, 1957).

When elderly clients perceive that the social worker is supporting them, they develop a sense of trust, and their natural ability to change is set in motion. Research findings suggest that interventions are more successful when practitioners believe their clients have the strengths and the resources necessary to solve their problems (Asay & Lambert, 1999; Hubble, Duncan, & Miller, 1999). Tallman and Bohart (1999) contended that a client's capacity to heal is the most potent common factor in any kind of intervention, the very "engine" that makes practice work.

Before you begin your initial interview, close your eyes and imagine yourself as 80 years old. Then answer the following questions:

- Where do you live?
  Describe your home.
  With whom do you live?
  Do you have friends or family nearby?
- What do you look like?
  How changed are you from your younger years?
  Are you attractive to others?
- In what activities do you engage?
  Do you cook for yourself?
  Do you read, watch TV, or garden?
  Do you exercise?
  How often do you get out?
  Where do you go?
  What form of transportation do you use?
  Do you have many friends?
  How often do you see family?
- How is your physical and mental health?
  Do you have any illnesses or disease?
  Are you on medication?
  Are you mobile?
  Do you often feel depressed?
- How will you celebrate your birthday?
  What foods do you eat?
  Who will be with you?
  What are the general customs?
- Have you aged successfully?
  Why or why not?

Other questions you may ask yourself include those that *picture yourself in need of care:*

- When will you need care? How old are you?
- Why do you need care?
  How mobile are you?
  Do you need help bathing?
  Are you on medications? If so, do you need supervision with your medications?

- What form will that care take?
  Do you receive Meals-on-Wheels? A friendly visitor?
  Are you on a ventilator?
  Can you change your bed linens?
- How will you go about making the arrangements for your care?
- Who is giving you the care?
  Is the care formal or informal?
  Is there more than one person?
- Where are you living?
- What do you most enjoy in life?

How do you feel about receiving help?

Initial Interviews

Initial interviews with older clients set the stage for the unfolding of a mutual helping process. It is important that, when appropriate, the social worker involves significant family members, partners, and friends at this time (Greene, 2000). If an older client has an impairment that affects communication, it may be necessary to modify the interview. For example, if a client wears a hearing aid, the practitioner will need to determine that the device is working, makes sure to face the client directly, and speaks at a normal conversational volume (do not shout). A client who has had a stroke may have totally or partially lost the power to use and understand words. Therefore, the social worker must allow that client plenty of time to communicate and to complete his or her thoughts. The best environment for an interview with clients having Alzheimer's disease is a quiet space without distractions. Use a low-pitched voice and ask one question at a time (http://www.ec.online.net/Knowledge/Articles/communication.html).

First meetings are important for both client and social worker. How does the practitioner begin, and what should he or she say? Important issues to cover include the following (see Shulman, 1999):

- Clarify the social worker's purpose and role. Offer a simple statement of the reason for the encounter and the services of the social worker's agency.
- Reach for client feedback; that is, make an effort to understand the client's perceptions of his or her needs.
- Partialize or separate into segments the client's concerns—help him or her break down sometimes overwhelming difficulties into manageable parts.
- Deal with issues of authority by striving to establish mutuality in the working relationship.

Assessing the Client System

Assessment of older adults is the process of gathering information about their everyday functioning to select appropriate interventions to enhance client (system) well-being.

This process includes appraising the current biological, psychological, and social attributes and spiritual well-being and how effectively they have functioned over time. Many times an assessment will also include the family system and an evaluation of a client's support network (Greene, 2000). An important feature of the assessment is gaining an understanding of the resources available to the client and learning whether the older adult engages effectively with other social systems, such as health care or recreational programs.

Assessment Teams

Assessments may be conducted by the social worker alone or by a team of geriatric specialists. In collaborative exchanges, the social worker will work with team members from different disciplines, for example, medicine, nursing, occupational therapy, nutritional counseling, and physical therapy. The team will collectively set goals and share responsibilities and resources (Merck & Co., 2005). Geriatric social workers will encounter blurring of professional boundaries and training across disciplines, requiring them to learn more about the roles of allied health professionals.

Geriatric Assessment

Geriatric assessment varies from an assessment with other age groups. Lichtenberg (2000) recommended four assessment principles for evaluating an older adult:

1. Chronological age alone does not necessarily reflect *functional age,* or a person's capacity to live effectively in his or her environment. Recognizing this ability is central to the geriatric assessment process (Greene, 2000). This person-in-environment perspective, which takes into account environmental press (see chapter 2), allows for a dynamic picture of the older adult's functioning as he or she adjusts to changes in the environment. From this perspective, the social worker gains information about how the individual responds and adjusts to changes in social setting (family and community), and the process of aging (physical and mental well-being) that influence functioning (Lawton, 1989; Lawton & Nahemow, 1973; Parmelee & Lawton, 1990).
2. Practitioners should use brief assessment instruments to supplement the traditional interview, and thus reduce the time it takes to evaluate older adults. He has pointed out that research demonstrates the reliability and validity of many of these assessment instruments. This chapter provides such instruments, including a depression scale and mental status exam.
3. Assessment, must result in a delineation of strengths and weaknesses (or risks and resilience). Knowledge of a client's unique characteristics and capacities can inform both the care-planning process and treatment recommendations.
4. Social workers need to use multiple assessment methods to improve the quality of information; see chapter 6. Because assessment instruments have rarely been validated with minority populations, geriatric social workers should use caution when adopting them (Tran, Ngo, & Conway, 2003; see chapter 3 for a further discussion of diversity).

Theory-Based Interview

Assessments not only relate to the aging population, but also they incorporate theory-based principles (see chapter 6). The use of a particular theory will allow the practitioner to interpret and organize the interview (see chapter 2 for a further discussion of theory for practice; see chapter 6 for an interview based on the resilience-enhancing model [REM]). However, the social worker can ask general questions to better understand how the older client is functioning within his or her environment:

- Is the older adult able to meet the demands presented, or is he or she overwhelmed?
- What is the nature of the stress that precipitated contacting the social agency?
- What biopsychosocial or spiritual factors stand in the way of effective functioning?
- What resources may permit the client to function better?
- What are alternative explanations for the perceived difficulties?
- What solutions have been tried?
- What actions are successful so far?
- Does the client agree with the practitioner's perceptions of the older adult's situation?

Strengths-Based Assessment

A general principle that guides social work assessment is that it should be strengths based. The strengths-based movement rests on a philosophy of helping in which "all [clients] must be understood and assessed in the light of their capabilities, competencies, knowledge, survival skills, visions, possibilities, and hopes" (Saleebey, 1997, p. 17). Social workers make a conscious decision to pay attention primarily to those factors of people's lives that can contribute to their growth and well-being. A strengths-based assessment requires that practitioners get to know their older clients and how they currently function and have functioned over time. Each client is unique, having his or her own psychosocial profile (Kivnick, 1993; Kivnick & Murray, 2001). Therefore, it is necessary to listen for each person's strengths and capacities, as well as client risks and constraints (see Appendix 5-A).

In addition to REM, presented throughout the text, there are several models used to foster client strengths (see chapter 6 for how REM guides the interview). For example, Graybeal (2001) argued that the traditional problem-based assessment used in the medical model conflicts with the alternative strengths-based assessment that explores a person's skills, capacities, and resilience. Consequently, he coined the acronym ROPES to guide practitioners' strengths-based interviews so that they will pay close attention to

Resources: personal, family, social environment, organizational, and community.
Options: present focus, with an emphasis on choice. What can be accessed now? What is available and hasn't been tried or used?

Possibilities: future focus, imagination, creativity, one's vision of the future, play. What have you thought of trying but haven't yet?

Exceptions: When is the problem not happening? When is the problem different? When will part of the hypothetical future solution occur? How have you survived, endured, or thrived?

Solutions: Focus on constructing solutions rather than solving problems. What is currently working? What are your successes? What are you doing that you would like to continue doing? What if a miracle happened? What can you do now to create a piece of the miracle? (Graybeal, 2001, p. 237)

The Interview: An Assessment Tool

As an assessment tool, the interview is a means for setting the helping process in motion. It is a "conversation with a deliberate purpose that the participants accept. . . . [It involves] both verbal and nonverbal communication between people during which they exchange ideas, attitudes, and feelings" (Kadushin & Kadushin, 1997, p. 4). Hepworth, Rooney, and Larsen (1997) have suggested that the purpose of the interview is to shed light on and to solve problems at the same time promoting client growth and improving quality of life. Assessment interviews also may be thought of as a way of "individualizing the person–situation configuration" (Northen, 1982, p. 60).

Interpretations of Client Answers

An effective social worker must possess good communication skills to interpret the client's responses to interview questions accurately. Practitioners need to send a specifically chosen message verbally and engage in "active listening," both of which require that they understand the client's story clearly. For example, on some occasions, the social worker may hear only a noncommittal response. The message the older client might be conveying is that he or she is still processing the information imparted, hence the client's hesitancy. Do not rush the client. Instead, a practitioner could indicate that he or she is unsure of the client's response. Client and social worker then might decide together whether they should discuss the issue further.

It might be helpful for the practitioner to acknowledge that the situation is difficult. Older adults may be sensitive to certain topics, such as their sexuality or finances, so it may be best to bring these up later in the helping process. The practitioner should remember that he or she is often younger than the client, who will have made many decisions and choices during his or her lifetime. Therefore, the social worker and client need to be collaborators in the helping process.

Assessment Components

Determination of Normal Aging

Aging is a process of gradual and spontaneous changes that result in maturation through childhood, puberty, and young adulthood. Then certain bodily functions begin to ebb (Merck & Co., 2005). Variations in physical and mental status increase as people age because individuals age at different rates. Even within one person, the signs of aging of organs and organ systems vary. Scientists believe that aging is a complex phenomenon arising from a combination of genes, lifestyle, and disease. Some generalizations, however, apply to all older adults—there is a gradual decline in bodily functions that tends to cause frailty (see Appendix 5-B).

Many of the changes that accompany aging, such as wrinkles and thinning and graying of hair, may seem to be cosmetic. But the social worker will need to learn from each client the particular meaning that person attaches to physical and social changes that accompany the aging process. Does the client seem to "go with the flow" and have vitality and grit? Does he or she seem sluggish or depressed? The great majority of people aged 65 years and older are healthy, happy, and fully independent. Some older adults will have made positive lifestyle choices, such as engaging in exercise. Others, though, may have problems of living that are severe enough to require the assistance of a geriatric practitioner. A comprehensive biopsychosocial and spiritual assessment is required to enable the social worker and client to make intervention decisions. Approaching the client system from a biopsychosocial–spiritual standpoint involves examining the client's physical and psychological functioning, economic and political factors affecting the client's life and his or her spiritual health, and looking at the risk and protective factors influencing each of these areas.

Biopsychosocial and Spiritual Assessment

A *functional-age assessment* enables geriatric social workers to understand the biopsychosocial–spiritual factors affecting a person's ability or competence to perform behaviors central to everyday life. Although many scientists continue to see older adults as going through a period of declining health and function, there is remarkable variability among individuals (Seeman & Chen, 2002). A functional-age assessment helps distinguish normal age-related changes from those requiring intervention by allowing the social worker to identify risk and protective factors for each area of functioning.

Biological factors are related to functional capacity and include health, physical capacity, or vital life-limiting organ systems; *psychological* factors encompass an individual's affect state or mood, cognitive or mental status, and the person's behavioral dimensions; and *sociocultural* aspects are the cultural, political, and economic components of life events (Greene, 2000). In addition, *spiritual* factors may include a person's relationship with his or her faith or religious community or an inner system of beliefs. Spiritual functioning is important because spirituality contributes to a person's ability to transcend the immediate situation and to discover meaning in events.

Biological Functioning

Although physicians generally diagnose a person's biological functioning, the social worker, through an assessment of the client's independence in activities of daily living, can address many physical attributes affecting everyday life (Appendix 5-C). Particularly in the client's home environment, the practitioner can quickly get a clear picture of the older adult's abilities and the risks involved in navigating that environment. Always take health complaints seriously. Note the medications a client has on hand. Are those medications current, and is the client using them properly?

Activities of Daily Living

The holistic assessment on how well an older adult fits with his or her home environment is measured by evaluating a client's capacity to perform activities of daily living (Iwarsson, 2005), which include feeding, toileting, dressing, bathing, cooking, shopping, cleaning, transferring (for example, from bed to chair), and using transportation.

Psychological Functioning

Older adults may be at risk for mental disorders: One in every five people aged 55 years and older experiences mental health concerns that are not part of the normal aging process. In addition, the suicide rate for people aged 65 years and older, especially among men, is higher than in any other age group (Gonyea, Hudson, & Curley, 2004). An assessment of psychological functioning involves examining, among other factors, the client's life satisfaction. For example, social workers might use the life history, a methodological tool, to explore an older adult's perceived identity (Appendix 5-D).

Depression

Practitioners also will want to assess their client's coping abilities, mood or affect, and past or current mental health problems. In particular, depression, or feelings of sadness or feeling "down," is common in late life, affecting nearly 5 million of the 31 million Americans aged 65 years and older. Both major and minor depression have been reported in 13 percent of community-dwelling older adults, 24 percent of older medical outpatients, and 43 percent of both acute-care and nursing-home-dwelling older adults. Left untreated, depression can lead to the onset of physical, cognitive, and social impairments as well as increased health care use, delayed recovery from medical illness and surgery, and suicide.

Contrary to popular belief, depression is not a natural part of aging; it is, however, often reversible with prompt and appropriate treatment. It is essential, then, that practitioners learn whether a client has had a history of depression (Appendix 5-E). Is the client depressed by perceived "damage"—such as surgery or a heart attack—to his or her body image? Is the depression associated with chronic or severe pain? Is the client suffering from a side effect of a medication? Geriatric social workers will want to assess what environmental factors, such as a diminishing social support system, may be playing a role in depression. They must be aware, however, that various cultural groups may conceptualize or describe depression differently. Clients who exhibit prolonged symptoms, for example, a lack of attention to personal care and feelings of discouragement or hopelessness, should be seen by a specialist who can administer medical tests and make a differential diagnosis.

Dementia

In their geriatric practice, social workers may encounter many different types of dementia among their clients. Dementia is a serious problem facing families of later years; the risk of developing dementia increases with old age. Alzheimer's disease, the most widely known form of dementia, is a process of degeneration of brain tissue that results in loss of intellectual reasoning and cognitive function. It is generally found in people 65 years of age and older. The causes of this degeneration of brain tissue are unknown but are thought to be a combination of genes and environmental factors.

The social worker may be the first professional to suspect that a client has dementia, based on the older adult's answers to questions about his or her mental status (Appendix 5-F). In such cases, the practitioner should discuss his or her concerns with the client and perhaps with the client's family. A referral to a qualified specialist must be made.

The social worker's suspicion of early Alzheimer's disease may lead to an improvement in the older adult's situation and that of his or her family (Appendix 5-G). Direct benefits to the older adult include a more definitive diagnosis of other potentially reversible causes of dementia, such as hypothyroidism. Furthermore, Alzheimer's disease sometimes is confused with depression and anxiety, both of which may be treated using pharmacological interventions. Family members also may benefit from early detection, which may provide them with more time to adjust to the diagnosis and plan for the future, and create an opportunity to obtain their older family member's input into decisions about advanced directives while that person is still at a mild stage of the illness (Cummings & Jeste, 1999; see also chapter 4 for a discussion of the social worker's role in ethical decision making).

Sociocultural Functioning

A client's *social age* comprises the roles and social habits that person performs in the family and other social structures. All cultures use age as a factor to prescribe role-appropriate behaviors: Deciding to retire and acting as a grandparent are both examples of age-appropriate behaviors and one's timing of life events (Greene, 2000). As people age, the meaning of various roles they play intensifies or becomes greater in importance (Krause, 2004). Given certain circumstances, such as insufficient income, some of these older adults may or may not find new meaningful roles in old age (for example, "After I retire, can I still afford to give presents to my grandchildren?").

Because having positive social supports and remaining connected to those support networks are protective factors to help buffer stress and contribute to older adults' well-being, learning how successful a client feels about fulfilling personal and social obligations is an important assessment task. As the geriatric social worker evaluates how much social support a client has, he or she will want to use the social network scale in Appendix 5-H to explore the structure and content of the older adult's social relationships.

Structure refers to the number, types, and interconnectedness of ties, and *content* describes the kind of assistance a person gives and receives (for example, "Does the client baby-sit or perform volunteer work?").

Spiritual Well-being

In an effort to address the person-in-environment, the helping professions are increasingly recognizing religion and spirituality as components of the helping process (Canda & Furman, 1999). Spirituality, or a person's quest "to transcend the self and discover meaning" (Conrad, 1999, p. 63), is an important protective factor and "serves as a modifiable resource that can be drawn upon during times of personal crises" (Angell, Dennis, & Dumain, 1998, p. 616). Hodge (2001) has provided a broad-based anthropological questionnaire to help geriatric social workers better understand their clients' spiritual lives (see Appendix 5-I).

Home Environment Assessment

Assessing older adults at home allows practitioners to observe firsthand clients' mobility and physical functioning in their own setting plus any safety concerns. However, conducting a home-based assessment presents both challenges and opportunities (Naleppa & Hash, 2001). When entering a client's home, one challenge is helping the client to maintain boundaries, that is, to be cognizant that the social worker is in his or her home as a professional, not as a friend. Practitioners frequently wonder if they should accept food, drink, or small gifts from a client in that person's home. The decision whether or not to take these items hinges on the context of the situation (Naleppa & Hash). Is accepting a cup of tea important in the client's culture? Distractions, such as a television running or an unexpected visitor, are other potential obstacles social workers face during home visits. And, occasionally, social workers may arrive at a client's home during an emergency and find themselves calling emergency personnel.

Yet, interviewing an older adult in his or her own home provides an opportunity for the client to feel more comfortable. Even though the state adult protection agency may conduct a complete evaluation of home safety, a home-based visit will allow the geriatric practitioner to survey the home for safety issues (see the checklist in Appendix 5-J).

Assessment of Client Competence Handling Environmental Issues

The ecological model of aging proposes that the older adult's ability to function with competence is an outcome of how that person meets environmental demands (Lawton, 1989). However, a biopsychosocial and spiritual assessment alone will not provide a complete picture of client competence. Rather, the social worker needs to determine the client's appraisal of critical life events. *Appraisal* has a special meaning referring to whether the older adult has perceived a demand as a threat, loss, or challenge, and whether he or she views a demand as controllable (Lazarus & Folkman, 1984). How a client appraises an event varies depending on his or her culture, role demands or conflicts, and belief systems or personal values. According to Janoff-Bulman and Berger (2000), the appraisal process, particularly following adverse events in the elder's life, may produce several outcomes, including a greater appreciation of life, taking little for granted, or being motivated to live life differently (see chapter 6).

Assessment of Client Resiliency

During one's lifetime, a person appraises and attaches meaning to critical events. In fact, meaning making may be a natural process people undergo to counter stress and strive for health (Antonovsky & Sourani, 1988). They want their worlds to be comprehensible, manageable, and meaningful. A time line is an assessment tool that allows the practitioner and the client to review the important events in the client's life (see Figure 2-2 in chapter 2). As older individuals reminisce about their lives, they decide whether their lives were "acceptable." Erikson (1959/1980) was one of the first theorists to argue that old age is a time of increased meaning making. He contended that in the last stage of life, people struggle with "how to grow old with integrity in the face of death" (p. 104). *Integrity* means having few regrets and coping well with failures as well as with successes.

In the final step in the assessment process, the practitioner learns how the client perceives his or her own life course. The practitioner will have examined how the client has appraised his or her life events. Has the older adult come to terms with those events? By listening to a client recount life events, the social worker will discover the client's degree of resiliency:

> What we call resilience is turning out to be an interactive and systemic phenomenon, the product of complex relationship of inner strengths and outer help throughout a person's life span. Resilience is not only an individual matter. It is the outward and visible sign of a web of relationships and experiences that teach people mastery, doggedness, love, moral courage and hope. (Butler, 1997, p. 26)

Assessment of the Family of Later Years and the Caregivers

Understanding how the older client's needs and capacities fit within a family context requires that the social worker conduct a family assessment. Initially, the practitioner needs to learn about the family. The genogram in Figure 5-1 will help the social worker visualize the family structure, and the ecomap in Figure 5-2 will enable the social worker to assess the relationship among family members and their social network.

To determine how changes in an older adult's functional capacity influence the family unit, the geriatric social worker may use the functional-age model of intergenerational treatment (Greene, 2000). The practitioner will assess the family as a (1) *social system*—that is, how group members interact with and influence each other; (2) *set of reciprocal roles*—that is, what members' behavioral expectations are for each other; and

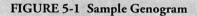

FIGURE 5-1 Sample Genogram

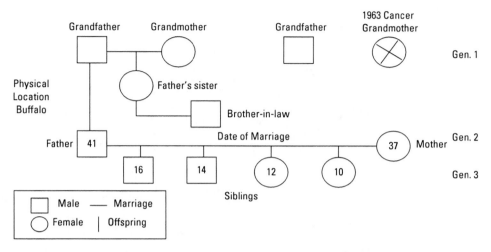

Source: Adapted with permission from Hartman, A., & Laird, J. (1983). *Family-centered social work practice* (p. 473). New York: Free Press.

(3) *developmental unit*—that is, how the family as a whole faces life transitions. The practitioner tries to determine the following during this assessment:

- Are family communication patterns viable enough for the family to make decisions?
- Is the family role structure sufficiently flexible to meet new demands?
- Is the family's shared history positive enough to face transitions? A crisis?

During a family assessment, it is also important to determine the caregiver's needs and level of stress. Typically, a primary caregiver provides "direct care" by doing the personal-care tasks such as bathing the older family member, giving medications, or checking and monitoring the older adult's behavior. A caregiver may also perform "indirect care" involving care management tasks, such as coordinating the use of services, and household tasks, such as shopping or bill paying. The caregiving role may be rewarding. However, caregiving tasks have the potential to adversely affect the caregiver's mental and physical well-being, be disruptive to marital or family relationships, or cause problems in meeting work and other social responsibilities. These conflicting responsibilities may result in caregiver burden (Pearlin, Aneshensel, & Leblanc, 1997; Riley, 2007).

Caregiver burden is a product of the financial, physical, psychological, and social demands of caregiving (George & Gwyther, 1986). It may be an *objective burden*, those

FIGURE 5-2 Example of an Ecomap to Be Filled Out during Assessment

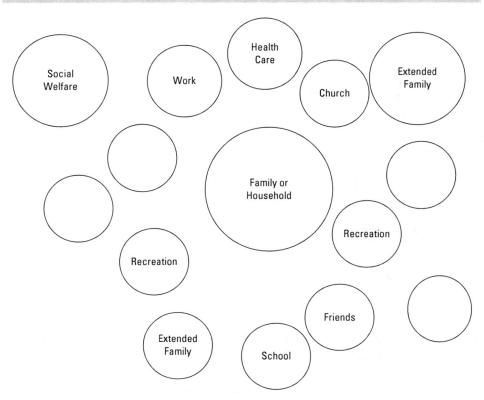

Note: Solid line = important or strong connection. Dotted line = tenuous connection. Line with slashes = stressful or conflict-laden connection. Arrows = direction of the energy flow.
Source: Hartman, A. (1978). Diagrammatic assessment of family relationships. *Social Casework*, 59, 465–476. Reprinted with permission from *Families in Society* (www.familiesinsociety.org), published by the Alliance for Children and Families.

events and activities that are associated with a negative caregiving experience, or a *subjective burden*, the caregiver's emotional reactions, including worry, anxiety, frustration, and fatigue (Pinquart & Sorensen, 2003). To help reveal the caregiver's attitudes toward his or her experience, the geriatric practitioner may wish to use the questionnaire shown in Appendix 5-K. As noted in chapter 2, caregiving may also provide rewards that give the caregiver a sense of accomplishment.

Conclusion: Services Plans and Evaluation of Client Goals

The final step in the assessment of older adults, their families, and their social supports is to develop clear, timely, appropriate services or care plans with measurable objectives. The client and social worker develop the plans together. They should take into account a client's functional status, life goals, symptom management, and financial and social supports and address financial, legal, housing, medical, and social needs (see chapter 7). Following the implementation of services or care plans, the geriatric social worker must be prepared to reevaluate and adjust the care plans on a continuing basis.

Suggested Exercise to Evaluate Student Competence

Students will demonstrate their practice effectiveness when they

- tape a role play of the opening interview for the professor to evaluate
- read the case history of the Gray family below and answer the questions posed at the conclusion of the study.

Mrs. Gray is a 77-year-old widow who had been living alone for the past 10 years. Recently, she began to exhibit signs of dementia such as wandering outside of her home at odd hours (for example, middle of the night), forgetting things on the stove, and so forth. Her son and daughter-in-law became very concerned about her functioning and had her move into their home across town. Mrs. Gray has been living with them for about six months.

In that time period, Mrs. Gray's condition has worsened. She is very disoriented and on a few occasions she has been confused in the household, for example, she urinated in a chair insisting it was the toilet, and she stores inappropriate items in the refrigerator (clothes, her purse, and so forth). She has her own bedroom as her 12-year-old granddaughter was moved to a sleeper sofa in the basement. The granddaughter has been quite vocal about her disappointment about leaving her bedroom.

The move of Mrs. Gray into the household has also had an impact on family activities. A planned vacation was cancelled because the family could not afford to hire someone to stay with Mrs. Gray during the time they were away. Currently, the daughter-in-law is considering decreasing her hours of work or quitting her job altogether because the family is concerned about having Mrs. Gray stay by herself all day. The family worries that a crisis may be "waiting to happen."

The impact on the family has been quite profound. They are trying to decide how to handle this situation—whether Mrs. Gray can continue to live with them or whether they need to investigate a nursing home for her.

Questions

- Care provision for an older family member often involves multiple stresses. Identify and discuss three sources of stress that are evident in the Gray family.
- What tools provided in this chapter would assist you in your assessment? Why?

References

American Psychiatric Association. (1994). *Diagnostic and statistical manual of mental disorders* (4th ed.). Washington, DC: Author.

Angell, G. B., Dennis, B. G., & Dumain, L. E. (1998). Spirituality, resilience, and narrative: Coping with parental death. *Families in Society, 79,* 615–630.

Antonovsky, A., & Sourani, T. (1988). Family sense of coherence and family adaptation. *Journal of Marriage and Family, 50,* 79–92.

Asay, T. P., & Lambert, M. J. (1999). The empirical case for the common factors in therapy: Quantitative findings. In M. A. Hubble, B. L. Duncan, & D. Miller (Eds.), *The heart & soul of change* (pp. 23–55). Washington, DC: APA Press.

Butler, K. (1997). The anatomy of resilience. *Family Therapy Networker, 3/4,* 22–31.

Canda, E. R., & Furman, L. D. (1999). *Spiritual diversity in social work practice.* New York: Free Press.

Conrad, A. P. (1999). Professional tools for religiously and spiritually sensitive social work practice. In R. R. Greene (Ed.), *Human behavior theory and social work practice* (2nd ed., pp. 63–72). New York: Aldine de Gruyter.

Council on Social Work Education, Gero-Ed Center. (2004). *Foundation gerontological social work competencies.* Retrieved November 16, 2006, from http://depts. washington.edu/geroctr/Curriculum3/ Competencies/FdnComp.doc

Cummings, J. L., & Jeste, D. V. (1999). Alzheimer's disease and its management in the year 2010. *Psychiatric Services, 50,* 1173–1177.

Erikson, E. H. (1980). *Identity and the life cycle.* New York: W. W. Norton. (Original work published 1959)

Farran, C., Miller, B., Kaufman, J., Donner, D., & Fogg, L. (1999). Finding meaning through caregiving: Development of an instrument for family caregivers of persons with Alzheimer's disease. *Journal of Clinical Psychology, 55,* 1107–1125.

George, L. K., & Gwyther, L. P. (1986). Caregiver well-being: A multidimensional examination of family caregivers of demented adults. *Gerontologist, 26,* 253–259.

Gonyea, J. G., Hudson, R. B., & Curley, A. (2004, Spring). The geriatric social work labor force: Challenges and opportunities in responding to an aging society. In *Institute for geriatric social work issue brief* (pp. 1–7). Boston: Boston University School of Social Work.

Graybeal, C. (2001). Strengths-based social work assessment: Transforming the dominant paradigm. *Families in Society, 82,* 233–241.

Greene, R. R. (2000). *Social work with the aged and their families* (2nd ed.). New York: Aldine de Gruyter.

Hartman, A. (1978). Diagrammatic assessment of family relationships. *Social Casework, 59,* 465–476.

Hartman, A., & Laird, J. (1983). *Family-centered social work practice.* New York: Free Press.

Hepworth, D. H., Rooney, R. H., & Larsen, J. A. (1997). *Direct social work practice.* Pacific Grove, CA: Brooks/Cole.

Hodge, D. R. (2001). Spiritual assessment: A review of major qualitative methods and a new framework for assessing spirituality. *Social Work, 46,* 203–207.

Hubble, M. A., Duncan, B. L., & Miller, D. (Eds.). (1999). *The heart & soul of change.* Washington, DC: APA Press.

Iwarsson, S. (2005). A long-term perspective on person–environment fit and ADL: Dependence among older Swedish adults. *Gerontologist, 45,* 327–336.

Janoff-Bulman, R., & Berger, A. R. (2000). The other side of trauma: Towards a psychology of appreciation. In J. H. Harvey & E. D. Miller (Eds.), *Loss and trauma: General and close relationship perspectives* (pp. 29–44). Philadelphia: Brunner-Routledge.

Kadushin, A., & Kadushin, G. (1997). *The social work interview: A guide for human services professionals.* New York: Columbia University Press.

Kahn, R. L., Goldfarb, L., & Pollack, M. (1964). The evaluation of geriatric patients following treatment. In P. H. Hoch & J. Zubin (Eds.), *Evaluation of psychiatric treatment* (pp. 106–121). New York: Grune & Stratton.

Kirst-Ashman, K., & Hull, G. H. (1999). *Understanding generalist practice* (2nd ed.). Chicago: Nelson-Hall.

Kivnick, H. Q. (1993, Winter/Spring). Everyday mental health: A guide to assessing life strengths. *Generations, 17,* 13–20.

Kivnick, H. Q., & Murray, S. V. (2001). Life strengths interview guide: Assessing elder clients' strengths. *Journal of Gerontological Social Work, 34*(4), 7–32.

Krause, N. (2004). Lifetime trauma, emotional support, and life satisfaction among older adults. *Gerontologist, 44,* 615–623.

Lawton, M. P. (1989). Behavior-relevant ecological factors. In K. W. Schaie & C. Scholar (Eds.), *Social structure and aging: Psychological processes.* Hillsdale, NJ: Lawrence Erlbaum.

Lawton, M. P., & Brody, E. M. (1969). Assessment of older people: Self-maintaining and instrumental activities of daily living. *Gerontologist, 9,* 179–186.

Lawton, M. P., & Nahemow, L. (1973). Ecology and the aging process. In C. Eisdorfer & M. P. Lawton (Eds.), *Psychology of adult development and aging* (pp. 619–674). Washington, DC: American Psychological Association.

Lazarus, R. S., & Folkman, S. (1984). *Stress, appraisal, and coping.* New York: Springer.

Lichtenberg, P. A. (Ed.). (2000). *Handbook of assessment in clinical gerontology.* New York: John Wiley & Sons.

Lubben, J. (1988). Assessing social networks among elderly populations. *Family & Community Health, 11,* 42–52.

Merck & Co., Inc. (2005). *The Merck manual of geriatrics.* Retrieved October 1, 2005, from http://www.merck.com/mrkshared/mmg/sec1/ch7/ch7a.jsp

Naleppa, M. J., & Hash, K. M. (2001). Home-based practice with older adults: Challenges and opportunities in the home environment. *Journal of Gerontological Social Work, 35*(1), 71–88.

Northen, H. (1982). *Clinical social work*. New York: Columbia University Press.

Parmelee, P. A., & Lawton, M. P. (1990). The design of special environments for the aged. In J. E. Birren & K. W. Schaie (Eds.), *Handbook of the psychology of aging* (3rd ed., pp. 465–489). San Diego: Academic Press.

Pearlin, L. I., Aneshensel, C. S., & Leblanc, A. J. (1997). The forms and mechanisms of stress proliferation: The case of AIDS caregivers. *Journal of Health and Social Behavior 38*, 223–236.

Pinquart, M., & Sorensen, S. (2003). Associations of stressors and uplifts of caregiving with Caregiver burden and depressive mood: A meta-analysis. *Journal of Gerontology: Psychological Sciences, 58B*(2), 112–128.

Rennemark, M., & Hagberg, B. (1997). Social network patterns among the elderly in relation to their perceived life history in an Eriksonian perspective. *Aging & Mental Health, 1,* 321–331.

Rogers, C. R., & Dymond, R. F. (1957). *Psychotherapy and personality change*. Chicago: University of Chicago Press.

Riley, J. (2007). Caregiving: A risk and resilience perspective. In R. R. Greene (Ed.), *Social work practice: A risk and resilience perspective* (pp. 239–262). Belmont, CA: Thomson Brooks/Cole.

Saleebey, D. (1997). *The strengths perspective in social work practice* (2nd ed.). New York: Longman.

Seeman, T., & Chen, X. (2002). Risk and protective factors for physical functioning in older adults with and without chronic conditions: MacArthur studies of successful aging. *Journal of Gerontology Social Sciences, 57B*(3), S135–S144.

Shulman, L. (1999). The skills of helping individuals, families, groups, and communities. Itasca, IL: F. E. Peacock.

Tallman, K., & Bohart, A. C. (1999). The client as a common factor: Clients as self-healers. In M. A. Hubble, B. L. Duncan, & S. Miller (Eds.), *The heart & soul of change* (pp. 91–131). Washington, DC: American Psychological Association.

Tran, T. V., Ngo, D., & Conway, K. (2003). A cross-cultural measure of depressive symptoms among Vietnamese Americans. *Social Work Research, 27,* 56–65.

APPENDIX 5-A Strengths Assessment Interview Guide

1. What makes a day a good day for you? What do you hope for at the start of a new day?

2. What are the things you do, each day or each week, because you really want to—not because you have to—when you get totally absorbed, forget about everything else, and the time seems to fly?

3. At what are you good? At what kinds of things did you used to be good? What about yourself has always given you confidence or made you proud?

   Now: _____

   Past: _____

4. What kinds of exercise do you do regularly? What kinds could you do to help you feel better?

   Do: _____

   Could Do: _____

5. What kinds of help, service, or assistance do you give? To whom? What help or service would you like to give?

6. When you get out, what do you like to do? Where do you like to go? What would you like to do? Where would you like to go?

   Like to Do? Go? _____

   Would Like to Do? Go? _____

7. What lessons have you learned about how to cope with life from day to day? Are there ways you wish you could cope better?

   Lessons, Cope: _____

   Cope Better: _____

8. Who are the people especially important to you these days? Tell me about these relationships.

9. What physical things or objects do you have that are most precious to you? What things do you save? Or take special care? If you had to relocate, what few things would you take with you?

10. To interviewer: What additional strengths, values, commitments, skills, or assets do you know (from whatever source) that this person has?

Source: Adapted from Kivnick, H. Q., & Murray, S. V. (2001). Life strengths interview guide: Assessing elder clients' strengths. *Journal of Gerontological Social Work, 34*(4), 32.

APPENDIX 5-B Normal Aging

Heart . . . . grows slightly larger, and oxygen consumption during exercise declines

Arteries . . . . stiffen with age, and fatty deposits build up

Lungs . . . . decline in terms of breathing capacity

Brain . . . . loses some cells and some may become damaged; the number of connections between cells may regrow

Kidneys . . . . become less efficient; if urinary incontinence occurs, it may be managed through exercise and behavioral techniques

Muscles . . . . may decline without exercise

Skin . . . . becomes less elastic and more lined and wrinkled

Hair . . . . turns grayer and thins

Height . . . . declines slowly to as much as two inches by 80 years of age

Eyesight . . . . declines, with loss of peripheral vision and decreased ability to judge depth

Taste, Touch, Smell . . . . decrease; taste decreases, sensitivity to touch lessens, and ability to smell declines

Hearing . . . . lessens, with loss of hearing acuity

Personality . . . . maintained; stability is expected

Source: Retrieved and summarized on February 13, 2006, from http://www.webmd.com/hw/healthy_seniors/tn722.asp and http://www.merck.com/mrkshared/mmg/sec1/ch1/ch1a.jsp

APPENDIX 5-C Index of Independence in Activities of Daily Living

Name _____ Date of evaluation _____

For each area of functioning listed below, check description that applies. (The word "assistance" means supervision, direction, or personal assistance.)

Bathing—either sponge bath, tub bath, or shower

☐ receives no assistance (gets in and out of tub by self if tub is usual means of bathing)

☐ receives assistance in bathing only one part of the body (such as back or legs)

☐ receives assistance in bathing more than one part of the body (or not bathed)

Dressing—gets clothes from closets and drawers, including underclothes and outer garments; uses fasteners (including braces, if worn)

☐ gets clothes and gets completely dressed without assistance

☐ gets clothes and gets dressed without assistance, but has assistance in tying shoes

☐ receives assistance in getting clothes or in getting dressed, or stays partly or completely undressed

Toileting—going to the "toilet room" for bowel and urine elimination; cleaning self after elimination; and arranging clothes

☐ goes to toilet room, cleans self, and arranges clothes without assistance (may use object for support such as cane, walker, or wheelchair and may manage night bedpan or commode, emptying same in morning)

☐ receives assistance in going to toilet room, or in cleaning self, or in arranging clothes after elimination, or in use of night bedpan or commode

☐ doesn't go to room termed "toilet" for the elimination process

Transfer

☐ moves in and out of bed as well as in and out of chair without assistance (may be using object for support such as cane or walker)

☐ moves in and out of bed or chair with assistance

☐ doesn't get out of bed

(Continued)

APPENDIX 5-C Index of Independence in Activities of Daily Living (*Continued*)

Continence—

☐ controls urination and bowel movements completely by self

☐ has occasional "accidents"

☐ has supervision to help maintain urine or bowel control; uses catheter; or is incontinent

Feeding

☐ feeds self without assistance

☐ gets clothes and gets completely dressed without assistance

☐ gets clothes and gets completely dressed without assistance

Scoring System

The Index of Independence in Activities of Daily Living is based on an evaluation of the functional independence or dependence of patients in bathing, dressing, going to the toilet, transferring, continence, and feeding.

A .... independent in feeding, continence, transferring, going to toilet, dressing, and bathing

B .... independent in all but one of these functions

C .... independent in all but bathing and one additional function

D .... independent in all but bathing, dressing, and one additional function

E .... independent in all but bathing, dressing, going to the toilet, and one additional function

F....... independent in all but bathing, dressing, going to the toilet, transferring, and one additional function

G .... dependent in all six functions

Other.... dependent in at least two functions, but not classifiable as C, D, E, or F.

Source: Reprinted with permission from Lawton, M. P., & Brody, E. M. (1969). Assessment of older people: Self-maintaining and instrumental activities of daily living. *Gerontologist, 9,* 179–186.

APPENDIX 5-D Research Questions for Life Histories: An Eriksonian Framework

Make a self-evaluation of good, neutral, or bad:

- Trust/autonomy: To what extent do you think you were well cared for and well guided through your first years? How easily do you interact with others without feeling shy or ashamed?

- Initiative: To what extent do you enjoy starting new activities? Were you easily kept back by feelings of guilt in your preschool years?

- Industry: Were you a hard-working pupil in the early school years? Did your teachers indicate that you were good enough?

- Identity: Did you belong to a group of friends in your teens? Did you feel like you knew yourself? Did you know how to behave toward other people?

- Intimacy: Do you remember your first love? Did you establish a close relationship with anyone? How do you remember that person?

- Early generativity: In the first half of your working life, did you do things that were meaningful for other individuals? For the next generation?

- Late generativity: In the second half of your working period, did you do things for other people? The next generation?

Source: Adapted from Rennemark, M., & Hagberg, B. (1997). Social network patterns among the elderly in relation to their perceived life history in an Eriksonian perspective. *Aging & Mental Health, 1,* 321–331.

APPENDIX 5-E DSM-IV Criteria for Major Depressive Episode

A. Five (or more) of the following symptoms have been present during the same two-week period and represent a change from previous functioning; at least one of the symptoms is either (1) depressed mood or (2) loss of interest or pleasure.

Note: Do not include symptoms that are clearly due to a general medical condition, or mood-incongruent delusions or hallucinations.

1. depressed mood most of the day, nearly every day, as indicated by either subjective report (for example, feels sad or empty) or observation made by others (for example, appears tearful); note that in children and adolescents, can be irritable mood
2. markedly diminished interest or pleasure in all, or almost all, activities most of the day, nearly every day (as indicated by either subjective account or observation made by others)
3. significant weight loss when not dieting or weight gain (for example, a change of more than 5 percent of body weight in a month), or decrease or increase in appetite nearly every day; note that in children, consider failure to make expected weight gains
4. insomnia or hypersomnia nearly every day
5. psychomotor agitation or retardation nearly every day (observable by others, not merely subjective feelings of restlessness or being slowed down)
6. fatigue or loss of energy nearly every day
7. feelings of worthlessness or excessive or inappropriate guilt (which may be delusional) nearly every day (not merely self-reproach or guilt about being sick)
8. diminished ability to think or concentrate, or indecisiveness, nearly every day (either by subjective account or as observed by others)
9. recurrent thoughts of death (not just fear of dying), recurrent suicidal ideation without a specific plan, or a suicide attempt or a specific plan for committing suicide.

B. The symptoms do not meet criteria for a Mixed Episode (see p. 335 [of the *DSM-IV*]).
C. The symptoms cause clinically significant distress or impairment in social, occupational, or other important area of functioning.
D. The symptoms are not due to the direct physiological effects of a substance (for example, a drug of abuse, a medication) or a general medical condition (for example, hypothyroidism).

    The symptoms are not better accounted for by bereavement (that is, after the loss of a loved one); the symptoms persist for longer than two months or are characterized by marked functional impairment, morbid preoccupation with worthlessness, suicidal ideation, psychotic symptoms, or psychomotor retardation.

Source: Reprinted with permission from American Psychiatric Association. (1994). *Diagnostic and statistical manual of mental disorders* (4th ed., p. 356). Washington, DC: Author.

APPENDIX 5-F Mental Status Questionnaire

1. Where are we now? _____

2. Where is this place located? _____

3. What is today's date? _____

4. What month is it? _____

5. What year is it? _____

6. How old are you? _____

7. What is your birthday? _____

8. What year were you born? _____

9. Who is president of the United States? _____

10. Who was president before [name given as answer to question 9]?

_____

Source: Reprinted from Kahn, R. L., Goldfarb, L., & Pollack, M. (1964). The evaluation of geriatric patients following treatment. In P. H. Hoch & J. Zubin (Eds.), *The evaluation of psychiatric treatment* (pp. 106–121). New York: Grune & Stratton, Elsevier.   Copyright 1964, with permission from Elsevier.

APPENDIX 5-G DSM-IV Diagnostic Criteria for Dementia of the Alzheimer's Type

E. The development of multiple cognitive deficits manifested by both

1. memory impairment (impaired ability to learn new information or to recall previously learned information), and

2. one (or more) of the following cognitive disturbances:

    i.   aphasia (language disturbance)

    ii. apraxia (impaired ability to carry out motor activities despite intact motor function)

    iii. agnosia (failure to recognize or identify objects despite intact sensory function)

    iv. disturbance in executive functioning (that is, planning, organizing, sequencing, abstracting).

F. The cognitive deficits in Criteria A1 and A2 [see Appendix 5-E] each cause significant impairment in social or occupational functioning and represent a significant decline from a previous level of functioning.

G. The course is characterized by gradual onset and continuing cognitive decline.

H. The cognitive deficits in Criteria A1 and A2 [see Appendix 5-E in this chapter] are not due to any of the following:

1. other central nervous system conditions that cause progressive deficits in memory and cognition (for example, cerebrovascular disease, Parkinson's disease, Huntington's disease, subdural hematoma, normal-pressure hydrocephalus, brain tumor)

2. systemic conditions that are known to cause dementia (for example, hypothyroidism, vitamin B_{12} or folic acid deficiency, niacin deficiency, hypercalcemia, neurosyphilis, HIV infection)

3. substance-induced conditions.

I. The deficits do not occur exclusively during the course of a delirium.

J. The disturbance is not better accounted for by another Axis I disorder (for example, major depressive disorder, schizophrenia).

Source: Reprinted with permission from American Psychiatric Association. (1994). *Diagnostic and statistical manual of mental disorders* (4th ed., p. 9). Washington, DC: Author.

APPENDIX 5-H Lubben Social Network Scale

Family Networks (*circle one*)

1. How many relatives do you see or hear from at least once a month?
   (*Note: Include in-laws with relatives.*)

0 = zero	**1** = one
2 = two	**3** = three or four
4 = five to eight	**5** = nine or more

2. Tell me about the relative with whom you have the most contact. How often do you see or hear from that person?

0 = monthly	**1** = monthly
2 = a few times a month	**3** = weekly
4 = a few times a week	**5** = daily

3. To how many relatives do you feel close? That is, how many of them do you feel at ease with, can talk to about private matters, or can call on for help?

0 = zero	**1** = one
2 = two	**3** = three or four
4 = five to eight	**5** = nine or more

Friends Networks (*circle one*)

4. Do you have any close friends? That is, do you have any friends with whom you feel at ease, can talk to about private matters, or can call on for help? If so, how many?

0 = zero	**1** = one
2 = two	**3** = three or four
4 = five to eight	**5** = nine or more

5. How many of these friends do you see or hear from at least once a month?

0 = zero	**1** = one
2 = two	**3** = three or four
4 = five to eight	**5** = nine or more

6. Tell me about the friend with whom you have the most contact. How often do you see or hear from that person?

0 = monthly	**1** = monthly
2 = a few times a month	**3** = weekly
4 = a few times a week	**5** = daily

(Continued)

APPENDIX 5-H Lubben Social Network Scale (*Continued*)

Confidential Relationships

7. When you have an important decision to make, do you have someone you can talk to about it? (*circle one*)

Always	Very often	Often	Sometimes	Seldom	Never
5	4	3	2	1	0

8. When other people you know have an important decision to make, do they talk to you about it? (*circle one*)

Always	Very often	Often	Sometimes	Seldom	Never
5	4	3	2	1	0

Helping Others

9. (a) Does anybody rely on you to do something for them each day? For example: shopping, cooking dinner, doing repairs, cleaning house, providing child care, and so forth.

   ☐ No— if no, go to 9b   ☐ Yes— if yes, question 9 is scored "5" and skip to question 10

   (b) Do you help anybody with things like shopping, filling out forms, doing repairs, providing child care, and so forth? (*circle one*)

Very often	Often	Sometimes	Seldom	Never
4	3	2	1	0

Living Arrangements (*circle one*)

10. Do you live alone or with other people?
    (*Note: Include in-laws with relatives.*)

    5 Living with spouse

    4 Live with other relatives or friends

    1 Live with other unrelated individuals (for example, paid help)

    0 Live alone.

Total Lubben Social Network Scale Score: _____

Note: The total Lubben Social Network Scale (LSNS) score is obtained by adding up scores from each of the 10 individual items. Thus, total LSNS scores can range from 0 to 50. Scores on each item were anchored between 0 and 5 to permit equal weighting of the 10 items.

Source: Adapted with permission from Lubben, J. (1988). Assessing social networks among elderly populations. *Family & Community Health, 11*, 42–52.

APPENDIX 5-I Framework for Spiritual Assessment

Initial Narrative Framework

- Describe the religious/spiritual tradition in which you grew up. How did your family express its spiritual beliefs? How important was spirituality to your family? Extended family?

- What sort of personal experiences (practices) during your years at home stand out for you? What made these experiences special? How have they informed your later life?

- How have you changed or matured from those experiences? How would you describe your current spiritual or religious orientation? Is your spirituality a personal strength? If so, how?

Interpretive Anthropological Framework

- *Affect:* What aspects of your spiritual life give you pleasure? What role does your spirituality play in handling life's sorrows? Embracing life's joys? Coping with life's pain? How does spirituality give you hope for the future? What do you wish to accomplish in the future?

- *Behavior:* Are there particular spiritual rituals or practices that help you deal with life's obstacles? What is your level of involvement in faith-based communities? How are they supported? Are there spiritually encouraging individuals with whom you maintain contact?

- *Cognition:* What are your current spiritual/religious beliefs? On what are they based? What beliefs do you find particularly meaningful? What does your faith say about personal trials? How does this belief help you overcome obstacles? How do your beliefs affect your physical health or mental health practices?

- *Communion:* Describe your relationship to the "Ultimate." What has been your experience of the Ultimate? How does the Ultimate communicate with you? How have these experiences encouraged you? Have there been times of deep spiritual intimacy? How does your relationship help you face life challenges? How would the Ultimate describe you?

- *Conscience:* How do you determine right or wrong? What are your key values? How does your spirituality help you deal with guilt or sin? What role does forgiveness play in your life?

- *Intuition:* To what extent do you experience intuitive hunches (that is, flashes of creative insight, premonitions, spiritual insight)? Have these insights been a source of strength in your life? If so, how?

Source: Adapted with permission from Hodge, D. R. (2001). Spirituality assessment: A review of major qualitative methods and a new framework for assessing spirituality. *Social Work, 46,* 208.

APPENDIX 5-J Home Safety Checklist

Examine	Appear Safe	Do Not Appear Safe
Electrical outlets and switches	☐	☐
Electrical and phone cords	☐	☐
Rugs, runners, and mats	☐	☐
Shelves secure and reachable	☐	☐
Telephone use and hearing	☐	☐
Emergency numbers and contacts	☐	☐
Doorbell	☐	☐
Smoke detector	☐	☐
Space heaters	☐	☐
Wood-burning stoves	☐	☐
Exits	☐	☐
Kitchen (stove)	☐	☐
Bathroom		
Tub/shower	☐	☐
Commode	☐	☐
General lighting	☐	☐
Steps	☐	☐
Garden	☐	☐

Source: Retrieved and summarized January 17, 2006, from http://www.aging-parents-and-elder-care.com/Pages/Checklists/Home_Safety_Chklst.html

APPENDIX 5-K Attitudes Toward Caregiving: A Questionnaire

This questionnaire contains a number of statements related to opinions and feelings about yourself, your impaired relative, and your caregiving experience. Read each statement carefully, then indicate the extent to which you agree or disagree with the statement. Check ☑ one of the alternative categories that are organized according to three subscales: I. Loss/Powerless Subscale (LP), II. Provisional Meaning (PM), III. Ultimate Meaning (UM). These categories are obtained through the statistical analysis, and numbered items will not appear sequentially.

	SA Strongly Agree	A Agree	U Undecided	D Disagree	SD Strongly Disagree
I. Loss/Powerless Subscale (LP)					
1. I miss the communication and companionship that my family member and I had in the past.	☐	☐	☐	☐	☐
2. I miss my family member's ability to love me as he/she did in the past.	☐	☐	☐	☐	☐
3. I am sad about the mental and physical changes I see in my relative.	☐	☐	☐	☐	☐
4. I miss the little things my relative and I did together in the past.	☐	☐	☐	☐	☐
5. I am sad about losing the person I once knew.	☐	☐	☐	☐	☐
6. I miss not being able to be spontaneous in my life because of caring for my relative.	☐	☐	☐	☐	☐
12. I miss not having more time for other family members and/or friends.	☐	☐	☐	☐	☐
13. I have no hope; I am clutching at straws.	☐	☐	☐	☐	☐
18. I miss our previous social life.	☐	☐	☐	☐	☐
19. I have no sense of joy.	☐	☐	☐	☐	☐
24. I miss not being able to travel.	☐	☐	☐	☐	☐
25. I wish I were free to lead a life of my own.	☐	☐	☐	☐	☐
30. I miss having given up my job or other personal interests to take care of my family member.	☐	☐	☐	☐	☐
31. I feel trapped by my relative's illness.	☐	☐	☐	☐	☐

(Continued)

APPENDIX 5-K Attitudes Toward Caregiving: A Questionnaire (*Continued*)

	SA Strongly Agree	A Agree	U Undecided	D Disagree	SD Strongly Disagree
I. Loss/Powerless Subscale (LP) (*continued*)					
34. We had goals for the future, but they just folded up because of my relative's dementia.	☐	☐	☐	☐	☐
36. I miss my relative's sense of humor.	☐	☐	☐	☐	☐
37. I wish I could run away.	☐	☐	☐	☐	☐
41. I feel that the quality of my life has decreased.	☐	☐	☐	☐	☐
7. My situation feels endless.	☐	☐	☐	☐	☐
II. Provisional Meaning (PM)					
8. I enjoy having my relative with me: I would miss it if he/she were gone.	☐	☐	☐	☐	☐
9. I count my blessings.	☐	☐	☐	☐	☐
10. Caring for my relative gives my life a purpose and a sense of meaning.	☐	☐	☐	☐	☐
14. I cherish the past memories and experiences that my relative and I have had.	☐	☐	☐	☐	☐
15. I am a strong person.	☐	☐	☐	☐	☐
16. Caregiving makes me feel good that I am helping.	☐	☐	☐	☐	☐
20. The hugs and "I love you" from my relative make it worth it all.	☐	☐	☐	☐	☐
21. I'm a fighter.	☐	☐	☐	☐	☐
22. I am glad I am here to care for my relative.	☐	☐	☐	☐	☐
26. Talking with others who are close to me restores my faith in my own abilities.	☐	☐	☐	☐	☐
27. Even though there are difficult things in my life, I look forward to the future.	☐	☐	☐	☐	☐

(*Continued*)

APPENDIX 5-K Attitudes Toward Caregiving: A Questionnaire (*Continued*)

	SA Strongly Agree	A Agree	U Undecided	D Disagree	SD Strongly Disagree
II. Provisional Meaning (PM) (*continued*)					
28. Caregiving has helped me learn new things about myself.	☐	☐	☐	☐	☐
32. Each year, regardless of the quality, is a blessing.	☐	☐	☐	☐	☐
33. I would not have chosen the situation I'm in, but I get satisfaction out of providing care.	☐	☐	☐	☐	☐
38. Every day is a blessing.	☐	☐	☐	☐	☐
39. This is my place: I have to make the best out of it.	☐	☐	☐	☐	☐
40. I am much stronger than I think.	☐	☐	☐	☐	☐
42. I start each day knowing we will have a beautiful day together.	☐	☐	☐	☐	☐
43. Caregiving has made me a stronger and better person.	☐	☐	☐	☐	☐
III. Ultimate Meaning (UM)					
11. The Lord won't give you more than you can handle.	☐	☐	☐	☐	☐
17. I believe in the power of prayer: without it I couldn't do this.	☐	☐	☐	☐	☐
23. I believe that the Lord will provide.	☐	☐	☐	☐	☐
29. I have faith that the good Lord has reasons for this.	☐	☐	☐	☐	☐
35. God is good.	☐	☐	☐	☐	☐

Source: Farran, C., Miller, B., Kaufman, J., Donner, D., & Fogg, L. (1999). Finding meaning through caregiving: Development of an instrument for family caregivers of persons with Alzheimer's disease. *Journal of Clinical Psychology, 55*, 1102–1125. Reprinted with permission from John Wiley & Sons, Inc.

Interventions | 6

RATIONALE: Social workers use a problem-solving process and select a target of intervention to maximize the coping capacity and innate resilience of the client system. Intervention is aimed at enhancing the well-being of individuals, families, groups, communities, organizations, and societies.

COMPETENCY: Students will develop clear, timely, and appropriate services or care plans with measurable objectives for older adults. They will

- apply evaluation and research findings to improve practice and program outcomes
- establish rapport and maintain an effective working relationship with older adults and family members
- assist caregivers to reduce stress levels and maintain their own mental and physical health
- mediate situations with angry or hostile older adults, family members, or both
- support persons and families dealing with end-of-life issues related to dying, death, and bereavement
- use educational strategies to provide older people and their families with information related to wellness and disease management (e.g., Alzheimer's disease, end-of-life care)
- re-evaluate and adjust service or care plans for older adults on a continuing basis
- apply skills to terminate work with older clients and their families. (Council on Social Work Education, Gero-Ed Center, 2004)

Continuum of Care

This chapter discusses interventions and services for individuals and families. It explores intervention strategies derived from various theories and schools of thought. Community-based services are discussed further in chapters 8 and 10. Services to older adults may be informal, those provided by family and friends, or formal, those provided by community-based agencies. The total delivery system for services to frail older adults who have some limits on biopsychosocial functional capacity that interfere with their autonomous functioning is generally termed long-term care.

Needs, services, and interventions form five continua: (1) a continuum of client need, or how independent or dependent an older adult is; (2) a continuum of services, that is, services suggested by need; (3) a continuum of services settings, or the degree of support for living the client requires; (4) a continuum of services providers, whether a person can manage without outside care, can conduct self-care, or requires professional care; and (5) a continuum of professional collaboration, whether the client requires help from more than one discipline (Hooyman, Hooyman, & Kethley, 1981; Figure 6-1). These continua help geriatric social workers visualize how to match a client with needed services and care along a *full* continuum of care. This encompasses a range of activities—from those with the most capacity to those with the least (Vourlekis & Greene, 1992). It also allows for practitioners to think about services that are least restrictive or those environments that permit the most independent functioning.

FIGURE 6-1 Continuum of Care

1. Continuum of Need

Independent (Little or no need)	Moderately dependent	Dependent (Multiple needs)

2. Continuum of Services

Health promotion/ disease prevention	Screening and early detection	Diagnosis and pretreatment evaluation	Treatment	Rehabilitation: skilled nursing services	Continuing care and hospice

3. Continuum of Service Settings

Own home, apartment, etc.	Friend or relative's home apartment, etc.	Congregate living situation	Subacute care facility (e.g., day hospital)	Acute-care facility (e.g., hospital)	Skilled long-term care facility (e.g., nursing home)	Continuing care and hospice

4. Continuum of Service Providers

Nonservice	Self-care	Family friends (support network)	Paraprofessionals	Professionals

5. Continuum of Professional Collaboration

Single discipline	Multidisciplinary	Interdisciplinary

Source: Reprinted with permission from Hooyman, N., Hooyman, G., & Kethley, A. (1981, March). *The role of gerontological social work in interdisciplinary care.* Paper presented at the annual program meeting of the Council on Social Work Education, Louisville, KY.

To arrive at a holistic picture of the older adult's functioning and an intervention plan that is acceptable to the older client (and the client's family), the social worker must synthesize the various elements of the assessment and integrate them into a plan. What do the biopsychosocial and spiritual assessments indicate? Are the demands of the client's environment putting the person at risk? What protective factors, such as a rich support network, exist? Has the client overcome many hurdles or adversities in his or her life? Would you think of the client as resilient?

What services and interventions does the client (and his or her family) appear to need? Is there general agreement on a plan of action? Are these services available in the client's community? Does the client need a day care program, a homemaker, or congregate meals? What interventions and services would promote client competence?

Health Education

A continuum of care should encompass health education that includes the goal of prevention. Prevention programs serve a couple of purposes: they aim to reduce a person's likelihood of becoming ill or disabled and promote a healthy lifestyle by improving eating habits, exercise, and health screenings (see http://www.merck.com/pubs/mmanual_ha/ sec2/ch04c.html). Public campaigns about the signs of depression and a hotline telephone number that connects a caller to someone who can provide information on how to get help for at-risk older adults are good examples of wellness programs and preventive services. Such programs may conduct outreach to older people in need and are designed to inform community organizations, religious groups, senior centers, and local businesses about the issues older adults face and where to seek help.

Prevention and health promotion require that practitioners rethink how they conduct assessment and intervention so that they follow the principle of basing the level of care on the individual's functional capacity—from the person who is most independent to the person who is least independent (Vourlekis & Greene, 1992). Greene (2005) has proposed that practitioners evaluate care needs, using *client triage,* a process by which the most frail or physically and mentally challenged clients receive the most intense service. Triage allows the practitioner to meet the challenges of those most in need. This process must be accompanied by an understanding that clients may reverse frailty and regain strength. Also, because caregivers often bear heavy responsibilities and frequently do not take care of themselves—for example, fail to take a break or eat properly, according to the National Alliance for Caregiving (2003)—geriatric practitioners should also assess whether caregivers are at risk for burnout and identify prevention programs for them.

Adult Protective Services

Adult Protective Services is at the other end of the care continuum from preventive services. These state agencies are mandated to ensure the safety and well-being of elders and adults with disabilities who may be in danger of being mistreated or neglected, and are unable to care for themselves, protect themselves from harm, or have no one to assist them (see Appendix 6-A). Similar to child protective services, social workers are mandated to report elder abuse.

Because self-neglect is the most prevalent type of abuse, it is important during an assessment of an older adult for the social worker to determine if the person has "the capacity to make an acceptable choice with respect to a specific decision" (Weisstub, 1990, p. 68). If the practitioner finds that the older adult is not mentally competent or tends to make faulty judgments, he or she should then collaborate with state and local protective agencies to develop a plan to ensure the adult's safety in the home (see Appendix 5-J in chapter 5 for a home safety checklist). Confidentiality may be difficult under such circumstances, presenting ethical dilemmas.

Evidence-Based Practice in Geriatric Mental Health Care

At least one in five people older than 65 years of age suffers from a mental disorder (U.S. Department of Health and Human Services, 1999). Consequently, during the past decade, research on treatments for mental illnesses experienced by people in their later years has grown dramatically (Bartels et al., 2002). Because social workers are often on the front lines, working directly with older adults and their families, they must keep abreast of the latest assessment instruments and research supporting the effectiveness of pharmacological and psychosocial interventions, particularly for clients with depression or dementia (Institute of Medicine, 2001). (For a more detailed description of instruments for assessing depression and other mental disorders, see chapter 5.) Distinguishing between evidence-based practice techniques and those that are less "proven" may prove beneficial to clients' well-being.

Geriatric social workers must make use of evidence-based practice or knowledge procured from literature reviews of aggregate meta-analyses of relevant randomized controlled trials. This approach includes being aware of relevant consensus statements and consensus reviews. According to Bartels et al. (2002), recent literature has revealed the following major findings about geriatric mental health:

- Researchers generally agree that antidepressants are an effective treatment for geriatric depression. More than half of older adults treated with such medications experienced at least a 50-percent reduction in depressive symptoms.
- In general, cognitive therapy, behavioral therapy, and cognitive–behavioral therapy have the greatest empirical support for effectiveness in treating geriatric depression.
- For patients with mild to moderate dementia associated with the early stages of Alzheimer's disease, evidence-based reviews and meta-analyses find that cholinesterase inhibitors, in contrast to placebos, have only a modest effect, delaying the decline of cognitive functioning of some patients by 6 to 12 months.

- Behavioral and environmental modifications have been found to be moderately effective in enhancing functioning and reducing problem behaviors of Alzheimer's patients. Effective treatment methods include regulating the amount of stimulation the person receives, having the older adult engage in light exercise, or listening to music (Beers, 2004).

Traditional Psychosocial Interventions and New Intervention Paradigms

Social workers were among the first professionals to engage in psychosocial interventions to enhance the coping capacity of older clients (Lowy, 1991). As they adopted new theoretical concepts and practice strategies, the way in which coping was conceived also evolved, providing a rich repertoire of treatment strategies (Greene & Cohen, 2005). Therefore, the practitioner may choose from the treatment strategies described in Appendix 6-B to develop his or her model of intervention, choosing from traditional or contemporary models as described below.

Traditional Interventions

Early in this evolution, caseworkers simply provided material or concrete services such as financial aid. However, during the 1950s and 1960s, the works of psychodynamic theorists such as Sigmund Freud and Erik Erikson came to the fore. Practitioners began to evaluate ego functioning and ego strengths, and they provided techniques for ego support. Although Freudian interventions were never widely used with older adults, Erikson's theory about coping style in old age—the resolution of the conflict between integrity versus despair—was, and it remains popular today.

Life Review

The idea that it is natural and possibly curative for older adults to talk about their past was first brought to light by Robert Butler, a geriatric psychiatrist who coined the term *life review* in 1963. He espoused a form of reminiscence therapy based on an Eriksonian psychodynamic perspective in which recall of the past was said to allow for the resolution and integration of past conflicts (Greene, 2000). Butler argued that older adults who were better adapted and able to deal with personal, social, and medical adversities experienced an improved resolution of life cycle stages. The fundamental issue involved in helping older adults was to set in motion a process of coping with death and loss.

Butler (1968) was optimistic that autobiographic processes could help people maintain self-identity and tranquility. Butler's words embody social work practice with older adults, thus foreshadowing a resilience approach:

> Psychotherapeutic work with older people involves the management of small deaths and intimations of mortality. Put succinctly, the psychotherapy of old age is the psychotherapy of grief and of accommodation, restitution, and resolution. "Coming to terms

with," "bearing witness," reconciliation, atonement, construction and reconstruction, integration, transcendence, creativity, realistic insight with modifications and substitutions, the introduction of meaning and of meaningful, useful, and contributory efforts: these are the terms that are pertinent to therapy with older people. (p. 237)

According to Erikson's theory of human development, at each of eight stages of life, people struggle to resolve a psychosocial crisis pertaining to how they see themselves and the world at large. Integrity versus despair, the eighth psychosocial crisis, takes place during old age, when the psychosocial crisis is "how to grow old with integrity in the face of death" (Erikson, 1959/1980, p. 104).

Integrity is realized by older adults who have few regrets, have lived fruitful lives, and cope equally well with failures as with successes. The person who has achieved a sense of integrity appreciates the continuity of past, present, and future experiences. He or she also comes to accept the life cycle, cooperate with the inevitabilities of life, and experience a sense of being complete (Greene, 2005). In contrast, *despair* is found in those who fear death and wish life would give them another chance. The older adult who has a strong sense of despair believes that life has been too short and finds little meaning in human existence. That person has lost faith in himself or herself, as well as in others. The person in whom despair dominates has little sense of world order or spiritual wholeness (Greene, 2007).

Life review may take many forms: an older adult's detailing his or her life to another person or use of the expressive arts such as bibliotherapy, journaling, memory books, and time capsules (Caldwell, 2005). Drawing pictures of important life events or tapping naturally occurring memories are examples of artistic life-review methods. Social workers frequently use creative techniques to engage their clients—for instance, suggesting that clients write poetry or attend antique fairs to help them remember past events (Malekoff, 2004).

The oral traditions of a people often guide life review. For example, social workers encouraged Hispanic people living in northern New Mexico to reminisce in a way that embodied their oral traditions. Practitioners used theatrical settings, food, drink, and proverbs to stimulate verbal accounts of historical events (Andrada & Korte, 1993).

To obtain older adults' complete life history, the social worker must ask them to describe what kind of person they think they are, the circumstances under which they have lived, and their relationships with significant others (these topics may also be addressed in the assessment process; see Appendix 5-D in chapter 5). Clients' responses may result in further discussion of what changes might lead to enhanced functioning.

The efficacy of life-review interventions has been well documented. Rennemark and Hagberg (1997) found that positive self-evaluations of Erikson's life stages were generally important for well-being, particularly when life events were understood within a context of significant others.

Ecological–Systems Thinking

Subsequent to psychodynamic approaches, family systems theory and its companion, the ecological perspective, have been used to better understand how older adults interact with others and with various social systems (see chapter 2 for details on these theoretical constructs). When bringing families of later years together, geriatric social workers generally use systems theory to improve communication and organization related to caregiving. These theories afford an understanding of an older adult's resource needs and form the basis for family-focused interventions (addressed later in this chapter under "Family Intervention").

Cognitive–Behavioral Approach

A scientific basis exists for conducting one-on-one psychotherapeutic-type interviews with older adults: A review of the literature documents that cognitive and behavioral interventions are efficacious for treating depressed older adults (Teri, Logsdon, Uomoto, & McCurry, 1997).

Cognitive interventions help a client recognize distorted thinking and learn to replace those thoughts with more realistic substitutes. For example, following a heart attack, an older adult may feel he or she has lost all meaning in life. The social worker would then reinforce that the client still has choices and would explore those possibilities with the client (see "Putting the Resilience-Enhancing Model into Action" later in this chapter). Interventions with depressed people might require social workers to explain the nature of the disorder, so that clients do not view themselves as crazy or weak. Because some older adults may expect their practitioners to be paternalistic, social workers must guide those clients to learn how to become active participants in their own care.

Interviews as part of the cognitive intervention process may cover fewer points, but the practitioner could enhance those points using visual or memory aids. He or she could adapt interventions to address older adults' *context,* or their social–environmental setting; *cohort differences,* that is, the specific historical period in which they lived; *maturity,* or their emotional complexity and wealth of experience; and their specific *challenges,* including chronic medical conditions and neurological disorders (Knight, 1999).

Despite these adjustments, the greatest barrier to effective treatment of older adults with mental illnesses such as depression is inadequate recognition of the disease by the elders themselves, or by their families or physicians (Karel & Hinrichsen, 2000). Behavioral interventions, which focus on modifying negative behaviors or helping clients to unlearn them rather than exploring the underlying causes of those behaviors, have proven efficacious in working with older adults, including those with mental illness. The primary purpose is to deal with immediate and specific problems and reward positive changes. Techniques include biofeedback, relaxation training, and disease self-management (Gage & Goreczny, 1998).

Advantages of the behavioral approach include avoiding *ageism*—the belief that aging is equated with inevitable decline. Because behavioral interventions focus on how to improve functional-age challenges, they offer an optimistic orientation to solving problems (such as urinary incontinence or paying attention to personal grooming). Behavioral techniques are particularly successful in nursing homes when the staff works together to develop and evaluate plans to modify disruptive behaviors (Dupree & Schonfeld, 1998). Behavioral approaches are also useful for training caregivers in the principles of management of troublesome behaviors at home (Gallagher-Thompson, Coon, Rivera, Powers, & Zeiss, 1998).

Paradigm Shift

Constructionist Therapy

Psychosocial interventions from the social constructionist school are intended to help clients appraise stressful life encounters by having them assign meaning to the stressors at hand and then help them cope with those encounters. By appraisal, we mean that clients weigh life events and assign meaning to them. The client and social worker come to understand stressful life encounters within the context of an individual's life purposes and goals (Park & Folkman, 1997).

Meaning systems orient, motivate, and guide people in actions they expect to take throughout the life course. When people encounter a specific stressful event, they measure that event against their expectations. The level of distress is determined by the degree of discrepancy between the meaning of the specific event and one's meaning system. For example, an older adult may be severely troubled about the death of an adult child, because the elder's expectations were that he or she would die before a child. Therefore, such a critical event would be highly stressful and particularly difficult to resolve (Greene, 2000).

Grief Counseling

The death of a significant person in an older client's life poses a tremendous challenge to his or her ability to adapt or cope. Social workers use a process called *normalizing* to help bereaved clients learn that the feelings of loss they are experiencing, such as anger, guilt, anxiety, helplessness, and sadness, are typical. Normalizing also means that each individual must go on to see his or her life without the deceased person. Practitioners must remember, though, that people may normalize the grieving process differently.

Grieving individuals struggle with how to affirm or reconstruct personal meaning in the face of loss (Neimeyer, 2001). Therefore, an effective intervention following the death of a loved one is a social constructionist conceptualization of grief resolution, which pays significant attention to the ever-present human ability to organize experience in narrative form and make sense of troubling events.

Narrative Gerontology

Narrative therapy, a psychotherapeutic approach in which an older adult recalls his or her life experiences (sometimes in writing), is another means for clients to make sense of their life events. This approach might be useful in both assessment and intervention. Increasingly, researchers are finding that maintaining a coherent narrative—one that makes sense to the client—is important to a person's well-being (McAdams, Diamond, Mansfield, & de St. Aubin, 1997).

Narrative therapy is closely aligned with constructionist therapy. Both approaches help clients to reconstruct what is important to them, to provide them with more choices for action. The time the social worker and client spend together is used to explore the client's meaning of life experiences. The practitioners attempts to see the world through the client's eyes, and when issues are perceived, alternatives or reinterpretations are sought (Viney, Benjamin, & Preston, 1988). Narratives benefit the client and practitioner alike because they help

- communicate hope
- build rapport
- establish connections
- inspire and encourage
- preserve cultural identity
- clarify emotions
- help clients cope with death, illness, and tragedy.

They contain an individual's story as well as macro-level or larger stories that reflect a client's "shared history, values, beliefs, expectations, and myths" (Webster, 2002, p. 143). Therefore, life histories provided through client narratives enable geriatric social workers to learn about their clients' critical life events (Greene & Cohen, 2005)—personal, interpersonal, sociocultural, and societal episodes (Appendix 6-C).

Resilience-Enhancing Model

As practitioners listen to and analyze critical life events, they will find opportunities to intervene and elaborate on the information provided. Social workers often learn how resilient a client is and what previous successes he or she has had. For example, in Appendix 6-C, PJ says that religion has helped her cope with life. That information may prompt an acceptable intervention tailored for PJ. Maybe she has not gone to church recently because she is in a wheelchair and lacks transportation. Can she imagine what it would be like to return to her congregation? Can she see herself taking a specialized van? Social constructionist models of change support intuitive client thinking and use positive emotions to promote resilience (Wartel, 2003). Such models also encourage an older client to see aging "as part of a new season, a journey one takes" (Ronen & Dowd, 1998, p. 83).

The resilience-enhancing model (REM) as developed by Greene (2007: see Figure 6-2) and other strengths-based approaches do not deny clients' problems and concerns. Rather, such interventions are carried out in an atmosphere in which clients can examine problems "from a perspective of enhanced dignity and sense of agency, . . . highlighting aspects of their lives that are going well" (Saul, 2003, p. 300). In putting together a resilience-enhancing practice model, the social worker

- uses critical thinking
- considers the practice context—that is, the societal cultural milieu and historical time
- subscribes to the purposes of the profession

FIGURE 6-2 Conceptual Framework of Risk and Resilience in Practice

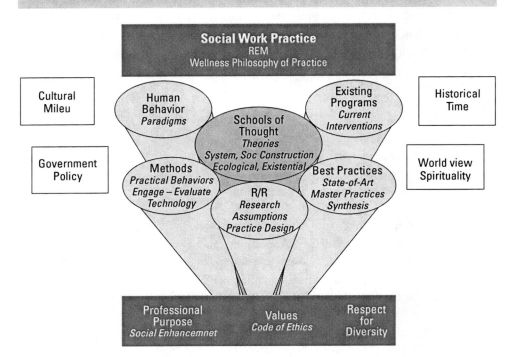

Source: Greene, R. R. (2007). Social work practice: A risk and resilience perspective. Belmont, CA: Thomson Brooks/Cole.

- bears in mind governmental policy
- applies human behavior theories
- draws from various schools of thought
- respects client diversity and spirituality
- struggles with ethical dilemmas
- uses evidenced-based practice protocols
- identifies and applies research findings
- calls on best practices or state-of-the-art interventions.

Family Intervention

Functional-Age Model of Intergenerational Therapy

Historically, interventions with older adults and their families have been based on systems theory and thus have addressed matters of intergenerational connectedness. What are expressions of family loyalty? Can the family resolve "old debts" (Boszormenyi-Nagy & Spark, 1973)? Can they continue to act as a system of mutual aid? Indebtedness varies by family, and in some instances family members may deny gratitude or recognition or may angrily express that another is indebted to them because of past "wrongs." Other families may foster loyalty through the cultural norms involving familism (see chapter 3).

One intergenerational intervention model that helps older adults and their families to resolve past or current issues is the Functional-Age Model of intergenerational therapy. Functional-Age Model (FAM) as developed by Greene [1986] 2000 allows the geriatric social worker to do the following:

- Observe the structure and communication patterns within the family. Who is the contact person for the older adult? Who has primary caretaking responsibilities? Does each family member communicate his or her needs? Does the older adult participate? As these patterns are revealed, the practitioner clarifies, reframes, and redirects communications. He or she encourages family members to direct their remarks to one another. When an apparent "failure" exists in mobilizing the family on behalf of the older adult, the social worker addresses the issue with the family explicitly.
- Develop a picture of how the family has functioned over time. Has it been able to meet crises before? If so, how? If it is currently experiencing difficulties, what are they? Does the family have ideas about how they will face these challenges?
- Learn about role responsibilities within the family. How does the family carry out caregiving roles and responsibilities? What is the division of labor? Is one family member overburdened? Does the primary caregiver have conflicts with work, child care, and adult caregiving responsibilities?
- Examine how the family deals with stress. How is caregiving proceeding? Who does what? Is there time for respite? Do family members experience any rewards?

Family Resilience

Walsh (1998) has promoted family well-being through interventions that "identify and fortify key interactional processes that enable families to withstand and rebound from disruptive life challenges" (p. 3). According to her, the family unit has the potential to meet crises through self-repair and growth. Practitioners examine and reframe *family belief systems*, the values and attitudes that form a family's ideas about how to act, and organizational and communication patterns. *Family organizational patterns*, which are based on behavioral expectations, reflect how the family is structured to carry out tasks, such as having the ability to rally together to cope with stress. *Communication patterns* point to the relationships in a family and how those relationships influence the exchange of information within that family.

Family-centered models call for social workers to take an active role in modifying and enhancing the way in which families perform their caregiving function. Practitioners typically carry out this role through family decision-making meetings, or semistructured gatherings of extended family members intended to open communications and facilitate services provider and family collaborations (Brodie & Gadling-Cole, 2003).

Caregiver Intervention

Caregivers' attitudes and feelings about the caregiving process and the recipients of their care influence their caregiving experience (see Appendix 5-K in chapter 5 for a questionnaire that helps assess attitudes toward caregiving). Is the caregiver able to find rewards in the experience? Is he or she gaining something from the experience that promotes coping and resilience? Because it is essential that caregivers maintain their emotional and physical health, an important role of the geriatric social worker is to assess the situation (see chapter 5) and subsequently discuss the range of interventions available to a caregiver. Is the caregiver taking care of himself or herself, or is the person at a risk of depression or physical illness?

Traditional interventions for caregivers include support groups, individual and family counseling, case management, respite services, skills training, or a combination of those strategies (Bourgeois, Schulz, & Burgio, 1996). Nontraditional caregiving interventions include tapping positive emotions, exploring spirituality, and discovering the benefits of caregiving (Riley, 2007). For example, a social worker and client may foster the following six rewards of caregiving:

1. The caregiver feels useful and needed, and that he or she is doing something meaningful.
2. The caregiver has a sense of competence and mastery.
3. The caregiver has an opportunity to share feelings of love and empathy with the care recipient.
4. He or she feels satisfied about being there for someone who took care of the caregiver in the past.
5. The caregiver feels appreciated by other family members and friends for what the caregiver is doing.
6. He or she has feelings of altruism and self-respect as a result of doing—without being asked—what needs to be done. (Toseland & Smith, 2001)

A recurrent theme in interviews with caregivers is that they use religious faith and prayer to find meaning in, and to cope with, the caregiving experience (Riley, 2007). Consequently, social workers need to understand how faith and faith-based practices contribute to client resilience. For instance, they may ask clients to describe their cultural practices and perceptions of how those practices have influenced their life experiences (see chapter 5).

Putting the Resilience-Enhancing Model into Action

The following is a case study showing how REM can guide a social worker in intervening with an older adult (Greene, 2007; Appendix 6-D). In this case, the social worker meets with her client Jim, an adult male, in the hospital. Jim had suffered a heart attack three days earlier.

■ The practitioner first acknowledges the client's loss, vulnerability, and future: She helps move him from "this could not happen to me" to "I must face this challenge." She makes an alliance with the client's hopes, vision, and values.

> The social worker assumes that now that Jim's condition has stabilized, he will feel a heightened sense of vulnerability. She avoids saying phrases such as "I know everything will be all right." She lets him talk about how frightening it was to recognize that he was having symptoms of a heart attack. She acknowledges that he has lost a sense of security—"I am no longer physically well." Once Jim's loss is acknowledged, she guides him to a discussion of the future. Can he still picture playing with his grandson? Taking a trip?

■ The social worker identifies the client's source of stress: She discovers what about the event made it most troubling. She wants to know how the client experienced the event.

> Jim would like to do positive things in the future, but he is worried about another heart attack. This is his major source of stress.

■ The practitioner recognizes client stress: She accepts the client's source of distress. The social worker wants the client to know that she has heard his "complaint."

> The social worker recognizes that Jim's concern about having another heart attack can be a worry. She wonders aloud about other family member concerns.

■ The social worker stabilizes or normalizes the situation: She helps the client understand that it is okay to feel a general tension. She wants to impart empathy and affirmation.

> The social worker explains that almost all the patients she sees following a heart attack have similar concerns. Jim talks about picturing himself in a helpless situation when in public.

■ The practitioner helps the client take control: She suggests that he is capable of carrying out his role responsibilities. The social worker wants to empower him to take control.

> The social worker asks if Jim has been to the patient education group. She explains the type of information available from the nurse educator. She also asks if Jim has talked with his doctor about the severity of his attack and his prognosis.

■ The social worker provides resources for change: She assures the client that resources are at hand to support his physical and psychological safety. Her goal is for the client to use the available resources.

At his bedside, the social worker leaves a number of pamphlets that discuss a patient's recovery following a heart attack. She says she will return the next day.

- The social worker promotes client self-efficacy: She communicates to Jim that he can manage his own affairs. She wants to reinforce the idea that he can solve his difficulty.

     The next day Jim says he has asked his doctor about his recovery. He tells the social worker that he was relieved to learn about the extent of the damage to his heart and that it was not as serious as he had thought.

- The practitioner collaborates in client self-change: She sets in motion a self-motivating process. She wants the client to know he can take charge of himself.

     The social worker wanted to know what else he had done. Jim said he had signed up for the nurse educator lecture that afternoon.

- The social worker strengthens the client's problem-solving abilities: She brings the client into the problem-solving relationship with her. The practitioner wants Jim to know that they are collaborators.

     The social worker asks Jim what his major questions are. She asks him, "What do you hope to learn?" Jim replies that he wants to know how much he can still roughhouse with his grandson.

- The practitioner addresses positive emotions: She helps the client escape from harsh realities to images of pleasure. She wants to reframe events so that the client can be hopeful.

     The social worker says Jim's grandson sounds like a rascal.

- The social worker listens to the client's stories and uses humor: She realizes that the story of the event contains a mixture of pain and joy. She wants to help the client put the problem outside of him.

     Jim and the social worker laugh about a story of Jim's grandson and how he got into trouble trampling his grandmother's rose bush.

- The practitioner achieves creativity: She discovers new ways for the client to meet his goals. The social worker hopes Jim will find creative ways to live with his illness.

     The social worker asks Jim in what activities do grandpa and grandson engage. Jim realizes that he and his grandson often sit and read. He suggests that he might have to "resort to" computer games!

- The social worker helps make meaning of the client's critical events: She helps Jim appraise the critical event with new eyes. The social worker hopes the appraisal process will lead to positive outcomes, such as a greater appreciation of life.

  Jim says, "I know one thing: I'll be playing with him every chance I get!"

- The practitioner helps the client to discern the benefits of adverse events: She guides him to resolving a negative event by finding a positive meaning.

  "I have learned one thing," Jim says. " I will never say I can't baby-sit!"

- The social worker attends to Jim's spirituality and to transcend the immediate situation: She determines if spirituality can be a personal strength. The social worker anticipates that the client will look for "greater" opportunities.

  "God willing," says Jim, " I will be at my grandson's high school graduation!"

Conclusion

Social work professionals are increasingly using risk and resilience theory to define and augment their practice because they consider this theory to be effective in alleviating distress and promoting well-being at the individual, family, and community levels. Their practice with various client systems is based on the belief that people possess a natural ability for self-change and self-correcting behaviors (Greene, 2007). Therefore, social workers begin the helping process with an assessment of client system strengths and challenges. Their intervention choices emphasize client self-determination (chapter 4), explore client resources, adopt a collaborative client–helper relationship, build on healthy tendencies, and take on an anti-ageist perspective (Ronch & Goldfield, 2003).

Suggested Exercise to Evaluate Student Competency

Based on the case study used in chapter 5 on assessment, students will develop a (mutually acceptable) care plan that includes an evaluation component.

References

Andrada, P. A., & Korte, A. O. (1993). En aquellos tiempos: A reminiscing group with Hispanic elderly. *Journal of Gerontological Social Work, 20*(3/4), 25–42.

Bartels, S., Dums, A. R., Oxman, T. E., Schneider, L. S., Areán, P. A., Alexopoulos, G. S., & Jeste, D. V. (2002). Evidence-based practices in geriatric mental health care. *Psychiatry Services, 53,* 419–431.

Beers, M. H. (2004). *The Merck manual of health & aging.* Retrieved May 1, 2007, from http://www.merck.com/pubs/mmanual_ha/sec2/ch04/ch04a.html

Boszormenyi-Nagy, I., & Spark, G. (1973). *Invisible loyalties*. New York: Harper & Row.

Bourgeois, M., Schulz, R., & Burgio, L. (1996). Interventions for caregivers of patients with Alzheimer' disease: A review and analysis of content, process, and outcomes. *International Journal of Aging: Human Behavior, 43,* 35–92.

Brodie, K., & Gadling-Cole, C. (2003). The use of family decision meetings when addressing caregiver stress. *Journal of Gerontological Social Work, 42*(1), 89–99.

Butler, R. N. (1963). The life review: An interpretation of reminiscence in the aged. *Psychiatry, 26,* 65–76.

Butler, R. N. (1968). Toward a psychiatry of the life-cycle: Implications of socio-psychologic studies of the aging process for the psychotherapeutic situation. In A. Simon & L. Epstein (Eds.), *Aging in modern society* (pp. 233–248). Washington, DC: American Psychiatric Association.

Caldwell, R. L. (2005). At the confluence of memory and meaning—Life review with older adults and families: Using narrative therapy and the expressive arts to remember and re-author stories of resilience. *Family Journal: Counseling and Therapy for Couples and Families, 13,* 172–175.

Council on Social Work Education, Gero-Ed Center. (2004). *Foundation gerontological social work competencies.* Retrieved November 16, 2006, from http://depts.washington.edu/geroctr/Curriculum3/ Competencies/FdnComp.doc

Dupree, L. W., & Schonfeld, L. (1998). The value of behavioral perspectives in treating older adults. In M. Hersen & V. B. Van Hasselt (Eds.), *Handbook of clinical geropsychology* (pp. 51–70). New York: Plenum Press.

Erikson, E. H. (1980). *Identity and the life cycle.* New York: W. W. Norton. (Original work published 1959)

Gage, M., & Goreczny, A. J. (1998). Behavioral medicine interventions with older adults. In M. Hersen & V. B. Van Hasselt (Eds.), *Handbook of clinical geropsychology* (pp. 351–380). New York: Plenum Press.

Gallagher-Thompson, D., Coon, D. W., Rivera, P., Powers, D., & Zeiss, A. M. (1998). Family caregiving: Stress, coping, and intervention. In M. Hersen & V. B. Van Hasselt (Eds.), *Handbook of clinical geropsychology* (pp. 469–493). New York: Plenum Press.

Greene, R. R. (2000). Social work with the aged and their families. New Brunswick, NJ: Aldine Transaction.

Greene, R. R. (2005). Family life. In L. W. Kaye (Ed.), *Perspectives on productive aging: Social work with the new aged* (pp. 107–122). Washington, DC: NASW Press.

Greene, R. R. (2007). *Social work practice: A risk and resilience perspective.* Belmont, CA: Thomson Brooks/Cole.

Greene, R. R., & Cohen, H. L. (2005). Social work with older adults and their families: Changing practice paradigms. *Families in Society, 86,* 367–373.

Hooyman, N., Hooyman, G., & Kethley, A. (1981, March). *The role of gerontological social work in interdisciplinary care.* Paper presented at the annual program meeting of the Council on Social Work Education, Louisville, KY.

Institute of Medicine. (2001). *Crossing the quality chasm: A new health system for the 21st century.* Washington, DC: National Academy Press.

Karel, M., & Hinrichsen, G. (2000). Treatment of depression in late life: Psychotherapeutic interventions. *Clinical Psychology Review, 20,* 707–729.

Kenyon, G. M., & Randall, W. (2001). Narrative gerontology: An overview. In G. Kenyon, P. Clark, & B. de Vries (Eds.), *Narrative gerontology* (pp. 3–18). New York: Springer.

Knight, B. (1999). The scientific basis for psychotherapeutic interventions with older adults: An overview. *JCLP/In Session, 55,* 927–934.

Lowy, L. (1991). *Social work with the aging: The challenge and promise of the later years.* New York: Harper & Row.

Malekoff, A. (2004). Remembering with and without awareness through poetry to better understand aging and disability. *Journal of Gerontological Social Work, 44*(1/2), 255–264.

McAdams, D. P., Diamond, A., Mansfield, E., & de St. Aubin, E. (1997). Stories of commitment: The psychosocial construction of generative lives. *Journal of Personality and Social Psychology, 72,* 678–694.

National Alliance for Caregiving. (2003). *Family caregiving and public policy principles for change.* Retrieved May 8, 2005, from www.caregiving.org

Neimeyer, R. A. (Ed.). (2001). *Meaning reconstruction and the experience of loss.* Washington, DC: American Psychological Association.

Park, C. L., & Folkman, S. (1997). The role of meaning in the context of stress and coping. *General Review of Psychology, 1,* 115–144.

Rennemark, M., & Hagberg, B. (1997). Social network patterns among the elderly in relation to their perceived life history in an Eriksonian perspective. *Aging & Mental Health, 1,* 321–331.

Riley, J. (2007). Caregiving: A risk and resilience perspective. In R. R. Greene (Ed.), *Social work practice: A risk and resilience perspective* (pp. 239–262). Belmont, CA: Thomson Brooks/Cole.

Ronch, J. L., & Goldfield, J. (2003). Mental health and aging: Strengths-based approaches. Baltimore: Health Professions Press.

Ronen, T., & Dowd, T. (1998). A constructive model for working with depressed elders. *Journal of Gerontological Social Work, 30*(3/4), 83–99.

Saul, J. (2003). Strengths-based approaches to trauma in the aging. In J. Ronch & J. A. Goldfield (Eds.), *Mental wellness in aging: Strengths-based approaches* (pp. 299–314). Baltimore: Health Professions Press.

Sijuwade, P. O. (1995). Cross-cultural perspectives on elder abuse as a family dilemma. *Social Behavior and Personality, 23,* 247–252.

Teri, L., Logsdon, R. G., Uomoto, J., & McCurry, S. M. (1997). Behavioral treatment of depression in dementia patients: A controlled clinical trial. *Journals of Gerontology: Psychological Sciences and Social Sciences, 52*B, P159–P166.

Toseland, R., & Smith, T. (2001). *Supporting caregivers through education and training.* Washington, DC: U.S. Department of Health and Human Services.

U.S. Department of Health and Human Services. (1999). *Mental health: A report of the surgeon general.* Rockville, MD: Author.

Viney, L. L., Benjamin, Y. N., & Preston, C. (1988). Constructivist family therapy with the elderly. *Journal of Family Psychology, 2,* 241–258.

Vourlekis, B., & Greene, R. R. (1992). *Social work case management.* New York: Aldine de Gruyter.

Walsh, F. (1998). *Strengthening family resilience.* New York: Guilford Press.

Wartel, S. G. (2003). A strengths-based practice model: Psychology of mind and health realization. *Families in Society, 84,* 185–191.

Webster, J. (2002). Reminiscence functions in adulthood: Age, race, and family dynamics correlates. In J. D. Webster & B. K. Haight (Eds.), *Critical advances in reminiscence work* (pp. 140–152). New York: Springer.

Weisstub, D. N. (1990). *Enquiry on mental competency: Final report.* Toronto: Ontario Ministry of Health.

APPENDIX 6-A Types of Abuse: General Definitions

- *Neglect,* the most common form of abuse, involves failure to provide essential physical or mental care for an older person. Neglect may be unintentional or intentional (withholding food, water, or medication).

- *Physical neglect* includes withholding food or water, failing to provide proper hygiene, or neglecting to offer physical aids or safety precautions.

- *Physical violence* involves actions that may result in pain, injury, impairment, or disease. Pushing, striking, slapping, pinching, force-feeding, or improper use of physical restraints or medications are examples of physical violence.

- *Psychological abuse* is any action by the caregiver that causes fear, isolation, confusion, or disorientation in an older person. These are acts intended to harm and may include verbal aggression using words that humiliate and infantilize.

- *Financial exploitation* is the misuse of an older person's income or resources for another's personal gain.

- *Violation of rights,* in which the older adult is deprived of legal rights and personal liberties, is a form of abuse.

- *Domestic abuse* refers to several forms of maltreatment of an older person in his or her home by someone who has a special relationship (often the caregiver) with that elder.

- *Self-neglect,* in which the elder does not take care of himself or herself, is often linked to the very old and cognitively impaired older adults, whereas physical and emotional abuse is often carried out by perpetrators with problems.

- *Institutional abuse* occurs in nursing homes and other long-term care settings. The perpetrator can be a staff member or family or friend.

Source: Adapted from Sijuwade, P. O. (1995). Cross-cultural perspectives on elder abuse as a family dilemma. *Social Behavior and Personality, 23,* 247–252.

APPENDIX 6-B Premises of Schools of Thought Relevant to a Resilience Perspective

Psychodynamic

- The ego distinguishes reality.

- The ego identifies possible courses of action.

- Anxiety is an ever-present state of tension. *Reality anxiety* is a fear proportionate to a real-world threat.

- Defenses protect the individual. Denial is a defense mechanism used to avoid threatening aspects of reality.

- Helping professionals time their interventions so the client can return to a sense of competence, contributing to ego resilience.

Cognitive

- People's emotions are based on how they think about themselves.

- Most people have irrational conceptions about themselves and their situation.

- People can overcome irrational beliefs and self-defeating behavior.

- Practitioners foster cognitive processes that identify and challenge misconceptions.

- Helping strategies are primarily educational.

- The purpose of intervention is to assist the client in developing cognitive tools, fostering his or her sense of mastery and control.

Systems

- Systemic interventions focus on group membership.

- Family and community systems have the capacity to adapt to stress.

- Adaptability rests on a system's organizational and communication patterns.

- Belief systems influence the capacity to maintain continuity and accept change.

- Practitioners foster positive group organizational and communication patterns.

- Family members have the ability to transform and explore alternative solutions.

Ecological

- Stress occurs when people believe they have inadequate internal and external resources to meet environmental demands.

- When people perceive stress, they engage in a coping process.

- Stress can be reduced by improving the level of person-in-environment fit.

(Continued)

APPENDIX 6-B Premises of Schools of Thought Relevant to a Resilience Perspective (*Continued*)

Ecological

* Social systems also contribute to enhancing person-in-environment fit.

* The practitioner can help clients manage stressors by reinforcing each client's natural problem-solving skills, optimism, and resilience.

Constructionist

* This approach assumes that there are no universal truths or singular reality; rather, knowledge is created through interaction at the local level.

* Constructionists provide a safe environment in which individuals and families explore their own meaning of events.

* Reflective questions help clients construct and reconstruct their sense of self.

* Clients are asked to view themselves as "free" from a difficulty so that they may develop alternative understandings and solutions.

* Clients may choose not to accept negative attributions, such as racism or victimization.

* Language and culture are the vehicles for the exchange of ideas and meaning.

* By creating new meaning, individuals and communities can overcome life challenges.

Narrative

* People are proactive and self-organizing.

* People's behavior is shaped by the meaning they give to events.

* As people create meaning in interactions with others, they develop and reconstruct their life stories.

* A person's life story contains information about how he or she has met critical events. The story gives life coherence and continuity.

* If a story is problem saturated, the client can be helped to re-author it and discover alternative solutions.

* Practitioners aim to broaden the client's view of reality and find alternatives ways to overcome an impasse.

Source: From *Social work practice: A risk and resilience perspective* (with CD-ROM)) 1st ed. by Greene, R. R. (2007). Reprinted with permission of Wadsworth, a division of Thomson Learning: www.thomsonrights. com. Fax 800-730-2215.

APPENDIX 6-C Four Levels of Narratives

1. Personal Meanings

Narratives can reflect the personal and unique meaning of individuals' lives and, at the same time, individuals "create and discover the meaning of [their] stories within a fundamentally social or interpersonal context" [Kenyon & Randall, 2001, p. 8]. Older adults develop competence, assets, and resiliency from their earlier experiences of learning to negotiate discrimination and oppression.

Personal factors associated with resilience include working for a brighter future and hoping for a better world.

As Mr. August S. recounts:

> Back to the forces that enabled me to cope. . . . I was the first grandchild on either side of the family to be born, a very special place. My father's name was August, my name was August; I'm a junior. If I had any reason to feel guilt, it was because of that special place. I received unequivocal love. There was some rivalry between grandparents as to where I would visit. My grandmother on my maternal side was such a very strong force, so there was no such thing as her babies going anywhere else but her house. I had a sense of belongingness, that "somebodiness," that sense of being special among people of color, black people in particular. A sense of belongingness, this sense of unconditional love, served as a bulwark to oppressive conditions, discrimination, segregation.

2. Interpersonal Factors

Interpersonal factors associated with resilience encompass mentoring others, taking an activist stand, or having a significant person in one's life.

Miss Patricia J. recalls how important her aunt was to her:

> Since I have grown older and had a family and experienced the changes, I look back and I don't realize how my aunt was able to maintain a home like she did and to keep us together. There was no man in the household. She was already a widow. Her daughter was married and was expecting her first child, and she and the husband was no longer together, so there was just a household of women. My aunt only had a third-grade education, but she had so much wisdom. That's what it was. I say godly wisdom.

(Continued)

APPENDIX 6-C Four Levels of Narratives (*Continued*)

3. Sociocultural Factors

Sociocultual aspects of resilience involve learning from one's culture of origin and creating coalitions.

Mrs. Sara J. candidly reveals the times in which she lived:

> Then when we went to the square of town, other kids could go in and sit at the ice cream counter where the soda fountains were. They could go and sit and drink and eat there, but if we bought something we had to get it and take it in our hands and go on out with it to eat. We couldn't even sit on the stoop.

4. Structural Factors

Structural aspects of resilience include participating in civil rights movements and accessing education and health care.

The striving for structural equality is captured in the following comment by Mr. Robert A.:

> Well, he went to buy the land and they said, "Well, we are thinking about not selling it." They didn't want to sell it to a black, so later they said, "We will sell it to you for more money an acre."

Source: Levels are based on Kenyon, G. M., & Randall, W. (2001). Narrative gerontology: An overview. In G. Kenyon, P. Clark, & B. de Vries (Eds.), *Narrative gerontology* (p. 8). New York: Springer.

APPENDIX 6-D Engage, Assess, Intervene, and Evaluate Using Resilience-Enhancing Model Competencies

Engage

Students will

- develop self-awareness about using a risk and resilience approach to helping older adults function in their environments:

  - Do they believe that the self is adaptive and strives toward personal growth?

  - Do they believe resilience is innate?

  - Do they believe they can help clients through a solution-focused approach?

  - Can they operationalize a strengths perspective?

- prepare to meet with older adults by developing anticipatory empathy with particular attention to the applicant or client's culture, race, social class, gender, sexual orientation, stage of development, physical and mental functioning, and to the agency or departmental context

- understand the behavior of older adults as a dynamic process of person-in-environment exchanges over time

- prioritize the target systems, and assess and intervene with the target system.

Assess

Students will

- assess an older adult's risk and resilience factors associated with problems of daily living

- attend (differentially) to client's culture, race, social class, gender, sexual orientation, stage of development, and physical and mental functioning

- use empathy as they listen and respond to an older adult's individual stories

- assess the level of fit between an individual's, family's, and group's strengths and limitations and social and physical environmental resources and gaps

- conduct assessments of older adults to determine what promotes or deters their well-being (for example, assets, risks, threats, and opportunities)

- assess how biopsychosocial functioning over the life course has contributed to or been a deterrent to an older adult's current functional capacity

- critically analyze and select interventions for older adults and their families that are informed by data, clinical trials, and best practices associated with risk and resilience research

(Continued)

APPENDIX 6-D Engage, Assess, Intervene, and Evaluate Using Resilience-Enhancing Model Competencies (*Continued*)

- understand that systems are resilient in their own right and be able to assess the systemic, resilient properties of families, schools, communities, and society; the assessment will include the system's assets and challenges as obtained from system members.

Intervene

Students will

- select and apply client-centered intervention techniques that make meaning of critical life events and promote an older adult's resilience

- help individuals, families, and groups to deal with life transitions and traumatic events

- attempt to address functional limitations and redress social and economic inequities

- reflect and seek solutions with older adults (and their families) who are facing ethical decisions regarding the risks and resilient nature of living environments

- identify organizational obstacles to effective and efficient services delivery and make recommendations for change

- use system-level interventions derived from community data and input

- analyze regulations and policies to determine how they promote or deter older adults' well-being

- advocate for resilience-enhancing policies.

Evaluate

- mutually determine and use a termination plan that is sensitive to the diversity and context of the client system.

- use strategies to evaluate programs, services delivery systems, and impact of professional services provided for the client system.

Source: Adapted for REM by Greene (2007) from curriculum developed by Alex Gitterman, EdD, professor of social work, University of Connecticut School of Social Work, and Nancy Humphreys, PhD, professor and director of the Institute for the Advancement of Political Social Work Practice, University of Connecticut.

Group Work

Addressing Issues of Later Adulthood 7

RATIONALE: Foundation social work practice encompasses professional knowledge, values, and skills with systems of all sizes.

COMPETENCY: Students will be able to prepare, engage, assess, intervene, and evaluate their work with groups. They will

- establish rapport and maintain an effective working relationship with older adults and family members.
- utilize group interventions with older adults and their families (e.g., bereavement groups, reminiscence groups).
- adapt psychoeducational approaches to enhance older persons' coping capacities and mental health.
- use educational strategies to provide older persons and their families with information related to wellness and disease management (e.g., Alzheimer's disease, end-of-life care).
- assist caregivers to reduce stress levels and maintain their own mental and physical health.
- address respectfully the cultural, spiritual, and ethnic values and beliefs of older adults and families. (Council on Social Work Education, Gero-Ed Center, 2004)

Social workers often practice with clients in group settings. Indeed, the process of bringing individuals together in a group format has been a part of social work since the early days of the profession. As outlined in Zastrow's (2001) frequently used text on group processes, social group work took root during the early 1800s in the Young Men's Christian Association/Young Women's Christian Association, Boy and Girl

Scouts, and Jewish community centers. Programs delivered in group formats provided opportunities for education, social interaction, recreation, and collective social action. Group participation promoted the development of social skills, helped members create a social network, or provided an opportunity to work with others to change the social environment (for example, advocate for additional community resources).

One reason that groups are an effective intervention method is that a group is the basic social unit within our social structure. An infant's first group affiliation is his or her family as membership begins during the prenatal period. Even before a baby is born, she or he is part of a family by transmission of genetic material, being exposed to cultural family practices (for example, food the mother eats) and other factors that begin to shape the child physically and emotionally. Typically after birth, a baby joins a family social system (for example, birth family, adoptive or foster family). Although family social structures vary considerably, most have multiple members, including parents, grandparents, siblings, cousins, and other kinship relations. Throughout life, children make other social connections by establishing friendship groups; joining sports or activity groups (such as Boy Scouts, debate club, choir, or band); and perhaps even joining gangs. Into adulthood, people add to their group affiliations through other memberships at work (for example, being part of a managerial or treatment team), in civic life (for instance, by serving on a board of directors), or in family life (such as marrying into a partner's family group or participating in a group for parents of children with disabilities). As these examples illustrate, both naturally and purposefully formed group affiliations exist across the life course.

What is the difference, though, between membership in these various social groups and being part of a group as a social work intervention? Gisela Konopka (1983), one of the founders of group work, defined that form of practice as "a method of social work which helps individuals to enhance their social functioning through purposeful group experiences, and to cope more effectively with their personal, group or community problems" (p. 18).

Adding to that definition is Lowy (1982), a pioneer in advancing aging issues within social work, who said that group work is "one method of social work which places emphasis on maximizing group process so that the group may become the instrument in which and through which the participating members may benefit, their interpersonal relationships may improve, and the participants may collaborate improving conditions in their environment" (p. 22). The power of group interventions is evident in the description of group work offered by Corey and Corey (1997): "Groups provide a natural laboratory that demonstrates to people that they are not alone and that there is hope for creating a different life. . . . Groups are powerful because they allow participants to experience some of their long-term problems being played out in the group sessions with opportunities to do something different from what they have been doing" (p. 5).

The relationships and dynamics within the group are paramount in all of the aforementioned definitions. Although group work may occur in several contexts, such as in psychotherapy centers, long-term care facilities, or senior centers, or as an intervention for multiple issues, a commonality is using group members' experiences with each other as a foundation for change.

Group Process and Outcome

In groups that function well, individuals have the opportunity to share similar life experiences and explore their uniqueness in a secure and accepting atmosphere. The benefits from participating in groups (Toseland, 1995), including during later life, are many:

- feelings of belonging and affiliation—with age, social networks often decrease; group members can counter the loss of other social roles by participating in a group
- validation and affirmation—members appreciate that their experiences, thoughts, and feelings are shared by other group members who may face similar circumstances
- ventilation and integration—in a group setting, members can openly share experiences and emotions with age cohorts who may more objectively listen and reflect than can spouses, adult children, or other close family members
- satisfying and meaningful roles—older members can assume meaningful roles within groups (for example, a member who may take on the role as group leader) to allow them to demonstrate capacities and competence
- interpersonal learning—through group discussions and activities, members learn about themselves, their roles (for instance, as grandparents relating to grandchildren), and functioning (such as ways to change behaviors after learning about a health diagnosis)
- information—groups provide information about specific issues (for example, learning to live with hypertension) and serve as forums for lifelong and adult education programs (such as finances after retirement or creative writing)
- problem solving—group settings promote opportunities for problem solving by sharing challenges, experiences, and successes with others.

As Greene (2000) has indicated, group participation can potentially offer older adults an opportunity to facilitate continued personal growth, provide support through crises or difficult challenges, provide rehabilitation, and positively affect mental health.

Although group work is beneficial for older clients, practitioners must consider some unique aspects of group interventions with this population. As Burnside and Schmidt (1994) have pointed out, group work with older clients is more directive, less confrontational, and more supportive than with other age groups. Younger cohorts of the "therapy generation" may feel comfortable sharing personal information with others. However, because older adults have lived during social eras in which people valued privacy more highly, social workers may need to take a more active and direct role in fostering interaction and cohesion among group members (Toseland, 1995).

Social workers must also be mindful of the fact that age-related changes may affect the group experience for older adults. Practitioners may observe a degree of cognitive slowing or impairment that is exacerbated in a group format, sensory changes that affect sight and hearing, or altered functional ability to physically negotiate the environment so an older adult may attend group sessions (Toseland & Rizzo, 2004). Not only must group leaders be aware that the meeting room environment is vitally important to accommodating the physical changes of aging, but also they must consider the potential for reduced stamina among group members. Therefore, social workers should be sensitive to the length of a group session and, if possible, make light refreshments available.

Resilience-Enhancing Model Approach to Facilitating Groups of Older Adults

The resilience-enhancing model (REM) (Greene, 2007) for social work practitioners who work with older adults is an effective method for increasing resiliency in group interventions. The principles of REM, described in chapters 1 and 6, are organized into the skill development areas of engagement, assessment, intervention, and evaluation. From a group work perspective, the skills of engagement are those required to convene the group. They include developing a group structure, assessing environmental issues, and determining the type of leadership style that will best facilitate the particular intervention group, such as a social support, psychoeducational, or activity group. The competencies related to assessment include paying attention to relationship development and determining what influences multicultural issues have on group members. When applying REM in group practice with older adults, practitioners must be aware that interventions will vary by type of group. In their evaluations of group interventions, social workers will look not only at a group's progress toward goals but also at how effective group interventions are in fostering resilience, coping, and functioning among group members.

Assembling the Group

Because the environment sets the context for a group's process and dynamics, selection of a meeting place is critical. Practitioners must consider physical space: Where will the group meet? How will participants feel about that meeting space? Is it conducive for recruiting all potential members of the group, for example, or does it send a message that might inhibit involvement? Is the environment welcoming to all potential members? Other factors, adapted from Pritchard (2004), that social workers need to take into account when selecting a meeting room for older adults are

- Privacy: Is there a glass door or window into the room?
- Room size: Taking into account that personal space may be very important, and depending on the emotional content being discussed, is there enough

space? Consider the needs of members who may wish to speak privately about a topic with the group leader.

- Chairs: Is there room for people who might be in wheelchairs or who use some other type of assistive device? Are the chairs hard or soft? Do they have arms? What is the height? Are group members able to easily get up and sit down?
- Tables: Are adequate tables available on which to rest drinks or food? Are larger tables handy so members may work in pairs?
- Noise: How noisy is the heating or air conditioning unit? Listen to the traffic and noise from hallways to determine if they may be disruptive.
- Amenities: Is the meeting location along a mass transportation line? Is parking convenient? Are restrooms nearby? (p. 34)

The following example emphasizes how important it is for social workers to be sensitive to the feelings, views, and perceptions of potential members about the context for group meetings:

A local aging services provider sponsored a support group for caregivers. The agency advertised that the meeting was open to any caregiver within the community and that the group would meet in a hall located in a local church building. Despite the open invitation, some potential members perceived that the group was affiliated with that particular faith organization and thus felt uncomfortable participating in a church that was outside their own faith experience. Because the aging agency did not provide enough explanatory information or use more personal recruiting techniques, potential members were reticent to join the group.

A practical factor to consider when choosing an appropriate physical environment for a group meeting is transportation, a major issue for many aging individuals. Some people may no longer drive or may have driving restrictions, such as being unable to negotiate difficult traffic patterns (that is, driving on freeways or high-volume roads); unable to drive in poor weather conditions; or unable to drive after dark. Group facilitators need to investigate alternate transportation methods, including locating the meeting place on a public transportation route; securing transportation services for participants, for example, using a community agency van; or arranging for shared transportation among members.

Group workers must also address the particular challenges and functional issues that might prevent people from affiliating with a group. For example, a group leader might hold meetings during school hours for a group of grandparents who are raising grandchildren, or might select a space where child care is available on-site. A suitable meeting place for a support group for people with health impairments would be one that participants could easily and conveniently access, with parking close by, wheelchair ramps, and handicap-accessible restrooms.

In addition to environmental issues, social workers need to think about leadership within a group (Toseland & Rizzo, 2004). In certain types of groups, such as a psychoeducational one that offers a curriculum, the practitioner might retain a more formal leadership role. That is, the social worker could provide some of the content by deliver-ing lectures or structuring role playing or other activities. In other types of groups, such as support or mutual aid groups, participants should assume a greater proportion of leadership responsibility. In support groups, for example, the members who have had the most experience with a particular issue (for instance, have been caregivers for sev-eral years) might assume the role of a veteran member. Others who are just beginning their caregiving role would look to the veterans for information, assurance, or hope.

How leadership dynamics potentially unfold is a process social workers ought to consider before a group first meets. Leadership, like listening and empathizing skills, is a learned behavior (Kottler, 2001). If the social worker wishes to function as group leader (such as in a psychoeducational group), he or she needs to incorporate ways to share power, authority, and decision making with the group members. The social worker might, for instance, ask the group about how to structure various sessions, perhaps by using outside speakers, integrating readings, and the like. If part of the group process involves developing leadership within the group, the social worker should strategize about identifying potential leaders and encouraging members to assume leadership roles.

Practitioners will need to determine the group structure in the early stages of the group's development. Several aspects of group structure are related to the type of group offered (Corey & Corey, 1997). One aspect is the group's composition, including the heterogeneity or homogeneity of group members. In a caregiver support group, for example, social workers might ask themselves: Is it appropriate to restrict the group to addressing one form of caregiving, such as family members caring for older family members or grandparents caring for grandchildren?

Even within caregiver categories there are subpopulations that would benefit from a group that could focus specifically on its unique issues. McCallion and colleagues (2000) have described an intervention approach specifically designed for grandparents who are raising grandchildren with disabilities. Although these caregivers have similar experiences as other grandparents who are rearing grandchildren, they face other issues related to their grandchildren's disabilities, such as educational options, and services delivery networks involving developmental disabilities or mental health. This type of group illustrates that social workers need to consider carefully how broadly or narrowly they have to define membership composition.

Heterogeneity of members may be a desirable characteristic in some groups, how-ever. Cusicanqui and Salmon (2004) detailed the development of an intergenerational singing group that brought together residents of a senior living facility with children in the community. This activity group had the dual goals of helping the residents feel more integrated into their community and providing the children with an opportunity for interaction with older adults. The groups rehearsed separately but gathered together periodically to meet and sing. In addition, the groups performed a program together at the end of the school year. Although the older adults and the children could have easily established independent singing groups, the intergenerational aspect provided each age cohort with greater opportunities for social interactions.

Other aspects of group structure worthy of examination by social workers in the early stages of group development include

- optimal size for group: If the group is too large, limited interaction among members will occur. If it is too small any attrition will significantly affect the group's numbers.
- duration of group session: How long will each session last? Participants who have limited functional abilities may not have the stamina for lengthy sessions ranging from two to three hours. Sessions that are too short, though, will limit the content or conversation that may develop. Will there be a fixed number of sessions (for example, 10 total), or will the group be ongoing?
- membership structure: Groups tend to be open or closed. With open groups, members can join throughout the life of the group as other members leave. This structure allows for a more consistent level of membership; that is, if two people leave, the group leader can invite two people to join. In contrast, members of closed groups generally remain until the group finishes. A closed group allows for a different type of dynamic among the members because relationships can potentially develop in greater depth than in open groups.

Relationship Building

As group members begin to meet, the social worker needs to assess various dimensions and dynamics. Within some groups, such as those in long-term care facilities, the members hold pre-existing relationships. In other groups, where relationships are not established, it is hoped that trusting and positive relationships will form. Important to the development of relationships within groups is the social worker's assessment of the dynamics that emerge among the group members and the worker's awareness of multicultural characteristics within the group. As REM principles state, the assessment process should include an understanding of the older adults' risk situations, resilience, functioning across the life course, and factors that promote or inhibit well-being.

To begin this assessment process, the social worker may structure pregroup meetings with the individuals expected to participate in the group (Corey & Corey, 1997). During these sessions, the practitioner could provide information about the group and evaluate the optimal fit among group members. At this initial session, the social worker could also prepare each member for the group experience and address members' questions. He or she may query the members about their perceptions, expectations, and goals related to the group experience. Pregroup meetings might also help the practitioner begin to assess how members' personalities and experiences may combine to shape the "group personality" as the members begin to develop relationships.

During the assessment process, social workers will also need to determine how to integrate multicultural characteristics and experiences into the group dynamic. Experiences might be quite different for group members from diverse backgrounds, and thus may affect the participants' behavior. For example, the older cohort in the southeastern United States lived through the Jim Crow era, a period when black men who looked at white women were potentially in danger of losing their lives. Although most people typically regard eye contact as an indication of positive communication patterns, even today that action may hold a different meaning for some black men in relationship to some white American women. In the group context, the social worker needs to be aware and sensitive to this dynamic and interpret it within its cultural context.

In addition, practitioners must strive to understand the language used in a group within a multicultural context. The following examples illustrate how language can create feelings of exclusion, alienation, or marginalization:

- An end-of-the-year party is called the "Group Christmas Party" by some members. Consider the effect on members who are of other faiths or religious communities that do not celebrate Christmas.
- Use of heterosexist language within the group, such as discussing members' "husbands" or "wives." Consider the effect on a member who is gay, lesbian, or is in a committed nonmarried relationship—that is, the person is cohabitating.
- Discussing later life sources of income such as pensions, home equity, and investments accounts. Consider how individuals from lower socioeconomic strata feel about their own financial conditions.

Instead of integrating differences in an exclusionary way, social workers should seek opportunities to enhance members' experiences with one another by stressing inclusion. They ought to use language to encompass the breadth of and diversity among group members. For instance, instead of a "Christmas Party," the social worker could take the lead by reclassifying the event as the "Holiday" or "End-of-the-Year Party." Within the group, members might brainstorm about an appropriate theme, such as integrating experiences from the cultural and spiritual traditions represented within the group to create a new type of celebration.

In the exclusionary language example, the social worker should strive to use inclusive relationship language by, for instance, describing committed relationships as "husband, wives, partners, and significant others." Although a bit more cumbersome, that phrasing will likely have a positive outcome: People in committed, nonmarried relationships will feel included.

The income example illustrates how important it is for social workers to be sensitive to issues of socioeconomic status. Because of longer life expectancies, lower wage structures, and a more sporadic labor force pattern, older women have fewer economic resources than older men, especially in later life. Because economic vulnerability is real for many older adults, social workers must avoid framing later-life economic matters from a middle-income perspective.

Types of Groups

From a resilience perspective, interventions should help individuals deal with life transitions and events to promote optimal functioning and make meaning of their situation. Regardless of the type of group offered, social workers need to be well grounded in theoretical frameworks for working with older members (see chapter 2). This section highlights several types of groups commonly used with older adults and provides examples of the issues they address.

Support Groups

Social workers frequently use support groups to assist older clients with transitions and changes related to the aging process. A support group is "attentive to the emotional needs of the membership as they pertain to a particular life event or challenge" (Ruffin & Kaye, 2006, p. 532). This type of group characteristically includes a great deal of interaction between members, a shared sense that members are dealing with a life situation that is not well understood by others outside the group, and a high level of self-disclosure among the group's participants (Toseland, 1995). Practitioners who lead support groups work to facilitate an atmosphere of trust and openness and help establish interaction patterns that include all group members.

Caregiver support groups typically strive to help relieve caregiver stress. Care provision is a significant role: Nearly 40 percent of the U.S. population older than 55 years of age spends an average of 580 hours annually caring for a family member (Johnson & Schaner, 2005). In addition to the responsibilities of providing care, many individuals juggle work and other family responsibilities. An extensive literature indicates that support groups can assist caregivers with the tasks of caring for older family members (Kaasalainen, Craig, & Wells, 2000; McCallion & Toseland, 1995; Toseland, Rossiter, & Labrecque, 1989), raising grandchildren (Kolomer, McCallion, & Overendyer, 2003; Minkler & Roe, 1993), or caring for children with disabilities (Goodman, 2004; Kelly & Kropf, 1995; Mengel, Marcus, & Dunkle, 1996). Being among caregivers facing similar issues, sharing successes and frustrations of caregiving, and being affirmed in one's role are the therapeutic outcomes support groups offer individual caregivers.

Support groups also assist older adults during transitions and periods of change. For example, support groups might be available for older adults who are dealing with non-age-specific challenges such as addictions or domestic violence. Evidence indicates that older adults facing these particular challenges are more responsive and have positive experiences when participating in a group specifically for their age cohort (Blow, Walton, Chermack, Mudd, & Brower, 2000; Brandl, Hebert, Rozwadowski, & Spangler, 2003; Brownell & Heiser, 2006; Lemke & Moos, 2002; Wolf, 2001). Salient factors for older adults include the primacy of isolation, feelings of depression, and health or functional declines that are associated with the abuse. Victims of violence or people with addictions may feel accepted and more comfortable about discussing these and other related issues with a group of similarly aged peers.

The integration of technology into the structures of support groups is an exciting development. Because many older adults have transportation or mobility issues, support groups have begun to use computers or telephones to help establish membership. For example, one intergenerational support program brought together by computer consisted of a group of older adults ages 80 years to 86 years and school-aged children as pen pals (Marx, Cohen, Renaudat, Libin, & Thein, 2005). The program promoted exchanges between different age groups and provided a social outlet for each of those groups. When it began including face-to-face visits, 88 percent of the adult members rated the program favorably.

Because today's older adults likely did not use a computer until sometime during their adulthood, they may be more comfortable with the use of a telephone in a technologically based group. Although implementing a successful telephone program can be challenging (see Appendix 7-A), social workers can structure groups so that greater opportunity for access exists. The benefits of successful telephone support groups are many: They can assist older adults with disabilities to feel a greater sense of social support and a decreased sense of loneliness, plus they can help strengthen older adults' coping skills (Stewart et al., 2001); they can provide caregivers with support, help them improve their problem-solving skills, and reinforce their coping skills (Smith, Toseland, Rizzo, & Zinoman, 2004); and they can assist the participants in managing health-related issues and provide disease-specific knowledge for older men and women with HIV or AIDS (Nokes, Chew, & Altman, 2003).

The following example highlights some positive outcomes of participation in a support group. After serving as a care provider for her husband, YA was widowed. As a result of her experience in a bereavement group, the social support available to her increased, she learned more about the normal process of grief and loss, and she was able to provide encouragement to others.

> After the death of her husband of 42 years, YA felt like a part of her own body was missing. During the past four years, she had been the primary caregiver for her husband, Ira, as he battled cancer and emphysema. Because he had received his diagnoses shortly after they had moved from their home in the northeast to Florida, there was little time to make new friends and become integrated into their new community. Now with all of her family still living in the northeast, YA was confused about whether she should stay in Florida or move back closer to her children.
>
> The hospice social worker encouraged YA to join a support group to help her deal with grief and bereavement issues, as well as to connect with others who have gone through similar experiences. A group offered through a local hospital was specifically for older adults who had undergone the loss of a spouse. Although reluctant initially, YA regularly attended the group. She was amazed at how helpful it was to hear other members' experiences and to be able to share her stories about "her Ira." Many of the

widows and widowers had also been in long-term marriages and were experiencing very similar adjustment issues. The social worker who led the group normalized YA's grief reactions—such as when she experienced hearing Ira's voice or would break into tears at unexpected moments.

Now YA says she no longer feels "like I'm going crazy," and others shared their own experiences about the grief process. Most important, YA reported that she feels she has found a place where she can hold on to the memories of her husband, share the laughter and the tears of her experience, and offer others in the group support and caring during their time of loss. Through her involvement in the group, YA has discerned that she does not want to permanently move back north and has discovered she has additional support in her community.

Mutual Aid and Empowerment Groups

Mutual aid and empowerment groups are discussed together because they share some similar characteristics; for example, both emphasize the shared use of skills, knowledge, and talents of the group members. In a group context, the terms *self-help* and *mutual aid,* often used synonymously, underline the reciprocal assistance provided among the members (Gottlieb, 2000). Mutual aid groups can be especially transforming for older adults because they are "an important substitute for lost social support, provide a vehicle for coping with a [sometimes] devastating life transition, restore diminished self-concept, prompt life review, and maximize strengths while promoting health and mental health" (Kelly, 2004, p. 114).

An empowerment group stresses the collaboration and shared resources that individuals bring to the group, and highlights the fit between individuals and their environments. Cox and Parsons (1996) have described the philosophy of empowerment as "emphasiz[ing] the importance of collaborative problem definition and decision-making, collective action, client strengths, education, *mutual aid and self-help activities,* and resource access" [italics added] (p. 130). Within this conceptualization, the mutual assistance provided among group members promotes empowerment because it leads to an increase in participants' experiences of social action and collaborative change.

Like support groups, mutual aid and empowerment groups appear across a broad spectrum of issues. For example, a health diagnosis may precipitate several behavioral or lifestyle changes influencing an older adult and his or her family. Diabetes, for instance, affects approximately 21 percent of the population older than 60 years of age, with even higher percentages for African and Hispanic Americans (American Diabetes Association, 2006). Because diabetes results in changes to a person's diet and eating habits, the older adult must comply strictly with medical instructions or face serious negative outcomes. Involvement with other group members who are dealing with a similar issue can be beneficial, according to DeCoster and George (2005), who studied a mutual group for older adults with diabetes. Group participants reported improvement in checking blood-sugar rates, maintaining their diets, and exercising regularly, among other positive outcomes.

Mutual aid groups also may assist with emotional issues involved in end-of-life care. Goelitz (2004) described how the ending of a time-limited group for caregivers of terminally ill family members provided a normative pathway into the more difficult topics of death, loss, and grief. As they discussed the upcoming ending of the group, care providers achieved greater insight into members' feelings about the impending death of a family member. Through extended discussions, they arrived at ways to commemorate the collective meaning of the group. In that way, each group member shared his or her own story, which was woven into a mosaic of shared experiences and emotions about their lives and losses.

The following example of an empowerment group demonstrates how the members provided each other with emotional, instrumental, and tangible support. The group, which consisted of 10 grandmothers who were raising their grandchildren, also focused on how members could work to change the social environment.

> The grandparent group, called the "Grand Group," met monthly at a local social services agency in a small city. Typically, the all-women group started a session—the beginning time—by singing a hymn, saying a prayer, or reading a devotional passage. Group members decided which one to do; spirituality was often a theme discussed within the group. The agency supplied coffee and the grandmothers shared the responsibility of bringing in additional light refreshments.
>
> During the beginning time, the members checked in with each other to find out what had happened in their lives and families since the previous meeting.
>
> The Grand Group had been meeting for about two years and had an open membership structure so grandmothers could join and leave over time. An ongoing goal of the group was to assist the grandmothers to feel a greater sense of empowerment as caregivers and community members. Through sharing their stories, they made several decisions whose implementation was of benefit to them and their families and that affected changes within their communities. Those decisions included
>
> - holding a celebration at the end of each school year so their grandchildren could interact with others who had similar family structures
> - developing a clothes co-op, which involved grandparents' bringing in outgrown clothes from their grandchildren to share with each other
> - inviting a local elected official to one of their group meetings to hear stories of his (or her) life and to discuss family support issues
> - undertaking fund-raising activities to attend the GrandRally in Washington, DC, a biennial event to influence lawmakers. (see http://www.grandrally.org)

The social work group facilitator assumed an active role in helping the group move from "storying" to "social action." She encouraged the Grand Group members to share their resources in an action-oriented approach and offered suggestions for doing so. Because of those and similar initiatives, the group members reported a greater sense of agency within their families and communities.

Psychoeducational Groups

Psychoeducational groups function as both emotional and informational support systems for members. They combine educational and psychosocial processes within an intervention to enhance knowledge or skill attainment (Schneider & Cook, 2005). Typically, this type of group has a greater degree of structure than a support group and may follow a specific curriculum. Because of issues people experience in later life, psychoeducational groups can be important interventions to enhance functioning.

Psychoeducational groups are often framed within the context of a particular theoretical perspective (see chapter 2) that is integrated into the group content and process. Hébert and colleagues (2003) described a psychoeducational group for caregivers of people with dementia that was based on the stress and coping model (Folkman et al., 1991; Lazarus & Folkman, 1984). In that theoretical perspective, a stressor is conceptualized as either a modifiable or nonmodifiable behavior or event. The group intervention began with group members' identification of those caregiving aspects that they found stressful; the members proceeded to determine if the particular aspects were modifiable or nonmodifiable. The objective of the second part of the intervention was to help care providers learn adaptive coping mechanisms. For modifiable events, the caregivers built solution-focused coping strategies and more emotion-focused coping (for example, reframing) for events they could not modify. Each group session was two hours long and the group ran for 15 weeks.

During the initial four meetings, caregivers examined their stressors, and their understandings shifted from global to specific stressors. In this particular example, a caregiver might have started the group by stating, "I always feel stressed," but later shifted to identifying specific stressful events related to caring for her mother. Specific stressful experiences might have been as follows: "I feel most stressed when my mother and my children require my attention at the same time" or "I feel stressed when my mother asks me the same question several times in a row." In the remaining sessions of the group, the caregivers determined which stressors were modifiable—one could be feeling simultaneously overwhelmed by one's children and the care recipient.

Through problem-focused solution coping, members worked collectively to entertain possible strategies to relieve their stress. For example, the caregiver who felt stressed juggling responsibilities involved in caring for both her mother and her children may have decided to put out cereal so the children could fix their own breakfast while the caregiver attended to her mother. In a nonmodifiable situation—for instance, when the older care recipient repeated the same question to her daughter—the social work group facilitator and other group members could help the caregiver rethink her responses. The group might help the caregiver reframe the annoying situation of repeated questioning by reminding her that her mother's behavior is not malicious but is the result of a disease process in the brain; by giving the caregiver permission to provide the same answer to her mother each time; and by helping the care provider seek support from other family members who might provide a respite from that behavior. This particular psychoeducational caregiver group helped participants learn new ways of understanding and handling the multiple and stressful experiences of caregiving for someone with dementia.

A contrasting example of a psychoeducational group for caregivers of people with dementia is the "Memory Club," which followed a structured curriculum (Zarit, Femia, Watson, Rice-Oeschger, & Kakos, 2004; see Appendix 7-B). The group was an intervention for individuals with early-stage dementia and their care partners. The group ran for 10 sessions and included eight to 10 caregiving dyads. Each session covered a topic related to dementia care provision, and the facilitator sought to develop cohesion among the members. In their evaluations of the Memory Club, members indicated they had found the group helpful in learning more about dementia, developing coping strategies to deal with the disease, and building social support.

Psychoeducational interventions can assist older adults and their care providers to enhance their functional status, as illustrated in the following example. In addition, this type of group may have a wellness and preventative focus, as revealed in the story about GB, who enrolled in a cardiac wellness group after a checkup with his doctor:

> GB is a 62-year-old male who is in overall good health. Although he has had no heart problems, his father and brother died of heart-related conditions when they were both in their fifties. After his last exam, GB continued to be bothered by fears and worries about his health even though his doctor found no major medical problems. Through a story in the newspaper, GB learned about a psychoeducational group called "Me and My Heart" offered through the local chapter of the American Heart Association. He decided to join the two-month-long program. Although it was not promoted as a program for older adults, GB was relieved to learn that most of the participants were in his age range. Just this aspect of participation helped normalize his feelings about wanting to learn more about his health, and take care of himself in the best way possible.
>
> During the first meeting, GB learned more about the heart and how it functions. In discussions with other members, he also felt validated because several other people were attending because of familial heart conditions. He learned basic information about cardiac issues, but he also felt "normalized" in his desire to take better care of his cardiac functioning (see chapter 6). In addition, the facilitators discussed various reasons older adults are at risk of cardiac conditions. A large part of the session was being proactive in taking care of oneself prior to the onset of cardiac problems.
>
> The group covered several topics in subsequent sessions: cardiac risk factors, including hereditary and lifestyle ones; a "heart-healthy" diet; the positive impacts of exercise; sexuality and cardiac functioning; ways to handle stress; and basic cardiopulmonary resuscitation techniques. Each session included delivery of content, through a lecture, film, or panel presentation, and an activity or discussion. After the eight-week course, GB reported that he learned information about his health and was able to clear up some of his questions with health care professionals who were guest speakers. In addition, he said that he learned some techniques to take better nutritional care of himself as well as deal with stressful situations in his life.

Activity Groups

Toseland (1995) has described activity groups as "social, recreational, and educational groups [to] provide members with an opportunity to become actively engaged with peers in activities that enhance enjoyment" (p. 184). From a resilience perspective, the opportunity for older adults to have satisfying social relationships, continue to learn and discover new ideas and skills, and remain actively involved in their communities are important components in preventing several physical, social, and emotional problems in later life.

This type of group is highly structured and typically is organized around a program or activity. The social worker involved with the group may assume a large portion of planning, such as dealing with logistics (getting transportation set up for an outing and the like); making contingency plans (for example, how to handle an outdoor activity if it rains); and addressing cost issues (for instance, paying for activities).

Such behind-the-scenes work may not feel like "real" social work practice, yet the outcome for the group is often quite powerful and reaches far beyond the completed project or program (Wright, 2002). Activity groups appeal to a variety of older adults, and topics of interest to them vary but may include exercise, music, games, health and legal issues, aging or memory problems, and movies (Cohen, Parpura, Campbell, Vass, & Rosenberg, 2005). A number of agencies or organizations may host activity groups: senior centers, faith-based organizations, senior living facilities, and others. Quite often, a social worker does not administer the activity or program; rather, someone with particular expertise in a topical area undertakes that effort.

Exercise programs provide positive health outcomes for older adults and an opportunity for social connection. In a randomized controlled trial, community-based seniors who were at risk of falling engaged in group exercise (Barnett, Smith, Lord, Williams, & Baumand, 2003). For one year, the treatment group attended a weekly exercise program to improve individual strength and balance. At the end of the intervention, participants in the activity group had 40 percent fewer falls and demonstrated better balance than those who did not participate in the activity group.

Social workers can structure activity groups so that they preserve functioning, even in situations in which members have significant impairments. In long-term-care settings, for example, residents can participate in structured activities that could help them preserve their cognitive functioning and enhance their integration and engagement with others. Offering activity groups to people with cognitive impairments requires additional considerations, however (Griffin, 2005). The group facilitator needs to keep the group size small, with fewer than eight members; steer away from activities that promote winning or losing; discourage interruptions by staff or others during the activity; be sensitive to participants' physical and cognitive capabilities; have enough staff assistance to help deliver the program; and distract or remove participants who disrupt the group.

Activity groups offer a way to integrate learning, socialization, and enjoyment. In addition, such groups may capitalize on the strengths and resources found in the community. The following is an example of a program on a university campus:

The Life-Long Learning Group (the "Triple Ls") was a lively bunch of senior adults who lived in a small university town. A social worker led the group, and the group elected an executive board that decided which programs and activities would be undertaken. Often, interesting topics emerged from events that were happening within the community. During the previous year, the university baseball team had a strong season and went to the college world series. That event sparked a great deal of interest among the group members.

During the following spring, the executive board capitalized on the group's excitement about baseball. The Triple Ls organized a program for learning about the sport and supporting the university's team. During one session, a history professor with expertise in sports gave a lecture on the history of baseball. At another session, a physical education professor talked about the strategy of the game. The third week, the group went on a behind–the-scenes tour of the dugout and field, and met the coaches and players. During the final week of the program, the group attended a baseball game.

The group members enjoyed the program. It struck the right balance of learning, enjoyment, and socialization. Because the university was a focal point of the town, the program provided an avenue for older adults in the community to feel connected to campus life.

Life Review and Reminiscence

For the most part, people like to tell stories about their past. It is natural to recall the "good old days" at high-school reunions, on birthdays or anniversaries, or during retirement parties. Chapter 6 discussed life review in relation to the psychosocial tasks of later life. Within Erikson's (1959/1980) theory of human development, older adulthood involves the psychosocial stage of integrity versus despair; that stage focuses on the integration of life stories and experiences from the past into a current understanding of self. From a narrative gerontological perspective, those life stories go beyond synthesizing parts of people's own narratives to situating them in the community of others. As Randall (1995) has put it,

Not only might we be *a* story, . . . but we might be *many* stories as well—of many kinds, on many levels, with many subplots and versions. Also, given [an] emphasis on the stories that *we* are, it points beyond the individual dimension of our existence to the communal one. It reminds us that, in the end, none of us is an island whose saga can be separated from the story of a particular family, from the stories of colleagues and friends, from the countless larger stories of which our world is constructed or indeed from history as a whole." [emphasis added] (p. 10)

As part of the life review, we share and blend our past with our present and future, and blend our narratives with those around us. From Randall's perspective, using review and reminiscence in a group format also blends life histories into a more collective whole.

Life review can be a positive part of group experiences for older adults. It involves reminiscence, yet is a professionally facilitated intervention that aims to reduce group members' unfinished issues, affirm their histories, and ultimately achieve integration (Molinari, 2002). To determine which participants might benefit best from this type of intervention, social workers need to assess group members for their level of motivation, ego functioning, and personality variables, such as openness to entertaining difference and change. In general, though, participation in reminiscence groups aids older adults.

Indeed, the incorporation of reminiscing and reflecting can assist older group members to recount positive accomplishments throughout their lives and their current ability to function despite losses and functional changes (Toseland & Rizzo, 2004). Consider the example of a group therapy that focused on depression in older women: Participants were individuals who live in subsidized housing units (Husaini et al., 2004). The group intervention incorporated reminiscence to reintroduce earlier life memories and experiences. Each group session concluded with a reminiscence theme, such as a favorite holiday or memories of early childhood or young adulthood. The social work facilitator structured some of the sessions around retaining and reliving the positive memories, but some sessions allowed participants to share and process earlier life pain, grief, or regret.

Social work group facilitators may also structure the sharing of life stories around important cohorts or periods. They might use relevant events as a way to examine self-histories within a group format. In the following example, a social work intern led a reminiscence group to engage male participants at a senior center:

> LM, a second-year intern in a master of social work program, was completing her practicum at a senior center. One of the internship goals was to deliver culturally and gender-sensitive interventions with her client population. With her supervisor and field liaison, she observed that male participants were less integrated into the center's programs. Because so many more women participated, men had few activities or programs that seemed to attract their interest. LM set this as her goal: offering an intervention with particular relevance to male participants.
>
> During LM's practicum, the center was completing a history of its new building, an old railway station. This subject seemed to spark an interest in the men at the center. They sat in clusters and talked about the old train station, thus giving LM an idea for a reminiscence group.
>
> LM did her homework about the station's history and implemented a group that centered on that subject. For two months, the men came together to reminisce about various related issues. Some of the topics elicited deep emotion, such as the men's stories of themselves as young soldiers who were leaving on the train to go to war. During one very emotional session, an black American man related his experience waiting in the "colored section" of the station, which prompted members to launch into a discussion about living in the segregated south.

Some lighter sessions included stories about playing with toy train sets with their fathers and grandfathers, and the brotherhood of fixing machinery. Although LM could not always add knowledge to the content (she reported that she was not mechanically inclined), she helped illuminate the themes of history, community, and relationships that the men shared. In the end, some of their stories were included in the monograph of the center's history.

Group Effectiveness

Although evaluation often refers to the outcome of a group, different types of evaluation may occur throughout a group's life. Social workers conduct a *formative,* or *process, evaluation* when a group is ongoing. Zastrow (2001) defined another type as the *group process evaluation,* which is "an assessment, generally by group members, of the aspects of the group that were useful or detrimental. Feedback about techniques and incidents that blocked or enhanced process is of immense value to the group leader" (p. 533). Based on the information derived from such evaluations, social workers can decide which techniques or processes will be most helpful to the members, refine their group work skills, and learn about group dynamics through members' perceptions.

Group facilitators may integrate process evaluations into a group in various ways. Certain sessions devote some time to member check-ins, in which participants share their impressions of the group. During the discussion time, members discuss their experiences in the group and identify both helpful and problematic aspects. A different strategy is a *peer evaluation,* in which one peer or more (typically other than the group leader) provides an evaluation. Sometimes the peer evaluates the group through a one-way mirror or by participating in a group session. A similar strategy involves audiotaping or videotaping part of a session, followed by a review of the tapes by someone with expertise in running groups. Of course, the social worker would need to inform participants that nonmembers would be viewing the group process and then request their consent to the use of this strategy.

Practitioners may also use quantitative measures in the formative evaluation process. An example is the Groupwork Engagement Measure (GEMS), a 37-item measure of engagement across multiple dimensions (Macgowan, 1997, 2003). Macgowan developed GEMS based on the social work literature on groups and designed the instrument for closed membership groups. The social worker administers GEMS after the third or fourth session. Macgowan's (2003) particular measurement strategy determines members' participation and integration across the following seven dimensions:

1. attending—"member arrives at or before start time"
2. contributing—"member contributes his or her share of talk time"
3. relating to worker—"member supports work that the worker is doing with other members"
4. relating to other members—"member helps other group members to maintain good relationships with others"

5. contracting—"member expresses continued disapproval about what the group members are doing together"
6. working on own issues—"member makes an effort to achieve his or her particular goals"
7. working on others' issues—"member talks with others in ways that help them focus on their issues" (p. 7).

Each group member receives an overall score and subscores on various dimensions. Using the data, the social worker can determine strategies to increase participants' engagement in very individualized ways.

At the end of the group, the social worker performs a *summative,* or *outcome, evaluation,* which typically answers this question: Did the group have a positive effect on group members' functioning? Or, did the group achieved anticipated outcomes such as reducing depression, increasing coping, increasing social support, and decreasing isolation? Cummings and Kropf (in press) have compiled evidenced-based treatments for older adults, including groups that deal with health, mental health, and cognitive status and social role functioning. Appendix 7-C describes effective group interventions with older adults in these three functional domains.

Group evaluation could comprise several designs ranging from a single subject ($N = 1$) to a random clinical trial. In single-subject designs, the group worker compares the baseline scores for each member of the group to scores at various points throughout and after the intervention. In the example of YA, the worker would hypothesize that grief and depression scores would decrease as a result of YA's participation in the support group. Another research design would involve comparing the aggregate score of a group participating in a group intervention with that of a group of nonparticipators, such as people on the waiting list. The hypothesis would be that group participants would have significantly better scores than the control group. With GB, for example, the group that participated in the "Me and My Heart" group would have significantly higher scores on cardiac health information test than a waiting group who had not yet participated.

The gold standard of research is the randomized clinical trial; however, the costs and level of control needed may prohibit a social worker from implementing such a research design within social services programs. In clinical trials, the researcher randomly assigns participants to two or more groups; one of which receives a particular group intervention. (In the section *Activity Groups,* the community-based exercise program described is a randomized clinic trial.) The random assignment provides a way to distribute differences among individuals to the groups before the intervention. Thus researchers have higher confidence that any differences after group treatment are a result of the group experience rather than because of other rival hypotheses (for example, differences in the two groups before intervention accounted for the differences). When reviewing evaluation studies about groups, social work group workers should keep in mind that randomized control designs, when available, typically provide the strongest outcome evidence.

From Roots to Future—Importance of Group Work

Group work clearly has been an enduring method of social work intervention throughout the history of professional practice. The method is particularly relevant in contemporary practice with older adults facing issues of later adulthood. Group work gives social workers an approach to increase older adults' social support, provide them with information and skill enhancement, offer members opportunities for new learning and shared enjoyment with peers, and introduce ways in which group participants may share resources and wisdom. For these and other reasons, many practitioners who work with older adults will facilitate one or more of the types of groups discussed in this chapter.

Although group work is a method of intervention that has been part of professional practice from our beginnings, it continues to hold promise for current and future generations of older adults. The relationships between group members are powerful, and provide curative and therapeutic qualities from the interactions. With age, individuals may have limited opportunity to enhance social networks through naturally occurring means (for example, the workplace, clubs). Group membership provides a method to be in relationship with others who have similar interests, needs, or experiences.

Conclusion

This chapter has presented an array of various types of groups that have particular utility with the older population. To learn about effective group strategies to promote physical, emotional, and social functioning of older adults, content was presented to help beginning practitioners prepare to launch a group, recruit members, and structure group formats to deal with germane issues (for example, bereavement, transitions, staying connected). In addition, a number of group structures was presented: support, mutual aid and empowerment, psychoeducational, activity, and reminiscence groups. For each one, examples were provided to illustrate how various groups would run and the type of activities or content that would be included.

It is critical for the next generation of social workers to have skills in working with groups of older adults. Even nontraditional settings (for example, schools, prisons) are being transformed by the population explosion of older adults. Clearly, our roots in group work are deep and will continue to have a hold on our profession.

Suggested Exercises to Evaluate Student Competence

Activity 1. Students will demonstrate their ability to develop a plan for leading a group in a nursing home. The plan will address

- Physical Space: Where will the group meet? How will participants feel about that meeting space? Is the locale conducive to recruiting potential members of the group? For example, does it send a message that might inhibit involvement, or is the environment welcoming to potential members?

* Optimal Size: Is the group too large or too small? Why?
* Length of the Session: How long will each session last? Will there be a fixed number of sessions or will the group be ongoing?
* Membership Structure: Will the group be open or closed?

Activity 2. Students will demonstrate their ability to work in small groups. Students will divide into small groups, and then each group will select a subpopulation of older adults that it believes will benefit from participation in a group experience. This group can be based upon life experiences that are shared (such as older gays or lesbians, Holocaust survivors, or older Korean Americans) or particular problems or challenges that are encountered (for example, older alcoholics, recently diagnosed diabetics, black American caregivers).

After selecting the subpopulation, address the following issues to determine how the group experience can be beneficial. Address the following questions:

* What type of group would be most beneficial for the population you selected? Why did you select this type of group?
* What type of setting (for example, hospital, senior center, gay or lesbian center) would you use for this group? Why do you think this setting would be most conducive to formation of the group?
* How would you recruit for this type of group? What might be some recruitment challenges?
* How would you structure the group?
* What are some of the goals the group can accomplish?
* How would you evaluate the success of the group?

References

American Diabetes Association. (2006). *Total prevalence of diabetes and pre-diabetes.* Retrieved June 10, 2006, from http://www.diabetes.org/diabetes-statistics/prevalence.jsp

Barnett, A., Smith, B., Lord, S. R., Williams, M., & Baumand, A. (2003). Community-based Group exercise improves balance and reduces falls in at-risk older people: A randomized controlled trial. *Age and Aging, 32,* 407–414.

Blow, F. C., Walton, M. A., Chermack, S. T., Mudd, S. A., & Brower, K. J. (2000). Older adult treatment outcome following elder-specific inpatient alcoholism treatment. *Journal of Substance Abuse Treatment, 19,* 67–75.

Brandl, B., Hebert, M., Rozwadowski, J., & Spangler, D. (2003). Feeling safe, feeling strong: Support groups for older abused women. *Violence Against Women, 9,* 1490–1503.

Brownell, P., & Heiser, D. (2006). Psycho-educational support groups for older women victims of family mistreatment: A pilot study. *Journal of Gerontological Social Work, 46*(3/4), 145–160.

Burnside, I., & Schmidt, M. G. (1994). *Working with older adults: Group process and techniques* (3rd ed.). Boston: Jones and Bartlett.

Cohen, J. F., Parpura, G. A., Campbell, K. M., Vass, J., & Rosenberg, F. R. (2005). Elderly persons' preferences for topics of discussion and shared interest groups. *Journal of Gerontological Social Work, 44*(3/4), 39–57.

Corey, M. S., & Corey, G. (1997). *Groups: Process and practice* (5th ed.). Pacific Grove, CA: Brooks/Cole.

Council on Social Work Education, Gero-Ed Center. (2004). *Foundation gerontological social work competencies.* Retrieved November 16, 2006, from http://depts. washington.edu/geroctr/Curriculum3/ Competencies/FdnComp.doc

Cox, E. O., & Parsons, R. R. (1996). Empowerment-oriented social work practice: Impact on late life relationships of women. *Journal of Women and Aging, 8*(3/4), 129–143.

Cummings, S. M., & Kropf, N. P. (Eds.). (in press). *Evidenced-based psychosocial treatments for older adults.* New York: Haworth Press.

Cusicanqui, M., & Salmon, R. (2004). Seniors, small fry, and song: A group work libretto of an intergenerational singing group. *Journal of Gerontological Social Work, 44*(1/2), 189–210.

DeCoster, V. A., & George, L. (2005). Empowerment approach for elders living with diabetes: A pilot study of a community-based self-help group—the Diabetes Club. *Educational Gerontology, 31,* 699–713.

Erikson, E. H. (1980). *Identity and the life cycle.* New York: W. W. Norton. (Original work published 1959)

Folkman, S., Cheney, M., McKusick, L., Ironson, G., Johnson, D. S., & Coates, T. J. (1991). Translating coping theory into an intervention. In J. Eckenrode (Ed.), *The social context of coping* (pp. 239–260). New York: Plenum Press.

Goelitz, A. (2004). Using the end of groups as an intervention at end-of-life. *Journal of Gerontological Social Work, 44*(1/2), 211–221.

Goodman, H. (2004). Elderly parents of adults with severe mental illness: Group work interventions. *Journal of Gerontological Social Work, 44*(1/2), 173–188.

Gottlieb, B. H. (2000). Self-help, mutual aid, and support groups among older adults. *Canadian Journal on Aging, 19,* 58–74.

Greene, R. R. (2000). *Social work with the aged and their families* (2nd ed.). New York: Aldine de Gruyter.

Greene, R. R. (2007). *Social work practice: A risk and resilience perspective.* Belmont, CA: Thompson Brooks/Cole.

Griffin, L. (2005). Friendship Club and the Chaplain's Lunch: Small-group activities for low functioning individuals. *Activities Directors' Quarterly for Alzheimer's and Other Dementia Patients, 6*(3), 4–8.

Hébert, R., Lévesque, L., Vézina, J., Lavoie, J. P., Ducharme, F., Gendron, C., Préville, M., Voyer, L., & Dubois, M. F. (2003). Efficacy of a psychoeducative group program for caregivers of demented persons living at home: A randomized controlled trial. *Journals of Gerontology: Social Sciences, 58B*(1), S58–S67.

Husaini, B., Cummings, S., Kilbourne, B., Roback, H., Sherkat, D., Levine, R., & Cain, V. A. (2004). Group therapy for depressed elderly women. *International Journal of Group Psychotherapy, 54,* 295–319.

Johnson, R. W., & Schaner, S. G. (2005). Many older Americans engage in caregiving activities. In *Perspectives on productive aging* (Brief No. 3). Retrieved June 20, 2006, from http://www.urban.org/publications/311203.html

Kaasalainen, S., Craig, D., & Wells, D. (2000). Impact of the caring for aging relatives group program: An evaluation. *Public Health Nursing, 17,* 169–177.

Kaslyn, M. (1999). Telephone group work: Challenges for practice. *Social Work with Groups, 21,* 68–75.

Kelly, T. B. (2004). Mutual aid groups for older persons with a mental illness. *Journal of Gerontological Social Work, 44*(1/2), 111–126.

Kelly, T. B., & Kropf, N. P. (1995). Stigmatized and perpetual parents: Older parents caring for adult children with life-long disabilities. *Journal of Gerontological Social Work, 24*(1/2), 3–16.

Kolomer, S., McCallion, P., & Overendyer, J. (2003). Why support groups help: Successful interventions for grandparent caregivers. In B. Hayslip & J. H. Patrick (Eds.), *Working with custodial grandparents* (pp. 111–126). New York: Springer.

Konopka, G. (1983). *Social group work: A helping process* (3rd ed.). Englewood Cliffs, NJ: Prentice Hall.

Kottler, J. A. (2001). *Learning group leadership: An experiential approach.* Needham Heights, MA: Allyn & Bacon.

Lazarus, R., & Folkman, S. (1984). *Stress, appraisal, and coping.* New York: Springer.

Lemke, S., & Moos, R. H. (2002). Prognosis of older patients in mixed-age alcoholism treatment programs. *Journal of Substance Abuse Treatment, 22,* 33–43.

Lowy, L. (1982). Social group work with vulnerable older persons: A theoretical perspective. *Social Work with Groups, 5,* 21–32.

Macgowan, M. (1997). A measure of engagement for social group work: The group-work engagement measure. *Journal of Social Service Research, 23,* 17–37.

Macgowan, M. (2003). Increasing engagement in groups: A measurement-based approach. *Social Work with Groups, 26,* 5–28.

Marx, M., Cohen, M. J., Renaudat, K., Libin, A., & Thein, K. (2005). Technology-mediated versus face to-face intergenerational programming. *Journal of Intergenerational Relationships, 3,* 101–118.

McCallion, P., Janicki, M. P., Grant-Griffin, L., & Kolomer, S. (2000). Grandparent caregivers II: Service needs and service provision issues. *Journal of Gerontological Social Work, 3*(3), 57–84.

McCallion, P., & Toseland, R. (1995). Supportive group interventions with caregivers of frail older adults. *Social Work with Groups, 18,* 11–25.

Mengel, M. H., Marcus, D., & Dunkle, R. E. (1996). "What will happen to my child when I'm gone?" A support and education group for aging parents as caregivers. *Gerontologist, 36,* 816–820.

Minkler, M., & Roe, K. M. (1993). *Grandmothers as caregivers: Raising children of the crack cocaine epidemic.* Newbury Park, CA: Sage Publications.

Molinari, V. (2002). Group therapy in long term care sites. *Clinical Gerontologist, 25*(1/2), 13–24.

Nokes, K. M., Chew, L., & Altman, C. (2003). Using a telephone support group for HIV-positive persons aged 50+ to increase social support and health-related knowledge. *AIDS Patient Care and STDs, 17,* 345–351.

Pritchard, J. (2004). *Support groups for older people who have been abused.* London: Jessica Kinsley Publishers.

Randall, W. L. (1995). *The stories that we are: An essay on self-creation.* Toronto: University of Toronto Press.

Ruffin, L., & Kaye, L. W. (2006). Counseling services and support groups. In B. Berkman (Ed.), *Handbook of social work in health and aging* (pp. 529–538). New York: Oxford University Press.

Schneider, J. K., & Cook, J. H. (2005). Planning psychoeducational groups for older adults. *Journal of Gerontological Nursing, 31,* 33–38.

Smith, T. L., Toseland, R. W., Rizzo, V. M., & Zinoman, M. A. (2004). Telephone caregiver support groups. *Journal of Gerontological Social Work, 44*(1/2), 151–172.

Stewart, M., Mann, K., Jackson, S., Down-Wamboldt, B., Bayers, L., Slater, M., & Turner, L. (2001). Telephone support groups for seniors with disabilities. *Canadian Journal on Aging, 20,* 47–72.

Toseland, R. W. (1995). *Group work with the elderly and family caregivers.* New York: Springer.

Toseland, R. W., & Rizzo, V. M. (2004). What's different about working with older people in groups? *Journal of Gerontological Social Work, 44*(1/2), 5–23.

Toseland, R. W., Rossiter, C. M., & Labrecque, M. S. (1989). The effectiveness of peer-led and professionally led groups to support family caregivers. *Gerontologist, 29,* 465–471.

Wolf, R. S. (2001). Support groups for older victims of domestic violence. *Journal of Women and Aging, 13,* 71–83.

Wright, W. (2002). But I want to do a real group: A personal journey from snubbing to theorizing to demanding activity-based group work. *Social Work with Groups, 25*(1/2), 105–110.

Zarit, S. H., Femia, E. E., Watson, J., Rice-Oeschger, L., & Kakos, B. (2004). Memory Club: A group intervention for people with early-stage dementia and their care partners. *Gerontologist, 44,* 262–269.

Zastrow, C. (2001). *Social work with groups* (5th ed.). Pacific Grove, CA: Brooks/Cole.

APPENDIX 7-A Barriers to Forming a Successful Telephone Support Group

Communication Obstacles

It may be difficult to attribute particular content to individuals. Participants may have problems identifying the speaker. Problems in hearing may impede communication.

Solutions

- During the first group sessions, ask individuals to state their names before they begin speaking.
- Mail the names of the group members to each participant before the call so that they may refer to the group roster during the call.
- If people have hearing difficulties, assistive devices may help. Use the first session of the group as a trial to determine if those with hearing difficulties are able to participate.

Impediments to Full Participation

Certain things in the participants' environment may distract them from engaging fully.

Solutions

- Keep a checklist of who has participated during the session to try and bring back "absent" members.
- Initially come up with ground rules about participating—for example, no eating, drinking, or side conversations during the session.
- Provide a call-in number in case a member is inadvertently disconnected from the call.

Membership Limitations and Time Constraints

Because of a lack of visual cues, a telephone group should remain small (about four to five members).

Solution

- The duration of a call should be kept short due to the lack of personal interaction.

Worker's Level of Activity

The social worker must increase his or her level of activity with this type of group.

Solutions

- Provide feedback more quickly on the telephone because, in this format, silence is more uncomfortable.
- Prompt others to provide information or feedback.

Source: Kaslyn, M. (1999). Telephone group work: Challenges for practice. *Social Work with Groups,* 21, 68–75. Adapted with permission by the Haworth Press, Inc.

APPENDIX 7-B Memory Club: A Psychoeducational Curriculum

Session	Topic	Summary of Content
1	Welcome	Create a comfortable, safe, friendly environment; set clear expectations for what is ahead; learn more about group members' stories and concerns
2	Dementia in Early Stages: Medical Information	Provide knowledge about Alzheimer's and other dementias; help families express their concerns, questions, thoughts
3	Dementia in Early Stages: Emotional Issues	Discuss the effects of memory loss on an older adult's sense of self and his or her family; validate challenges and experiences in daily living
4	Talking About Feelings	Discuss feelings related to the diagnosis and the effects on self and social relationships; examine commonalities and differences in experiences
5	"I Get by with a Little Help from My Friends"	Explore trust, communication, role changes, and task sharing; work on using activities to decrease stress resulting from those issues; discuss issues of giving and receiving assistance
6	It's Hard Enough Dealing with My Own Changes!	Build on sessions 4 and 5 by continuing to raise awareness of concerns facing the other half of dyad; expose and validate concerns that the partner has about the other by carefully confronting the issues; explore whether to tell friends and coworkers of the diagnosis
7	Keeping the Faith: Taking Care of Yourself	Explore ways in which members may find peace, comfort, and strength/resilience; discuss coping; identify benefits of self-care; begin to prepare members for the group's end
8	Community Resources	Provide information on resources and plan for the future (for example, legal, financial, medical)
9	Looking to the Future	Review previous information covered and explore implications for the future, the changing nature of the disease, and needs for ongoing support or guidance
10	Graduation	Recognize the completion of growth—accomplishment, learning, and challenges; evaluate the group

Source: Adapted with permission from Zarit, S. H., Femia, E. E., Watson, J., Rice-Oeschger, L., & Kakos, B. (2004). Memory club: A group intervention for people with early-stage dementia and their care partners. *Gerontologist, 44,* p. 264.

APPENDIX 7-C Effective Group Interventions with Older Adults in Three Domains

Domain	Condition	Chapter Authors[a]	Outcomes
Physical Health	Cancer	Maramaldi, Dungan, & Poorvu	Decreased depression and improved family functioning due to cognitive behavioral groups; less stress among partners of patients; improved marital quality, enhanced social networks; improved quality of life for patients; increased adherence to physical health management protocols; improved self-efficacy and coping strategies
	Cardiac conditions	Peck & Ai	
	Diabetes	DeCoster	
	Chronic pain	Yoon & Doherty	
	HIV/AIDS	Emlet & Shippy	
Mental Health and Cognitive Status	Dementia	Sanders & Morano	Decreased depression and anxiety; enhanced treatment compliance; increased relaxation; enhanced communication; decreased agitation
	Depression and anxiety	Adamek & Slater	
	Substance abuse	Cummings, Bride, & Rawlins-Shaw-	
Later Life Social Roles	End of life	Waldrop	Enhanced social adjustment; reduced depression; enhanced coping; decreased depression and anxiety; improved knowledge of and access to resources; improved quality of life among care providers; enhanced leisure choices; enhanced life satisfaction
	Family caregivers	Cassie & Sanders	
	Grandparent caregivers	Kolomer	
	People with developmental disabilities & care providers	McCallion & Nickles	

[a] Refers to authors of specific chapters contained in the book cited in the source note below.

Source: Cummings, S. M., & Kropf, N. P. (Eds.). (in press). *Handbook of evidence-based psychosocial treatments for older adults.* New York: Haworth Press. Adapted with permission by the Haworth Press, Inc.

Geriatric Case Management

Assembling a Broad Repertoire of Practice Skills

8

RATIONALE: Foundation social work practice encompasses brokering and advocacy roles. Effective case management involves linking clients to needed resources and designing services delivery systems on a continuum of care—including prevention and health promotion—to meet the needs of specific populations.

COMPETENCY: Students will be able to engage, assess, and broker needed services for older adults. They will monitor their progress in meeting client needs and in maintaining client functionality. They also will

- provide social work case management to link elders and their families to resources and services and to conduct long-term planning.
- develop clear, timely, and appropriate service plans with measurable objectives for older adults.
  Such plans are to be based on functional status, life goals, symptoms management, and financial and social supports of older persons and their families and are to address financial, legal, housing, medical, and social needs.
- re-evaluate and adjust service plans for older adults on a continuing basis.
- advocate on behalf of older adults with agencies and other professionals to help them obtain quality services.
- identify ways to outreach to older adults and their families to ensure appropriate use of the services continuum (e.g., health promotion, long term care, mental health).
  This competency includes understanding the diversity of elders' attitudes toward the acceptance of services.
- identify and develop strategies, including intergenerational approaches, to address services gaps, fragmentation, discrimination, and barriers that have an impact on older persons.

● identify the availability of resources and resource systems for older adults and their families.
● apply evaluation and research findings to improve practice and program outcomes. (Council on Social Work Education, Gero-Ed Center, 2004)

Case managers may come from various disciplines and backgrounds. They are typically either graduate-level nurses or social workers having professional designations or certifications—for example, the National Academy of Certified Case Managers, Certified Advanced Social Work Case Manager, or Certified Social Work Case Manager (Naleppa, 2006). Case, or care, management is strongly rooted in the social work profession. According to historical records, case coordination—the precursor to the current practice method—is one of the earliest forms of professional social work practice. A part of the first Board of Charities, case coordination involved organizing services and conserving funds to provide care for sick and impoverished people. It also played an important role in the settlement house movements in New York and Chicago from the late 19th century through the Great Depression (Frankl & Gelman, 1998; Naleppa & Reid, 2003).

Today, an increasingly aging population calls for even greater numbers of case managers. Social workers, with their dual focus on the person-in-environment configuration, have the requisite knowledge and skill set to function as geriatric case managers or to serve other populations that may be considered vulnerable because of limited cognitive or physical ability (Rothman, 1994).

The competencies defined in this chapter address the social work roles and skills necessary for effective case management practice. As case manager, the social worker must be able to complete a comprehensive biopsychosocial assessment of the older client to determine that person's needs or challenges and strengths or assets. Too often, case management services focus primarily on an older client's limitations or problem situations. Older adults, however, are resilient; therefore, case managers must include clients' survivorship within their understanding of each older adult's history and current life situation. Lewis and Harrell (2002) offered a model to foster resilience in practice with older adults. The model, which provides a framework for case management with that particular population, has three components:

1. promoting affiliations, which involves expanding the meaning of social relationships; being sensitive to issues related to one's culture, ethnicity, and sexual orientation; and creating culturally responsive services for the older population within services systems

2. enhancing safety and support, such as including the client's perception of his or her interpersonal functioning; promoting trust within the worker–client relationship; exploring environmental and cultural dynamics; and being sensitive to the client's expression of self-determination
3. fostering altruism; that is, focusing on reciprocity within the client's social relationships; exploring the client's need for social connectedness and related values; and identifying the client's linkages with extended family and indigenous groups, including clubs, self-help groups, churches, synagogues, mosques, and the like.

These three principles assist the case manager in understanding the older client's social and emotional values and history as they relate to that person's physical and environmental resource needs.

Effective case managers must have a thorough knowledge of resources within the environment that may benefit the client and family. To enhance client functioning, managers may use formal sources of support (for example, respite care, volunteer opportunities, or health care options) and informal sources (such as social support systems or personal assets). They can then construct the information they have acquired from those resources into a services plan with measurable goals and objectives to be evaluated later. Furthermore, they can be change agents, helping to transform fragmented services delivery practices into comprehensive services systems.

What Is Geriatric Case Management?

Case Management Defined

Several definitions of the case management role exist within social work, human services, and health care literature. Indeed, Sullivan and Fisher (1994) have pointed out that "case management, as implemented and described in professional literature, suggests such widely diverse activities and desired outcomes that the term now has no innate meaning" (p. 65).

In an attempt to determine the core content of case management, Genrich and Neatherlin (2001) performed a content analysis of published literature on that practice method. After reviewing a total of 228 published articles, they determined that the common role components were

- being able to establish strong interpersonal relationships
- developing plans that foster appropriate use of resources
- engaging in the study of populations for problem identification and plans of action
- pursuing activities directed at monitoring and tracking institutional and community efforts
- implementing research to measure outcomes

- developing and implementing plans that reflect awareness of fiscal issues and trends
- conducting cost-effectiveness analysis.

In a similar study, Bowers and Jacobson (2002) interviewed long-term care case managers who were identified as "excellent" or "very good" by professional supervisors, colleagues, and consumers of their services. The goal of the interviews was to determine how this small group of case managers ($N = 16$) viewed their positions. An analysis of the transcripts revealed a number of common principles identified by the highly rated case managers (see Appendix 8-A).

Geriatric Case Management

Although geriatric case management is certainly a form of case management practice, some of its practice aspects are unique. An important focus of case management with the older population is the preservation of functioning and emphasis on quality-of-life issues for both the older adult and family members. Cress (2001) defined the geriatric case management role as "a preventative service rendered on demand, increasing the quality of an older person's life, managing all of the players rendering services to the older person, and offering assurance and peace of mind to the adult children of the older individual" (p. 3). Furthermore, Cress defined other unique aspects of geriatric case management, including

- smaller caseloads than case managers with other populations to be able to respond more individually to clients
- uniqueness of working with families who might be "at a distance" from where an older parent lives
- personalized services plans to promote and preserve functioning with the older client.

Other authors have promoted strengths-based case management models for older adults. Fast and Chapin (2000) stressed that illness, disease, or other challenges in functioning are only one part of the picture—and not the most important part! In their conceptualization, "problems become a backdrop rather than the foreground of the client–care manager relationship. The client is perceived as having a range of experiences, characteristics, and roles that determine who he or she is, rather than as someone who is old, disabled, or chronically ill" (pp. 1–2). Optimal outcomes achieved through strengths-based case management include optimizing client living arrangements, vocational activities, and use of leisure time (Sullivan & Fisher, 1994). Fast and Chapin (2000) presented those principles forming the foundation of strengths-based case management practice as

- discovering and building on strengths rather than problems facilitates hope and self-reliance

- recognizing that older adults have the power to learn, grow, and change
- realizing that relationship-building is essential to effective efforts to help clients
- encouraging older people to participate in decisions, make choices, and determine the direction of the helping process
- reaching out assertively to all community agencies for resources. (pp. 7–9)

Contexts

As people age, physical, emotional, and social issues may present challenges requiring resources beyond those currently available to them. Geriatric case managers can assist older adults during transitions—such as when a client retires and is seeking volunteer opportunities or following the death of a client's spouse—by connecting them to additional sources of support, providing continuous monitoring to determine if current levels of support and functioning are adequate, and offering assistance to care providers. Case managers may also support families in their decision making about issues involving possible transitions; for instance, they may help older parents of children with disabilities by addressing the need for permanency planning.

Crises and transitions are frequently a gateway for case managers to intervene and assist older clients to deal with complex care plans or comorbidity issues. A recent health diagnosis, for example, may necessitate that an older adult restructure lifestyle patterns by increasing exercise or using supportive or adaptive equipment, or the diagnosis may lead to a struggle with the onset of other challenges, such as depression or fatigue. After summarizing several case management models for older diabetics, DeCosta (in press) reported that case management is effective in reducing depression, enhancing functional abilities, and increasing knowledge about the disease. Naleppa and Reid (2000) described a task-centered case management model suitable for integration into acute-care settings such as a hospital. Using this model, the goals of which are to avoid hospitalization, rehospitalization, or entry into a nursing home, case managers may assess for potential in-home accidents or monitor for compliance with discharge care plans.

Other case management programs focus on care provision. Project Healthy Grandparents is one such program that has received national attention (Whitley, White, Kelley, & Yorker, 1999). Using a strengths-based model, practitioners partner with medical and legal professionals to provide health, social, and legal services to grandparents who are raising their grandchildren. Program results have suggested that the model fosters a sense of independence and self-assurance among grandparents, thus enhancing their level of confidence to nurture and support their grandchildren, and enables social workers and grandparents to establish linkages and supports with other families and resources within the community (Kelley & Whitley, 2003; Robinson, Kropf, & Myers, 2000).

Case Manager's Repertoire of Skills

To serve older adults who are fast becoming part of a number of services delivery sectors effectively, the case manager will need to assemble a broad repertoire of practice skills. Because the focus of case management is on both the individual and the larger environment, social workers striving to become effective, competent geriatric case managers must draw skills from their work with individuals, families, and the community, and from their roles as advocates and change agents.

Sensitive Relationship Building

The skill of engagement is critical to social work practice; therefore, it is not surprising that case managers must be especially sensitive in initial interactions with their clients. Managers may intervene during major transitions or crises when an older adult is dealing with change on many levels. As the strength-based model indicates, the client is an individual with a unique life history, a current set of strengths and resources, and particular needs and challenges. These client dimensions are an essential part in structuring the initial engagement and relationship-development phases.

For many reasons, a case manager may first engage with an older adult in the client's home. One reason is that the home may be a dangerous environment for elders: 55 percent of all falls for people aged 55 years and older occur in this environment, and 23 percent occur outside, near the home. Twenty-eight percent of all falls result in short- or long-term limitations of activities of daily living or independent activities of daily living (Kochera, 2002). With age, the older body may be less able to manage some of the more difficult household tasks—for example, carrying laundry into the basement, reaching top shelves, or navigating dark hallways—as efficiently as during younger years. Case managers work within an older adult's home environment to keep the client safe and reduce the risk of accidents. As people face increasingly difficult living conditions, managers can assess what environmental modifications or required home maintenance are necessary to help older adults remain in their homes and communities. Appendix 8-B provides a task-centered case management example from Naleppa and Reid (2000) for working with older clients living in households with deteriorating conditions.

Case managers not only work with community-based clients, but also serve older adults in long-term-care facilities. In this practice context, they may be responsible for coordinating services, for example, acute-care and long-term-care resources. In an evaluation of case manager services in rural long-term-care models, Schrader and Britt (2001) found that working in long-term care, especially in areas with limited resources, requires an integrated model of care. Case managers play a vital role: They may provide information across multiple and geographically disparate health care providers.

Furthermore, they may help clients and older adults with decision making about when to consider a residential relocation, such as a move into an assisted-living facility or a nursing home (Ritchie et al., 2002). Although older adults may prefer to remain in their communities, a case manager's comprehensive assessment may indicate that a more supportive and secure environment might be appropriate for a client who is unable to safely remain in his or her current residential setting.

Regardless of the context, a challenge for a case manager is to engage with clients who may be challenging or resistant to intervention. As part of the assessment process, the practitioner should consider these dynamics within the relationship. That is, what might be happening with the older client that could create a sense of mistrust or reluctance to receive assistance or aid?

There are many possible reasons that should be considered within the assessment process. One possibility is that older clients fear that their independence might be curtailed. If the reason is to provide additional support, such as contracting with home care providers, the older adult might be hesitant to engage with the practitioner. Another reason might be transference or countertransference issues between the older client and case manager. In these situations, an older client might believe that the case manager cannot possibly be helpful—for example, she or he is too young to understand, is of a different race or ethnicity, or gender. Likewise, the case manager might display countertransference that also hinders relationship development. If the case manager is experiencing challenges in developing a relationship, it is a good practice for him or her to seek supervision about the situation. The perspective of a supervisor can be helpful in understanding the dynamics and providing useful assistance in this phase of building a relationship with the client.

Appropriate Resources and Services

A recent study of older adults and their care providers found that the most important skill that social workers provided was assisting clients to locate needed resources (Naito-Chan, Damron-Rodriguez, & Simmons, 2004). On face value, linking clients and their families with resources within their environment may sound like a relatively simple task— The client presents with a particular need, the social worker finds a resource in the community that delivers services in that area, and the two are connected. That process, though, is frequently much more involved and complicated than it might appear at first.

To link clients with resources successfully requires that case managers possess a multitude of skills, including preparing and motivating clients to access resources, preparing clients to accept help, and being an advocate to ensure that clients' needs are adequately served. Consider the older adult who requires support from in-home services, such as a homemaker or a home health care worker. Although such services may be necessary to ensure the client's safety and well-being, the older adult may find it difficult to accept such a level of "intrusion." In such a case, the compassionate case manager can assist with the client's perceptions of his or her own declining health or functional status—termed "brokenness" by Nowitz (2005). The following example from Nowitz illustrates how a geriatric case manager assisted an 80-year-old client with her perceptions of the changes that she was experiencing:

> EG, a woman who was a former alcoholic, lived a very unhappy life and now suffered from dementia. The case manager arranged for her to receive 24-hour Medicaid homecare. EG lived in a tiny apartment and found it difficult to have caretakers around the clock in her home. After sharing her bitter feelings about her life during bimonthly visits by a care manager for a few years, the client showed a shift in attitude and feelings. She began to appreciate her caregivers and now welcomes the care manager's visits. (p. 191)

It is apparent that case managers must intervene in the psychosocial issues that clients face in receiving services. Instead of viewing clients as "resistive" or "uncooperative," managers must listen for ways in which clients are asking for help in relinquishing aspects of their independence.

Case managers also need to intervene to ensure that older clients do indeed receive services. *Ageism*, oppression and discrimination based on chronological age, can compromise older adults' ability to receive adequate services, particularly in health care. The cartoon in Figure 8-1 illustrates how ageism may lead to insidious neglect of an elderly client. Although the issue is portrayed in a seemingly humorous way, the cartoon depicts an aspect of ageism that older patients may encounter when they present with medical symptoms. When health care providers use age to explain the cause of an older adult's health condition, that health issue, and perhaps other conditions that might be amenable to treatment or cure, might go undiagnosed.

Sadly, inattention or neglect is not limited to an elderly client's physical health. Only about 4 percent to 5 percent of older adults receive any type of mental health services (Schulberg, Pilkonis, & Houck, 1998), yet mental health issues are present in an estimated 15 percent to 25 percent of the older population (Gallo & Lebowitz, 1999). The disparity in these percentages cannot be explained by a lack of treatment options, because evidenced-based treatment has consistently demonstrated that psycho-

FIGURE 8-1 A Physician and an Older Patient

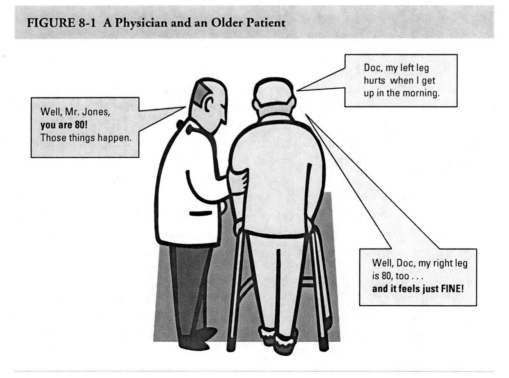

social interventions are effective in the older population (Adamek & Slater, in press; Gellis, 2006). More likely, many of today's cohort of older clients do not have knowledge about possible treatment options, have undiagnosed conditions such as depression or anxiety, feel uncomfortable receiving mental health services, or receive services that inadequately or inappropriately meet their needs.

Case managers play an essential role in coordinating health and mental health providers to ensure comprehensive care of older clients. An example of a geriatric case management system for adults who are depressed was described by Enguidanos, Davis, and Katz (2005). In their model, the case manager performed a number of tasks, including communicating with the primary care physician about the client's mental health issues, obtaining a referral to a geriatrician for psychiatric evaluation of the client, holding a family conference to discuss treatment issues, and identifying safety issues for remaining in the home. Clearly, the case manager plays an important role in ensuring that older clients receive comprehensive and appropriate support in dealing with depression.

A Network of Alliances

Knowledge about resources within the community is a vital case management tool. Case managers must develop positive relationships with other services providers to create a robust network of alliances within the community (see Appendix 8-A). Such relationships are invaluable when working to connect clients with existing resources.

Ample opportunities exist to be creative in securing resources. Case managers, however, need to look beyond the "usual suspects" of available services to other sources of support for families. For example, consider the situation of an older couple who was raising their grandson (Myers, Kropf, & Robinson, 2002). The family lived in a rural county and was very isolated. As part of the services plan, the case manager identified recreational and leisure opportunities for the grandson. The grandson decided that he wanted to join a Little League baseball team, so the case manager assisted the grandparents with getting him signed up, secured a donation of a uniform (which the family could not afford), and even attended a few games with the family. That recreational outlet provided the grandparents with a respite from the caregiving role, a social outlet to meet other families with similarly aged children, and integration into their community. The most poignant moment came when their grandson hit a home run—and got to be the team hero! The sense of pride shared by the whole family was immeasurable.

Clients themselves may have resources to contribute to a care management plan, and case managers can assist them in identifying those potential resources, which may include friends and neighbors. Moreover, managers can help older clients and their families handle the coordination of informal support systems. For example, the manager may work with "distant caregivers" who live away from their older family member. In such a situation, the social worker might ask the older adult to identify neighbors who could keep an eye on the older adult and contact the family if something seems amiss (for example, if newspapers and mail pile up or no lights are on in the home). If a risky situation should arise, the case manager could mobilize the client's informal network to articulate an action plan.

The Services Plan

An important case management role is assessing clients' level of functioning and presenting need, and investigating available resources and supports. The case manager and the client, with the family, if appropriate, should establish the services plan together. According to systems theory, one can achieve an outcome in a number of ways—a concept known as *equifinality* (Anderson & Carter, 1990). Therefore, in choosing a particular course of action, the case manager should encourage the older client's input as much as possible and allow the client to state his or her preferences. For example, some older adults may find that support groups are extremely helpful in enabling them to cope after a significant loss such as the death of a spouse or partner. Other older individuals, though, may not be "joiners" and thus may perceive group interactions as stressful or intrusive. If a goal is to enhance the older adult's coping skills, strategies might include suggesting the client participate in an online discussion board or group; read helpful works on grief, loss, and recovery; or engage in journaling.

Even the most comprehensive services plans need periodic review and re-evaluation. For some clients, the services plan may provide relief or have a restorative function, or a review of the plan might indicate it is no longer needed. For example, a widowed client may reach a point at which he or she is incorporating the loss and is ready to resume relationships and roles. After attending a grief and loss support group, the client might decide he or she is ready to leave the group and assume a volunteer position within the community. Such an outcome is a good indicator that the intervention successfully provided support to the client when needed during the grief process.

The case manager, though, must continually re-evaluate services plans addressing physical or cognitive changes that are part of a disease process—especially for clients with dementia, a progressive and incurable condition. Services plans must take into account multiple factors, including clients' level of safety in the current environment, other existing health issues, and care providers' quality of life (Merrick, 2001). As a client's condition changes, the case manager will need to review and revise the services plan to ensure it is relevant and continues to meet the client's and family's level of need.

Cost-Effectiveness of Services Delivery

The competencies discussed thus far have described practice-related knowledge and skills. Another major case management responsibility, though, involves work from a more fiscal or budgetary point of view: determining cost-effective methods of delivering services to clients. As health care services continue to shrink, services are being organized around acute-care versus chronic-care needs. However, many older adults require case management for long-term and progressive conditions, such as dementia. Therefore, the case manager will need to assemble outcome data to demonstrate the effectiveness of case management services to funding agencies or payees. For example, the manager must document positive outcomes such as delaying nursing home placement or alleviating comorbid conditions (for example, depression).

A variety of sources may pay for case management services (Cress, 2001; Hyduk, 2002). Some services are funded by federal dollars from agencies such as the U.S. Department of Veteran Affairs; the Health Care Financing Administration; or the National Heart, Lung, and Blood Institute. In addition, various community-based aging agencies have case management programs within the array of services provided to older clients. Other identified funding sources are foundations or the clients themselves (private pay). In dealing with cost issues, case managers can be creative in leveraging current resources to garner additional sources of support. For example, the Brookdale Foundation provides funds to institute support groups for relatives who are raising children (http://www.brookdalefoundation.org/relativesasparents.htm). Other sources fund local agencies to provide support services and enhance coordination among various service sectors, for example, aging, mental health, and child welfare. Although such grants are fairly small (currently about $10,000), the funds may enhance existing services and allow for start-up services and expansion into new services areas.

Changes in Services Delivery

Quality services delivery systems are essential for older adults. To ensure that the delivery of services is responsive to this population, case managers must actively promote changes that support the client, such as modifying programs to be more accessible to or appropriate for older clients. Because many older adults cannot access programs, or programs are unavailable in their communities, these adults are faced with particular challenges. Consider the basic issue of transportation, for example, which is a major barrier to services provision for a number of older adults residing in communities with limited resources. If a client cannot physically get to a senior center, for example, there is no probability that he or she can benefit from the services provided at the site.

Geriatric case managers are in a good position to determine ways to eradicate gaps such as this one in neighborhoods and communities. By having a good knowledge of resources, they could locate untapped resources that could be used, such as having a local church assist with transporting older adults to a senior center in their church bus. In addition, case managers might also be able to coordinate individual clients' resources into a plan—such as forming a cooperative in which families share responsibilities for transportation of older adults. Although it might not be possible to institute a comprehensive system of public transportation within the community, case managers can creatively construct other methods of providing service.

Changes to the services delivery environment are rarely done alone. Kropf (2006) has described several examples of community-level initiatives to enhance older adults' lives. One model program is a coalition approach throughout Georgia to support caregivers within their communities and raise awareness of caregiving issues and needs within the context of diverse communities around the state. The goal of the comprehensive statewide system is to further caregiving capacity within all communities in

Georgia. Established by the Rosalynn Carter Institute for Caregiving and funded by a grant from the Administration on Aging, that initiative has enabled the formation of partnerships within 12 regions of Georgia, a caregivers' system called CARE-NET (http://www.rosalynncarter.org/CARE-Net-ga.htm). Each CARE-NET is a collaborative network of representatives from a variety of constituencies, including family care providers, aging agencies, educational institutions, businesses, and other interested groups (Dodd, Talley, & Elder, 2004). Several case managers from multiple services settings are members of the various CARE-NET coalitions.

Case managers can also be change agents within their own programs and agencies. Sobolewski and Marren (2000) have argued for modifications to home care services delivery to focus more on client or patient satisfaction, involve multidisciplinary services teams, and emphasize patient outcomes. The services delivery model they provided departs from the traditional independent operation of a case manager who is evaluated on his or her individual performance. Rather, their model institutes a true team-delivery approach: A "team coach" oversees the various responsibilities of all team members. This approach ensures review and coordination of services across various dimensions of a client's case.

Advocacy Role

Advocacy, according to Frankl and Gelman (1998), is when "a case manager acts on behalf of clients who are unable or unwilling to act on their own behalf . . . or when clients are able to act on their own, but when it is judged that a case manager could intervene more effectively" (p. 38). The advocacy role is a vitally important part of case management; Frankl and Gelman have argued, compared with the role of advocate, other case management roles are subsidiary. The example of Mr. Jones and his doctor, as depicted in Figure 8-1, illustrates one reason why older adults may require a case manager as their advocate. Unfortunately, ageism is a part of our culture, and other professionals are not immune to engaging in oppressive behaviors. Therefore, in addition to helping connect clients with various resources, case managers may need to advocate for improved responsiveness of those resources to their clients.

Acting as an advocate requires numerous social work skills. Fast and Chapin (2000) have suggested that a case manager first needs to acquire thorough knowledge about available resources in the client's environment, the client's preferences for using services, and any barriers or obstacles to using or accessing these services. The manager then must use his or her influence to assist the client in connecting with these resources. Consider the example of older adults with developmental disabilities—these clients receive services through aging initiatives, such as leisure-based options or meal programs. As adults with lifelong disabilities age, it makes little sense for them to continue with vocational or habilitation services, such as supported employment or workshops. Yet few agencies offer later life leisure-based options, thus leaving many older adults with nothing to do.

In the mid-1990s in Georgia, the Division of Aging Services and the Governor's Council on Disabilities instituted an initiative to bridge the gap between the aging and disabilities networks to promote a more comprehensive array of options for older adults (Smith, Thyer, Clements, & Kropf, 1997). Case managers within the disability services sector led the way as advocates by creating structures that would allow their older clients to "cross over" to aging services at a comparable time of life as their nondisabled counterparts. Although this particular initiative met with only limited success because of a lack of resources to coordinate referrals, services providers in both networks came to appreciate the idea.

Clearly, geriatric case managers must have a set of competencies to practice with older adults successfully and effectively. As the older population grows in both size and diversity, case managers will continue to play increasingly important roles in services delivery. They must have the skills to intervene effectively with older clients and their families, provide needed linkages to traditional and innovative resources, and serve as change agents to promote a comprehensive system of programs and services. Although case coordination was one of the earliest functions within the social work profession, this role continues to hold an important place in today's services delivery systems.

Conclusion

Case management has been a part of social work practice since the earliest days of the profession. Beginning with the Settlement House Movement, this type of intervention approach continues to be an important part of our professional role. Geriatric case managers tend to focus on promoting functioning with older adults and providing linkage to needed resources within the environment.

Because the issues faced by older adults often straddle multiple services sectors (for example, health, mental health, aging services), case managers need to have an extensive network of other providers. A person who has dementia, for example, may require a safe residence, support for care providers, and linkage to health care providers who understand this disease. An effective case manager will have skills to assess and intervene effectively with the older client and family, as well as be able to attend to issues in services delivery. The competencies that are part of this chapter highlight the breadth of skills that the geriatric case manager must possess.

Suggested Exercise to Evaluate Student Competency

Students will write a care plan to meet the needs of Mrs. Vishnick and her daughter Meta.

> Mrs. Vishnick is an 87-year-old widow who is the primary caregiver for her 64-year-old daughter, Meta, who has mental retardation. Meta has very limited functional ability, as she requires total support in all activities of daily living including dressing, feeding, toileting, and bathing. Meta does not participate in any services for people with developmental disabilities and has never been involved in any community programs.
>
> This family approached the county developmental disability service when Mrs. Vishnick became ill and required hospitalization. The only other family member is Mrs. Vishnick's

younger daughter, Teresa, who is married and lives in the same neighborhood. Although Teresa spends time with Meta, she has been adamant that she and her husband will not become the primary care providers for Meta when their mother can no longer function in this role. Teresa was the person who contacted the disability services agency in the present situation.

In understanding the family history, several events and situations have important meaning for the family's current situation. First of all, Mrs. Vishnick and her husband immigrated to the United States from Eastern Europe when they were first married. When the couple arrived in this country, Mr. Vishnick secured a job at an automotive manufacturing plant and they had Meta. When she did not seem to be making developmental progress, the Vishnick's physician encouraged them to place her in an institution, which they did not do. After the birth of Teresa, the demands of raising two children became overwhelming for Mrs. Vishnick and Meta was moved to the state institution, about 75 miles from the family home. One year after this move, a fire destroyed much of the institution, although Meta was uninjured. However, Mrs. Vishnick was so consumed with anxiety about her daughter's safety that Meta returned to the family home. Since this time, Meta and Mrs. Vishnick have not spent a single night apart until the recent hospitalization.

If you were the case manager in the agency, how would you proceed in working with this family? Consider the following questions:

- How would you develop a relationship with the family? What might be some issues or challenges in developing a trusting relationship?
- What resources would be appropriate for this family? How would you link to services in different networks (for example, aging services, health resources, and so forth)?
- From a macro practice perspective, what are some ways that case managers from different services delivery networks could work more effectively to assist families like the Vishnicks?
- How would you evaluate your practice as a case manager with this family? What would be some measurable outcomes that you could establish?

References

Adamek, M. E., & Slater, G. Y. (in press). Evidenced-based psychosocial interventions for older adults with depression and anxiety. In S. M. Cummings & N. P. Kropf (Eds.), *Evidenced-based psychosocial treatments for older adults.* New York: Haworth Press.

Anderson, R. E., & Carter, I. E. (1990). *Human behavior in the social environment: A social Systems approach* (4th ed.). New York: Aldine de Gruyter.

Bowers, B. J., & Jacobson, N. (2002). Best practice in long-term care case management: How excellent case managers do their jobs. *Journal of Social Work in Long-Term Care, 1,* 55–72.

Council on Social Work Education, Gero-Ed Center. (2004). *Foundation geronto-logical social work competencies.* Retrieved November 16, 2006, from http://depts. washington.edu/geroctr/Curriculum3/ Competencies/FdnComp.doc

Cress, C. (2001). *Handbook of geriatric care management.* Gaithersburg, MD: Aspen Publishers.

DeCosta, V. (in press). Evidenced-based psychosocial treatments for older adults with diabetes: A review of interventions. In S. M. Cummings & N. P. Kropf (Eds.), *Handbook of evidenced-based psychosocial treatments for older adults.* New York: Haworth Press.

Dodd, J., Talley, R., & Elder, T. (2004). *Caregivers together: Establishing your own CARE-NET—The community caregivers network* [Report]. Americus, GA: Rosalynn Carter Institute for Caregiving. Retrieved from http://www.rosalynncarter.org/ UserFiles/File/Caregiverstogether.pdf

Enguidanos, S. M., Davis, C., & Katz, L. (2005). Shifting the paradigm in geriatric care management: Moving from the medical model to patient-centered care. *Social Work in Health Care, 41*(1), 1–16.

Fast, B., & Chapin, R. (2000). *Strengths-based care management for older adults.* Baltimore: Health Professions Press.

Frankl, A. J., & Gelman, S. R. (1998). *Case management: An introduction to concepts and skills.* Chicago: Lyceum.

Gallo, J. J., & Lebowitz, B. D. (1999). The epidemiology of common late-life mental disorders in the community: Themes for a new century. *Psychiatric Services, 50,* 1158–1166.

Gellis, Z. (2006). Older adults with mental and emotional problems. In B. Berkman (Ed.), *Handbook of social work in health and aging* (pp. 129–139). New York: Oxford University Press.

Genrich, S. J., & Neatherlin, J. S. (2001). Case manager role: A content analysis of published literature. *Care Management Journals, 3,* 14–19.

Hyduk, C. A. (2002). Community-based long-term care case management models for older adults. *Journal of Gerontological Social Work, 37*(1), 19–47.

Kelley, S. J., & Whitley, D. (2003). Psychological distress and physical health problems in grandparents raising grandchildren: Development of an empirically based intervention model. In B. Hayslip & J. H. Patrick (Eds.), *Working with custodial grandparents* (pp. 127–144). New York: Springer.

Kochera, A. (2002, March). *Falls among older persons and the role of the home: An analysis of cost, incidence, and potential savings from home modification* (Issue Brief No. 56). Washington, DC: AARP Public Policy Institute.

Kropf, N. P. (2006). Community caregiving partnerships promoting alliances to support care providers. *Journal of Human Behavior in the Social Environment, 14*(1/2), 327–340.

Lewis, J. S., & Harrell, E. B. (2002). Older adults. In R. R. Greene (Ed.), *Resiliency: An integrated approach to practice, policy, and research* (pp. 277–292). Washington, DC: NASW Press.

Merrick, B. J. (2001). Geriatric care management approach to a treatment plan for dementia. *Journal of Geriatric Psychiatry, 34,* 233–245.

Myers, L., Kropf, N. P., & Robinson, M. M. (2002). Grandparents raising grandchildren: Case management in a rural setting. *Journal of Human Behavior in the Social Environment, 5,* 53–71.

Naito-Chan, E., Damron-Rodriguez, J. A., & Simmons, W. J. (2004). Identifying competencies for geriatric social work practice. *Journal of Gerontological Social Work, 43*(4), 59–78.

Naleppa, M. (2006). Case management services. In B. Berkman (Ed.), *Handbook of social work in health and aging* (pp. 521–528). New York: Oxford University Press.

Naleppa, M. J., & Reid, W. J. (2000). Integrating case management and brief-treatment strategies: A hospital-based geriatric program. *Social Work in Health Care, 31*(4), 1–23.

Naleppa, M. J., & Reid, W. J. (2003). *Gerontological social work: A task-centered approach.* New York: Columbia University Press.

Nowitz, L. (2005). Geriatric case management: Spiritual challenges. *Journal of Gerontological Social Work, 45*(1/2), 185–201.

Ritchie, C., Wieland, D., Tully, C., Rowe, J., Sims, R., & Bodner, E. (2002). Coordination and advocacy for rural elders (CARE): A model of rural case management with veterans. *Gerontologist, 42,* 399–405.

Robinson, M. M., Kropf, N. P., & Myers, L. (2000). Grandparents raising grandchildren in rural communities. *Journal of Aging and Mental Health, 6,* 353–365.

Rothman, J. (1994). *Practice with highly vulnerable clients: Case management and community-based service.* New York: Prentice-Hall.

Schrader, C., & Britt, T. (2001). Case management issues in rural long-term care models. *Journal of Applied Gerontology, 20,* 458–470.

Schulberg, H. C., Pilkonis, P., & Houck, P. (1998). The severity of major depression and choice of treatment in primary care practice. *Journal of Consulting and Clinical Psychology, 66,* 932–938.

Smith, G. S., Thyer, B. A., Clements, C., & Kropf, N. P. (1997). An evaluation of coalition building training for aging and developmental disability service providers. *Educational Gerontology, 23,* 105–114.

Sobolewski, S., & Marren, J. (2000). Home care and the new economy: Creating a new model for service delivery. *Care Management Journals, 2,* 248–252.

Sullivan, W. P., & Fisher, B. J. (1994). Intervening for success: Strengths-based case management and successful aging. *Journal of Gerontological Social Work, 22*(1/2), 61–73.

Whitley, D. M., White, K. R., Kelley, S. J., & Yorker, B. (1999). Strengths-based case management: The application to grandparents raising grandchildren. *Families in Society, 80,* 110–119.

APPENDIX 8-A Best Practice Principles in Long-Term-Care Case Management

- *Honoring the spirit of the rules:* Case managers will have a good understanding of the particular rules and regulations, but will hold up the *philosophy* (spirit) versus the precise *letter* of the law. Without being flagrant rule-breakers, excellent case managers may use liberal interpretations or "rule bending" when necessary.

- *Risk taking:* It is important that case managers support their clients who must assume the risk for their decisions.

- *Nurturing the personal side of relationships:* It is essential that case managers maintain positive relationships with their clients and cultivate good relationships with co-workers, supervisors, families, and other service providers.

- *Managing without formulas:* Excellent case managers do not use a specific "recipe" or "formula" to complete their work. They do not establish number of hours per case but, rather, determine time based on client need.

- *Listening and knowing:* Excellent case managers report listening to their clients, being familiar with who the clients are, and engaging with them.

- *Relating to supervisors:* Case managers have stressed the importance of excellent supervisors. They rely on their supervisors' support, good will, and advice. Excellent supervisors are "collaborators" rather than "overseers."

Source: Bowers, B. J., & Jacobsen, N. (2002). Best practices in long-term case management: How excellent case managers do their job. *Journal of Social Work in Long-Term Care,* 1(3), 61–67. Adapted with permission by the Haworth Press, Inc.

APPENDIX 8-B Task-Centered Approach to Home Safety and Repairs

Elderly homeowners often live in older structures of which the size was suitable when their children lived with them. Now those homeowners may no longer be able to carry out regular maintenance or required repairs, thus leading to safety problems. If these situations are left unchanged, deteriorating conditions may lead to the condemnation of the houses.

Reasons for not undertaking needed maintenance and repairs include high cost, inability to repair due to poor health, and not knowing how to make repairs. Types of formal assistance include the following programs: neighborhood conservation, emergency repair, repair and maintenance, and weatherization. Local private businesses may undertake smaller repair and maintenance jobs.

Task Menu for the Geriatric Case Manager

1. Assess the home for safety and need for repairs. As necessary, refer to a resource index on home safety issues such as the Safety for Older Consumers: Home Safety Checklist (document no. 701), available online from the U.S. Consumer Productive Safety Commission at http://www.cpsc.gov/cpscpub/pubs/older.html.

2. Discuss potential repairs with the client and indicate which ones are health and safety priorities.

3. Assist the client in selecting the repairs that should be undertaken.

4. Identify whether informal support systems can help with the repairs.

5. If the home requires professional repair or maintenance is needed, assist with the contact as needed and help the client research prices. (Note that the AARP or Area Agencies on Aging, among other organizations, may provide information on discount plans.)

6. Establish whether maintenance or repair programs are available and establish eligibility.

7. Assist the client with arranging for repairs to be completed.

Source: Naleppa, M. J., & Reid, W. J. (2000). Integrating case management and brief-treatment strategies: A hospital-based geriatric program. *Social Work in Health Care,* 31, 22–23. Adapted with permission by the Haworth Press, Inc.

A Shift in Organizational Practice

Meeting the Needs of an Increasingly Aging Society

9

RATIONALE: Social workers can influence organizational policies, procedures, and resources to facilitate and maximize the provision of services. They can contribute to crafting innovative and open work environments and organizational responsiveness. They also will need to address the dynamics of a changing workforce and intervene in organizations to advance resilient organizational environments.

COMPETENCY: Students will develop strategies for creating an elder-friendly organizational environment. They will

- adapt organizational policies, procedures, and resources to facilitate the provision of services to diverse older adults and their family caregivers.
  This competency can encompass health, mental health, and long-term care policies.
- include older adults in planning and designing programs.
- identify and develop strategies, including intergenerational approaches, to address services gaps, fragmentation, discrimination, and barriers that have an impact on older persons.
- apply evaluation and research findings to improve practice and program outcomes.
- evaluate the effectiveness of practice and programs in achieving intended outcomes for older adults. (Council on Social Work Education, Gero-Ed Center, 2004)

Organizations provide the context and structure in which social workers provide services to individuals, families, groups, and communities. Social workers, whether they are working with individuals or communities, need to understand the interdependency of social welfare organizations and their environment and that "the organization's legitimacy . . . depends on the external environment" (Pillari & Newsome, 1998, p. 133).

The mission, services and services delivery, and funding differ among the three types of human services organizations—public, nonprofit, and for profit. Although public and nonprofit organizations have been the most common sources of service delivery to older adults, for-profit agencies are increasingly assuming an active role in areas such as home health care, assisted living, and geriatric care management.

The aging of U.S. society is challenging many organizations that serve older adults to shift from an inflexible administrative style—"this is the way things always have been done"—to a more nurturing role—"how should we do things here to meet our clients' needs?" Social workers can help an organization respond to this transition by engaging the organization as a client, a target of change, or as an ally in the change process. This chapter addresses the role of organizations in serving older clients and the responsibility of organizations to older workers.

A Closer Look at Organizations

Characteristics

Healthy communities comprise a network of organizations that carry out seven basic functions: (1) production, distribution, and consumption; (2) socialization; (3) social control; (4) social participation; (5) mutual support (Warren, 1978); (6) defense; and (7) sense of community (Pantoja & Perry, 1998; for more information about community functions, see chapter 10). Organizations, including those serving older adults, share some characteristics. For example, they are made up of people who bring their own values, personalities, experiences, and beliefs into the work environment. Moreover, each organization has its own values, expectations, and beliefs about the people it serves, the people who do the serving, the types of services it offers, and how it provides those services. Is the organization's staff diverse? Do the workers, committee members, clients, and volunteers reflect the population served by the organization?

The organization should have a clearly stated mission and purpose. The organization's mission should include serving older adults and the involvement of older adults in decision making. The structure of organizations should include a division of responsibility and policies that dictate how they will be governed. Social workers, particularly those who serve as staff, board or committee members, or volunteers, can advocate for older adults by helping to increase their visibility within the organizational structure. In meetings and on an individual basis, social workers can promote the image of positive aging.

Organizations do not exist in isolation; rather, they are constantly interacting with other organizations, agencies, and individuals in the broader community. An organization may participate in community coalitions in order to address the fragmented health and social services delivery network for older adults and the lack of coordination of services (Kirst-Ashman, 2000). In general, "a strong organization has a solid mission, a good reputation in the community, family-friendly personnel policies and practices, sound financial management, well-maintained facilities, and receptive administrators" (Miley, O'Melia, & DuBois, 2007, p. 228). Furthermore, a successful organization creates services delivery alliances by building interagency coalitions, developing working relationships with other professionals, working on teams, and leading effective meetings (Miley et al.).

Organizations willing to improve services delivery are called *open systems.* These organizations receive *inputs,* which in social services agencies typically are "critical resources such as funding, staff, and facilities" (Netting, Kettner, & McMurtry, 2004, p. 231). "More subtle but also vital are inputs such as values, expectations, and opinions about the agency that are held by community members, funding agencies, regulatory bodies, and other segments of the environment" (p. 231). The agency then takes the *throughput* step, in which it processes the inputs and produces *outputs*—its final products or outcomes.

Open systems have feedback loops; they are self-correcting or cybernetic systems, meaning each organization is "able to garner information from its surroundings, interpret this information, and adjust its functioning accordingly" (Netting et al., 2004, p. 232). Consequently, open organizations are in constant contact with their environment. Later, this chapter will describe in more detail open systems such as resilient and elder-friendly organizations.

Structural and Cultural Lag

In contrast to open systems, *closed systems* are organizations or agencies that are stuck on how they respond to, or offer limited responses to, shifts in individual or environmental circumstances. *Structural lag,* the "tendency of social structures and norms to lag behind people's rapidly changing lives" (Burkhauser & Quinn, 1994, p. vii), results when social institutions resist transforming social and economic conditions quickly. Consequently, tension or mismatches occur between entrenched existing institutions and desired best practices (Foner, 1994). An example of structural lag, according to Roberts (2003), is the United States' lack of preparation for societal aging and the related fiscal stress in major entitlement programs—Medicaid, Medicare, and Social Security.

According to the 2005 White House Conference on Aging, 50 resolutions were passed on the pressing aging issues of today and the future, thereby indicating the need to develop strategies for implementation. A press release from the White House presenting the top 10 resolutions (M. Thompson & Wesolowski, 2005) can be found in Appendix 9-A.

When technological and material changes in an organization clash with an organization's customs, culture, and symbolic meanings, *cultural lag* has occurred (Bolman & Deal, 1997; Foner, 1994). Structural and cultural lag are like wearing clothes a size too small. No matter how hard we try to make the clothes fit, they are constricting. Apply this imagery to the structural and cultural lag of social structures. Until recently, age-differentiated structures had compartmentalized education for young people, work for young and middle-aged adults, and retirement for older adults. People received their formal education when they were young, worked during midlife, and were forced to retire between ages 62 and 65 years; retirement symbolized the end of their careers (Reeves, 2005). Thus, compartmentalization resulted in clear role expectations for people across the life span (Riley, Kahn, & Foner, 1994b; Riley & Riley, 1994).

Many of today's employers and organizations still think in terms of linear, age-stratified approaches to careers, preventing them from preparing creatively for an aging workforce. This translates into limited opportunities for a healthy, active, and diverse workforce that can continue contributing its knowledge and skills beyond retirement age. Such options might include flexible work hours, such as part-time work or time off to care for relatives or friends (Achenbaum, 2005; Haight, 2003; Mosner, Spiezle, & Emerman, 2003; Reeves, 2005; Riley, Kahn, & Foner, 1994a; Ruiz, 2006).

Age-integrated structures can provide opportunities for education, work, and leisure or retirement to people of all ages across the life span (McCarthy, 2005; Riley & Riley, 1994; see Figure 9-1). Age integration can alter the person-in-environment fit by tapping into older workers' strengths and assets and by building individual and organizational capacity, reducing the "prolonged 'roleless role' of retirement" (Riley & Riley, p. 24). As system change agents and advocates, social workers can educate organizations and communities about the advantages of age-integrated organizations that build on the strengths of older adults, rather than limit their contributions because of preconceived notions and stereotypes about older adults.

A Changing, Aging Workforce

Americans' perception of aging is shifting. In the survey *American Perceptions of Aging in the 21st Century* conducted in 2000, more than 73 percent of the respondents indicated that a decline in physical activity and mental functioning, rather than chrono-

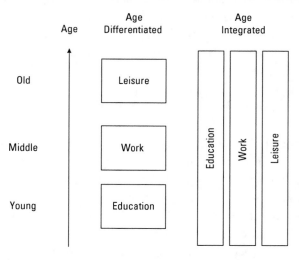

FIGURE 9-1 Types of Social Structures: Age Differentiated Versus Age Integrated

Source: Adapted with permission from Riley, M. W., & Riley, J. W. (1994). Structural lag: Past and future. In M. W. Riley, R. L. Kahn, & A. Foner (Eds.), *Age and structural lag: Society's failure to provide meaningful opportunities in work, family, and leisure* (p. 26). New York: John Wiley & Sons.

logical age, was the most significant indicator of old age (National Council on Aging, Inc., 2002). However, cultural and structural lags still exist in understanding older workers, some of whom are healthy and active and others who will continue working despite various limitations (Merleen, 2006; Ruiz, 2006).

The older workforce today is more heterogeneous. Baby boomers, who will cross the age 65 threshold in 2011, will have experienced geographic mobility, career opportunities, increased longevity, advances in technology and communication, and sociocultural and historical changes (Mosner et al., 2003; Reeves, 2005; see chapter 1). They joined the workforce at the beginning of the technology explosion, which influenced them both positively and negatively. Baby boomer women encountered the women's movement when they were in their twenties or thirties, challenged gender role assignments, and sought to further their education and careers. Political and social movements in the 1960s and again in the 1990s opened the doors for people of color and those with disabilities. Today's older workforce reflects older adults' diverse life and work experiences; family responsibilities; economic, human, and social capital, and a "one size does not fit all" mentality for recruiting and retaining older workers (Pitt-Catsouphes & Smyer, 2006b).

People still face age discrimination despite the enactment in 1967 of the Age Discrimination in Employment Act, which protects employees and job applicants aged 40 years and older from discrimination in hiring, firing, training, compensation, benefits, promotion, and job assignments based on age (Leven, 2004; Pethokoukis, 2006; see chapter 11 for more details). The legislation applies to organizations, including local, state, and federal governments, with 20 or more employees (Pitt-Catsouphes & Smyer, 2006a, 2006b). However, there is still no consensus about the terms to use for people who have moved from mid-career into the later years of working for pay (Pitt-Catsouphes & Smyer, 2006a).

Bureau of Labor Statistics estimates indicate that, between 1998 and 2008, approximately 25 million people will leave the workforce because of death, disability, and retirement—88 percent of those aged 45 years and older. By 2010, more than 51 percent of the workforce is expected to be at least 40 years old (Toosi, 2002). This shift in age in the workforce will dramatically affect services delivery to older adults by public administration, education, and health and social services organizations.

Building Blocks of an Elder-Friendly, Culturally Competent Organization

Characteristics of Elder-Friendly Institutions

Elder-responsive organizations are those agencies, institutions, and corporations whose policies and practices, external and internal structure, cultural norms, rituals, staff, and internal and external lighting, signage, and interior design convey an openness to and affirmation of older adults as customers, consumers, employees, and volunteers. Such organizations acknowledge that people of all ages can contribute and they take responsibility for providing resources to allow older adults to age in place and maintain their quality of life. An *aging-in-place* philosophy recognizes that people prefer to stay in their community as they age rather than move when their physical, cognitive, or psychological health changes (see chapter 10 for further details about the elder-friendly movement). Social workers may track individual and community resources, as well as organizational assets that can support successful or productive aging by older members of the community. (Appendix 9-B delineates tools for assessing the strengths and resources that individuals might bring to the organization, Appendix 9-C for community participation and leadership, and Appendix 9-D for organizational assets.)

Elder-responsive organizations are critical to the creation of elder-friendly communities because they recognize that the aging process is not linear. Some changes may be progressive, such as Alzheimer's disease, whereas others may improve over time, for example, through a combination of medications and physical activity. Organizations that promote aging in place communicate to older adults and their families and caregivers that they are concerned with the whole person; they do not have a limited view of the person as an aging body and the organization as a pass-through for people on their way to a nursing home. Practitioners can assess the organizational culture for friendliness using the guidelines in Appendix 9-E and can work to develop an elder-friendly, culturally competent organization using the strategies outlined in Appendix 9-F. Assessing and assisting in positive change in an organization might begin with a determination of how older adults fit within the organization. It may be that older adults are seen as clients, but cannot have any decision-making responsibilities. Based on this assessment, a few interventions might be selected, such as involving older adults in the planning, development, and evaluation of services and proposing changes in policies and procedures to reflect the organization's commitment to older adults as resources as well as clients.

Resiliency Principles

Building organizations that serve older adults effectively and addressing issues related to an aging workforce are critical to a successful response to societal aging. *Organizational resiliency* is the ability of an organization to handle unforeseen or unplanned changes actively, adapt to changing situations, and reinvent strategies and tactics in response to changing circumstances in order to "bounce back—bounce forward—with speed, grace, determination and precision" as required by changing circumstances or setbacks (Bell, 2002, p. 2; Center for Organization Effectiveness, 2005a; Curran, 2004; Kline, Schonfeld, & Lichtenstein, 1995). Resilience is "neither ethically good nor bad, it is merely the skill and the capacity to be robust under conditions of enormous stress and change" (Coutu, 2002, p. 52).

An organization that "hopes to become resilient must address four types of challenges: cognitive, strategic, political and ideological" (Hamel & Välikangas, 2003, p. 54). The organization must remember that change is constant and dynamic; what worked yesterday may not work tomorrow. An exploration of alternatives rather than the provision of answers will support organizations in their efforts to adapt to changing internal and external pressures. For example, organizations serving older adults who spent their adulthood during World War II may need to adjust their services or opportunities to prepare for the contributions of aging baby boomers.

An organization has met political challenges when it shows its willingness to move resources from the products of yesterday to the programs and services of tomorrow (Curran, 2004; Hamel & Välikangas, 2003) by investing in human capital and resources, such as building on the skills and knowledge that older adults bring to the agency, rather than limiting those adults to a role of care recipient or frail elder. As an organization moves from yesterday's best practices to developing "risky" or novel ideas for experimentation, it is addressing ideological challenges. For example, when private geriatric care managers start to charge for their services and assisted living facilities build luxury housing for high-income older adults, they have begun testing assumptions about older recipients of services.

The application of the five principles of leadership, culture, people, systems, and settings (all of which are related) that build resilient organizations will enable those organizations to transform themselves in an increasingly complex and changing environment (Akabas & Gates, 2006; Azzarto & Smith, 1994; Bell, 2002; Coutu, 2002; Greene, 2007; Hamel & Välikangas, 2003; Kaplan, 2000; Network, 2004; Pulley, 1997). Although these principles are found in business management literature, they are also social work concepts that provide a framework for assessing and intervening in organizations, particularly organizations that are on the forefront of supporting older adults to age in place (American Association of Retired Persons, 2005).

Leadership

Leaders in organizations "can identify and articulate future directions, persevere in the face of obstacles, treat staff with dignity, communicate well, engender trust and inspire top level performance" (Brody & Nair, 2003, p. 203). Strategic leaders need to know when to collaborate and when to compete (Rothman, Erlich, & Tropman, 2001). Effective leaders must be able to define an organization's key values clearly, set priorities, invest in human capital and allocate resources fairly, balance risk and safety, and cultivate resiliency in themselves and their workforce (Curran, 2004; Kline et al., 1995; Pulley, 1997; Schoenberg, Coward, & Albrecht, 2001; Shirey, 2006; N. Thompson, 2005). In organizational practice with older adults, leadership is about envisioning elder-friendly, intergenerational communities that hear and respect older adults' voices, along with those of all generations, in the planning, implementation, and evaluation of current programs and that build support for current and future programs.

Culture

Organizational culture is "the way we do things around here" (Deal & Kennedy, 1982, p. 4). In resilient organizations, culture represents the core, shared values that guide the organization and the way staff behaves and thinks. Culture encompasses a shared mission, a commitment to learning, and partnerships and strategic alliances with other organizations (Rothman et al., 2001). Organizations may demonstrate those shared values through their mission statements, rituals and ceremonies, traditions, beliefs, metaphors, humor, and stories (Bolman & Deal, 1997; Brody & Nair, 2003; Deal & Kennedy, 1982). Although organizational culture may differ between agencies, many health and human services agencies foster a sense of a higher purpose, emotional bonding, trust, stakeholder involvement, and pride in work. Because cultural values "are entrenched as traditional ways of thinking and doing and are developed over a long time period" (Brody & Nair, p. 73), organizations may need to review those values periodically.

Sometimes internal or external circumstances, such as those related to structural or cultural lag, may challenge the existing organizational culture, but value systems of resilient organizations vary little over time and are used as scaffolding when times are difficult (Coutu, 2002). For example, many nursing homes are now undergoing a cultural change. They are working to improve the quality of life and care for their residents through organizational shifts and environmental modifications (Vourlekis & Simons, 2006). These improvements build on their core value of providing quality care to residents. The Green House and Eden Alternative projects, for example, help nursing homes become more resilient rather than extinct. The Green House project involves group homes that use a social and habilitative model of care and maximum staff to serve elders needing skilled nursing care. The Eden Alternative is a reconfiguration of the environment for older adults, including a more home-like environment and gardens. These projects also aim to give residents and family members increased rights in decision making; develop and nurture intergenerational relationships; and design a more homelike, community atmosphere rather than an institutional environment (Kane, 2006; Lustbader & Williams, 2006; Vourlekis & Simons).

People

Resilient organizations need a resilient workforce in which all participants in the organization share decision-making authority rather than having only upper management make the decisions. Organizations must give staff and older adults the skills, support, and services to make decisions and take action to meet the local community's needs (Waite & Richardson, 2004).

Systems

Organizations face challenges as they prepare for an aging workforce, and need to plan how to respond with trained staff to the rapid expansion of information and communication technologies. As the baby boomers move toward the traditional retirement age, organizations must have systems in place to support these older workers. For instance, they will need to make workplace accommodations, devise ways to pass on knowledge and wisdom accumulated over the years, and provide options for continued employment.

Resilient organizations must use technology as an asset rather than a barrier to services delivery (Bell, 2002).

Just as organizations need to improve their planning in the face of an aging workforce, health and social services organizations must plan for a significant increase in volunteers as retired baby boomers seek ways to continue to contribute to society. Health and social work professionals generally recognize that older adults are assets to agencies because of their participation in the planning, development, and evaluation of services. These professionals also realize that organizations must put systems in place to allow older adults to contribute their time, energy, and resources as employees or as volunteers, and allow them to move freely between those roles. Local health and social services organizations and programs such as Literacy Volunteers of America or Volunteers of America recruit older adults to respond to critical needs in their communities. They are responsible for developing an infrastructure that permits the organization to match older adults' skills and abilities with the needs of the local community, so older adults will no longer be retiring *from* something but *to* something.

Settings

Older adults are found in multiple settings and environments, and continuous changes in these settings affect both work and retirement. Development of organizational resilience involves confronting and overcoming structural lag within organizations through, for example, cultural changes, much as the Eden Alternative or Green House projects are proposing, or through collaborative alliances to develop elder-friendly communities that provide an environment for older adults to age in place. A social worker concerned with the lack of aging-friendly resources for clients might meet with staffs from other agencies to assess their leadership, culture, people, systems, and settings before referring clients to those agencies.

In sum, elder-friendly organizations are resilient organizations characterized by mutual trust and respect, skilled communication, real collaboration, effective decision making, environments for successful change, and authentic leadership (Center for Organization Effectiveness, 2005b; Pulley, 1997; Shirey, 2006). Such organizations allow older adults to "flourish in ambiguous and uncertain environments" (Bell, 2002, p. 4) while creating ways to train and retain culturally competent workers to meet the growing demands of the 21st century.

Accessible Technology and Increased Work Flexibility

Elder-friendly organizations address physiological changes as the body ages, including changes in vision, hearing, mobility, and dexterity; and disabling conditions, such as arthritis or occupational injuries (Haight, 2003). A reduction in the number of physically demanding jobs will allow older workers to remain in the workforce longer. Accessible technology can support employment longevity by, for instance, making working environments more accessible. For example, technology makes possible that computer operating systems, software, hardware, and other assistive products are compatible. Technology can also serve "as an equalizer for people with disabilities, removing workplace barriers and increasing employment opportunities while reducing social isolation" (Mosner et al., 2003, p. 12).

Increasing work hour flexibility is another means of addressing structural lag as it relates to older workers. Most employed people, young and old, would like flexible work hours, varying starting and stopping times, the ability to move from full-time to part-time status and back again, time off for education or training, flexibility to exit and reenter the workforce, and extended career breaks to care for family or handle personal responsibilities (Bond, Galinsky, Pitt-Catsouphes, & Smyer, 2005; Kahn, 1994; Mosner et al., 2003; Pitt-Catsouphes & Smyer, 2006b). A balanced relationship between social structures and human lives (Riley & Riley, 1994) might include

> a future society in which retirement as we know it today will be replaced by periods of leisure interspersed throughout the life course with periods of education and work; a society in which lifelong learning replaces the lockstep of traditional education; a society in which opportunities for paid work are spread more evenly across all ages; a society in which older people, as well as children, will be productive assets, not burdens; a society in which work is valued as much for its intrinsic satisfactions as for its economic returns; a society that can give new meaning not only to leisure but also to all of life—from birth to dying and death. (p. 33)

Organizational Analysis

Social work assessment, a skill competent practitioners must possess, is a complex process and product of learning about an individual's or organization's potential and capabilities, the environmental or community resources and characteristics, and changes that will enhance functioning. Just as an individual assessment helps shed light on a person's strengths and resources (see chapter 5), an assessment of an organization's external and internal environment will help social workers identify strategies to assist it to work in partnership with older adults and other community agencies. An organization may be the client, target of the change, or part of the change agent system. Analysis of an organization is an ongoing and mutual process involving the worker, older adults, community members, and others, depending on the nature of the concern requiring attention (Johnson & Yanca, 2007). To assess an organization's readiness for change, the social worker might follow the guidelines shown in Appendix 9-G.

An examination of an organization's external environment involves gaining an understanding of sources of revenue, regulatory and accrediting agencies, other services providers, and clients and referral sources, and discovering what its reputation is in the community. An external analysis might reveal that other agencies are interested in developing a collaborative alliance with the organization to explore how to transform the community into an elder-friendly one. Organizations that traditionally serve older adults might join with others that have never before been part of an aging network.

An internal environmental analysis should focus on "corporate authority and mission; administrative, management and leadership style; organizational and program structure; planning; delivery and evaluation of programs and services; personnel policies and practices; and adequacy of technology and resources" (Netting et al., 2004, p. 280). For example, if the Alzheimer's Association were considering creating a weekend respite program, a social worker might first conduct an internal assessment, followed by an analysis of the external environment, to determine the level of support in the community for such a service (Appendix 9-H).

Strategies that Increase Organizational Effectiveness

A thorough assessment is needed to plan interventions for organizational change. Such an assessment should determine how ready the organization is for change (Appendix 9-G). Organizational change strategies should include engaging external systems to benefit the clients, workers, or both; removing procedures that inhibit services; developing or modifying programs and projects; and involving clients in setting the direction of the agency (Homan, 1999). The change process may at times require collaborative strategies; at other times, it may call for adversarial strategies or a combination of the two. Both approaches build on an organization's strengths and environmental resources, and may be successful in creating change and empowering organizations and older adults.

Collaborative strategies work to establish partnerships. Partner groups contribute resources and move toward common goals, while keeping open the possibility of addressing future community problems in new ways. Such strategies include providing information, presenting alternative courses of action, requesting support for experimentation, establishing study committees, creating new opportunities for interaction, making appeals to conscience or professional ethics, using logical arguments and data, and pointing out negative consequences (Johnson & Yanca, 2007; Resnick & Patti, 1980). For example, community agencies that traditionally serve older adults, such as senior centers, may meet to discuss intergenerational programming that would benefit youths as well as older adults. Agencies that traditionally provide housing for older adults might join with older adults, bankers, and administrators of governmental agencies to discuss intergenerational housing arrangements for grandparents raising grandchildren.

Adversarial or *confrontational strategies* may come into play when decision makers such as agency administrators, legislators, or leaders of social services organizations are unresponsive to older adults, their allies, and their advocates, thus requiring confrontation to initiate change. Adversarial strategists may submit petitions, confront decision makers in open meetings, bring sanctions against an agency, engage in public criticism through the use of the media, encourage noncompliance, go on strike, picket a an agency, initiate litigation, or bargain for change (Homan, 1999; Johnson & Yanca, 2007; Resnick & Patti, 1980). For instance, one might confront absentee landlords about unsatisfactory housing conditions for community-dwelling older adults. Whether collaborative or confrontational strategies are used to achieve change, interventions require careful and thoughtful planning (Appendix 9-I).

Use of Traditional and Alternative Evaluation Methods

Traditionally, evaluations of organizations serving the elderly focus on their ability to provide a "continuum of care" of home- and community-based services to frail and vulnerable older adults, with the goal of preventing premature and inappropriate institutionalization. Program evaluation encourages fiscal responsibility, identifies areas of weakness or concerns that need attention, and provides ethical accountability to boards of directors, funding sources, clients, and the larger community regarding an organization's strengths and resources in meeting its stated goals and objectives (Miley et al., 2007). The NASW *Code of Ethics* (2000) states that programs, or the organizations implementing them, should not claim they can achieve more than they can deliver. Common tools for evaluating programs include consumer satisfaction questionnaires, review of client files, and peer reviews, often using outside experts (Miley et al.). In addition to applying traditional program evaluation approaches, it is critical that evaluators ask about how an agency is planning for, and responding to, older clients, aging staff, and policies affecting older adults, as well as about the organization's participation in the provision of services to help older adults age in place.

An alternative to traditional program evaluation methods is the *empowering evaluation* approach, which is designed to assist people helping themselves and improving programs using a form of self-evaluation and reflection (Fetterman, 2007). This form of evaluation encourages self-determination and supports successful aging, vital involvement, and elder-friendly paradigms by fostering the involvement of clients (that is, consumers or customers) as partners in all aspects of the evaluation process and by building organizational capacity (Miley et al., 2007).

The initial step in conducting an empowerment evaluation is to establish a mission or vision that focuses on the results clients or consumers would like and to specify the tasks and processes to accomplish these results. In the second step, staff and program participants work together to identify the most critical program activities and then meet to discuss the activities' strengths and weaknesses. During the third step, staff and participants address program improvement by identifying future directions for the program and strategies to help them achieve their goals, and discuss how they will evaluate their progress (Fetterman, 2007). Empowerment evaluation not only involves assessment of the external, but also includes an internal component, which includes the input from the program participants themselves (Brown, 1997). Agencies that serve older adults and use empowerment evaluation affirm, empower, and demonstrate "respect for people's capacity to create knowledge about, and solutions to, their own experiences" (Fetterman, 2007, p. 147) and strengthen the organization's capacity for services delivery in the community. In addition to the three steps of the empowerment evaluation, Chinman, Imm, and Wandersman (2004) identified 10 questions that help to establish accountability in organizations. Older volunteers, board members, and community members can participate in this empowerment evaluation by answering these questions and providing feedback in program planning, implementation, evaluation, and sustainability, making the organization more elder friendly. Chinman et al.'s 10 questions are:

1. What are the needs and resources in my organization/school/community/state? (NEEDS and RESOURCES)
2. What are the goals, target population, and desired outcomes (objectives) for my school/community/state? (GOALS)
3. How does this program incorporate knowledge of science and best practice in this area? (BEST PRACTICE)
4. How does this program fit with other programs already being offered? (FIT)
5. What capacities do I need to put this program into place with quality? (CAPACITIES)
6. How will this program be carried out? (PLAN)
7. How will the quality of program implementation be assessed? (IMPLEMENTATION)
8. How well did the program work? (OUTCOMES)
9. How will continuous quality improvement strategies be incorporated? (CQI)
10. If the program (or components of the program) is successful, how will the program be sustained? (SUSTAINING) (p. 24)

Conclusion

Finally, integral to the empowerment evaluation technique are the following five dimensions identified by Fetterman (2007): (1) training, (2) facilitation, (3) advocacy, (4) illumination, and (5) liberation. *Training* involves teaching participants how to conduct their own evaluations and increasing their skills, knowledge, and confidence as evaluators. *Facilitation* is the process of empowering program participants by offering suggestions and assisting them to create the evaluation design. *Advocacy* involves helping marginalized people to advocate for themselves and disenfranchised people regarding policies, economic development, and services. *Illumination* means that program participants have gained insight and understanding in their ability to assess problems and develop intervention strategies. *Liberation* "enables participants to find new opportunities, see existing resources in a new light, and redefine their identities and future roles" (Fetterman, p. 16), thereby taking charge of their own lives (Miley et al., 2007). According to Putnam (2000),

> In the end, however, institutional reform will not work—indeed, it will not happen— unless you and I, along with our fellow citizens, resolve to become reconnected with our friends and neighbors. Henry Ward Beecher's advice a century ago to "multiply picnics" is not entirely ridiculous today. We should do this, ironically, not because it will be good for America—though it will be—but because it will be good for us. (p. 414)

Suggested Exercise to Evaluate Student Competency

Select an organization and use Appendix 9-E, "Guidelines for Assessing Organizational Culture for Elder Friendliness" to evaluate its elder-friendly organizational environment.

References

Achenbaum, W. A. (2005). *Older Americans, vital communities: A bold vision for societal aging.* Baltimore: Johns Hopkins University Press.

Akabas, S. H., & Gates, L. B. (2006). The workplace. In B. Berkman & S. D'Ambruoso (Eds.), *Handbook of social work in health and aging* (pp. 499–508). New York: Oxford University Press.

Aldag, R., & Reschke, W. (2000). *Leading change.* Madison, WI: Center for Organization Effectiveness. Retrieved August 10, 2006, http://www.greatorganizations.com/leadingchange.htm

American Association of Retired Persons. (2005). *Reimagining America: How America can grow older and prosper.* Retrieved June 3, 2006, from http://www.aarp.org/research/blueprint

Azzarto, J., & Smith, M. F. (1994). Should health and human services be decentralized into neighborhood social health centers managed by the community? In M. J. Austin & J. I. Lowe (Eds.), *Controversial issues in communities and organizations* (pp. 73–85). Boston: Allyn & Bacon.

Beaulieu, L. J. (2002). *Mapping the assets of your community: A key component for building local capacity.* Mississippi State, MS: Southern Regional Development Center.

Bell, M. A. (2002, January 7). *The five principles of organizational resilience.* Retrieved August 10, 2006, from http://www.gartner.com/1_researchanalysis/focus_areas/special_reports/rvo/bmit_rvo.html

Bolman, L. G., & Deal, T. E. (1997). *Reframing organizations: Artistry, choice, and leadership* (2nd ed.). San Francisco: Jossey-Bass.

Bond, J. T., Galinsky, E. M., Pitt-Catsouphes, M., & Smyer, M. A. (2005, November). The diverse employment experiences of older men and women in the workforce. *Research Highlights, 2.* Retrieved August 8, 2006, from http://agingandwork.bc.edu/documents/Center_on_Aging_and_Work_Highlight_Two_000.pdf

Brody, R., & Nair, M. D. (2003). *Macro practice: A generalist approach* (6th ed.). Wheaton, IL: Gregory.

Brown, J. W. (1997). Empowerment evaluation: Knowledge and tools for self-assessment and accountability [Book Review]. *Health Education & Behavior, 24,* 388–391.

Burkhauser, R. V., & Quinn, J. F. (1994). Changing policy signals. In M. W. Riley, R. L. Kahn, & A. Foner (Eds.), *Age and structural lag: Society's failure to provide meaningful opportunities in work, family, and leisure* (pp. 237–263). New York: John Wiley & Sons.

Center for Organization Effectiveness. (2005a). *Guidelines for assessing organizational culture.* Retrieved August 10, 2006, from http://www.greatorganizations.com/pdf/spGuidelinesCulture.pdf

Center for Organization Effectiveness. (2005b). *Leading change.* Retrieved August 10, 2006, from http://www.greatorganizations.com/leadingchange.htm

Chinman, M., Imm, P., & Wandersman, A. (2004). *Getting to outcomes: Promoting accountability through methods and tools for planning, implementation, and evaluation.* Santa Monica, CA: Rand Corporation.

Council on Social Work Education, Gero-Ed Center. (2004). *Foundation gerontological social work competencies.* Retrieved November 16, 2006, from http://depts. washington.edu/geroctr/Curriculum3/ Competencies/FdnComp.doc

Coutu, D. L. (2002). How resilience works. *Harvard Business Review, 80,* 46.

Curran, C. R. (2004). Bad news for the custodians of convention. *Nursing Economics, 22,* 109–110.

Deal, T. E., & Kennedy, A. A. (1982). *Corporate cultures.* Reading, MA: Addison-Wesley.

Fetterman, D. M. (2007). *Collaborative, participatory, & empowerment evaluation* [Empowerment Evaluation Blog]. Available at http://www.stanford.edu/~davidf/ empowermentevaluation.html#

Foner, A. (1994). Endnote: The reach of an idea. In M. W. Riley, R. L. Kahn, & A. Foner (Eds.), *Age and structural lag: Society's failure to provide meaningful opportunities in work, family, and leisure* (pp. 263–280). New York: John Wiley & Sons.

Greene, R. R. (Ed.). (2007). *Social work practice: A risk and resiliency perspective.* Belmont, CA: Thomson Brooks/Cole.

Haight, J. M. (2003). Human error & the challenges of an aging workforce [Electronic version]. *Professional Safety, 48,* 18–24. Retrieved August 6, 2006 from http:// www.asse.org

Hamel, G., & Välikangas, L. (2003). The quest for resilience. *Harvard Business Review, 81,* 52–63.

Homan, M. S. (1999). *Promoting community change: Making it happen in the real world* (2nd ed.). Pacific Grove, CA: Brooks/Cole.

Johnson, L. C., & Yanca, S. J. (2007). *Social work practice: A generalist approach* (9th ed.). Boston: Pearson Education.

Kahn, R. L. (1994). Opportunities, aspirations, and goodness of fit. In J. W. Riley, R. L. Kahn, & A. Foner (Eds.), *Age and structural lag: Society's failure to provide meaningful opportunities in work, family, and leisure* (pp. 37–56). New York: John Wiley & Sons.

Kane, R. A. (2006). A social worker's historical and future perspective on residential care. In B. Berkman & S. D'Ambruoso (Eds.), *Handbook of social work in health and aging* (pp. 591–600). New York: Oxford University Press.

Kaplan, C. P. (2000). A case study of resiliency enhancement interventions with an African American woman. In E. Norman (Ed.), *Resiliency enhancement: Putting the strengths perspective into social work practice* (pp. 55–69). New York: Columbia University Press.

Kirst-Ashman, K. K. (2000). *Human behavior, communities, organizations, and groups in the macro social environment: An empowerment approach.* Belmont, CA: Wadsworth/Thomson Learning.

Kline, M., Schonfeld, D. J., & Lichtenstein, R. (1995). Benefits and challenges of school-based crisis response teams. *Journal of School Health, 65,* 245–249.

Leven, C. (2004). *Older workers: Opportunity at our doorstep.* Tokyo: Nikkei Senior Work-Life Forum.

Lustbader, W., & Williams, C. C. (2006). Culture change in long term care. In B. Berkman & S. D'Ambruoso (Eds.), *Handbook of social work in health and aging* (pp. 645–652). New York: Oxford University Press.

McCarthy, J. (2005). Planning a future workforce: An Australian perspective. *New Review of Academic Librarianship, 11,* 41–56.

Merleen, R. (2006). Workforce crisis. *Computerworld, 40,* 34–35.

Miley, K. K., O'Melia, M., & DuBois, B. (2007). *Generalist social work practice: An empowering approach* (5th ed.). Boston: Pearson Education.

Mosner, E., Spiezle, C., & Emerman, J. (2003). *The convergence of the aging workforce and accessible technology: The implications for commerce, business and policy.* Retrieved August 2, 2006, from http://download.microsoft.com/download/d/2/3/d23515f3-2d73-49f4b3b36fae6ac975ce/agingworkforce.doc

National Association of Social Workers. (2000). *Code of ethics of the National Association of Social Workers.* Retrieved July 21, 2006, from http://www.socialworkers.org/pubs/code/code.asp

National Council on Aging, Inc. (2002). *American perceptions of aging in the 21st century: The NCOA's continuing study of the myths and realities of aging.* Retrieved August 7, 2006, from http://www.ncoa.org/Downloads/study_aging.pdf.pdf

Netting, F. E., Kettner, P. M., & McMurtry, S. L. (2004). *Social work macro practice* (3rd ed.). Boston: Pearson Education.

Network, G. R. (2004). *What is resiliency?* Retrieved August 5, 2006, from http://www.globalresiliency.net/brochure.0604.pdf

Pantoja, A., & Perry, W. (1998). Community development and restoration: A perspective and case study. In F. G. Rivera & J. L. Erlich (Eds.), *Community organizing in a diverse society* (pp. 220–242). Boston: Allyn & Bacon.

Pethokoukis, J. M. (2006). The economy may face a SHORTAGE of qualified workers. *U.S. News & World Report, 140,* 46–47.

Pillari, V., & Newsome, M. (1998). Human behavior in the social environment families, groups, organizations, and communities. Pacific Grove, CA: Brooks/Cole.

Pitt-Catsouphes, M., & Smyer, M. A. (2006a, February). *How old are today's older workers?* (Issue Brief No. 4). Retrieved August 7, 2006, from http://agingandwork.bc.edu/static/documents/Center_on_Aging_and_Work_Brief_Four.pdf

Pitt-Catsouphes, M., & Smyer, M. A. (2006b, March). *One size does not fit all: Workplace Flexibility* (Issue Brief No. 5). Retrieved August 8, 2006, from http://agingandwork.bc.edu/static/documents/Center_on_Aging_and_Work_Brief_Five.pdf

Pulley, M. L. (1997, November 4). Leading resilient organizations [Electronic version]. *Leadership in Action, 17,* 1–5. Retrieved August 10, 2006 from http://216.239.33.104/search?q=cache:xuqGJKZmRMUC:www.linkages.com/resilient_orgs_LiA.pdf+rsilient+organizations&hl=en&ie=UTF-8

Putnam, R. D. (2000). *Bowling alone: The collapse and revival of American community.* New York: Simon & Schuster.

Reeves, S. (2005, September 29). *An aging workforce's effect on U.S. employers.* Retrieved August 2, 2006, from http://www.forbes.com/2005/09/28/career-babyboomer-workcx_sr_0929bizbasics_print.html

Resnick, H., & Patti, R. J. (Eds.). (1980). *Changes from within: Humanizing social welfare organizations.* Philadelphia: Temple University Press.

Riley, M. W., Kahn, R. L., & Foner, A. (Eds.). (1994a). *Age and structural lag: Society's failure to provide meaningful opportunities in work, family, and leisure.* New York: John Wiley & Sons.

Riley, M. W., Kahn, R. L., & Foner, A. (1994b). Introduction: The mismatch between people and structures. In M. W. Riley, R. L. Kahn, & A. Foner (Eds.), *Age and structural lag: Society's failure to provide meaningful opportunities in work, family, and leisure* (pp. 1–14). New York: John Wiley & Sons.

Riley, M. W., & Riley, J. W. (1994). Structural lag: Past and future. In M. W. Riley, R. L. Kahn, & A. Foner (Eds.), *Age and structural lag: Society's failure to provide meaningful opportunities in work, family, and leisure* (pp. 15–36). New York: John Wiley & Sons.

Roberts, A. (2003). In the eye of the storm? Societal aging and the future of public-service reform. *Public Administration Review, 63,* 720–733.

Rothman, J., Erlich, J. L., & Tropman, J. E. (Eds.). (2001). *Strategies of community intervention.* Itasca, IL: F. E. Peacock.

Ruiz, G. (2006). Gray eminence. *Workforce Management, 85,* 32–36.

Schoenberg, N. E., Coward, R. T., & Albrecht, S. L. (2001). Attitudes of older adults about community based services: Emergent themes from in-depth interviews. *Journal of Gerontological Social Work, 35,* 3–19.

Shirey, M. R. (2006). Authentic leaders creating healthy work environments for nursing practice. *American Journal of Critical Care, 15,* 256–267.

Thompson, M. B., & Wesolowski, B. (2005). *2005 White house conference on aging closes.* [Press Release]. Retrieved July 10, 2006, from http://www.whcoa.gov/about/resolutions/top%2010.pdf

Thompson, N. (2005). Holding fast: The struggle to create resilient caregiving organizations [Book Review]. *Community Care,* (1562), 46.

Toosi, M. (2002). A century of change. The US laborforce, 1950–2050. *Monthly Labor Review, 125*(5), 15–28.

Vourlekis, B., & Simons, K. (2006). Nursing homes. In B. Berkman & S. D'Ambruoso (Eds.), *Handbook of social work in health and aging* (pp. 601–614). New York: Oxford University Press.

Waite, P. J., & Richardson, G. E. (2004). Determining the efficacy of resiliency training in the work site. *Journal of Allied Health, 33,* 178–183.

Warren, R. L. (1978). *The community in America* (3rd ed.). Chicago: Rand McNally.

APPENDIX 9-A Top 10 Resolutions of the 2005 White House Conference on Aging

The following is a press release disseminated on December 14, 2005.

2005 WHITE HOUSE CONFERENCE ON AGING CLOSES

Top 10 Resolutions Announced

WASHINGTON, DC—The 2005 White House Conference on Aging (WHCoA) officially closed today, with delegates sharing recommendations to be sent to the President and Congress on the pressing aging issues of today and the future. Delegates in attendance selected the top 50 resolutions to present and participated in working groups to develop strategies for implementing the resolutions. The top 10 resolutions as voted by the delegates are:

- Reauthorize the Older Americans Act Within the First Six Months Following the 2005 White House Conference on Aging

- Develop a Coordinated, Comprehensive Long-Term Care Strategy by Supporting Public and Private Sector Initiatives that Address Financing, Choice, Quality, Service Delivery, and the Paid and Unpaid Workforce

- Ensure that Older Americans Have Transportation Options to Retain Their Mobility and Independence

- Strengthen and Improve the Medicaid Program for Seniors

- Strengthen and Improve the Medicare Program

- Support Geriatric Education and Training for All Healthcare Professionals, Paraprofessionals, Health Profession Students, and Direct Care Workers

- Promote Innovative Models of Non-Institutional Long-Term Care

- Improve Recognition, Assessment, and Treatment of Mental Illness and Depression Among Older Americans

- Attain Adequate Numbers of Healthcare Personnel in All Professions Who are Skilled, Culturally Competent, and Specialized Geriatrics

- Improve State and Local Based Integrated Delivery Systems to Meet 21st Century Needs of Seniors

- By statute, the final report from the conference will be presented to the President and Congress by June 2006.

- For a full listing of the 50 resolutions, visit www.whcoa.gov

Source: Adapted with permission from Thompson, M. B., & Wesolowski, B. (2005). 2005 *White House conference on aging closes.* [Press release]. Retrieved July 10, 2006, from http://www.whcoa.gov/about/resolutions/top%2010.pdf

APPENDIX 9-B Capacity Inventory for Individuals

Part 1: Skills Information

Please indicate which of the following skills you have by placing a check mark ☑ in the column under "Skills You Have." These talents and skills include those you have developed from training or from experiences at home, church, work, or in community activities. If you don't have this skill or would like to receive additional training in this area, please place a check mark ☑ in the column under "Want to Learn This Skill."

Skills	Skills You Have	Want to Learn This Skill
Health		
Caring for elderly individuals	☐	☐
Caring for mentally ill individuals	☐	☐
Caring for sick individuals	☐	☐
Caring for physically or developmentally challenged individuals	☐	☐
Office		
Typing (words per minute_____)	☐	☐
Operating an adding machine or calculator	☐	☐
Working with office files	☐	☐
Taking phone messages	☐	☐
Writing business letters (not typing)	☐	☐
Receiving phone orders	☐	☐
Operating several phone lines	☐	☐
Keeping track of supplies	☐	☐
Shorthand or speed writing	☐	☐
Bookkeeping	☐	☐
Entering information into a computer spreadsheet	☐	☐
Preparing computer graphics	☐	☐
Word processing	☐	☐
Construction and Repair		
Painting	☐	☐
Home construction or repair	☐	☐
Tearing down buildings	☐	☐
Knocking out walls	☐	☐
Wallpapering	☐	☐

(Continued)

APPENDIX 9-B Capacity Inventory for Individuals (*Continued*)

Skills	Skills You Have	Want to Learn This Skill
Construction and Repair (*Continued*)		
Furniture repairs	☐	☐
Furniture refinishing	☐	☐
Repairing locks	☐	☐
Building garages	☐	☐
Bathroom modernization	☐	☐
Building room additions	☐	☐
Tile work	☐	☐
Installing drywall and taping	☐	☐
Plumbing repairs	☐	☐
Electrical repairs	☐	☐
Bricklaying and masonry	☐	☐
Cabinetmaking	☐	☐
Kitchen modernization	☐	☐
Furniture making	☐	☐
Installing insulation	☐	☐
Soldering and welding	☐	☐
Concrete work (sidewalks)	☐	☐
Installing floor coverings	☐	☐
Heating/cooling system installation	☐	☐
Installing windows	☐	☐
Building swimming pools	☐	☐
Carpentry skills	☐	☐
Roofing installation or repair	☐	☐
Maintenance		
Window washing	☐	☐
Floor waxing and mopping	☐	☐
Washing and cleaning carpets/rugs	☐	☐
Routing clogged drains	☐	☐
Using a hand truck in business	☐	☐
Caulking	☐	☐
General household cleaning	☐	☐

(*Continued*)

APPENDIX 9-B Capacity Inventory for Individuals (*Continued*)

Skills	Skills You Have	Want to Learn This Skill
Maintenance (*Continued*)		
Fixing leaky faucets	☐	☐
Mowing lawns	☐	☐
Pruning trees and shrubbery	☐	☐
Cleaning/maintaining swimming pools	☐	☐
Floor sanding and stripping	☐	☐
Wood floor stripping/refinishing	☐	☐
Food		
Catering	☐	☐
Serving food to large number of people (more than 10)	☐	☐
Preparing meals for large number of people (more than 10)	☐	☐
Clearing/setting tables for large number of people (more than 10)	☐	☐
Washing dishes for large number of people (more than 10)	☐	☐
Operating commercial food preparation equipment	☐	☐
Meat cutting	☐	☐
Baking	☐	☐
Child Care		
Caring for infants (0–1 year of age)	☐	☐
Caring for toddlers (1–3 years of age)	☐	☐
Caring for preschool children (3–5 years of age)	☐	☐
Caring for children (5–11 years of age)	☐	☐
Taking children on field trips	☐	☐
Transportation		
Driving a van	☐	☐
Driving a bus	☐	☐
Driving a tractor trailer	☐	☐
Driving a commercial truck	☐	☐
Driving a vehicle to deliver goods	☐	☐
Hauling	☐	☐

(Continued)

APPENDIX 9-B Capacity Inventory for Individuals (*Continued*)

Skills	Skills You Have	Want to Learn This Skill
Transportation (*Continued*)		
Operating farm equipment	☐	☐
Driving an ambulance	☐	☐
Repairing Machinery		
Repairing radios, TVs, video/tape recorders, CD players	☐	☐
Repairing small appliances	☐	☐
Repairing automobiles	☐	☐
Repairing trucks/buses	☐	☐
Auto body repairs	☐	☐
Repairing large household appliances (for example, refrigerator, washer/dryer)	☐	☐
Repairing heating and air-conditioning system	☐	☐
Supervision		
Writing reports	☐	☐
Filling out forms	☐	☐
Planning work for other people	☐	☐
Developing a budget	☐	☐
Keeping records of activities	☐	☐
Interviewing people	☐	☐
Sales		
Operating a cash register	☐	☐
Selling wholesale or manufacturing products (if YES, what products? _____)	☐	☐
Selling products retail (if YES, what products? _____)	☐	☐
Selling services (if YES, what services? _____)	☐	☐
How have you sold these products or services?	☐	☐
Door to Door	☐	☐
Telephone	☐	☐
Mail	☐	☐
Store	☐	☐

(Continued)

APPENDIX 9-B Capacity Inventory for Individuals (*Continued*)

Skills	Skills You Have	Want to Learn This Skill
Sales (*Continued*)		
From home	☐	☐
Music		
Singing	☐	☐
Play an instrument (what instrument? _____)		
Other Skills	☐	☐
Upholstering	☐	☐
Sewing	☐	☐
Dressmaking	☐	☐
Knitting	☐	☐
Tailoring	☐	☐
Moving furniture/equipment to different locations	☐	☐
Managing property	☐	☐
Assisting in the classroom	☐	☐
Tutoring students	☐	☐
Hairdressing	☐	☐
Hair cutting	☐	☐
Phone surveys	☐	☐
Jewelry and watch repair	☐	☐

Are there other skills you have that are not listed here? If YES, what are those skills? Just write them on the following lines.

1. _____
2. _____
3. _____

Priority Skills

- Given everything you have checked in the skills inventory above, what three things would you say you do best? Please list them.

1. _____
2. _____
3. _____

(Continued)

APPENDIX 9-B Capacity Inventory for Individuals (*Continued*)

- Which of all of your skills are good enough that other people would hire you to do them?

    1. _____

    2. _____

    3. _____

- Are there any skills that you have that you could teach to others?

    1. _____

    2. _____

    3. _____

- What skills would you most like to learn?

    1. _____

    2. _____

    3. _____

Part 2: Community Skills

Have you ever organized or participated in any of the following community activities? Please place a check mark ☑ by those activities that you have been involved in.

Boy Scouts/Girl Scouts	☐
Hobby clubs	☐
Coached or assisted a sports team	☐
Church fundraisers	☐
Parent–Teacher Association or Organization	☐
Camp trips for kids	☐
Field trips	☐
Worked on political campaigns	☐
Neighborhood clubs or programs	☐
YMCA/YWCA or 4-H programs	☐
Religious organizations	☐
Civic or service clubs	☐
Veterans organizations	☐
Participated in community improvement activities	☐
Worked in support of or opposition to a local issue	☐

(*Continued*)

APPENDIX 9-B Capacity Inventory for Individuals (*Continued*)

Part 3: Enterprising Interests and Experience

Business Interest

• Have you ever considered starting a business?

   ☐ NO (if NO, skip to the next section on *Business Activity*)

   ☐ YES (if YES, what kind of business? _____)

• Did you plan to start it alone or with other people?

   ☐ ALONE   ☐ WITH OTHERS

• Did you plan to operate it out of your home?

   ☐ NO   ☐ YES

• What obstacles are keeping you from starting this business? _____

_____

Business Activity

• Are you currently earning money on your own through the sale of services or products?

   ☐ NO   ☐ YES (If YES, what are the services or products you sell?)

_____

• To whom do you sell these services or products?

_____

• How do you get customers?

_____

• What would help you improve your business?

_____

Part 4: Personal Information

Name _____

Address _____

Phone _____ Year of birth _____

Sex: ☐ FEMALE ☐ MALE

Number of years you've lived in the community: _____

_____

APPENDIX 9-C Community Participation and Leadership Inventory

Political and Government-Related Activities

- Have you ever written or talked to a public official about a public issue that was of concern to you?

  ☐ YES   ☐ NO

- Have you ever spoken out in a public meeting on a community or neighborhood issue of concern to you?

  ☐ YES   ☐ NO

- Have you ever worked actively for the election of any political candidate?

  ☐ YES   ☐ NO

- Have you ever been elected or appointed to a position in the local government?

  ☐ YES   ☐ NO

Involvement in Voluntary Organizations

- Do you currently belong to, or have you ever been a member of, any of the following organizations:

A. *Community civic and service organizations*

	YES	NO
Jaycees	☐	☐
Kiwanis	☐	☐
Lions	☐	☐
Rotary	☐	☐
Council on Aging	☐	☐
March of Dimes	☐	☐
Salvation Army	☐	☐
United Way	☐	☐
League of Women Voters	☐	☐
American Cancer Society	☐	☐
American Heart Association	☐	☐
American Red Cross	☐	☐

B. *Religious organizations*

Christian Women's Fellowship	☐	☐
Christian Men's Fellowship	☐	☐
Habitat for Humanity	☐	☐
Knights of Columbus	☐	☐
House of worship outreach and other groups	☐	☐

(Continued)

APPENDIX 9-C Community Participation and Leadership Inventory (*Continued*)

C. *Social and recreational organizations*

	YES	NO
Hobby clubs	☐	☐
Athletic boosters	☐	☐
Recreational clubs	☐	☐
Sports leagues	☐	☐

D. *Patriotic and fraternal organizations*

American Legion	☐	☐
Daughters of the American Revolution	☐	☐
Elks	☐	☐
Masons	☐	☐
Veterans of Foreign Wars	☐	☐
Shriners	☐	☐

E. *Education and youth organizations*

Parent–Teacher Association or organization	☐	☐
School advisory committee	☐	☐
School volunteer committee	☐	☐
Boys Scouts/Girl Scouts	☐	☐
Boys/Girls Club	☐	☐
4-H Club	☐	☐

Leadership in Voluntary Organizations

If you answered YES to any of the voluntary organizations listed above, have you served as an officer or committee chair in any of these organizations?

☐ YES   ☐ NO

Involvement in Local Issues

Over the past five years, have you been involved in any type of community project(s) or issue(s)? This could be an issue taking place in your neighborhood or community.

☐ YES   ☐ NO

IF YES, please place a check mark ☑ by the items below that best represent the type of involvement you may have had in this issue(s) or project(s).

☐ Helped bring an issue or project to the attention of my community, neighborhood, or local government

(*Continued*)

APPENDIX 9-C Community Participation and Leadership Inventory (*Continued*)

☐ Helped investigate the issue or project (for example, gathered facts about the issue, tried to find out what people felt about the issue/project, asked other people to help work on the issue or project)

☐ Helped decide what was to be done about the issue or project (for example, what approaches would be best to deal with the issue or project)

☐ Worked on putting the plan of action together (for example, helped figure out who would be responsible for carrying out different parts of the plan, helped determine when activities related to the plan would be started and completed)

☐ Helped carry out activities to get the project off the ground and completed, or to get the local issue settled.

Background Information

Name _____

Address _____

Phone _____

Number of Years You Have Lived in the Community: _____

Gender: ☐ FEMALE ☐ MALE

Source: Adapted with permission from Beaulieu, L. J. (2002). *Mapping the assets of your community: A key component for building local capacity.* Mississippi State, MS: Southern Regional Development Center. Retrieved August 4, 2005, from http://srdc.msstate.edu/publications/227/227_leadership_inventory.pdf.

Copyright © 2002 by the Southern Rural Development Center, Series #227.

APPENDIX 9-D Organization Inventory

Name of formal organization: _____

Type of community institution (check the category that best matches):

☐ Kinship/family   ☐ Economic   ☐ Education

☐ Political/governmental   ☐ Religious   ☐ Association

1. Mission or purpose of the formal organization:

_____

_____

_____

2. Number of members and/or employees: _____ # members

                                       _____ # employees

3. The organization's major activities/programs in the community:

_____

_____

_____

_____

4. Local groups the organization works most closely with:

_____

_____

_____

_____

5. New projects, programs, and/or activities this formal organization would like to become involved in over the next few years that would benefit the community:

_____

_____

_____

_____

_____

(Continued)

APPENDIX 9-D Organization Inventory (*Continued*)

6. Current profile of the formal organization's resources:

Equipment owned (that is, computers, vehicles)		
Type of purchases made locally and outside the community	*Locally*	*Outside the Community*
Number of employees (if applicable) who live in or outside the community	*In the Community*	*Outside the Community*
Major areas of expertise of persons involved in the work of this organization		
Resources (foundations, grants, in-kind donations) available to support community projects		
Links the formal organization has with resources located outside the community		

Source: Adapted with permission from Beaulieu, L. J. (2002). *Mapping the assets of your community: A key component for building local capacity.* Mississippi State, MS: Southern Regional Development Center. Retrieved August 5, 2006, from http://srdc.msstate.edu/publications/227/227_institutionsinventory.pdf.

APPENDIX 9-E Guidelines for Assessing Organizational Culture for Elder Friendliness

Gathering Information

* Look around. What do the headquarters and other buildings look like? How are people dressed? How much interaction is there? Who is talking to whom? How does the place "feel"? *How welcoming is the agency for older adults, for people with disabilities, for a diverse population?*

* Read newsletters and other internal documents. What values are emphasized? Who is held up for praise? Are parties, celebrations, or other ceremonies mentioned? What sorts of things are discussed? *Are older adults visible in newsletters, pictures, and at parties? Are they recognized for their contributions to the organization?*

* Look at annual reports or other communications to others outside the firm. What "face" is being presented to the world? *Does the "face" represent the clients served, the community, and the organizational values?*

* Ask, Can you tell me anything about what the culture is like here? Are there any stories that people here tell about _____? *It is often older adults who have the institutional memory. Are the stories they tell the same as the younger workers? Why or why not?*

* Ask, What values are stressed in _____? How are they communicated? How are they reinforced? *Older adults often pass on the culture and the values to others. Who passes the values in the organization? What do those values say about older adults, about retirement, about the organization's willingness to accommodate people with limitations?*

* Ask, Who is looked up to in _____? *Where are the older adults?*

* See what you can learn about rites and ceremonies in the organization. What happens when people accomplish something? Are there rites of passage, such as promotion ceremonies and retirement parties? Are there regular get-togethers, such as holiday parties, social events, and company softball games? *Who is included in the celebrations and who is left out? Are old, young, people of color, and Anglos invited? Who comes? What does retirement look like? When does retirement planning begin? Is retirement an individual choice or an organizational decision?*

* Ask, What sorts of behaviors are expected and rewarded here? What sorts of behaviors are punished?

* Ask people outside the firm what they think of it. *Ask older adults in the community about their experiences. Ask retired employees about their experiences.*

* Check magazines, newspapers, and other sources to get clues about the culture.

* As appropriate, use quantitative measures such as the QFIT-C, Organizational Culture Profile, Organizational Culture Inventory, or a tailored culture survey.

(Continued)

APPENDIX 9-E Guidelines for Assessing Organizational Culture for Elder Friendliness (*Continued*)

Making Sense of the Information

- Overall, how salient is the culture?

  - Do leaders mention culture, values, and heroes in their messages?

  - Do organizational members talk much about culture and its elements?

- What primary themes emerge?

- Are responses consistent across people, levels, and units?

- How does everything fit together?

  - Are valued behaviors rewarded?

  - Are symbols, stories, heroes, and ceremonies consistent?

Note: The author of this chapter is the source of the questions and comments in italic type.

Source: Adapted with permission from Aldag, R., & Reschke, W. (2000). *Leading change.* Center for Organization Effectiveness. Madison: WI. Retrieved August 10, 2006, http://www.greatorganizations.com/leadingchange.htm

APPENDIX 9-F Strategies to Develop Elder-Friendly, Culturally Competent Organizations

- Involve older adults in the planning, development, and evaluation of services.

- Use older adults of color and older lesbian, gay, bisexual, and transgender people as cultural guides so the organization can be accountable to diverse minority communities.

- Provide services and programs that diverse communities can access easily and that have a strong educational and prevention focus.

- Train staff in culturally competent assessment and intervention strategies with older adults that adhere to the cultural integrity of the ethnic group's values, beliefs, and lifestyles.

- Hire bilingual, bicultural, or indigenous staff, or staff who are experienced translators. Ensure that these staff members are culturally and age sensitive and can develop relationships with individuals and with communities.

- Build coalitions with other organizations, including minority-owned newspapers, media, and civic and religious organizations that serve minority older adults.

- Provide employed caregivers with workplace time flexibility; education about resources; stress management classes; and geriatric care managers (see chapter 8) who can help access, manage, and coordinate care and services (U.S. Department of Health and Human Services, Administration on Aging, 2003).

- Change polices and procedures to reflect the organization's commitment to older adults as resources as well as clients.

- Audit the organization for elder friendliness and cultural competence and make ongoing changes as needed.

APPENDIX 9-G Assessing System Readiness for Change

	Systems promoting change: initiator, client change agent, support, action	Systems to be changed: controlling, host, implementing, target
General openness to change	Probably not an issue, because these groups are promoting change.	If these systems have shown tendencies in the past to resist changes of this type, this should serve as an early warning.
Anticipated or actual response to proposed change	How committed are those promoting change to the type of change being proposed? What are the differences, if any? Are some committed only to a highly specific solution?	Is there consensus or disagreement about the type of change being proposed? How strong are feelings for or against it?
Availability of resources	Do the systems promoting change have the skills and human resources to see the change effort through to completion, even if there is resistance?	Do the systems to be changed have the funding, staff, facilities, equipment, or other resources needed to implement the proposed change?
Opposition to change	What forces outside these systems are opposing change? How strong is the opposition?	What is the source of outside opposition? How strong are the pressures to reject the proposed change? What significant people are most vulnerable to pressures?

Source: From Netting, F. E., Ketter, P. M., & McMurtry, S. L. *Social work macro practice* (3rd ed., p. 326). Published by Allyn and Bacon, Boston, MA.

APPENDIX 9-H Framework for Organizational Assessment

Organizational Goals and Structures

- Identify the organization's mission, purpose, goals, and history.

- Describe the organizational governance and decision-making structures.

- Define the perspectives or principles that guide leadership and managerial staff.

- Characterize the organizational culture and membership or constituencies.

Organization–Environment Relations

- Detail the organization's economic, political, demographic, fiscal, cultural, legal or governmental, and technological environments.

- Characterize the fit between organizational purpose and tasks and between the needs and resources of the environment.

- Describe the opportunities available in the environment and threats posed by the environment.

- Identify relevant policy issues that affect organizational functioning.

Organizational Competence

- Describe how the organization evaluates its achievement of its purpose and goals, and how the organization uses that feedback to enhance effectiveness.

- Assess the organizational capacity for innovation or change.

- Identify mechanisms for strategic planning and continuous quality improvement.

Source: From Miley, Karla Krogerud, et al. *Generalist social work practice: An empowering approach* (5th ed., p. 274). Published by Allyn and Bacon, Boston, MA.

APPENDIX 9-I Principles for Increasing Effectiveness of Organizational Change

- Know your issues well so that you can determine who to include in your coalition and what is your target for change. Does the organizational or community issue involve legislation, budget allocation, transportation, development of a new agency program, or a change in an internal agency policy? Could you frame the issue as an intergenerational one that might help you access a different group of partners than if it were identified as an "aging issue"?

- Involve clients or community members as participants on the team to help identify the issue or issues and to become valuable partners in determining intervention strategies.

- Gain the support of external advocacy groups. Access local coalitions through the area agencies on aging or local chapters of national organizations that serve older adults, such as AARP, Older Women's League, Gray Panthers, or Alzheimer's Association.

- Capitalize on external threats and opportunities. Demographic trends have consistently indicated an increase not only in the older adult population in general, but also in that of older adults of color. Can you identify retired or semiretired, healthy older adults who might be wonderful resources for the agency?

- Create support systems that sustain social worker involvement in the change. Assess potential risks and benefits of involvement to the worker, the agency, and older adults. Does the organization value workers who are change-agent practitioners and recognize their contributions to the community by allowing them to use regular work hours to participate?

- Identify stakeholders, attract investors, and secure allies. Think creatively about who might be potential allies, such as clergy, local business people, foundations, or banks.

- Understand the organizational culture. What factors support change? What are the barriers to change?

- Expect, identify, and deal with resistance.

- Reduce personal risk.

- Implement and confirm the change.

Source: From *Promoting community change: Making it happen in the real world* (2nd ed.) by Homan, M. S. (1999). Reprinted with permission of Wadsworth, a division of Thomson Learning: www.thomsonrights. com. Fax 800-730-2215.

Community Capacity Building

Macro Perspective on the Person in Environment

10

RATIONALE: Social workers include community organizers who seek to find sustainable solutions congruent with locale and community stakeholders. They collaborate with community-based agencies and seek consultation from natural helpers.

COMPETENCY: Students will prepare to organize communities, seeking means of creating an aging-friendly environment. They will

- advocate and organize with service providers, community organizations, policy makers, and the public to meet the needs and issues of a growing aging population.
  The competency encompasses strategies to address age discrimination in relation to health, housing, employment, and transportation.
- identify the availability of resources and resource systems for older adults and their families.
- identify the major sources of funding for meeting the needs of older adults. (Council on Social Work Education, Gero-Ed Center, 2004)

No More "One Size Fits All"

Advances in medical and health care, behavioral changes that support healthy lifestyles, enhanced environmental conditions, and increased longevity of older ethnic minorities have resulted in an older adult population that chooses to age in place in their homes and communities, living more active, productive, or successful lives. Much has been written about the development of the older adult and the effects of psychological, biological, and social systems on later adulthood (see chapters 1 and 5). Occasionally, scholars will make reference to the effect of older adults' living environments, but usually do not examine how communities and neighborhoods influence physical, social, and psychological adjustment in older adulthood (Berk, 2004; Glicken, 2004; Hutchison, 1999; Kirst-Ashman, 2000).

Until recently, gerontological social work used a social planning model that relied on "experts" and "professionals" in the planning, development, or implementation of home- and community-based services, without recognizing the assets and contributions that older adults bring to the community (Atchley & Barusch, 2004; Kochera, Straight, & Guterbock, 2005; Netting, Kettner, & McMurtry, 2004; Richardson & Barusch, 2006; Rybash, Roodin, & Santrock, 1985). That one-size-fits-all model for creating aging-friendly communities is increasingly ineffective, and presents new challenges and opportunities to the social work profession.

How can community practitioners develop sufficient strategies to support older adults who want to be creative and remain active members of their communities (Austin, Camp, Flux, McClelland, & Sieppert, 2005; Cox, 2001; J. L. Johnson & Grant, 2005; Zastrow & Kirst-Ashman, 2004)? For example, numerous national and international initiatives have explored the effects of aging on industrial societies; however, scholars and academicians have failed to differentiate "between individual development and societal aging" (Achenbaum, 2005, p. xvii). *Societal aging*, a term coined by Bernice Neugarten, refers to the mix of individual and population aging at the same time as the aging of institutions and social mores (Achenbaum). Societal aging is the tapestry that reveals older adults in their relationship with young and middle-age adults; the community values, traditions, and rituals; and the network of agencies, programs, and services that support the community.

Societal ageism pits generation against generation and limits ways that older adults can contribute to their community (Achenbaum, 2005; see chapter 1). Furthermore, in the past social ageism also affected social work education and practice. As a result, older adults were viewed as recipients of services and not as contributing members of society. The social work profession's efforts to plan proactively for ways to engage older adults as active community members were limited. The response of older adults and others to adverse conditions created by societal ageism has played a significant role in hindering the development of individual and community resiliency.

Because the aging process knows no race, ethnicity, gender, class, sexual orientation, or geographic location boundaries, older adults and community members are challenged to determine a vision and plan that builds on assets and resources unique to their community. Because there is a wide variety of community change practice models, and a renewed openness to changing definitions of community, a great opportunity exists now and in the future for revitalizing communities (Cox, 2001). In addition, A. K. Johnson (1998) has predicted that decentralization by the federal government and more opportunity for local decision making and resource development may result in further opportunity to revitalize community practice.

In response to the fears of declining communities (Breton, 2001; Cox, 2001; Putnam, 2000) and the lack of adequate planning and preparation for a growing and increasingly diverse aging population (Hooyman & Kiyak, 2005; Wilson, 2006), social work, with its focus on the person in environment (Kirst-Ashman, 2000), must position itself to take advantage of the opportunities for rebuilding and revitalizing communities using community members' skills and talents (Saleebey, 2002). By recognizing and using older adults' resources and assets, social workers can foster individual and community resiliency (Greene, 2007).

The new paradigm of successful community aging (Greene & Cohen, 2005) shifts the social work lens from a limited view of older adults as vulnerable, burdensome, and a drain on community resources to a larger, embracing one that recognizes older adults as community assets, having the capacity and desire to make communities better places in which to live, work, and play (Achenbaum, 2005; Austin et al., 2005; Billig, 2004). This new perspective recognizes vital communities that support older adults aging in place and includes a vision of resilient, intergenerational communities that support all members.

To best assist these communities, social workers need to apply new forms of community practice. For instance, they may work in collaboration with nontraditional partners, define multiple targets of change, try alternative strategies in the change process, and address issues of ethnicity and cultural diversity and other areas of cultural competence, with the goal of using all community members' contributions and talents to build and sustain community capacity (Cox, 2001; Rivera & Erlich, 1998).

This chapter explores new approaches to social work practice with older adults and communities, based on an understanding that communities are changing, aging, and engaged in a transformative process that recognizes the contributions of older adults as valuable community resources. Although certain roles and tasks have been associated with past community practice, the knowledge, skills, and values—the competencies—presented in this chapter will assist microsystem and macrosystem practitioners to learn how to influence the environment in the person-in-environment perspective.

Social work students will investigate how intergenerational livable communities can contribute to successful aging and improve the quality of life for all their residents, developing strategies to help older adults become community resources, not just services recipients. The chapter also highlights those communities that have made aging well a priority.

History of Social Work in Community Practice

Early practitioners faced challenges as they worked among the marginalized and voiceless populations, such as those living in poverty, immigrants, and children and families of war veterans (Berg-Weger, 2005; Netting et al., 2004). Settlement houses, which opened in the late 1880s, enabled social workers to improve others' lives by actively participating to change the clients' community (Berg-Weger; Netting et al.). However, during the early part of the 20th century, Freudian psychology and the publication of Mary Richmond's *Social Diagnosis* (L. C. Johnson & Yanca, 2007) shifted the social work profession away from an emphasis on changing communities to embracing individuals and families as the target of change.

Not until the 1960s was community organizing again recognized as a "legitimate concentration" (Rivera & Erlich, 1998, p. 3). Many community activists who assisted traditionally marginalized groups gain political power and social and economic justice later became social workers. Many of those activists were also involved in governmental social programs that provided strategies for community-level intervention to address economic and social injustice (Netting et al., 2004). Social workers began to organize communities and develop social programs that affected the quality of life for people of color, children and families living in poverty, older adults, and the physical and mental health needs of individuals and families across the life span.

Community organization subsequently became an official method of social work practice. Social legislation, including the Civil Rights Act of 1964, Economic Opportunity Act of 1964, Community Mental Health Centers Act of 1963, Food Stamp Act of 1964, and Older Americans Act of 1965, influenced the nature of community life for today's older adults. Now, at the beginning of the 21st century, society is preparing for the increasingly aging population by creating intergenerational, livable communities.

Through public and private funding sources, local communities, state government, and national organizations are seeking to create a bold vision of intergenerational, livable communities that can capitalize on the assets and contributions of all members and can support those who need additional assistance by creating opportunities for interdependent relationships. Social workers have been involved in leadership positions in the past and have a responsibility—and they have the skills and knowledge—to expand community capacity and foster healthy communities in which individuals and families can contribute to and receive from their environment (Kirst-Ashman & Hull, 2006).

What Is Community?

Definitions

According to Shaffer and Anundsen (1993), *community* is a "dynamic whole that emerges when a group of people participate in common practices, depend on one another, make decisions together, identify themselves as a part of something larger than the sum of the individual relationships, or commit themselves for the long term to their own, one another's and the group's well-being" (p. 10). Community may be a "state of being," or a sense of community might be "found at the intersection of the inward and outward life" (Homan, 1999, p. 110).

The oldest definitions of community come from Ferdinand Tonnies, who described the move from gemeinschaft (rural) communities, in which identification with the community is strong and informal, relationships are personal, and authority is based on tradition, to gesellschaft (structured) communities, in which people have limited identification with community, authority is rational, and relationships are impersonal (Hutchison, 1999; L. C. Johnson & Yanca, 2007). After years of discussion about the breakdown of communities (Putnam, 2000; van Wormer, Besthorn, & Keefe, 2007), the development of elder-friendly communities is a return to the sense of belonging that is a signature feature of gemeinschaft communities.

Communities are often multifaceted and complex and can "shape, provide opportunities, and limit clients' behavior" (Hardcastle, Wenocur, & Powers, 1997, p. 3). People may belong to several different communities; membership in some may overlap, whereas others may have select distinct memberships. Physical boundaries define the geographic community or community of place. Identification or interest defines some "nonplace" communities, such as sororities or fraternities or certain ethnic or cultural groups, such as the black community or the Jewish community. Communities of personal networks may include professional associations, such as the National Association of Social Workers (Homan, 1999; L. C. Johnson & Yanca, 2007; Netting et al., 2004). This chapter defines *community* as a social system with shared values and beliefs, a defined population, and significant relationships between members of the community and between community members and community institutions (L. C. Johnson & Yanca).

Functions

Warren (1978) has identified five functions of a healthy community: (1) production, distribution, and consumption; (2) socialization; (3) social control; (4) social participation; and (5) mutual support. Two additional functions are defense and communication (Pantoja & Perry, 1992). *Production, distribution, and consumption* may be determined by whether a community provides or lacks accessible, affordable, or available transportation, health care, work, and volunteer activities. *Socialization* is the process of understanding a community's customs, values, and traditions and asking whether older adults are frail, vulnerable, and physical and economic drains on the community or integral and contributing members.

The health, social, and aging services delivery system in any community is based on *social controls,* frequently defined by legislators or funding sources and developed by professionals or "experts" without including the consumer or recipient's voice. Such controls reflect the attitude that older adults are frail and dependent. Vehicles that assist older community residents in *social participation* and help them feel that others value their knowledge and experience include senior centers, civic and volunteer organizations, and religious institutions.

Mutual support is demonstrated by the care that black or Hispanic American communities provide to their older members by recognizing them as "turnaround people." Turnaround people are caring members of society who "recognize existing strengths, mirror them back, and help young people see where they are strong" (Saleebey, 2002, p. 217). However, according to Kretzmann and McKnight, (1993), professional health and social services agencies have filled a similar function in many communities and consequently may have weakened older members' roles and responsibilities in providing mutual aid and support.

The community *defense* function may include training the mail delivery person or meter readers to act as gatekeepers, watching for lack of activity in homes of older residents and knowing to whom to report their concerns. Such *communication* can help older adults feel more connected to a world outside of their own homes and thereby helps them feel safe and remain in their homes and community longer. They may talk with the grocery clerk, bank teller, and friends and family; read newsletters, mail, and e-mail; and participate in public forums and meetings.

Although these functions are important aspects of a healthy community, "it is far more common to find out that these functions are carried out in a way that falls short of meeting the needs of at least some community members" (Netting et al., 2004, p. 132). For older adults, the community may be a deciding factor in determining whether they are able to remain in the community because the older adults' "range of adaptive behaviors to a stressful environment becomes constrained because of changes in physical, social and psychological functioning" (Hooyman & Kiyak, 2005, p. 384), making the stability and strength of the environment more critical for older adults than for other populations.

Social Work's Role in Community Practice

Since the late 19th century, community organization, the foundation of social work practice, has struggled to define and redefine itself in relation to the larger society. Currently, community practice involves changing policy, practice, or legislation by working directly with clients to identify and address community projects and by advocating for community change, although community residents may not participate in that effort (Shulman, 2006). The focus of community practice may address strategies to improve the community's social, economic, and physical health or to enhance the well-being of individuals and families living in the community.

According to the NASW *Code of Ethics* (NASW, 2000), all social workers are ethically obligated to advocate for social and economic justice, attending to the well-being of members of their community. The *Code of Ethics* specifically charges social workers to help individuals and families in need directly and to address community and social problems. Social workers confront social and economic injustice by acting as partners and advocates for oppressed and marginalized individuals, families, and communities. The *Code of Ethics* also mandates that social workers recognize the importance of relationships and act as partners to enhance and strengthen relationships to improve the well-being and level of functioning for all levels of systems.

Standard 6 of the *Code of Ethics* spells out social workers' responsibility to the broader society in the areas of social welfare, public participation, public emergencies, and social and political action for underserved and vulnerable individuals and communities. The code requires that all social workers engage in community practice to empower vulnerable, disadvantaged, oppressed, and exploited people and groups (NASW, 2000).

Although community practice is articulated in the *Code of Ethics* and has continued to evolve, disagreements about the social work role in community work continue to exist (Homan, 1999; Hutchison, 1999). In particular, the following four areas of tension discussed below affect community work with older adults.

Community as Context for Practice versus Target of Practice

In practice, social workers may view community as both the target of and the vehicle for change (Long & Holle, 1997; Lyons & Zarit, 1999). The position that the community is the context in which work with families and individuals occurs emphasizes the need to create healthy individuals, recognizing that communities and organizations can create both challenges and assets for clients. Practitioners demonstrate the importance of the community as context by enhancing the assets of older adults, reducing their liabilities, and allowing them to age in place (Kivnick & Murray, 1997).

In contrast, the view that the community is the target of practice or is the client stresses the importance of developing healthy communities. Homan (1999) explained:

> Just like an individual or a family, a community has resources and limitations. Communities have established coping mechanisms to deal with problems. To promote change, the community must believe in its own ability to change and must take responsibility for its actions or inactions. (p. 20)

For example, neighborhood watch programs, a community coping mechanism, increases the safety and reduces victimization of older adults and other community members.

Hardcastle and colleagues (1997) have suggested that social workers view community as **both** the context and the target of practice. The elder-friendly community initiative (discussed later in this chapter and in chapter 9), which supports the empowerment of older adults and enables the community to begin recognizing its older members' contributions, incorporates this integrated approach.

Agency-Based Model versus Social Action Model

The tension between the agency-based and social action models results from a controversy between two beliefs: the view, which evolved from Jane Addams's settlement house movement, that social reform efforts and change are necessary to improve community functioning, versus the belief that community services are best delivered through a coordinated network of social and human services. Although this conflict is sometimes framed as an either–or dilemma, social workers can more effectively address community problems and use community resources by following an "integrated approach to community social work practice that enhances community-based services, builds sense of community, and advocates for social reform" (Hutchison, 1999, p. 346).

Older adults, for instance, have benefited from a network of home- and community-based services provided through area agencies on aging. Moreover, grassroots organizations have supported the elder population. For example, the Older Women's League, founded in 1980 after a White House miniconference on aging, creates social change by raising awareness about older women. The Gray Panthers, started by Maggie Kuhn in

1970, advocates for older adults and educates others about both intergenerational issues and the marginalization and oppression of older women.

Conflict Model versus Collaborative Model

The conflict model emphasizes the need to challenge social and economic injustice and to fight for and at the side of marginalized and oppressed populations. An illustration of this model in action is the Gray Panthers' work with the U.S. Food and Drug Administration to help reform the pharmaceutical market so that less costly generic drugs are more readily available.

The development of nontraditional, collaborative partnerships that cross economic, religious, age, and cultural lines may lead to the identification of creative new problem-solving approaches (Hutchison, 1999). The Gray Panthers, for example, has built a coalition of more than 125 local, state, and national organizations to address a number of issues and to build community capacity. The elder-friendly community movement also illustrates the effective use of the collaborative model by bringing community members together with formal and informal organizations to create and implement a common vision of the community.

Social Worker as Expert versus Partner in the Change Process

The social worker may be viewed as either an expert or a partner, depending on his or her approach to a community—its resources, strengths, and assets. Although social workers may have expertise in areas such as public and private funding and work within formal systems, community members also are the experts on their own community's resources and solutions. Community work involves recognizing and affirming the strengths that each partner—community and social worker—brings to the relationship (Hutchison, 1999). In the new paradigm of successful aging and livable communities, practitioners view older adults as partners and contributors to the development and implementation of a community vision that supports and nurtures all members (McNulty, 2005). Social workers can help reduce or remove the psychological, social, and physical obstacles restricting older adults from contributing to the community.

A more positive view of the preceding four areas of tension is as eight possible intervention strategies discussed later. After assessing the community, social workers, in collaboration with older adults, can choose which strategy would most effectively support the community development and change process.

Older Adults and Community Practice

New Approaches

Social workers with community practice skills and gerontological social workers are currently in demand (Berk, 2004; Berkman & D'Ambruoso, 2006; Damron-Rodriguez, 2006). Communities are often multifaceted and complex and can "shape, provide opportunities, and limit clients' behavior" (Hardcastle et al., 1997, p. 3). In social work practice, the individual and family are usually the starting place for assessment, surrounded by the community or communities, larger society, and global concerns. A. K. Johnson (1998) has identified a different perspective through the Community Practice Pilot Project (CPPP). Students who participated in the CPPP reported that by first assessing the "environment-surrounding-the-person"—that is, the multiple communities to which the individual or family belonged before assessing the individual or family—they could better understand the individual and the family.

Traditionally, gerontological social work and community practice have overlooked older adults as partners in building community capacity and social capital (Austin et al., 2005). The basis of that traditional approach is the medical model, a problem-oriented framework whose users mediated psychosocial concerns and saw older adults as generally in need of care and as an economic drain on community resources. Social workers may still view many interventions through that medical-model lens. On the other hand, they must "understand the linkage between health and social services, . . . pursue the creation of client-centered, seamless systems, and . . . develop a range of community-based, long-term care services that can provide choices for an increasingly ethnically diverse older population" (Austin et al., p. 402).

The traditional medical model does not give sufficient attention to the development of community capacity, even when practitioners consider older adults to be key informants. Instead, in that model, social workers conduct a community needs assessment by identifying unmet needs and community problems (L. C. Johnson & Yanca, 2007). The model acknowledges social workers as "experts" who should plan for older adults; professionals conduct the assessment and frequently gather the data.

In contrast, contemporary approaches to community practice give more attention to building community capacity, social justice, and empowerment. Social workers, who have successfully implemented new community practice models with minority and disenfranchised populations, can also use these models as effective strategies to engage and empower older adults. Community workers can learn to become effective change agents with older adults by focusing on "the capacities and strengths within a community, for doing so empowers people in the community" (Corey, Corey, & Callanan, 2007, p. 446). *Asset mapping,* which begins with a practitioner's assessment of local community members' capacity, skills, and resources, is an effective assessment tool and an intervention strategy within the resilience-enhancing framework (see Appendix 10-A).

More than simple semantics, shifting from community needs assessment to community assessment, which is the foundation for developing aging-friendly communities, reflects a philosophical and practical transformation in the role of social workers who are involved in community development. The move to an increasingly participatory, strengths-based resilience approach to gathering information about the community begins with an identification of community *assets,* not community problems or needs.

Social work practitioners engaged in new models of community practice with older adults apply principles about older adults and the social work role within the community that recognizes community members' assets and talents. Furthermore, following these principles, practitioners encourage multiple perspectives on the creation of elder-friendly communities (Appendix 10-B; see chapter 9). Rather than comprising discrete phases, the community engagement, assessment, intervention, and evaluation processes are interactive, dynamic, and overlapping. They involve older adults and other community members in defining the community, designing and implementing the assessment, and making decisions about community interventions (Gutierrez & Lewis, 1998; Homan, 1999; Rivera & Erlich, 1998).

Relationship Building

Social work practice with older adults in communities involves developing professional relationships with community members and understanding what role the practitioner is expected to perform and what goals he or she is trying to achieve. Social workers need to engage and access older adults where they live and engage informal and formal public and private organizations where they conduct business (Appendix 10-C). Doing so will enable social workers to understand how older community members perceive and give meaning to their communities and allow practitioners to appreciate the benefits and challenges of community in the lives of older adults and their families (Shulman, 2006). According to Rose (2000), in working with any community population,

> the challenge [is] to create relationships in which meaning [is] being produced, not received, where the participants [are] equally valid contributors to defining and shaping the process, product, and purpose of their interaction, not simply functional consumers of concealed, still dominated relationships, and where action [is] derived from the entire dynamic and [is] reflected [in] its values. (p. 411)

The engagement process supports the beginning of collaboration building among potential community partners. Factors critical to the development of healthy community collaboration include an understanding of the environment, membership, process or structure, communication, purpose, and resources (see Appendix 10-D). The creation of collaborative partnerships may involve assessment, intervention, and evaluation skills, and knowledge. The engagement of older adults, their families, and other community members empowers all of them, and increases older adults' capacity to participate in the change process, thereby enhancing community capacity.

Recognition of a Community's Strengths and Assets

Assessment, a critical component of the social work process with individuals, families, and groups, is equally fundamental in working with communities. It is just as essential to involve community members and the community as an entity in decision making as it is to include individuals. According to Saleebey (2002), "there is a growing sense that individual and familial resilience and the characteristics of the communities in which people live are inseparable" (p. 233). Assessment allows community members to tell their stories; that story telling may lead to the emergence of community resiliency (Greene & Cohen, 2005).

Different approaches to community assessment are needed based on the purpose for conducting the assessment. Traditionally, a problem-focused approach to community assessment was used. However, the strengths perspective in community practice has shifted the focus from identifying unmet needs to recognizing community assets and strengths (Glicken, 2004; Greene, 2007; Gutheil & Congress, 2000; Norman, 2000), a process that Beaulieu (2002) called the "development of the community"— that is, the transformation of the community. Community nonpractitioners may wish to use Corey et al.'s (2007) questions to learn about a community; Appendix 10-E provides the questions, modified for work with older adults, and includes questions from a strengths-based and resiliency approach.

Community assets are the individuals, formal and informal organizations, physical environment, and other resources that can improve a community's quality of life (Saleebey, 2002). They may also include capacities of individuals; gifts of "strangers" that recognize the contribution of both young and old; associations of community members; local, public, private, and not-for-profit institutions; physical assets; and community resource developers (Kretzmann & McNight, 1993). Older adults bring a wealth of resources to the community setting. According to Kretzmann and McKnight these include: economic potential; culture, history, and tradition; knowledge gained from a variety of personal and professional life experiences; time; and a connection with other older adults through senior centers, living arrangements, or social ties.

Identifying community assets means looking at not only what older adults can provide the community, but also what the community can offer older adults. For example, the community may assist older adults to develop skills and learn new ways of contributing to the community, whether through their income, education, or social or professional stature. Appendix 10-F provides examples of intergenerational mutual community assets.

An Integrated Model

The social work approach to community typically comprises three models or ideal types of intervention: (1) locality development, (2) social planning or policy, and (3) social action (Rothman, Erlich, & Tropman, 2001; Warren, 1978). The *locality development model* fosters community building and social integration by bringing diverse groups and constituencies together to resolve community issues and concerns (Miley, O'Melia, & DuBois, 2007; Rothman et al.) The *social planning model* uses outside experts to research community needs and to plan and coordinate the delivery of services. Examples of agencies that follow the social planning approach include the United Way; federal- or state-funded agencies; and the aging services delivery network, providing a continuum of home community-based services that frequently have been fragmented and limited. The *social action model* uses confrontational strategies to advocate for social justice and shifts in decision making and power structures in communities. The Gray

Panthers, for instance, has created social change by facing social issues from an intergenerational perspective.

Rivera and Erlich (1998) have reported that these three models of intervention are "color blind." Consequently, for social workers to achieve community change, provide a culturally competent community, and challenge institutional racism, they have recommended that community practitioners understand the heterogeneity, including the racial, ethnic, and cultural characteristics, of ethnic and cultural minority communities; use cultural guides (Green, 1999) to serve as liaisons with and cultural experts for the outside community; and remove barriers to empowerment for community members.

As local, state, and national conditions change and communities' strengths and resiliency emerge, community practice has by necessity become multifaceted and complex. "Sharpening of change methods is an endless and evolving process" (Rothman et al., 2001, p. 61), thus requiring community practice in the 21st century to incorporate aspects of all three ideal models into an integrated, rather than discrete, approach to community interventions. In doing so, community practitioners must ensure that they consider the ethnic, cultural, and racial perspectives and contributions of people of color; understand how diverse cultures affect leadership roles, family dynamics, and communication patterns; and recognize the "process of empowerment and the development of critical consciousness" (Rivera & Erlich, 1998, p. 10).

New paradigms for community practice promote culturally competent practice with older adults, are asset based, and use grassroots organizing. *Asset-based community development* builds on the assets of local residents who can develop and manage resources at the local level. *Community development corporations* are another type of culturally competent community practice model. Such businesses help families create local organizations—such as the Dudley Street Neighborhood Initiative in Massachusetts and the Annie E. Casey Foundation's Rebuilding Communities Initiative—which train people for community leadership and promote economic growth. The *grassroots organizing intervention* method, which is similar to the social action model but without the confrontational approach, comes into play when local leaders and the community initiate action (Miley et al., 2007).

Discovery of Community Resiliency

Resiliency is "the potential that comes for the energy and skill required by ongoing problem solving" (Netting et al., 2004, p. 149). Community resiliency is similar to individual and family resilience in that it builds on the "strengths and talents of the residents and members of the community" (Saleebey, 2002, p. 233) and "[there is a] growing sense that individual and familiar resilience and the characteristics of the communities in which people live are inseparable" (p. 233). "The stock of human and social capital characteristic of resilient neighborhoods," said Breton (2001), "consists of: (1) neighbor networks and the trust they generate, (2) active local voluntary associations through which residents mobilize for action, (3) stable local organizational networks, and (4) the services typical of an adequate social infrastructure" (p. 22). It is important therefore that social workers work toward the achievement of community resiliency.

Practitioners may accomplish this goal through social empowerment and the strengths perspective. *Social empowerment practice* is a process of assisting communities to increase their "personal, interpersonal, or political power" (Gutierrez & Lewis, 1998) and ensuring that members make their own decisions, have access to resources and opportunities, and take some control to improve their environment or community (Kirst-Ashman, 2000; Netting et al., 2004). To use a strengths-based community approach, social workers should conduct a community assessment by identifying assets and resources, determining what social and human capacity exists internally in the community, and recognizing relationships—that is, any community effort will involve developing and sustaining relationships with community members (Saleebey, 2002).

Community-Based Research

Community-based participatory research views community members, whether formal organizations or informal groups of community residents, as research partners—not research subjects. Community members bring their perspective of and hope for their community to the table as full participants in the planning, design, and implementation of research and distribution of the final report. The community-based participatory research model recognizes a community's resources and assets by acknowledging community members as experts and consultants and by building community capacity (U.S. Department of Health and Human Services, Agency for Healthcare Research and Quality, 2003).

Community practice with older adults is a process of building trusting relationships and community capacity as members learn how to relate to each other and the social worker learns how best to work with the community. Through asset mapping, practitioners identify the capacity of individuals and formal and informal groups, and use that information during the community assessment and intervention process, which in turn builds capacity for later interventions. The strengths-based perspective and resiliency approach provide social workers with tools to help communities define and implement a vision that builds on the strengths of all community members and supports older adults and their families to age in place.

Aging in Place

The national movement to promote aging in place began in the United States during the early years of the 21st century with the realization that communities need to prepare proactively for the aging baby boom population. Founders of the movement saw that community-based long-term-care networks were often fragmented. Consequently, they recognized that communities were ill prepared to meet long-term-care demands of an aging society (Bolda, Lowe, Maddox, & Patnaik, 2005).

The "broader social fabric is aging," says Achenbaum (2005) and will consequently influence communities and result in their transformation. Although many people assume that the majority of older adults reside in nursing homes, in reality only about 3 percent to 5 percent of people aged 65 years and older live in such facilities (Hooyman & Kiyak, 2005; Stahlman & Kisor, 2000), whereas 95 percent live in their communities. The nature of the community, whether robust or weak, can dramatically affect older adults' quality of life. This idea is grounded in the person-in-environment lens that emerged from the ecological perspective and systems theory (A. K. Johnson, 1998), and "enables social workers to understand the complexities of clients' lives by emphasizing the impact of the physical and social environment on the person" (Berg-Weger, 2005, p. 152). For older adults, it can determine whether they can age in place or will be forced to leave the community because of lack of support. Communities have since started to transform themselves, planning the services and programs they must develop, modify, or expand to create elder-friendly communities that can respond to the dramatic increase in the older population.

Research has indicated that aging in place has a number of advantages over moving older adults into long-term-care facilities (McNulty, 2005). For one, many older adults want to stay in their own homes and communities, in which the environment and relationships are familiar and predictable. In addition, home- and community-based services are more cost-effective than residential and institutional ones, and because these services support older adults aging in place, they frequently prevent premature or inappropriate institutionalization. Furthermore, older adults who stay in their homes and communities may have increased opportunities to remain socially and civically engaged as contributing members of the community. The development of aging-in-place communities is consistent with the social work value of the right of self-determination (NASW, 2000), as long as older adults have access to needed resources and services.

Elder-Friendly Communities

Social workers have the professional skills and knowledge to support communities as they transform into aging-friendly ones. National aging organizations and city and county government agencies have joined with formal and informal organizations, local government, private foundations, and the federal government to fund demonstration projects to help communities initiate dialogues with older adults. The goals of these partnerships are to create a mutually agreed-on vision for aging in place and to develop a plan of action.

These innovative community demonstration projects, based on the strengths perspective or resiliency approach, are called Community Partnerships for Older Adults (CPFOA), Livable Communities for All Ages, and the Aging in Place Initiative. This chapter uses elder-friendly communities as an umbrella term for communities that share an underlying philosophy centered on positive beliefs about, and images of, older adults as valuable members of society (to view the components of an elder-friendly community, see Figure 10-1). These communities strive to create a place in which community

FIGURE 10-1 Components of an Elder-Friendly Community

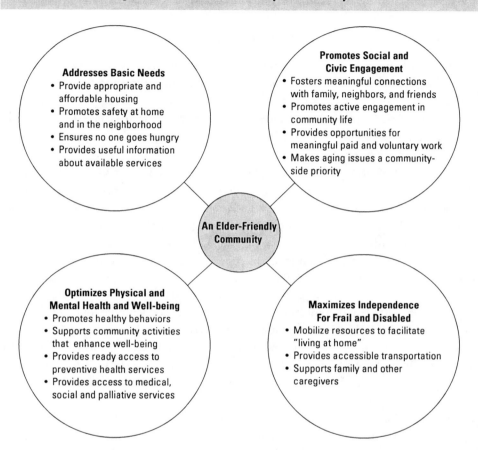

Addresses Basic Needs
- Provide appropriate and affordable housing
- Promotes safety at home and in the neighborhood
- Ensures no one goes hungry
- Provides useful information about available services

Promotes Social and Civic Engagement
- Fosters meaningful connections with family, neighbors, and friends
- Promotes active engagement in community life
- Provides opportunities for meaningful paid and voluntary work
- Makes aging issues a community-side priority

An Elder-Friendly Community

Optimizes Physical and Mental Health and Well-being
- Promotes healthy behaviors
- Supports community activities that enhance well-being
- Provides ready access to preventive health services
- Provides access to medical, social and palliative services

Maximizes Independence For Frail and Disabled
- Mobilize resources to facilitate "living at home"
- Provides accessible transportation
- Supports family and other caregivers

Source: Reprinted with permission from Feldman, P. H., & Oberlink, M. (2003). The advantage initiative: Developing community indicators to promote the health and well-being of older people. *Family Community Health, 26,* p. 269.

residents of all ages can live comfortably, enjoy meaningful work and volunteer experiences, and have access to health, educational, and supportive services, as defined in the Older Americans Comprehensive Services Amendments of 1973 (see Appendix 10-G).

For elder-friendly communities to develop successfully and sustain themselves, they must have the following nine characteristics, according to L. C. Johnson and Yanca (2007): (1) at least some primary relationships must exist; (2) the community must be comparatively autonomous; (3) it needs to have the capacity to face problems and engage in problem solving; (4) a broad distribution of power must be apparent; (5) citizens must be committed to the community; (6) citizen participation is possible and the community encourages it; (7) more homogenous than heterogeneous relationships exist; (8) community members have developed ways of dealing with conflict; and

(9) the community tolerates and values diversity. These characteristics are embodied in the seven functions of a healthy community, as discussed earlier.

Successful Aging-in-Place Communities

Livable communities or successful aging-in-place communities are "places where people of all ages can live comfortably," according to the Administration on Aging (AOA) (2005). The AOA, National Association of Area Agencies on Aging, Partners for Livable Communities, and AARP have identified a number of factors, listed in Appendix 10-H, that define livable communities and, at the same time, represent opportunities and challenges for successful aging in place.

Creative pilot communities highlight the importance of developing collaborative approaches with community partnerships comprising traditional health and human services agencies, organizations in the public and private sectors, government agencies, businesses, and older adults and their families. These projects enable communities to address complex and multifaceted issues in planning, implementing, and sustaining a new vision. Furthermore, community demonstration projects move from traditional community intervention models to the newer asset-based community development, grassroots organizing, and community development corporation models of community intervention. These contemporary models integrate aspects of the traditional models but address community practice and older adults from a strengths perspective and resiliency approach.

The Aging in Place Initiative assists communities to "improve their livability for older persons and in turn, increase livability for all people" (Aging in Place Initiative, n.d.). This project strives to develop accessible and affordable services through collaborative community and organizational efforts. Another national program, the CPFOA, funded by the Robert Wood Johnson Foundation, emphasizes building collaborative community and organizational partnerships to explore new ways to build and sustain the community-based long-term-care network by enhancing social capital and developing a sense of collective efficacy (Bolda et al., 2005). The CPFOA communities follow a variety of approaches to learning about a community, such as training older adults to canvas door to door in select neighborhoods and conducting focus groups and town hall meetings, with the results of those efforts forming the basis for community priority setting (Bolda et al.). Appendix 10-I provides additional details on these and other pilot projects.

AARP has developed a "Six-Point Call to Action" that offers government and private-sector recommendations for developing livable communities and points out the policy implications of such an effort (Kochera et al., 2005; see Appendix 10-J). The call to action addresses social engagement within the community, design and modification of homes to meet older adults' physical and social needs, affordable housing options and environments, enhancement of safety for all people and all abilities, modification of the travel environment and expansion of affordable transportation, and mobility options to meet diverse needs and preferences.

AARP has created a 10-point interactive community tool designed to assess community livability in the areas of transportation, workability, safety and security, shopping, housing, health services, recreation and cultural activities, and care (Kihl, Brennan, Gabhawala, & Mittal, 2005). This self-assessment community questionnaire is available online (Pollack, 1999).

Conclusion

Community practice with older adults builds on the new gerontology paradigm, which begins by identifying community assets or resources, rather than unmet needs and deficits, through a community assessment (Greene & Cohen, 2005). An assessment of community capacity embraces older adults as members of society who have the ability to make communities better places to live and work, and in which they can connect with others. This empowerment approach provides an environment for older adults to remain engaged in their community and age in place. Social workers bring to this new paradigm their knowledge and experience with assessment and intervention, a strengths approach and resiliency perspective, an understanding of the person in environment, values of self-determination, cultural competence, and skills in communication, problem solving, negotiation, and advocacy, all of which are critical to the successful development of elder-friendly communities.

Changes in the community will occur only if social workers join as partners with community members of all ages and with public and private community organizations to make significant structural and attitudinal changes with the goal of developing elder-friendly and livable communities. "The vision of a livable community is more than a goal; it is a call to boomers and their parents to become involved in their community as well as to public officials to seek out residents when planning and making change" (Kochera et al., 2005, p. 90).

Social work practice has its roots in the settlement house movement (Berg-Weger, 2005), and it is time to return to those roots as the 21st century vision of settlement houses evolves—now called livable or resilient communities. Older adults have expressed their strong desire to age in place. Social workers are well equipped as leaders and advocates to intervene in communities and assist older adults and other community members to create livable communities that will improve the quality of life for older adults and people of all ages.

Suggested Exercise to Evaluate Student Competency

Students will use Appendix 10-C, "Questions to Consider Before the Engagement Process," and Appendix 10-E, "Questions (by Type of Community Practice Approach) for Community Nonpractitioners," to explore the feasibility of their community action plan.

References

Achenbaum, W. A. (2005). *Older Americans, vital communities: A bold vision for societal aging.* Baltimore: Johns Hopkins University Press.

Administration on Aging. (2005). *Winners of livable communities for all ages competition announced.* Retrieved June 3, 2006, from http://www.aoa.gov/press/pr/2005/05_Sep/09_20_05_pf.asp

Aging in Place Initiative. (n.d.). *n4a and Partners for Livable Communities—Aging in Place Initiative.* Retrieved June 4, 2006, from http://aipi.n4a.org/

Atchley, R. C., & Barusch, A. S. (2004). *Social forces and aging: An introduction to social gerontology* (10th ed.). Belmont, CA: Wadsworth/Thomson Learning.

Austin, C. D., Camp, E. D., Flux, D., McClelland, R. W., & Sieppert, J. (2005). Community development with older adults in their neighborhoods: The elder friendly communities program. *Families in Society, 86,* 401–409.

Beaulieu, L. J. (2002). *Mapping the assets of your community: A key component for building local capacity.* Mississippi State, MS: Southern Regional Development Center.

Berg-Weger, M. (2005). *Social work & social welfare: An invitation.* Boston: McGraw-Hill.

Berk, L. E. (2004). *Development through the lifespan* (3rd ed.). Boston: Allyn & Bacon.

Berkman, B., & D'Ambruoso, S. (2006). *Handbook of social work in health and aging.* New York: Oxford University Press.

Billig, M. (2004). Supportive communities, an optimum arrangement for the older population? *Journal of Sociology and Social Welfare, 31,* 131–151.

Bolda, E. J., Lowe, J. I., Maddox, G. L., & Patnaik, B. S. (2005). Community partnerships for older adults: A case study. *Families in Society, 86,* 411–418.

Breton, M. (2001). Neighborhood resiliency. *Journal of Community Practice, 9,* 21–36.

Corey, G., Corey, M. S., & Callanan, P. (2007). *Issues and ethics in the helping professions* (7th ed.). Belmont, CA: Thomson Brooks/Cole.

Council on Social Work Education, Gero-Ed Center. (2004). *Foundation gerontological social work competencies.* Retrieved November 16, 2006, from http://depts.washington.edu/geroctr/Curriculum3/ Competencies/FdnComp.doc

Cox, E. O. (2001). Community practice issues in the 21st century: Questions and challenges for empowerment-oriented practitioners. *Journal of Community Practice, 9,* 37–55.

Damron-Rodriguez, J. (2006). Moving forward: Developing geriatric social work competencies. In B. Berkman & S. D'Ambruoso (Eds.), *Handbook of social work in health and aging* (pp. 1051–1064). New York: Oxford University Press.

Feldman, P. H., & Oberlink, M. (2003). The advantage initiative: Developing community indicators to promote the health and well-being of older people. *Family Community Health, 26,* p. 269.

Glicken, M. D. (2004). *Using the strengths perspective in social work practice: A positive approach for helping professions.* Boston: Pearson Education.

Green, J. (1999). *Cultural awareness in the human services.* Englewood Cliff, NJ: Prentice Hall.

Greene, R. R. (Ed.). (2007). *Social work practice: A risk and resiliency perspective*. Belmont, CA: Thomson Brooks/Cole.

Greene, R. R., & Cohen, H. L. (2005). Social work with older adults and their families: Changing practice paradigms. *Families in Society, 86,* 367–373.

Gutheil, I. A., & Congress, E. (2000). Resiliency in older people: A paradigm for practice. In E. Norman (Ed.), *Resiliency enhancement: Putting the strengths perspective into social work practice* (pp. 40–54). New York: Columbia University Press.

Gutierrez, L. M., & Lewis, E. A. (1998). A feminist perspective on organizing with women of color. In F. G. Rivera & J. L. Erlich (Eds.), *Community organizing in a diverse society* (3rd ed., pp. 97–116). Boston: Allyn & Bacon.

Hardcastle, D. A., Wenocur, S., & Powers, P. R. (1997). *Community practice: Theories and skills for social workers*. New York: Oxford University Press.

Homan, M. S. (1999). *Promoting community change: Making it happen in the real world* (2nd ed.). Pacific Grove, CA: Brooks/Cole.

Hooyman, N. R., & Kiyak, H. A. (2005). *Social gerontology: A multidisciplinary perspective* (7th ed.). Boston: Pearson Education.

Hutchison, E. D. (1999). *Dimensions of human behavior: Person and environment*. Thousand Oaks, CA: Pine Forge Press.

Johnson, A. K. (1998). The revitalization of community practice: Characteristics, competencies, and curricula for community-based services. *Journal of Community Practice, 5*(3), 37–62.

Johnson, A. K. (2000). The community practice pilot project: Integrating methods, field, community assessment, and experiential learning. *Journal of Community Practice, 8*(4) 5–25.

Johnson, J. L., & Grant, G. (2005). *Community practice*. Boston: Pearson Education.

Johnson, L. C., & Yanca, S. J. (2007). *Social work practice: A generalist approach* (9th ed.). Boston: Pearson Education.

Kihl, M., Brennan, D., Gabhawala, N., & Mittal, P. (2005). *Livable communities: An evaluation guide*. Washington, DC: American Association of Retired Persons.

Kirst-Ashman, K. K. (2000). *Human behavior, communities, organizations, and groups in the macro social environment: An empowerment approach*. Belmont, CA: Wadsworth/Thomson Learning.

Kirst-Ashman, K. K., & Hull, G. H. (2006). *Generalist practice with organizations & communities* (3rd ed.). Belmont, CA: Thomson Brooks/Cole.

Kivnick, H. Q., & Murray, S. V. (1997). Vital involvement: An overlooked source of identity in frail elders. *Journal of Aging and Identity, 2,* 205–223.

Kochera, A., Straight, A., & Guterbock, T. (2005). *Beyond 50.05: A report to the nation on livable communities—Creating environments for successful aging*. Washington, DC: AARP Public Policy Institute.

Kretzmann, J. P., & McKnight, J. L. (1993). *Building communities from the inside out: A path toward finding and mobilizing a community's assets*. Chicago: Assertive Community Treatment Association.

Long, D. D., & Holle, M. C. (1997). *Macro systems in the social environment.* Itasca, IL: F. E. Peacock.

Lyons, K. S., & Zarit, S. H. (1999). Formal and informal support: The great divide. *International Journal of Geriatric Psychiatry, 14,* 183–196.

McNulty, R. H. (2005). *Livable communities & aging in place.* Retrieved June 6, 2006, from http://www.aarp.org/research/international/gra/gra_special_05/aging_in_place.html

Miley, K. K., O'Melia, M., & DuBois, B. (2007). *Generalist social work practice: An empowering approach* (5th ed.). Boston: Pearson Education.

Mizoguchi, N., Luluquisen, M., Witt, S., & Maker, L. (2004). *A handbook for participatory community assessments: Experiences from Alameda County.* Oakland, CA: Alameda Public Health Department.

National Association of Social Workers. (2000). *Code of ethics of the National Association of Social Workers.* Retrieved July 21, 2006, from http://www.socialworkers.org/pubs/code/code.asp

Netting, F. E., Kettner, P. M., & McMurtry, S. L. (2004). *Social work macro practice* (3rd ed.). Boston: Pearson Education.

Norman, E. (Ed.). (2000). *Resiliency enhancement: Putting the strengths perspective into social work practice.* New York: Columbia University Press.

Older Americans Comprehensive Services Amendments of 1973, P.L. No. 93-29, title I, § 101, 87 Stat. 30 (1973); Pub. L. 97-115, § 3(d), 95 Stat. 1597 (1981). Retrieved June 2, 2006, from http://frwebgate.access.gpo.gov/cgi-bin/getdoc.cgi?dbname=browse_usc&docid=Cite:+42USC3003

Pantoja, A., & Perry, W. (1992). Community development and restoration: A perspective and case study. In F. G. Rivera & J. L. Erlich (Eds.), *Community organizing in a diverse society* (pp. 220–242). Boston: Allyn & Bacon.

Pollack, P. B. (1999). *Livable communities: An evaluation guide.* Washington, DC: AARP Public Policy Institute.

Putnam, R. D. (2000). *Bowling alone: The collapse and revival of American community.* New York: Simon & Schuster.

Richardson, V. E., & Barusch, A. S. (2006). *Gerontological practice for the twenty-first century: A social work perspective.* New York: Columbia University Press.

Rivera, F. G., & Erlich, J. L. (1998). *Community organizing in a diverse society* (3rd ed.). Boston: Allyn & Bacon.

Rose, S. M. (2000). Reflections on empowerment-based practice. *Social Work, 45,* 403–412.

Rothman, J., Erlich, J. L., & Tropman, J. E. (Eds.). (2001). *Strategies of community intervention.* Itasca, IL: F. E. Peacock.

Rybash, J. W., Roodin, P. A., & Santrock, J. W. (1985). *Adult development and aging* (2nd ed.). New York: Wm. C. Brown.

Saleebey, D. (2002). *The strengths perspective in social work practice* (3rd ed.). Boston: Allyn & Bacon.

Shaffer, C., & Anundsen, K. (1993). *Creating community anywhere: Finding support and connection in a fragmented world.* London: Putnam.

Shulman, L. (2006). *The skills of helping individuals, families, groups, and communities* (5th ed.). Belmont, CA: Thomson Brooks/Cole.

Stahlman, S. D., & Kisor, A. J. (2000). Nursing homes. In R. L. Schneider, N. P. Kropf, & A. J. Kisor (Eds.), *Gerontological social work: Knowledge, service settings and special populations* (pp. 225–256). Belmont, CA: Brooks/Cole Thomson Learning.

U.S. Department of Health and Human Services, Agency for Healthcare Research and Quality. (2003). *Creating partnerships, improving health: The role of community-based participatory research.* Retrieved May 14, 2007, from http://www.ahrq.gov

van Wormer, K., Besthorn, F. H., & Keefe, T. (2007). *Human behavior and the social environment, macro level: Groups, communities, and organizations.* New York: Oxford University Press.

Warren, R. L. (1978). *The community in America* (3rd ed.). Chicago: Rand McNally.

Wilson, N. L. (2006). Educating social workers for an aging society: Needs and approaches. In B. Berkman & S. D'Ambruoso (Eds.), *Handbook of social work in health and aging* (pp. 1041–1050). New York: Oxford University Press.

Winer, M., & Ray, K. (1997). *Collaboration handbook: Creating, sustaining and enjoying the journey.* St. Paul, MN: Amherst H. Wilder Foundation. (Available from the Wilder Publishing Center, 919 Lafond Avenue, St. Paul, MN 55104)

Zastrow, C. H., & Kirst-Ashman, K. K. (2004). *Understanding human behavior and the social environment* (6th ed.). Belmont, CA: Thomson Brooks/Cole.

APPENDIX 10-A Contrasting "Needs" Versus "Assets" Approach to Community Enhancement

Needs	Assets
Focuses on deficiencies	Focuses on effectiveness
Results in fragmentation of responses to local needs	Builds on interdependence
Makes people consumers of services; builds dependence	Identifies ways that people can give of their talents
Residents have little voice in deciding how to address local concerns	Seeks to empower people

Source: Mapping the Assets of Your Community: A Key Component for Building Local Capacity was developed by Lionel J. Beaulieu, Southern Rural Development Center. Copyright 2002 by the Southern Rural Development Center, Series #227. For more information, visit http//srdc.msstate.edu/publications/227/227_asset_mapping.pdf

APPENDIX 10-B Seven Principles to Adapt for Community Work with Older Adults

1. It is important to develop internal leaders from among the clients and to avoid taking over the leadership when problems occur.
2. The client must control the goals, objectives, and strategies even though the social worker may have other views.
3. A key role of the social worker is to help the group members develop and own structures and a culture for effective work.
4. The social worker must respect the existence of both current barriers and those that may emerge from previous experiences, which may make it difficult for the group members to take the next step until they are ready.
5. The social worker needs to know when to help clients to speak "softly" to a system in an effort to reach for the system's strength (that is, negotiate) and when to speak "loudly" to move a system to respond (that is, confront).
6. The social worker must understand the importance of shifting from confrontation to collaboration once he or she has obtained the system's attention and response.
7. The social worker needs to fully understand that the dynamics and skills crucial for clinical work are equally important when the client is a community. The purpose and goals may differ, but the process does not.

Source: From The skills of helping individuals, families, groups, and communities (with The interactive skills of helping CD-ROM, Engaging and working with the hard-to-reach client CD-ROM, and InfoTrac®) (5th ed., p. 542) by Shulman, L. (2006). Reprinted with permission of Wadsworth, a division of Thomson Learning: www.thomsonrights.com. Fax 800-730-2215.

APPENDIX 10-C Questions to Consider Before the Engagement Process

* What has been the community's past experience with social workers?

* Have I been brought into the community to solve a community problem or to help build community capacity? What information do I have available to answer this question?

* How will I develop a relationship with the community? How will I build a trusting relationship with older community members? Where and how will I learn about the community's cultural, social, economic, and historical trends?

* How can I support older adults and other community members as they make the transition from service recipients or service provider to participants in planning and implementation of an elder-friendly community?

* Using the strengths perspective and resiliency approach, how will I engage older adults and their families and community partners?

* What can I say or do as a culturally competent practitioner to convey my belief that each community, each older person, and each local provider is unique and needs time to share his or her own story and to be affirmed?

* As I engage and begin working with communities, how can I recognize barriers and resistance to the change process? When I get excited about the possibilities for an inter-generational community that welcomes and respects all members, how can I remember that I am not the expert in this community, and regardless of how frustrated and impatient I may feel, remember that the community-change process involves building collaborative relationships and meeting any outcome goals? Older adults and community members need time to connect and may need time to heal negative relationships from the past.

* How can I communicate in oral and written form in a language that community members and older adults can understand without a lot of social work jargon? Information is a powerful tool. Empowered people and communities have the information they need to make informed decisions.

APPENDIX 10-D 19 Factors Influencing Successful Collaborations

A review of the research literature revealed the following factors, which are grouped into six categories:

Factors Related to the Environment

1. history of collaboration or cooperation in the community
2. collaborative group seen as a leader in the community
3. favorable political/social climate

Factors Related to Membership Characteristics

4. mutual respect, understanding, and trust
5. appropriate cross-section of members
6. members view collaboration as being in their best self-interest
7. ability to compromise

Factors Related to Process/Structure

8. members share a stake in process and outcome
9. multiple layers of decision making
10. flexibility
11. development of clear roles and policy guidelines
12. adaptability

Factors Related to Communication

13. open and frequent communication
14. established informal and formal communication links

Factors Related to Purpose

15. concrete, attainable goals and objectives
16. shared vision
17. unique purpose

Factors Related to Resources

18. sufficient funds
19. skilled convener

Sources: Reprinted with permission from Winer, M., & Ray, K. (1997). *Collaboration handbook: Creating, sustaining and enjoying the journey.* St. Paul, MN: Amherst H. Wilder Foundation. (Available from the Wilder Publishing Center, 919 Lafond Avenue, St. Paul, MN 55104)

APPENDIX 10-E Questions (by Type of Community Practice Approach) for Community Nonpractitioners

10 Questions from a Problem-Focused Approach	10 Questions from a Strengths-Based and Resiliency Approach
What sense do you have of the social and psychological needs of older adults and their families in your community and whether those needs have been met?	What does an elder-friendly community look like? How do you engage the diversity of your community?
What are the special needs of older adults at various socioeconomic levels?	What are the assets and resources that older adults can provide their community? What do older adults need from the community in order to be fully contributing members?
What are some pressing economic needs and mental health concerns for older adults living in the community?	How can older community members participate in the design and implementation of community-based participatory research that will help the community learn about how to support all community members?
If your older adult clients or their family members ask what resources are available to assist them to stay in their own homes, would you know where to refer them?	How can collaborative relationships be developed between older community members and formal and informal organizations to assess which resources are accessible, affordable, and available?
What forces within your community exacerbate the problems older adults and their families are experiencing?	How can your community build a social infrastructure that supports successful aging and that facilitates aging well throughout the life span?
What are the main assets available to assist older adults in your community?	What opportunities are available for older adults to contribute to the community? How will the community engage and empower diverse older adults in your community?
What factors contribute to the strength and development of your community?	Who are the community partners, and how can new partners be recruited? How will you measure community strength?

(Continued)

APPENDIX 10-E Questions (by Type of Community Practice Approach) for Community Nonpractitioners (*Continued*)

10 Questions from a Problem-Focused Approach	10 Questions from a Strengths-Based and Resiliency Approach
What are the current attitudes of people in your community about the range of services available to older adults and their families?	What are the current attitudes of community members about older adults? How will you communicate your vision of an elder-friendly community and priorities to community members?
What role do you play or want to play in improving your community?	What knowledge, values, and skills do you bring to the community setting in your work with older adults and other community members to bring about social justice and community change?
Do you believe you have a broader responsibility to address the conditions that create problems for older adults and their families who you see?	As a social worker, how can you work collaboratively with members of the community to improve the quality of life for everyone? What do you want your community to look like today, next year, and in 10 years?

Note: The questions in the left-hand column illustrate a problem-focused orientation to community assessment. The questions in the right-hand column provide a strengths-based self- and community assessment.

Source: From *Issues and ethics in the helping professions* (7th ed.) by Corey, G., Corey, M. S., & Callanan, P. (2007). Reprinted with permission of Wadsworth, a division of Thomson Learning: www.thomsonrights. com. Fax 800-730-2215.

APPENDIX 10-F Examples of Intergenerational Community Assets

Qualities of Residents and the Community	Intergenerational Assets
Residents who like to read	Can mentor children, read to blind people or to frail older adults
Residents who like to garden	Can share information about gardening with others, watch to be sure children are walking across the street safely or are playing safely, help plan gardening projects for community spaces, take flowers to people who are shut in
Residents who like to volunteer and who are retired	May be willing to participate in community assessment and intervention for the benefit of the community, donate time to new businesses or community endeavors, participate in a neighborhood watch, donate time and expertise to local social services and health agencies
Churches and synagogues and other houses of worship	May be willing to offer space for community meetings and notify members about community meetings and community news
Schools and educational institutions	May be willing to distribute fliers about community meetings, provide access to parents as research participants and partners, offer support groups for grandparents raising grandchildren
Other resources and organizations	May donate time, expertise, money, services, or space

Source: Mizoguchi, N., Luluquisen, M., Witt, S., & Maker, L. (2004). *A handbook for participatory community assessments: Experiences from Alameda County* (p. 8). Oakland, CA: Alameda County Public Health Department. Reprinted with permission of the author.

APPENDIX 10-G Elder-Friendly Communities and the Older Americans Comprehensive Services Amendments of 1973

The key assumptions of the elder-friendly community approach are articulated in the Older Americans Comprehensive Services Amendments of 1973 (see Title 42: Public and Health, Chapter 35: Programs for Older Americans, Subchapter I—Declaration of Objectives). That legislation states:

> The Congress finds that millions of older citizens in this Nation are suffering unnecessary harm from the lack of adequate services. It is therefore the purpose of this Act, in support of the objectives of this chapter, to
>
> 1. make available comprehensive programs which include a full range of health, education, and supportive services to our older citizens who need them;
>
> 2. give full and special consideration to older citizens with special needs in planning such programs, and, pending the availability of such programs for all older citizens, give priority to the elderly with the greatest economic and social need;
>
> 3. provide comprehensive programs which will assure the coordinated delivery of a full range of essential services to our older citizens, and, where applicable, also furnish meaningful employment opportunities for many individuals, including older persons, young persons, and volunteers from the community; and
>
> 4. insure that the planning and operation of such programs will be undertaken as a partnership of older citizens, community agencies, and State and local governments, with appropriate assistance from the Federal Government.

Sources: Reprinted with permission from Older Americans Comprehensive Services Amendments of 1973. Pub. L. No. 93-29, title I, § 101, 87 Stat. 30 (1973); Pub. L. 97-115, § 3(d), 95 Stat. 1597 (1981). Retrieved June 2, 2006, from http://frwebgate.access.gpo.gov/cgi-bin/getdoc.cgi?dbname=browse_usc&docid=Cite: +42USC3003

APPENDIX 10-H Factors Defining Livable Communities

AOA	AARP	n4a and PLC
Affordable, appropriate, accessible housing	Dependable public transportation	Health, social, and public safety services
Physical environment adjusted for inclusiveness and accessibility	Safe, well-designed sidewalks	Economic development
Access to key health and supportive services	Roads designed for safe driving	Housing
Accessible, affordable, reliable, safe transportation	Transportation options	Educational, cultural, and social opportunities
Ample work, volunteer, and educational opportunities	Security and safety	Recreational opportunities
Participation in civic, cultural, social, and recreational activities encouraged	Affordable housing options and home design that allows for maximum activities of daily living if mobility is limited	Local leadership
	Well-run community centers, recreation centers, parks, and other places where older people can socialize	Transportation
	Ample opportunities to become a volunteer	Community design and planning

Notes: AOA = Administration on Aging; AARP = American Association of Retired Persons; n4a = National Association of Area Agencies on Aging; PLC = Partners for Livable Communities.

APPENDIX 10-I Livable Communities Initiatives and Demonstration Communities

n4a and PLC: Aging in Place Initiative	AOA: Livable Communities for All Ages	CPFOA: Implementation Grantees (Feb. 1, 2004, to March 2008)	CPFOA: Implementation Grantees (May 2, 2006, to April 2010)
Battle Creek, MI	Atlanta, GA	Aging Atlanta, Atlanta, GA	Aging Well—An Initiative of Greater Lyons Township, Oak Park, IL
Evansville, IN	Broome County, NY	Aging Futures, Broome County, NY	Aging: The Ultimate Adventure—Journeying Together, Fremont, CA
Fort Wayne, IN	Central, VA	Boston Partnership for Older Adults, Boston, MA	Community Advocates for Rural Elders, Port Angeles, WA
Hillsborough, FL	Dunedin, FL	Care for Elders, Houston/Harris County, TX	Haywood County Aging Partnership, Waynesville, NC
Lexington, KY	Milwaukee, WI	Connecting Care Communities, Milwaukee County, WI	Rappahannock Rapidan Elder Care Coalition, Culpeper, VA
Martinsville, VA	New York City	Maui Long Term Care Partnership, Island of Maui, HI	Seniors Count!, Manchester, NH
Rochester, NY	Tamarac, FL	Successful Aging Through Long-Term Strategic Alliances, El Paso County, TX	The Blueprint for Aging, Ann Arbor, MI
Syracuse, NY		San Francisco Partnership for Community-Based Care and Support, San Francisco County, CA	The Life: Act 2 Community Partnership, Jacksonville, FL

Notes: n4a = National Association of Area Agencies on Aging; PLC = Partners for Livable Communities; AOA = Administration on Aging; CPFOA = Community Partnerships for Older Adults, a national program of the Robert Wood Johnson Foundation.

APPENDIX 10-J Beyond 50.05—A Report to the Nation on Livable Communities: Creating Environments for Successful Aging

Section V. Recommendations

Unless America makes a commitment to livable communities, baby boomers and other persons of a range of ages and with a variety of abilities will find it difficult to age successfully and remain engaged with their communities. The shortage of affordable and well-designed housing, mobility options, and opportunities for community engagement make it difficult for persons to maintain independence and a high quality of life. On the other hand, those communities that design for livability empower their residents to remain independent and engaged, and offer a better quality of life.

This design does not come about by accident; it must be carefully considered, promoted, and supported. At every level of government, appropriate actions are needed to promote communities' livability. And an integral part of successful community planning is the active solicitation and participation of older Americans. The vision of a livable community is more than a goal; it is also a call to boomers and their parents to become involved in their community as well as to public officials to seek out residents when planning and making change.

Community Recommendations: A Six-Point Call to Action

This research report has shown that livable communities are vital to the successful aging of people age 50 and older. To promote this livability and the active engagement of residents, AARP encourages government and the private sector to respond to a Six-Point Call to Action. AARP believes that this action agenda can help focus attention on community needs for persons of all ages and abilities. AARP also recognizes that many groups can contribute additional ideas to promote livable communities, and that the policy implications listed within each action item are just first steps toward achieving those goals.

1. **Communities should encourage community engagement by facilitating various forms of social involvement, such as organizational membership and volunteering, and should actively solicit the contributions of persons of all ages and abilities in community decision making.**

Policy Implications

- Localities should evaluate the inventory of settings for social involvement (e.g., public spaces in town centers, libraries, community and recreation centers, people-oriented parks and plazas) and should expand the supply and improve the design of settings as appropriate.
- Localities and nongovernmental organizations should create and expand opportunities for volunteerism and community service.
- Localities should promote activities such as farmers' markets, walking groups, etc., that support residents' interaction.

(*Continued*)

APPENDIX 10-J Beyond 50.05—A Report to the Nation on Livable Communities: Creating Environments for Successful Aging (*Continued*)

- States and localities, including regional planning organizations, should enhance opportunities for citizen participation in planning meetings and other decision-making processes.

2. **Communities should promote the design and modification of homes that meet the physical needs of older individuals.**

Policy Implications

- States and localities should promote universal design and visitability [sic] through incentives to both the public and private sectors and encourage private partnerships to explore new and innovative approaches to home design.
- Communities should develop a clearinghouse through their area agencies on aging, community services departments, or centers for independent living for information on suitable home modifications, potential funding sources, and finding a licensed, qualified remodeler.

3. **Communities should encourage stability by ensuring an adequate supply of diverse and affordable housing environments.**

Policy Implications

- All levels of government should contribute to adequate funding for a range of affordable housing options, including those with services.
- States and local jurisdictions should include the housing needs of low-income and older people and people with disabilities in state and local development strategies.
- Localities should review local plans and zoning requirements periodically to assess their impact on the availability of affordable and diverse housing options for older people.
- Localities should remove zoning barriers to such housing alternatives as accessory apartments and shared housing.

4. **Communities should promote community features expressly intended to enhance safety and inclusiveness for persons of all ages and abilities.**

Policy Implications

- Localities should carefully consider efficient mixed-use development to reduce distances between residences, shopping sites, recreation, health care facilities, and other community features. Zoning requirements should be reviewed in this context.
- Localities should work with citizens and neighborhood groups to promote and improve safety and security.

(Continued)

APPENDIX 10-J Beyond 50.05—A Report to the Nation on Livable Communities: Creating Environments for Successful Aging (*Continued*)

- Localities should adequately fund programs and incentives to promote the availability of community-based services (such as home care) to persons of limited means. In addition, they should coordinate service activities with other programs (e.g., by coordinating with area agencies on aging to provide common space in subsidized housing developments for service coordinators or group meals).

5. **Communities should facilitate driving by older individuals by improving the travel environment, supporting driver education, and promoting safe driving throughout the life span.**

Policy Implications

- State and local areas should evaluate existing streets and roads, and plan for new ones, in accordance with design developed to promote safe driving for older drivers.
- Federal, state, and local jurisdictions, as well as private entities such as insurance companies, should offer incentives for individuals to take driver education courses.

6. **Communities should take positive steps to enhance mobility options, including public transportation, walking and bicycling, and specialized transportation for individuals with varied functional capabilities and preferences.**

Policy Implications

- State and local areas should work to expand transportation choices and evaluate the impact of state and local regulations and land-use policy on transportation systems.
- State and local jurisdictions should create or adapt complete public transportation systems designed to meet the needs and preferences of diverse community residents, and communities should coordinate all agencies with an interest in transportation and the infrastructure that supports transportation.
- State and local jurisdictions should design and retrofit the travel environment for walking and bicycling for safety, connectivity, and accessibility.
- States and local jurisdictions should include transportation needs of people with low incomes, older people, and people with disabilities in state and local development strategies and should actively involve citizens in long- and short-range planning.
- State and local areas should promote a range of affordable transportation and mobility options that meet diverse needs and preferences.
- Transportation providers should be encouraged to market their services to older residents, and private retailers and medical providers should be encouraged to help arrange for transportation service for older customers.

Source: Reprinted with permission from Kochera, A., Straight, A., & Guterbock, T. (2005). *Beyond 50.05 A report to the nation on livable communities: Creating environments for successful aging* (pp. 91–93). Washington, DC: AARP Public Policy Institute.

Policy Practice

*Advocating for
Older Adults*

11

RATIONALE: Social workers need to be informed about the history and current status of policy and how it affects individual and social well-being. Attention is given to marginalized groups and those living in poverty, as social workers analyze the impact of policies on creating resources, institutions, and conditions that are humane, equitable, and just. They advocate for social justice and adopt strategies to redress social inequities.

COMPETENCY: Students will be able to analyze how policy influences people at risk. They will

- identify how policies, regulations, and programs impact older adults and their caregivers, particularly among historically disadvantaged populations (e.g., women and elders of color).
- identify and develop strategies, including intergenerational approaches, to address service gaps, fragmentation, discrimination, and barriers that impact older persons.
- evaluate the effectiveness of practice and programs in achieving intended outcomes for older adults.
- advocate and organize with services providers, community organizations, policymakers, and the public to meet the needs and issues of a growing aging population.

The competency encompasses strategies to address age discrimination in relation to health, housing, employment, and transportation. (Council on Social Work Education, Gero-Ed Center, 2004)

A Policy Practice Framework

Social workers practice within a larger environment—regarded as a set of systems—that encompasses organizations, communities, and the general society. A *system* comprises objects that are ordered and bound together by a form of regular interaction or interdependence (Bardill & Ryan, 1973). A *social system,* according to Greene (1999), is a defined structure of interacting and interdependent parts that has the capacity for organized activities. Each system possesses unique characteristics, and each member of a system carries out specific but different roles. Systems theory informs social workers that a social system is more than the sum of its parts and the activities of any one member. Rather, it is a network of differing interlocking relationships with discernable structural and communication patterns.

Services delivery systems for older adults are entities within the community that provide structured programs and resources based on that population's needs. Each organization within a system delivers services that are influenced by a particular entity and its rules or guidelines. Further affecting the services delivery systems are organizational and public policy, which bring order and provide direction to those systems. In a systems model of policy development, the policy process is a total system—the various parts, including governmental representatives, legislatures, organizations, interest groups, and political parties, operate together to determine policy (Brueggemann, 2002).

Because policy organizes and affects systems, a practitioner's competency in influencing, revising, and developing policy is important to the well-being of older adults within the larger context of society. The profession calls this *policy practice.* What policy practice functions do social workers perform? The following framework, provided by Jansson (1999), offers an organized approach to engaging in policy practice:

- know the contextual setting of the environment to identify factors that affect policy
- be prepared to analyze and use multiple participants in the process who will shape choices and outcomes—allow policy deliberations to occur
- become familiar with and undertake these tasks of policy practice: agenda setting, problem analysis, proposal writing, policy enactment, policy implementation, and policy assessment
- become familiar with and use analytical, political, interactional, and value-clarifying policy practice skills
- become familiar with and develop policy competency skills. (p. 64)

Social workers must not only become acquainted with this framework, but also learn about services providers within a community. To practice effectively, it is critical that practitioners have working knowledge of community agencies and their policies. They need to seek information such as the type of services an agency offers, an agency's eligibility criteria, its services delivery restrictions, whether a waiting list exists, and the length and duration of services. Practitioners also must educate themselves about local, state, and federal policies. Primary policies, such as the Older Americans Act of 1965, protect older adults' interests and well-being, whereas secondary policies, such as kinship care bills, indirectly affect those elders. Practitioners need to be aware of the consequences policies may have for the older adult population in terms of creating opportunities and constraints.

Furthermore, as the aging population increases, older adults will need more policies and programs created or modified to meet their needs. Therefore, social workers will find they must keep abreast of these new or revised policies and programs so they may evaluate whether those policies or programs assist or hinder the helping process. To assess policies and services effectively, practitioners will need to develop skills in policy identification, analysis, development, and advocacy.

The practice competencies described in this chapter will help social workers learn how to identify the following: advantages and disadvantages of a policy, the target populations affected by a policy, the gaps in services created by a policy, how a policy addresses community and individual well-being, and the skills needed to effect policy change at both the organizational and societal levels. Practitioners may use Jansson's (1999) policy practice framework in conjunction with these competencies.

Information Gathering

An important role for any social worker is to identify and tap into resources that will enable clients to function optimally. To connect a client to needed resources, the practitioner must first assess the client's needs (see chapter 5 for a discussion on assessing the client system). The next task is to familiarize oneself with the specific policies and programs in the community where the client resides and determine what resources are available to meet those needs.

Community Resources and Programs

Practitioners have a number of tools at their disposal to assist them in their information gathering. Community-developed resource booklets provide basic information about available services. These resources often include contact information that allows social workers to seek more detailed data from a service provider.

Another resource is the professional network of social workers and other human services providers that exists within the practice community. This network might include members of the local chapter of the National Association of Social Workers (NASW), members of community welfare organizations or other professional organizations, or special interest groups. Participation in this network will ensure connection with experts who not only may have invaluable knowledge about community resources, but also may work in the very agencies that provide services to older adults. To locate professional, organizational, and advocacy resources, social workers may wish to consult directories such as those provided in Appendix 11-A.

Along the same lines as the professional network, the practitioner's employer and network of fellow employees are other resources available to the social worker. Social workers may ask their colleagues what resources they use. They may follow up with questions such as: What are the difficulties and successes you have encountered with other agencies? What are the admissions criteria, and do these criteria fit the client's needs?

Other information about services and programs is available on the Internet. Social workers can search for admissions criteria, agency location, hours of operation, and so forth. Using this medium, practitioners may locate services for older adults more expeditiously by entering key words or phrases, such as the name of the community or "services for older adults."

After gathering information about available community resources for their older adult clients, social workers then assess whether any gaps exist in those services and if the services apply to all older adults. If needs are identified through this process, social workers and the human services community can collaborate and advocate for additional services or reduce resource gaps that exist and reduce the number of gaps that exist.

Federal, State, and Local Policies

As part of their knowledge base, social workers require an operating knowledge of federal, state, and local policies affecting older adults. Information on regulations, policies, laws, and codes is generally available in public and law libraries, which typically have copies of federal and state codes, and through the Internet. Appendix 11-B contains a list of informative Web sites for policy practitioners. Several sites enable users to search for specific federal regulations and bills that have been introduced to the U.S. Congress. The home pages of state governments customarily provide information on regulations and pending legislation. Similarly, county regulations appear on the home pages of county governments.

Appendix 11-C describes key federal laws that mandate the provision of services and resources to older adults. It is essential that gerontological social workers gain familiarity with these key policies. Obtaining knowledge about how they translate into services for older clients will help social workers to become more responsive to meeting the needs of individuals and the community.

Objective Approach to Policy Analysis

To avoid having political reactions or emotional responses bias decision making on policy, practitioners can ensure a more objective process using a framework that systematically analyzes existing or proposed policies. A *policy analysis framework* is a model that proffers a set of questions whose answers will help practitioners determine if the policy addresses the problem. An analysis of policy affecting older adults should focus on ascertaining whether a policy adequately attends to the needs of that population or a target group. As advocates for older adults, social workers must ask how this policy will affect older Americans.

Policy Analysis Models

Karger and Stoesz Model

A number of policy analysis models exist. Karger and Stoesz (2002) broke down their framework into four sections:

1. historical background of the policy, focusing on identifying the historical events that led up to the policy's development
2. description of the problem that necessitated the policy, identifying the problem's parameters: What is the nature, scope, and magnitude of the problem? How is the aging population affected by the problem?
3. description of the policy, providing critical information such as how the policy works, the resources or opportunities it provides, who is covered by the policy, how it is to be implemented, expected goals and outcomes, funding issues, organizational auspices, policy time frames, and so forth
4. policy analysis, involving an in-depth and systematic examination of the policy goals and its political, economic, and administrative feasibility.

After examining these four areas, social workers then identify alternative policy options. It is recommended that social workers move forward with the policy alternative that is the most feasible from a political, economic, and administrative standpoint (Karger & Stoesz, 2002). Appendix 11-D outlines the Karger and Stoesz model and its applications to Medicare Part D policy.

Kraft and Furlong Model

The straightforward model of Kraft and Furlong (2004) followed these five steps:

1. define and analyze the problem
2. identify policy alternatives
3. develop criteria to evaluate the policy alternatives
4. use established evaluative criteria to assess the policy alternatives
5. make recommendations based on the assessment results.

Appendix 11-E illustrates how practitioners may use this model to analyze independent living options for older adults, including what type of information they may obtain.

DiNitto Rational Model

DiNitto (2003) offered a rational model of policy analysis, which emphasizes a cost–benefit approach to evaluation. The policy alternative that presents the most benefit for the least cost is the one recommended for adoption. Users of this model typically measure benefits and costs in economic terms; however, they may also apply this model to an evaluation of the social values of an approach. DiNitto's rational model follows six steps:

1. identify and define the social problem
2. identify and weigh all the values of society
3. identify and consider all alternative policies
4. weigh the consequences of each alternative as it relates to the target group affected and to society, and consider the effects each alternative will have on the present and future
5. conduct a cost–benefit analysis for each alternative
6. choose the policy alternative that yields the greatest benefit for the lowest cost. (p. 5)

Appendix 11-F provides an example of how this model might be applied to policies on elder abuse.

Bounded Rationality

The rational model required the policy analyst to identify all of the values of society and all possible alternative policies. Such an effort, including weighing the consequences of each alternative, is frequently more time-consuming than is feasible for the average practitioner. Consequently, policy analysts often use the more practical bounded rationality approach instead. In this model, developed by Herbert A. Simon (1945), the practitioner uses the principles of the rational model to analyze only a select number of alternatives. The practitioner then evaluates a reasonable number of consequences and values, and subsequently chooses the alternative that offers a desired benefit at the most reasonable cost (Simon).

Evaluation Frameworks

Social workers must systematically evaluate programs that provide services to older adults to determine whether these programs are meeting their goals and objectives and whether they are indeed providing services as intended. This process, called *program evaluation,* focuses on policy results or outcomes. One model, created by Rossi and Freeman (1989, 1998), suggests these seven steps:

1. identify program goals
2. identify the means by which the practitioner can measure the goals
3. identify the target group for which the program was designed—older adults in general or older adults who meet some predetermined criteria, such as income level or disability
4. identify the nontarget groups that might be affected by the program, such as family members, neighbors

5. using the measures developed in step 2, evaluate the program's effects on both the target and nontarget groups
6. evaluate the costs of the program compared to the allocated resources
7. identify indirect costs.

Appendix 11-G provides a summary of the questions to ask in the program evaluation process.

Using evaluation frameworks, social work practitioners can make informed decisions about which policies and programs are most effective and responsive to older adults. They can determine whether the available resources within a community are indeed meeting the needs of older adults and family members. Furthermore, evaluation frameworks allow social workers to analyze proposed revisions to existing policies to ascertain the benefits those revisions may have for older citizens.

Fairness in Practice

An evaluation may reveal inequities in the provision of resources and services to older adults. According to Estes (2001), inequities related to gender and class still exist. For instance, the American retirement system currently disregards the contributions of both retired female caregivers and women who were career homemakers but were not compensated monetarily for their accomplishments. Similarly, the labor market devalues working-class elders as they age (Estes).

Social workers can infuse equity into policy practice in a number of ways. One way is through the decision-making process involved in policy development (Kraft & Furlong, 2004). Practitioners may consider whether that process was fair and open. Did the decision makers come to their decision voluntarily or were they coerced into making the decision? If practitioners find that the decision-making process did indeed meet the criteria of being fair, open, and voluntary, they may conclude that the process was equitable. This means of applying equity to policy practice concerns the policy-making process only; practitioners may judge the process as equitable, even though some individuals may fare better or worse as a result of the process (Noziak, 1974).

Social workers may also measure equity in terms of outcomes: Were the outcomes just or was there a fair distribution of goods and services (Rawls, 1971)? Practitioners focus on programmatic equity—that is, how, from a services perspective, individuals are treated and how goods are distributed—and whether one group of individuals fares better or worse than another. Key to this focus is *fair treatment,* which Flynn (1985) defined as "the extent to which situations in similar circumstances are dealt with similarly" (p. 54). A program is inequitable, Chipungu (1991) has pointed out, if two people receive different services even though all other factors are the same.

Policy analysis frameworks may include equity—as a process or outcome criterion. When analyzing a policy, an appropriate step for practitioners is to review equity and its relationship to proposed policies and policy revisions systematically. Equity is an important criterion for the evaluation of redistribution policies, such as tax reforms, enhancement of health services, or assistance to poor people, and in debates in which one population clearly gains while another loses, such as the intergenerational equity debate about what is fair to future generations (Kraft & Furlong, 2004). An examination of equity in a particular policy might involve determining which group or category of people gains or loses as a result of the policy and which pays for the cost of the program.

Equity issues are dominant in the intergenerational equity debate (Kraft & Furlong, 2004), which, for example, is central in the dialogue about whether to preserve social security and Medicare. One side views these programs as a contract between the U.S. government and workers—a promise made to the older generation. The other side views the programs as an unfair burden to future generations, who will need to manage debt that they had no role in creating (Kraft & Furlong).

Clearly, intergenerational equity issues are present in many national debates, including those on environmental and conservation issues. As our country continues to contend with the distribution of scarcer social and natural resources to accommodate a growing aging population, the intergeneration equity debate will continue to gain importance in policy practice.

Attention to Well-Being

Like equity in practice, another factor in the policy analysis process deserves social workers' attention: whether a policy benefits individual and societal well-being. How one defines well-being varies, making it difficult to ensure the well-being of all because policies affect people differently. Therefore, applying the teleological theory of utilitarianism to policy analysis may be the most effective way to protect the well-being of most older adults.

Users of a utilitarian approach decide what action to take and what rule to create by determining which one they expect will promote the greatest good (Frankena, 1973). The principle of utility directs that the result achieved be the greatest balance of good over evil (Frankena). Whatever satisfies that principle, Mill (1863/1957) has argued, also satisfies the principle of justice, which, according to Frankena, is built into the principle of utility. Rule utilitarianism directs geriatric social workers to consider which rule, or in this case which policy or policy alternative, will advance the general good for older adults. A critical question to ask is how we achieve the greatest good for the greatest number of individuals.

Shaping Policy through Macro Practice

Social problems such as racism, sexism, classism, and ageism affect individuals and groups and may be embedded in institutions, policies, regulations, and communities. Therefore, they require broad intervention. Of all these problems, ageism has the widest effect on older adults, especially among minority elders. *Ageism,* or *age prejudice,* is a negative attitude toward or disposition about aging and older people based on the belief that aging makes people unattractive, unintelligent, asexual, unemployable, and mentally incompetent (Comfort, 1976). Ageism may lead to *age discrimination,* the act of treating people unjustly based on their chronological age or older appearance (Atchley, 1997), which promotes the exclusion of older adults from society.

To meet the needs of the older adult population effectively, practitioners may address ageism and age discrimination in practice using political advocacy and community organization skills. These skills form what is called *macro social work practice,* defined by Brueggemann (2002) as "the practice of helping people solve social problems and make social change at the community, organizational, societal, and global levels" (p. 3).

Political Advocacy

The intent of political advocacy is to eliminate or lessen the inequalities that exist in society for older adults. Inequalities, according to Jansson (1999), result from a deprivation of material resources; mental, emotional, or cognitive abilities; opportunities; interpersonal connections; personal rights; and physical abilities. Political advocacy focuses on efforts to help powerless individuals and groups improve their situations (Jansson, 2003).

Social workers as political advocates must start with this question: What are the structural or environmental factors that create or intensify the problems of older adults? Once they have identified the problem, practitioners must establish what policies or regulations require change. Does policy change need to occur at the federal, state, local, or organizational level? To be effective in changing policy, advocates must be skilled at

- developing a vision: They must ask what is the ideal state for which they strive. The ideal state is shaped by values, beliefs, and ideology.
- seeking opportunities for policy advocacy: Practitioners must identify where change needs to occur. They might join interest groups or other organizations to effect policy change. They might help mobilize change by participating in community forums, writing letters, working with the media, or using other resources.
- taking sensible risks: They ought to assess what is a doable and reasonable change and move toward effecting that change.
- balancing flexibility with planning: Political advocates need to develop a plan of action that includes tasks to be accomplished, but must be prepared to change the plan based on the situational realities they encounter.
- developing multiple skills: Social workers must possess analytic, political, interactional, and value-clarification skills to affect the policy process.
- being persistent: Perseverance is required even when facing defeats and obstacles. Practitioners must be mindful of their original vision.
- tolerating uncertainty: The political process is unpredictable. Advocates must learn to deal with changes in the process.

■ combining pragmatism with principles: Frequently, people must make mutual concessions during the political process. Political advocates must be able to consider alternative choices and choose the best choice that in the least way compromises their vision (Jansson, 1999, 2003).

Political advocacy requires skills and competencies that are different from social work practice skills used with individuals. Political advocacy is a much needed intervention that, when used appropriately, can protect the rights of older adults and move society toward equality of treatment of elders.

Community Organization

Community organization is another practice method that allows social workers to lessen the effects of ageism. It is a process by which people in neighborhood organizations, associations, and places of worship join forces to combat community social problems and, with the help of government and corporations, implement solutions to those problems.

The following five-step model, proposed by Brueggemann (2002), enables social workers to help resolve community issues affecting older adults:

1. Define the problem: Assist the community in identifying areas of oppression on which they wish to work. Keep in mind it is important that the members of the community themselves define the problem. For example, they might choose a senior housing project in need of repair, recommend that the community's senior center increase services, or suggest that the community develop an intergenerational day care program.

2. Engage the community: Gain an understanding of the community and its people. How do they really feel about an issue? How can the practitioner or organizer join with the community so that he or she is perceived as a helping agent rather than an intruder?

3. Empower forces of change: Enable people to mobilize so they may move their community into a position of change. The organizer needs to think of ways to entice people to be a part of the solution. Perhaps he or she may point out the injustices that older adults experience or emphasize how important community members' involvement is in effecting change.

4. Build an organization: As people become interested in being part of the change process, schedule a series of meetings to build a structure, such as a task force or coalition, to guide the operation, assignments, strategies, and time lines. The focus of the meetings should be on moving people toward decision making and action. Help participants to identify leaders and then train those leaders. Review and evaluate strategies, celebrate victories, regroup, and move on to other issues.

5. Evaluate and terminate: Evaluate progress toward resolving the problem and facilitate an organizational assessment. It is important that the organizer spend considerable time disengaging from the process.

Conclusion

Finally, practitioners may involve a number of community organizations in efforts to evoke positive change. Those organizations known for their advocacy work on behalf of older adults include the AARP (formerly called the American Association of Retired Persons); Gray Panthers; and Older Women's League. Among the professional organizations that advance the aging agenda are the American Society on Aging, National Council on Aging, Gerontological Society of America, and Association for Gerontology in Higher Education (see Appendix 11-B for a brief description of the aforementioned organizations' Web sites). Many of the professional and advocacy organizations listed in this appendix have been and continue to be instrumental in moving the aging agenda forward, and engage in political activism. Connecting with these groups is a good starting point for gerontological social workers to become politically active so they may begin defining the problems and issues requiring change.

As the United States grapples with an increasing older adult population, society will be in a quandary about how it can continue to provide needed services, at an affordable level, to elders. Public retirement income, private pensions, the financing of health care, and how to encourage older people to remain in the workforce are but a few of the policy issues our society will face (Atchley & Barusch, 2004). Social workers, having much to contribute to the debates on these issues, are in an important position to influence and shape policy affecting older adults.

Suggested Exercise to Evaluate Student Competence

Using Janson's (1999) policy analysis framework discussed in this chapter, students will select and analyze a policy under consideration nationally or in their state. The following framework offers an organized approach to engaging in policy practice:

- Learn the contextual setting of the environment and identify factors that affect policy.
- Obtain, analyze, and use the opinions of multiple participants engaged in policy formation.
- Perform at least one policy practice task: agenda setting, problem analysis, proposal writing, or policy assessment.

References

Atchley, R. C. (1997). *Social forces and aging.* Belmont, CA: Wadsworth.

Atchley, R. C., & Barusch, A. S. (2004). *Social forces and aging* (10th ed.). Belmont, CA: Wadsworth.

Bardill, D. R., & Ryan, F. J. (1973). *Family group casework.* Washington, DC: National Association of Social Workers.

Brueggemann, W. G. (2002). *The practice of macro social work* (2nd ed.). Belmont, CA: Brooks/Cole.

Chipungu, S. (1991). A value-based policy framework. In J. E. Everett, S. S. Chipungu, & B. R. Leashore (Eds.), *Child welfare: An Africentric perspective* (pp. 290–305). New Brunswick, NJ: Rutgers University Press.

Comfort, A. (1976). Age prejudice in America. *Social Policy, 7,* 3–8.

Council on Social Work Education, Gero-Ed Center. (2004). *Foundation gerontological social work competencies.* Retrieved November 16, 2006, from http://depts.washington.edu/geroctr/Curriculum3/ Competencies/FdnComp.doc

DiNitto, D. M. (2003). *Social welfare: Politics and public policy* (5th ed.). Boston: Allyn & Bacon.

Estes, C. L. (2001). *Social policy and aging: A critical perspective.* Thousand Oaks, CA: Sage Publications.

Flynn, J. P. (1985). *Social agency policy: Analysis and presentation for community practice.* Chicago: Nelson-Hall.

Frankena, W. (1973). *Ethics* (2nd ed.). Englewood Cliffs, NJ: Prentice Hall.

Greene, R. R. (1999). General systems theory. In R. R. Greene (Ed.), *Human behavior and social work practice* (pp. 215–249). New York: Aldine de Gruyter.

Jansson, B. S. (1999). *Becoming an effective policy advocate: From policy practice to social justice* (3rd ed.). Pacific Grove, CA: Brooks/Cole.

Jansson, B. S. (2003). *Becoming an effective policy advocate: From policy practice to social justice* (4th ed.). Pacific Grove, CA: Brooks/Cole.

Karger, H. J., & Stoesz, D. (2002). *American social welfare policy* (4th ed.). New York: Longman.

Kraft, M. E., & Furlong, S. R. (2004). *Public policy: Politics, analysis, and alternatives.* Washington, DC: CQ Press.

Mill, J. S. (1957). *Utilitarianism.* New York: Bobbs-Merrill. (Original work published 1863)

Noziak, R. (1974). *Anarchy, state, and utopia.* New York: Basic Books.

Older Americans Act of 1965, P.L. 89-73, 79 Stat. 218.

Rawls, J. (1971). *A theory of justice.* Cambridge, MA: Harvard University Press.

Rossi, P. H., & Freeman, H. E. (1989). *Evaluation: A systematic approach* (4th ed.). Newbury Park, CA: Sage Publications.

Rossi, P. H., & Freeman, H. E. (1998). *Evaluation: A systematic approach* (6th ed.). Newbury Park, CA: Sage Publications.

Simon, H. (1945). *Administrative behavior.* New York: Macmillan.

APPENDIX 11-A Directories of Professional, Organizational, and Advocacy Resources

Encyclopedia of associations: Regional, state and local organizations—An association's unlimited reference (17th ed., Vols. 1–5). (2006). Farmington Hills, MI: Thomson Gale.

National trade and professional associations of the United States (41st ed.). (2006). Washington, DC: Columbia Books.

Swartout, K. (Ed.). (2006). *Encyclopedia of associations: National organizations of the U.S.—An association's unlimited reference* (43rd ed., Vols. 1–3). Farmington Hills, MI: Thompson Gale.

Washington information directory. (2005–2006). Washington, DC: Congressional Quarterly.

World directory of trade and business associations (4th ed.). (2002). London: Euromonitor International.

APPENDIX 11-B Web Sites of Professional and Advocacy Organizations

The following listings are arranged alphabetically by URL.

www.aarp.org AARP, formerly known as the American Association of Retired Persons, is an advocacy organization for older Americans. This Web site contains data and research on a variety of issues.

www.access.gpo.gov This site provides access to the federal government's printing office and is a source for locating government documents.

www.aghe.org The Association for Gerontology in Higher Education features programs and resources to advance aging content in higher education curricula.

http://agingsociety.org The National Academy on an Aging Society, a nonpartisan public policy institute, contains information on issues related to population aging.

http://asaging.org The American Society on Aging offers educational resources for professionals working in gerontology.

http://cbo.gov The Congressional Budget Office provides analyses of economic and budget issues.

http://cms.hhs.gov The Health and Human Services Web site of the federal government features access to the Centers for Medicare and Medicaid Services. It includes links to federal and state health care programs.

http://csg.org The Council of State Governments features links to the government home pages for all 50 states and to public policy think tanks.

www.fedstats.gov This site contains federal data on policy problems.

www.firstgov.gov This Web site is the portal to federal government sites. It includes links to the governmental home pages for all 50 states and for national associations.

www.gao.gov The Government Accountability Office, formerly called the General Accounting Office, provides access to government agency and program reports, including evaluation studies.

http://geron.org The Gerontological Society of America provides information on research and educational resources that focus on older adults.

http://graypanthers.org The Gray Panthers, an advocacy group that works on a variety of issues affecting older adults, offers information and resources on advocacy and includes a guide to local networks.

(Continued)

APPENDIX 11-B Web Sites of Professional and Advocacy Organizations (*Continued*)

http://ncoa.org The National Council on Aging, which is dedicated to improving the health and independence of older people, provides information on programs, action alerts, and policies affecting older adults.

http://owl-national.org The Older Women's League, the only organization that currently focuses on issues unique to women as they age, features advocacy and policy information, and contains a directory of local chapters.

http://publicagenda.org This Web site features nonpartisan briefings on policy, polls, news, legislation, studies, and research.

http://socsec.org The Social Security Network features reports and analyses on social security and offers links to other Web sites containing information on social security.

http://ssa.gov The Social Security Administration offers comprehensive information on the social security program.

http://thomas.loc.gov This site features a comprehensive search engine for locating congressional documents in the Library of Congress collection.

www.uscourts.gov The Web site for the U.S. judiciary system.

www.whitehouse.gov The Web site for the White House.

APPENDIX 11-C Federal Aging Policies

Social Security Act (enacted 1935)

* a sweeping federal policy passed to help ensure economic security for the aged and, later, indigent populations; and for surviving spouses and children, and individuals with disabilities
* originally included social insurance, unemployment insurance, old age assistance, and aid to dependent children; later additions included Medicare, Medicaid, Supplemental Security Income, and Supplemental Security Disability Income
* 2006 financial status of social security

  See http://www.socialsecurity.gov/OACT/TRSUM/trsummary.html

Food Stamp Program (enacted 1961 by Executive Order)

* relief program, administered by the U.S. Department of Agriculture, to help people buy food
* eligibility rules less stringent for elderly people because of their generally high medical costs and fixed-income status
* 2005 budget: $30.5 billion

  See http://www.usda.gov/agency/obpa/Budget-Summary/2005/08.FNS.htm

Older Americans Act (enacted 1965)

* for individuals aged 60 years and older; provides access, in-home, senior center, nutrition, employment, and legal assistance services, and additional services based on local needs and resources
* establishes the federal Administration on Aging and the aging network comprising federal, state, and area agencies on aging
* 2006 appropriations: $1.36 billion

  See http://www.hhs.gov/budget/07budget/aoa.html

Medicare (established in 1965 under Social Security Act—Title XVIII)

* makes those eligible for old age insurance (commonly called social security) also eligible for the following health benefits:
  * Part A: coverage for hospital care
  * Part B: voluntary supplemental health insurance
  * Part C: Medicare + Choice—private insurance companies offer alternatives to the original Medicare plan.
  * Part D: subsidization of prescription medication purchases for seniors
* 2004 federal spending: $256 billion

  See http://www.kff.org/medicare/upload/7305.pdf

(Continued)

APPENDIX 11-C Federal Aging Policies (*Continued*)

Medicaid (established in 1965 under Social Security Act—Title XIX)

- a means-tested medical assistance program for categorically needy populations
- pays a significant amount of long-term care expenses and other health-related expenses for the elderly population
- 2004 federal spending: $256 billion

  See http://statehealthfacts.org/cgi-bin/healthfacts.cgi?action=compare&category= Medicaid+%26+SCHIP&subcategory=Medicaid+Spending&topic=Total+ Medicaid+Spending%2C+FY2004&gsaview=1

Tax Code Provisions Related to Older Americans

- social security benefit payments taxed if individual's income is above a certain threshold
- credit given for elderly or disabled individual if person is 65 years of age or older and if individual's income is below a certain threshold

Age Discrimination in Employment Act (enacted 1967)

- promotes the hiring of workers based on ability, not age, and to prohibit age discrimination in employment
- later includes government employers under these requirements

Housing and Community Development Act (enacted 1974)

- introduces Section 8 subsidy program
- eligible individuals pay 30 percent of their adjusted monthly income for rent, and government subsidy pays the rest
- reinstates Section 202, which offers low-interest loans for construction of residential projects and resulted in reduced rental costs

Employee Retirement Income Security Act (enacted 1974)

- strengthens workers' rights regarding private pension plans
- requires employers to inform participants of their pension plan status, outlaws discrimination regarding who may participate, sets minimum standards for vesting, requires accountability in management of pension plans, and guarantees payment of certain benefits on termination of a plan

(*Continued*)

APPENDIX 11-C Federal Aging Policies (*Continued*)

Consolidated Omnibus Budget Reconciliation Act (1986 and 1987)

* 1986: requires employers to continue accruing benefits for workers who continue past the normal retirement age
* 1987: lays out requirements for nursing homes, including minimum standards of care, staffing, and training; protects residents' rights and imposes a survey and certification process

Americans with Disabilities Act (enacted 1990)

* intends to end discrimination for individuals with disabilities
* prohibits discrimination in employment and in services, such as transportation, provided by public entities
* requires private businesses to be accessible for individuals with disabilities when it is "readily achievable"
* mandates access to telecommunications for those with hearing or speech-related disabilities

National Affordable Housing Act (enacted 1990)

* separates housing development programs for elderly people from those of people with disabilities
* provides block grants for housing project improvements and rehabilitation

Family and Medical Leave Act (enacted 1993)

* requires employers with 50 or more employees to offer eligible workers up to 12 weeks of unpaid leave for various emergencies, including the care of an ill parent

Health Insurance Portability and Accountability Act (enacted 1996)

* includes protections for individuals who may have difficulty obtaining insurance due to health conditions

APPENDIX 11-D Application of Policy Analysis Model to Medicare Part D

Steps	Analysis of Specific Issues	Applications to Medicare Part D
Examine the historical background	• What historical problems led to the policy, and how important have these problems been? • What is the historical background or legislative history of the policy (i.e., was it introduced several times before being passed)? • How has the original policy changed over time?	• For how long has the cost of prescription drugs been a societal concern? • What measures were taken to address the problem before Medicare Part D was implemented? • How has Part D changed since its implementation?
Describe the problem necessitating the policy	• What is the nature of the problem? • Who is affected by the problem and how? • What are the causes of the problem? • How will the policy remedy the problem?	• What percentage of the elderly population is affected by unaffordable medication costs? • How will Medicare Part D assist seniors with varying prescription drug costs?
Describe the policy	• How is the policy intended to work? • What resources, opportunities, or services does it provide? • Who is covered by the policy and how? • Who administers the policy and what are their specific roles? • How will it be funded? • What are its intended outcomes? What criteria will determine its effectiveness and appropriateness? • What is the knowledge base or scientific grounding for the policy?	• How will potential beneficiaries be identified, notified, and educated about Medicare Part D? • Who administers the program? • What medications are covered under the plan? • What are the costs to the federal government? To the states? To enrollees?

(Continued)

APPENDIX 11-D Application of Policy Analysis Model to Medicare Part D (*Continued*)

Steps	Analysis of Specific Issues	Applications to Medicare Part D
Analyze the policy	<ul><li>What are the implied goals of the policy?</li><li>What values underlie the policy?</li><li>What is the political, economic, and administrative feasibility of the policy?</li><li>Will the policy effectively solve the problem instigating it?</li><li>Is the policy the most efficient way to solve the problem compared with alternative measures?</li></ul>	<ul><li>What political motivations underlie the Medicare plan?</li><li>What economic classes benefit most from Medicare Part D?</li><li>Have seniors been able to make an informed decision about enrollment?</li><li>How much money do enrollees save using this plan?</li></ul>

Source: From Karger, Howard Jacob & David Stoesz. *American social welfare policy: A pluralist approach,* 4/e. Published by Allyn and Bacon, Boston, MA. Copyright © 2002 by Pearson Education. Adapted by permission of the publisher.

APPENDIX 11-E Analysis of Older Adults' Independent Living Options Using Policy Analysis Model

Step	Analysis of Specific Issues	Applications to Living Options
Define and analyze the problem	• What is the problem? • How did it develop? • Who is affected by it? • What are the major causes? • How might policy options affect the problem?	• How can older adults remain independent in the community after experiencing functional impairments? • How can older adults remain in the community safely? • Are family and friends affected by increased dependency?
Construct policy alternatives	• What are the policy options to consider?	• Does Medicare reimburse for assisted living to avoid nursing home placement? • Does Medicare pay for extended home care services to avoid nursing home placement? • Will the Seniors Independence Act of 1996 provide enough resources to support older adults in the community?
Develop evaluative criteria	• What are the costs? • How are societal values impacted? Effectiveness? Efficiency? Equity? Social and political feasibility?	• What is the expense to society to preserve an older adult's independence? • Is it feasible for older adults to remain in the community with services? From a social perspective? From a political perspective? • What are the resources needed to keep older adults in the community?

(Continued)

APPENDIX 11-E Analysis of Older Adults' Independent Living Options Using Policy Analysis Model (*Continued*)

Step	Analysis of Specific Issues	Applications to Living Options
Assess alternatives	• How does one distinguish between better and worse alternatives? • Does enough evidence exist to assess the alternatives? • Which are the better alternatives?	• Is it less expensive to provide community services over nursing home placement? • Are there enough community resources to enable elders to remain in the community? • Will the creation of aging and disability resource centers provide the support needed by older adults in the community?
Draw conclusions	• Which is the best or most desirable option given the political circumstances? • Which option performs the best in the evaluative criteria established?	• Could Medicare charge additional fees to support an increase in community services? • Are the services included under the Senior Independence Act comprehensive enough to enable older adults to remain at home?

Source: Kraft, M. E., & Furlong, S. R. (2004). *Public policy: Politics, analysis, and alternatives* (p. 116). Washington, DC: CQ Press. Adapted with permission of the publisher.

APPENDIX 11-F Application of Rational Model to Policies on Elder Abuse

Step	Analysis of Specific Issues	Applications to Living Options
Identify and define the social problem	• Is there a consensus that a problem exists? • Does the problem require an urgent fix?	• What are the causes of elder abuse? • Who are the victims? • How widespread is this injustice?
Identify and weigh societal values	• What barriers exist to solving this problem? • What provisions must be included in a policy to ensure its support?	• How do victims of abuse want the issue addressed? • Does the public need to be educated about it? • How do family members, younger generations, service providers, and the like view this issue?
Identify and consider all alternative policies	• How does each policy define the target group? • How well does each option meet the identified needs?	• What are the strengths and weaknesses of each policy? • What policies have been successful historically in preventing abuse?
Understand the consequences of each alternative for the target group as well as society at large—in terms of costs and benefits both in the present and the future	• What unintended consequences may result from each policy? • When will benefits and costs be experienced? • Can the policy adapt to meet changing needs in the future?	• Will greater monitoring of elder caregivers impose on individuals' privacy? • Will there be a reduction in care attendants because of stricter agency policies? • Would stricter penalties for abuse result in less reporting of cases?
Calculate a cost-to-benefit ratio for each alternative	• What social, political, and economic values does the policy achieve or sacrifice?	• Are restrictions of freedom justified if cases of abuse can be reduced through oversight? • Are finances available to support a policy's enforcement?
Choose the alternative yielding the greatest benefit for the lowest cost	• Which options promise the best social, political, and economic results for the least cost?	• Do resources exist that can be tapped into to efficiently meet the need?

Source: From DiNitto, Diana M. *Social Welfare: Politics and Public Policy,* 5/e. Published by Allyn and Bacon, Boston, MA. Copyright © 2000 by Pearson Education. Reprinted by permission of the publisher.

APPENDIX 11-G Questions to Ask in Rational Evaluation

Peter Rossi and Howard Freeman suggested that rational evaluation include three important types of questions:

1. Program Conceptualization and Design Questions

- Is a social problem appropriately conceptualized?
- What is the extent of the problem and the distribution of the target population?
- Is the program designed to meet its intended objectives?
- Is there a coherent rationale underlying it?
- Have chances of successful delivery been maximized?
- What are the projected or existing costs?
- What is the relationship between costs and benefits?

2. Program Monitoring Questions

- Is the program reaching the specified target population?
- Are the intervention efforts being conducted as specified in the program design?

3. Program Utility Questions

- Is the program effective in achieving its intended goals?
- Can the results of the program be explained by some alternative process that does not include the program?
- What are the costs of delivery of services and benefits to program participants?
- Is the program an efficient use of resources compared with alternative uses of resources?

Source: Rossi, P. H., & Freeman, H. E. (1989). *Evaluation: A systematic approach* (4th ed., pp. 45–46, 52). Newbury Park, CA: Sage Publications. Copyright 1989 by Sage Publications, Inc. Reprinted by permission of Sage Publications, Inc.

Index

About the Authors

Harriet L. Cohen, PhD, LCSW, is assistant professor in the Department of Social Work at Texas Christian University (TCU) in Fort Worth. She currently serves in national leadership roles in social work and aging, such as a John A. Hartford Geriatric Social Work Faculty Scholar. Her social work practice experience spans 26 years in a variety of nonprofit organizations to build community and organizational capacity to serve older adults and their families. Her research and publication interests include forgiveness and older Holocaust survivors, spirituality in midlife and older adults, and older lesbians and gay men issues.

JoAnn A. Damron-Rodriguez, PhD, LCSW, of the University of California, Los Angeles, in 2007 was awarded the UCLA Distinguished Teaching Award. She is currently Co-PI of a Archstone Foundation funded project for a California initiative in geriatric social work and is an evaluator for the Hartford Practicum Partnership Program. She is an appointed member of the Department of Veteran Affairs Geriatrics and Gerontology Advisory Committee, which reports to Congress. She was a recipient of the AGE-SW Leadership Award.

Colleen M. Galambos, DSW, is a professor at the School of Social Work at the University of Missouri-Columbia. She is editor-in-chief of the *Journal of Social Work Education* and served as the former editor-in-chief of *Health & Social Work*. She was a curriculum consultant to the John A. Hartford Faculty Development Institute Project with the Council on Social Work Education and was a member of the Joint Commission on Accreditation of Health Care Organizations Professional and Technical Advisory Committee on Long-Term Care. She has written numerous journal articles and book chapters in gerontology.

Roberta R. Greene, PhD, MSW, is professor and Louis and Ann Wolens Centennial Chair in Gerontology at the School of Social Work, University of Texas-Austin. Dr. Greene is author of numerous publications, including *Resiliency: An Integrated Framework for Practice, Research, and Policy* (NASW Press, 2002); *Social Work with the Aged and Their Families* (Aldine De Gruyter, 2000); *Social Work Practice: A Risk and Resilience Perspective* (Thompson/Brooks/Cole, 2007); and *Contemporary Issues of Care* (Haworth Press, 2007). She currently is conducting research for the John Templeton Foundation.

Nancy P. Kropf, PhD, formerly at the University of Georgia, is now professor and director of the School of Social Work at Georgia State University. Her area of research and scholarship is late-life caregiving relationships, including rural grandparents raising grandchildren. She was a John A. Hartford Geriatric Social Work Scholar (1999–2001). Dr. Kropf has published numerous articles and books, including *Teaching Aging: Syllabi, Resources & Infusion Materials for the Social Work Curriculum* (Council on Social Work Education, 2002); *Gerontological Social Work: Knowledge, Service Settings, and Special Populations* (Wadsworth, 2000); and *Developmental Disabilities: Handbook for interdisciplinary practice* (Brookline Books, 1995).

Youjung Lee, MSW, is a doctoral candidate at the University of Texas-Austin School of Social Work. Her dissertation research is on dementia caregivers and their rewards in a multicultural perspective. She has published on this topic in the *Journal of Human Behavior and the Social Environment*.

Olivia Lopez, PhD, is assistant professor in the Psychology/Sociology Department at Texas A & M University-Kingsville. Her dissertation research was on self-care practices and Hispanic women with diabetes, and a discussion of this issue is published in the *Journal of Human Behavior and the Social Environment*.